T0305686

Innovation from Emerging Markets

In recent years, emerging markets have come to represent the largest share of global GDP and have made gains in economic development and political influence. In turn, emerging-market companies have taken on a new level of importance in driving innovation, local development, and global competition. Advancing an integrative view that captures the diversity of innovation among companies in emerging markets, this book highlights the rapid evolution of emerging markets from imitators to innovation leaders. Building upon research conducted by the Emerging Multinational Research Network (EMRN) in collaboration with several universities in North and South America, Europe, and China, this rich and expansive collection includes studies of innovation in regions yet to receive focused analysis in the field. The authors also re-examine dominant theories of innovation and capability creation based on a broad range of case studies and research insights. Offering a taxonomy of emerging-market innovations, this collection reveals the unique drivers, types, and outcomes of innovation in emerging markets.

FERNANDA CAHEN is Assistant Professor of Management at FEI University Center, Brazil, and Visiting Researcher at the University of Southern California – Marshall School of Business. She is a member of the Emerging Multinationals Research Network (EMRN) under the Emerging Markets Institute at the S. C. Johnson School of Management, Cornell University. She coedited the book *Startups and Innovation Ecosystems in Emerging Markets: A Brazilian Perspective* (2019).

LOURDES CASANOVA is Senior Lecturer and Gail and Roberto Cañizares Director of the Emerging Markets Institute, Cornell University. She is the coauthor of *The Era of Chinese Multinationals: Competing for Global Dominance* (with Anne Miroux, 2020), *Entrepreneurship and the Finance of Innovation in*

Emerging Markets (2017), and *The Political Economy of an Emerging Global Power* (2014) and also the coauthor of the EMI reports (https://ecommons.cornell.edu/handle/1813/66953).

ANNE MIROUX is Faculty Fellow at the Emerging Markets Institute, Cornell University, and former Director of the Technology Division in the United Nations Conference on Trade and Development (UNCTAD). She is the coauthor of *The Era of Chinese Multinationals: Competing for Global Dominance* (with Lourdes Casanova, 2020) and also the coauthor of the EMI reports (https://ecommons.cornell.edu/handle/1813/66953).

Innovation from Emerging Markets

From Copycats to Leaders

Edited by

FERNANDA CAHEN
FEI University Center

LOURDES CASANOVA
Cornell University

ANNE MIROUX
Cornell University

CAMBRIDGE
UNIVERSITY PRESS

CAMBRIDGE
UNIVERSITY PRESS

University Printing House, Cambridge CB2 8BS, United Kingdom

One Liberty Plaza, 20th Floor, New York, NY 10006, USA

477 Williamstown Road, Port Melbourne, VIC 3207, Australia

314–321, 3rd Floor, Plot 3, Splendor Forum, Jasola District Centre, New Delhi – 110025, India

79 Anson Road, #06–04/06, Singapore 079906

Cambridge University Press is part of the University of Cambridge.

It furthers the University's mission by disseminating knowledge in the pursuit of education, learning, and research at the highest international levels of excellence.

www.cambridge.org
Information on this title: www.cambridge.org/9781108486866
DOI: 10.1017/9781108764407

© Cambridge University Press 2021

First published 2021

A catalogue record for this publication is available from the British Library.

ISBN 978-1-108-48686-6 Hardback

Contents

Figures

Tables

Boxes

Contributors

Editors and Authors – Emerging Multinationals Research Network (EMRN):

Veneta Andonova – Dean and Associate Professor of Business Strategy, School of Management, University of Los Andes, Colombia. Previously Associate Professor at the American University in Bulgaria. EMRN member.

Fernanda Cahen – Assistant Professor of Management at FEI University Center and Visiting Researcher at the University of Southern California. EMRN member.

Lourdes Casanova – Senior Lecturer and Gail and Roberto Cañizares Director, Emerging Markets Institute, Cornell S. C. Johnson College of Business, Cornell University. EMRN leader.

Anabella Davila – Professor of Strategic Human Resource Management and Strategy and Management in Latin America at the EGADE Business School, Monterrey Institute of Technology, Mexico. EMRN member.

Diego Finchelstein – Assistant Professor at the University of San Andrés (Argentina) and a researcher at the National Scientific and Technical Research Council (CONICET), Argentina. EMRN member.

Juana García Duque – Assistant Professor at the University of Los Andes, Colombia. Visiting Scholar, Harvard University. EMRN member.

Moacir de Miranda Oliveira Jr. – Full Professor and Head of the Business Administration Department at the University of São Paulo, Brazil. EMRN member.

Anne Miroux – Faculty Fellow at the Emerging Markets Institute at Cornell University and former Director of the Technology Division in the United Nations Conference on Trade and Development (UNCTAD), United States and Switzerland. EMRN member.

Invited authors:

Felipe Borini – Associate Professor at the Business Department, the University of São Paulo – (FEA-USP), Brazil.

Kristin Brandl – Assistant Professor at the University of Victoria, Peter B. Gustavson School of Business, Canada.

Yu Chen – Associate Professor at the Chinese Academy of Science and Technology for Development (CASTED), the Institute of Science and Technology Statistics and Analysis, China.

María Emilia Correa – 2019 Fellow in the Advanced Leadership Initiative at Harvard University. Board member of the for-profit companies Colbún, Córpora, and Explora in Chile and for the not-for-profit Fundación Bancolombia and Fundación Gaia in Colombia.

Peter Gammeltoft – Professor of International Business at the Department of International Economics, Government and Business, Copenhagen Business School, Denmark.

Victor Ragazzi Isaac – Professor at the Centro Universitário Senac – Campos do Jordão. PhD in International Business from the Superior School of Advertising and Marketing (ESPM), Brazil.

Itiel Moraes – Assistant Professor at the Federal University of Western Bahia, Brazil, and member of the GLORAD Center for Global R&D and Innovation, Brazil.

Ram Mudambi – Frank M. Speakman Professor of Strategy at the Fox School of Business, Temple University, and the Executive Director of the Temple CIBER, United States.

Ravi Ramamurti – University Distinguished Professor of International Business and Director, Center for Emerging Markets, Northeastern University, Boston.

Max von Zedtwitz – Professor of International Business and Innovation at CBS Copenhagen Business School, Southern Denmark University, and Kaunas University of Technology; Director of GLORAD Center for Global R&D and Innovation, Lithuania and Denmark.

Zhaohui Xuan – Professor at the Chinese Academy of Science and Technology for Development (CASTED), Director of the Institute of Science and Technology Statistics and Analysis, China.

Unless otherwise noted, the names of the editors and authors are listed by alphabetical order

Foreword

Ravi Ramamurti

For the two centuries since the Industrial Revolution, technological and other breakthrough innovations have occurred in industrialized Europe and North America and then diffused to other parts of the world. After World War II, a few other countries, such as Japan and South Korea, joined the exclusive club of cutting-edge innovators. But since 2000, a number of emerging economies have started to produce innovations of their own. In our work on reverse innovation, Vijay Govindarajan and I argued that we may be at the cusp of a new era in which important innovations could emanate from emerging economies and then diffuse to the rest of the world, including, sometimes, to industrialized countries.

The initial wave of innovations from emerging economies, such as China and India, was largely based on process innovations, particularly to make products much more affordable, often at costs that were 80–90 percent lower than in the industrialized countries. Other innovations attempted to make products simpler to use and easier to maintain in the harsh and underdeveloped conditions found in most low-income countries. While accomplishing these results did not usually require technological breakthroughs, it was based on a lot more than the cheap labor in emerging economies. For instance, it also involved new processes and business models that were asset-light and leveraged alliances among multiple partners. Local companies often took the lead in pursuing affordability innovation because they understood the needs of emerging-market customers better than foreign multinational corporations (MNCs), they had a low-cost mindset, and they had no legacy of high-margin products to defend. Foreign multinationals reluctantly joined this kind of innovation to defend their position in rapidly growing emerging economies and to

guard against future challenges by emerging-market firms in the
MNCs' own backyards (i.e., developed-country markets).

A decade ago, the full scope of innovation in emerging markets
was still unclear. Would these countries ever go beyond affordability
innovation to actually developing products and technologies that
were new-to-the-world? Could they muster the talent, capital, and
ecosystems necessary for such innovation? And so on. The essays in
this volume suggest that the answer to these questions is yes. As
Casanova, Miroux, and Cahen point out, innovation in emerging
markets has expanded in scope, going beyond process and cost
innovations to more fundamental technological innovations, based on
R&D spending, patenting, and the like. They draw attention to the
fact that emerging-market firms are turning from copycats to leaders.
This is a very important trend and deserves the attention of
management scholars and business leaders everywhere. China, in
particular, is taking very seriously the goal of catching up with the
West on technology and scientific research. The "Made in China
2025" program, which has generated much controversy in the United
States, reflects the scale of China's ambition and strategic intent.
China is investing heavily in educational and research institutions
and in the R&D programs of Chinese firms, including state-owned
enterprises. It has taken several measures to build top talent in key
fields, including attracting returnees with deep technical know-how
back to China. Its companies are now filing more patent applications
than US companies, although the quality of these patents is in
dispute. China is producing nearly half as many unicorns – startups
with a market valuation of $1 billion or more – as the United States,
and the venture industry is pouring sums comparable to that spent in
the United States into Chinese startups. China is also creating
ecosystems to support the development and adoption of future
technologies, such as autonomous driving or electric vehicles,
through imaginative public–private partnerships. Other emerging
economies, including Brazil, India, Mexico, and Turkey, are making
similar attempts in a more limited and piecemeal fashion, but

collectively these initiatives could add up to significant challenges to industry leaders in the United States, Europe, and Japan.

Given these trends, this book is timely and comprehensive. It asks all the important questions about innovation in emerging markets and tries to marshal thoughtful answers. It reflects on the past, yet is forward-looking. It includes in-depth studies of key emerging economies, such as Brazil, China, and India, and key industries, such as pharmaceuticals, financial services, and digital businesses. It draws on experts from around the world to grapple with the empirical and analytical issues raised by this new trend. Casanova, Miroux, and Cahen are to be congratulated for assembling an excellent team of scholars and academics to tackle different aspects of this important phenomenon. This volume adds greatly to our understanding of where innovation is heading in emerging markets and how companies and policy makers should respond to these developments. Scholars and practitioners everywhere should give it a careful reading.

Acknowledgments

This book was born out of the discussions in the Emerging Multinational Research Network (EMRN), a group of scholars who started meeting in 2014 under the auspices of the Emerging Markets Institute (EMI) at Cornell S. C. Johnson College of Business, Cornell University, and in collaboration with the University of Los Andes in Colombia; Monterrey Institute of Technology in Mexico; University of São Paulo and FEI University Center in Brazil; and University of San Andrés in Argentina.

The book became global when experts in innovation from the Chinese Academy of Science and Technology for Development (CASTED) in China, Copenhagen Business School in Denmark, Kaunas University of Technology in Lithuania, Temple University in the United States, and the University of Victoria in Canada joined the project in late 2018. The book also benefits from numerous exchanges and enriching discussions among a global team of eighteen scholars from nine different countries who contributed chapters to the book.

We thank the Emerging Markets Institute (EMI) at Cornell S. C. Johnson College of Business for supporting this project. We are grateful to Jennifer Wholey for leading the copy editing efforts, PhD student Eudes Lopes for all his valuable suggestions, Daniel dos Anjos for data analytics expertise, and Kelsey O'Connor for editing. The book would not have been possible without their cumulative efforts.

Special thanks go to the Global Innovation Index team: lead researcher Rafael Escalona Reynoso and coeditors Soumitra Dutta and Bruno Lanvin, who provided valuable insights on innovation. The research of Professor Ravi Ramamurti, Northeastern University, on emerging markets has been very inspiring, and we thank him for writing the Foreword to this book.

The book also benefited from discussions at Cornell University, especially with Andrew Karolyi, deputy dean of the college, and also members of the advisory council at EMI, especially Rob Cañizares, Henry Renard, and Timothy Heyman, and in particular from the EMI team. Founded in 2010, Cornell University's Emerging Markets Institute at the Cornell S. C. Johnson College of Business provides thought leadership on the role of emerging markets – and emerging-market multinationals – in the global economy.

The Institute brings together preeminent practitioners and academics from around the world to develop the next generation of global business leaders and create the premier research center on the role of emerging markets in the global economy.

And last but not least, the authors are indebted to their families, who have supported us through this busy period. This book is also theirs.

Introduction

Fernanda Cahen, Lourdes Casanova, and Anne Miroux

At the turn of the millennium, emerging markets (EMs) bent the arc of the global economy. China, India, Latin America, and Africa witnessed over a decade of growth, increased foreign direct investments (FDIs), and pro-market reforms. These shifts gave cause and effect for the expansion of consumer markets and the accumulation of wealth.

Led by China, emerging market multinational companies (EMNCs) rose to ever greater heights, powering local development, innovation, and competition (Casanova et al., 2019; Casanova & Miroux, 2020). Research on innovation gained momentum, meanwhile, stimulated by the global interest for EM issues: how innovation takes place and how countries rank globally. It is now imperative to understand the effectiveness of innovation policies across EMs and their implications beyond.

Innovation is a major contributor to economic and social transformation. EM companies have successfully honed such capabilities and no longer depend solely on foreign technology from advanced economies (Amann & Cantwell, 2012). It is notable that while not all companies have made the pivot from copycats to leaders, a substantial number have crossed the Rubicon. Table I.1 depicts cases and examples examined throughout this book. These leaders are wide ranging, yet all revealing, with distinctive origins, ages, and routes in their trajectories.

Most of the cases and examples in this book are from the E20, a group of top twenty emerging countries established by Cornell University Emerging Markets Institute (see Chapter 13) and including as of 2019: Argentina, Brazil, Chile, China, Colombia, India, Indonesia, Iran, Malaysia, Mexico, Nigeria, Pakistan, Philippines, Poland, Russia, Saudi Arabia, South Africa, South Korea, Thailand, and Turkey (Casanova & Miroux, 2019).

Table I.1 *Emerging markets companies covered in the book*

Company	Sector	Country	Chapter in the book
Alibaba Group Holding	Digital platform	China	5
América Móvil	Telecom	Mexico	1
Artecola	Adhesives	Brazil	9
Bancolombia	Bank	Colombia	12
Bharat Forge	Conglomerate	India	3
Bharti Airtel	Telecom systems and services	India	1
Cemex	Cement	Mexico	1
Crepes & Waffles	Food	Colombia	12
Dr. Reddy's Laboratories	Pharmaceutical	India	3
Embraer	Aircraft	Brazil	13
Eurofarma	Pharmaceutical	Brazil	8
Flipkart	E-commerce	India	5
Glenmark	Pharmaceutical	India	1
Grupo Bimbo	Food	Mexico	1
HCL Technologies	Information technology	India	10
Haier	White goods	China	1
Huawei	Electronics	China	13
INVAP	Satellites	Argentina	4
Jiangsu Hengrui Medicine	Pharmaceutical	China	8
Jumia	E-commerce	Nigeria	5
M-Pesa	Mobile payment platform	Kenya	1
Mercado Libre	Digital platform	Argentina	5
Natura	Cosmetics	Brazil	11
Nubank	Digital bank	Brazil	1
Ping An	Insurance	China	1
Postobon	Conglomerate	Colombia	12
Samsung	Telecoms	South Korea	13

Table I.1 (cont.)

Company	Sector	Country	Chapter in the book
State Grid	Energy	China	4
Sun Pharma	Pharmaceutical	India	8
Suplicy Cafés	Coffee shop franchise	Brazil	9
Suzlon Energy LTD	Wind turbine	India	3
Tata	Conglomerate	India	1
Tencent	Digital services	China	13

Sources: Choice made by the authors based on different rankings: Forbes World's Most Innovative Companies 2018; Fortune Global 500 2018; 2018 BCG Global Challengers; Fast Company Most Innovative Companies, 2018.

At the heart of this volume reside the following inquiries: What is driving this phenomenon? What types of innovations are being undertaken? What are the outcomes with, for, and beyond EMs?

By way of response, this book probes the leadership of note-worthy EM economies and companies. Drawing on cases from Africa (Nigeria and Kenya), Asia (China, India, and Korea), Emerging (Eastern) Europe (the Balkans), and Latin America (Argentina, Brazil, Colombia, and Mexico), it describes the capabilities and external conditions that give rise to such developments in both local and global contexts. At its core, this work revisits innovation through the prism of the growing reach of EMs in the global innovation landscape.

And yet, innovation in EMs varies significantly. Some still rely on an incipient process, or on harnessing an incremental process. Others pursue more radical R&D-based innovation toward global dominance, while for others, innovation lies in the development of new business models. Local and regional players develop solutions in terms of cost, with a high level of responsiveness to local needs (frugal innovation, social innovation, and bottom-of-the-pyramid innovation, among others).

In all, the picture of innovation leaders in EMs is complex, and the scant consensus around such issues proves a challenge. From firm-level studies focused on innovation capability formation and on innovation related to local needs to studies concerning the flow between subsidiaries located in EMs and their multinational company (MNC) headquarters, innovation – broadly defined – is now fashionable in EM literature. National systems of innovation and technology catch-up have been well explored, but are devoid of a more integrative approach. Indeed, most works rely on a more singular analysis, missing connections to particular institutional environments and firm capabilities, as well as the differential impacts of innovation. An integrated view of the complex diversity at hand entails more than a lone unit of analysis and gestures toward an interdisciplinary and multilevel understanding.

This book takes such a gambit. It lays bare the profound imprint of EMs on the global economy by way of its grasp of the workings of innovation in these contexts. We discuss distinctive manifestations, the relevance of institutional environments, their impact on social development, and "catch-up" dynamics.

The chapters reflect the broad, and now increasingly accepted, definition of innovation: including not only technology and R&D-based innovation but also new managerial processes and business models as well as specific types of innovation related to local needs (e.g., frugal innovation, social innovation). Such a starting point makes visible new types and mechanisms of innovation in addition to alternative institutional resources for competitive advantage, social development, and interlocking types of innovation in EMs.

The book provides an expansive view of how the EM landscape fits into overall research on innovation. We highlight the significant progress made by EMs as innovation leaders in some industries over the past two decades (2000–2020) and also point to a number of areas demanding attention. The project is the first of a series and part of a wider research schedule of the Emerging Multinational Research Network (EMRN) on issues related to the surge of EMs. The EMRN is a research initiative since 2014 under the auspices of the Emerging Markets Institute (EMI) at S. C. Johnson College of Business, Cornell University, with the Universidade de São Paulo in Brazil, Universidad de los Andes in Colombia, Tec de Monterrey in México, and Universidad de San Andrés in Argentina. The chapters in this book are written by EMRN members and invited experts from CASTED in China, Copenhagen University, and Temple University. EMRN relies on the extensive results of its case studies, survey-based research, and the annual EMI Report on Emerging Market Multinationals.

I.I   BOOK STRUCTURE

The book begins by presenting the theoretical and empirical context for the study of innovation in EMs. Throughout, we base our framework (Chapter 1) at the bridge between theory and practice, curating the literature so as to resignify the drivers, types, and outcomes of innovation in EMs. The structure of the book reflects the three key dimensions of our framework.

Part I aims to answer the question: What drives innovation leadership in EMs? The response resides in the cases. Some depend on traditional factors (e.g., innovation capabilities, industry competition, and the efforts of other innovators) and on the relationships forged within their innovation ecosystems. Others, still plagued by institutional voids, social demands, high transaction costs, and operational challenges, innovate out of necessity as local challenges give way to business opportunities. The five chapters in Part I explore these nuances.

Chapter 2 opens with the leading EM: China. Two decades of rapid growth and focused innovation policies have powered its companies to invest in key areas that drive innovation. Chinese firms, in particular, have profoundly altered the global competitive landscape, displacing trade and investment flows and implementing a new geography of innovation. This chapter presents the types, industries, and regional structures. It reveals that Chinese companies not only enjoy informal types of innovative activities (e.g., business model, organizational innovation, among others), but also increasingly embrace R&D-related terrains.

Chapter 3 turns to another major engine of global economic growth, India and its companies. The country represents the seventh-largest GDP. Its national system of innovation (NSI) is rising, reflecting a speedy catch-up process toward innovation standards on par with advanced economies. The chapter draws on comparisons in the wind turbine, pharmaceutical, and auto-parts industries to ascertain the impact of endogenous and exogenous pressures on the Indian NSI.

In the context of EM, well-known approaches to innovation such as technology and R&D-based innovation can be unique in their manifestations. For instance, R&D in advanced economies is typically performed by the private sector (local and multinational companies). However, this domain in EMs faces significant financial and institutional constraints. As a result, innovation is often still championed by government or state-owned companies (Finchelstein, 2017). Chapter 4 explores the role of government involvement as a driver of innovation. The chapter examines the dynamic through the cases of State Grid Corporation of China (SGCC), a state-owned company in the electricity sector and the second-largest global firm by revenues in 2018, and INVAP, an innovation-based state-owned Argentine company specializing in nuclear reactors and satellites. Both are samples of a wider universe of highly competitive state-owned enterprises (SOEs), whose growth rests on innovation buoyed by the state.

The rise of entrepreneurial ecosystems drives much of the increase in the number of innovative start-up companies and so-called unicorns (start-up companies with a valuation of US$1 billion or more). The combination of digital intensity and high connectivity lends credence for rapid innovations, particularly in digital technologies and business models. The latter turns on organization capabilities to improve, recombine, or change, giving rise to new organizational functions, structures, and processes for the reinvention of the business itself. Chapter 5 examines this phenomenon through the lens of e-commerce and mobile payments, which have become so pervasive through EMs. The case studies include Alibaba (China), Flipkart (at its origin, an Indian firm), Jumia (Nigeria), one of the e-commerce leaders in Africa, and Mercado Libre, the largest Latin American e-commerce company. These companies' business models have adapted to the regions they have incubated in, resulting in innovations such as new modes of delivery and payment systems. The extent to which these firms disrupt their respective markets, expand regionally or globally, and show how emerging countries have become innovation leaders in certain industries is the focus of the chapter.

Chapter 6 explores how entrepreneurial ecosystems become drivers of innovation and leadership in EMs. The chapter turns to the experience of eleven Balkan markets and provides evidence of the dynamism of their entrepreneurial ecosystems despite the short-comings of the national institutions and low public spending in R&D. Balkan nations score comparatively high on measures of innovation. The chapter emphasizes the role of finance and technical talent as well as the culture and connectedness of the entrepreneurial commu-nity as the major drivers behind entrepreneurial ecosystems in the Balkans.

Part II is dedicated to understanding the types of innovation EM leaders are undertaking. The chapters unpack unique manifestations of technology-driven and R&D-based innovation, including reverse, organizational, and business model innovation. Part II, "Types of Innovation in Emerging Markets," rounds out with innovations related to resource scarcity and the fundamental needs of EMs.

There has been remarkable progress of EMNCs in R&D inter-nationalization. Chapter 7 opens Part II and considers a core aspect of innovation: how EMNCs access and leverage knowledge from R&D internationalization. China has seen a particularly strong increase in R&D investments. The country not only successfully attracts foreign firms in R&D but also encourages its own. The chapter presents the internationalization of R&D as a product of the interplay of firm strategies, domestic government policies, and international affairs.

Chapter 8 discusses the market leadership of pharmaceutical companies from EMs and their efforts to move from generic producers to innovators. Since the 1950s, R&D investments in the pharmaceutical sector were based on large MNCs from advanced markets. Over the past thirty years, the pharmaceutical industry has been shaken by profound changes. Investments in R&D for drug development are more expensive than ever before, accelerating digitalization and spurring competition in EMs. Chapter 8 presents the evolution of the industry in China, India, and Brazil and explains how firm-level capabilities of the local companies have evolved. It compares the strategies of innovation by China's Jiangsu Hengrui Medicine, India's Sun Pharma, and Brazil's Eurofarma. It emphasizes the specific capabilities and external conditions that foster the growth of generic drugs by EM pharmaceutical companies in the last twenty years, as well as strategies and paths for their march to competitiveness.

The presence of subsidiaries of MNCs in EM is an important source of innovation and, in many cases, demonstrates significant implications for companies that seek foreign knowledge for innovation. Knowledge transfers from subsidiaries to the headquarters (reverse innovation) have come to garner attention in the last decade. However, an understanding of how foreign subsidiaries integrate with local partners and generate benefits for both sides still proves to be underexamined. Chapter 9 analyzes how the quality of the relationship – relational embeddedness – that subsidiaries of MNCs from developed countries cultivate with local partners influences the development of reverse innovations in EMs.

Chapter 10 explores how EM firms capture value through organizational innovations and comprise changes in the structure and processes for implementing new managerial and working practices. The chapter analyzes the innovations in human resource management systems of one of the largest IT consulting Indian multinationals: HCL Technologies. The chapter presents the "Employees First, Customer Second" (EFCS) management philosophy at HCL

Technologies. The case presents an emerging model of innovation based on value co-creation with employees.

A closer look at innovation in EMs reveals a variety of different terms such as frugal innovation, low-cost innovation, social innovation, bottom-of-the-pyramid innovation, good-enough innovation, resource-constrained innovation, and many others. The interconnection of these terminologies is that they describe innovations that are considerably less expensive than their peers in developed countries, typically triggered by the economic realities of EMs. The last chapters of Part II focus on innovations related to scarcity and constraints.

Chapter 11 turns to the case of frugal innovation in EMNCs. The chapter outlines how Brazilian multinationals employ the frugal innovation strategy to consolidate their international competitiveness. Frugal innovation is not limited to a new product or a redesign of products using fewer resources; it can also involve new production processes and new business models.

Some types of innovation from EMs generate prosperity not from growth per se, but also in combating inequality or promoting peace and social stability.

Chapter 12 examines such practices in places where social demands create opportunities for deep societal transformations. The chapter describes how companies in EMs often operate in territories riddled with conflicts. These companies innovate alongside their stakeholders and undertake initiatives that benefit both the business environment and local communities. Colombia is taken as an example, where armed conflict and postconflict gave rise to innovation in the military and business domains.

Finally, Part III covers innovation outcomes in EMs by drawing on the preceding chapters. Chapter 13 examines innovation performance at the macro-level, analyzing the progress made by emerging countries in global innovation mainly using the Global Innovation Index (GII). At the firm level, we examine the most innovative firms in different rankings, including the European Union industry scoreboard. We also take stock of the importance of industrial policies and coordinating policies among different stakeholders. The last chapter highlights the lessons from EM innovators and encapsulates the lessons that can be drawn from discussions in this book.

This book highlights innovation success stories in EMs, many of which are moving from copycats to becoming innovation leaders. Today, innovation is not anymore a migration of ideas from the North to the South. Innovation has become global in nature, and there is a need to learn both across developed and emerging economies and also within EMs.

REFERENCES

Amann, E., & Cantwell, J. (2012). *Innovative firms in emerging market countries.* (E. Amann & J. Cantwell, eds.). Oxford: Oxford University Press.

Casanova, L., Cahen, F., Miroux, A., Finchelstein, D., Davila, A., García, J., Andonova, V., & Oliveira Jr., M. M. (2019). Innovation in emerging markets: The case of Latin America. *AIB Insights, 19*(2), 8–12. Retrieved September 2019, from https://aib.msu.edu/publications/insights/volume/19/issue/2.

Casanova, L., & Miroux, A. (2019). Emerging Market Multinationals Report 2019. Building constructive engagement. Retrieved November 9, 2018, from www .johnson.cornell.edu/wp-content/uploads/sites/3/2019/11/EMR-2019.pdf.

(2020). *The era of Chinese multinationals: How Chinese companies are conquering the world.* San Diego, CA. Academic Press. Elsevier.

Finchelstein, D. (2017). The role of the state in the internationalization of Latin American firms. *Journal of World Business, 52*(4), 578–590.

1 A Framework for Innovation in Emerging Markets

Lourdes Casanova, Anne Miroux, and Fernanda Cahen

1.1 INNOVATION: THE SINE QUA NON OF GROWTH AND DEVELOPMENT

Innovation is the key to productivity gains and sustained economic growth. It has expanded beyond its roots as a key concept in economics in the 1980s and become a household term. Nations, companies, and leaders now routinely make headlines as "innovative," but robust definitions of innovation are less well known. In this chapter, we seek to lay out a holistic framework for thinking about innovation and its key components in the context of emerging markets.

Our understanding of innovation stems from the seminal work of J. A. Schumpeter in the 1930s, one of the first scholars to emphasize the concept, stressing its role in economic development not only through the creation of new products and processes, but also through new markets, new sources of supply for raw materials and semifinished products, and new industry structures (Schumpeter 1934, 1939, 1942). Though the concept of innovation has evolved, and various researchers have advanced new definitions since Schumpeter, his work remains foundational in the field.

In 2005, the Organisation for Economic Co-operation and Development (OECD) defined innovation as:

> The implementation of a new or significantly improved product (good or service), or process, a new marketing method, or a new organization method in business practices, workplace organization or external relations.
>
> *(OECD/Eurostat, 2005, p. 46)*

The latest revision of the *Oslo Manual* in 2018 broadens the definition:

> An innovation is a new or improved product or process (or combination thereof) that differs significantly from the unit's previous products or processes and that has been made available to potential users (product) or brought into use by the unit (process).
>
> *(OECD/Eurostat, 2018, p. 68)*

In the new definition, the term *unit* refers to "the actor responsible for Innovations and refers to any institutional unit in any sector, including households and their individual members" (OECD/Eurostat, 2018, p. 20). We adhere to the same definition in this book.

While the academic literature on innovation has most frequently examined research and development (R&D) expenditures, patent applications, and intellectual property (Amann & Cantwell, 2012), since the mid-1990s other forms such as process innovation (Pisano, 1996), service innovation (Gallouj & Weinstein, 1997), business model innovation (Chesbrough, 2007), and management innovation (Birkinshaw, Hamel, & Mol, 2008) have merited attention. This was the result of a more inclusive understanding of the term – a trend reflected in the *Oslo Manual*, which further expanded its definition to include the social sphere.

This broader perspective on innovation is especially useful in the context of emerging markets, where innovation in and beyond products and processes often spurred emerging markets to catch up with developed countries in specific domains such as mobile technology (Chapter 5), electric vehicles, solar panels, facial recognition, and beyond.

1.1.1 The National System of Innovation (NSI)

The concept of the National System of Innovation (NSI) has been central to the study of innovation and economic growth and development since the late 1980s (Edquist, 2005). The NSI-based approach rests on the premise that innovation and technological development are the result of a complex set of relationships among stakeholders in the system, including enterprises, universities, public and private firms, and government (or private) research institutes. The expression originally referred to "the network of institutions in the public and private sectors whose activities and interactions initiate, import, and diffuse new technologies" (Freeman, 1987, p. 1). A more general NSI definition includes "all important economic, social, political, organizational, institutional and other factors that influence the development, diffusion and use of innovations" (Edquist 1997, p. 14).

One key contribution of the NSI concept is that innovation is now viewed not simply as a linear process, but rather as an interactive one engaging a wide array of stakeholders. In other words, to improve innovation performance, policies must go beyond R&D expenditures to consider areas such as taxes, finance, competition, intellectual property, and much more.

NSI discussions have traditionally focused on advanced countries, mainly the United States and Germany (Lundvall, Joseph, Chaminade, & Vang, 2011), where NSIs are far more developed. In these environments, scientific knowledge is the key criterion for innovation, and formal R&D is seen as the source of innovation, especially in high-tech sectors, with large multinational corporations (MNCs) driving most radical innovation. However, the NSI concept is useful for analyzing innovation in emerging economies. (Johnson, Edquist, & Lundvall, 2003; UNCTAD 2019).

1.1.2   Measuring Innovation Performance

Measuring innovation activities and their impacts has become increasingly important as innovation has garnered more and more attention. The OECD's efforts are of particular importance: In 1963, it published the *Frascati Manual (Proposed Standard Practice for Surveys of Research and Experimental Development)*, the first manual of its type. The *Frascati Manual* focuses on the measurement of innovation inputs, such as the resources committed to R&D or number of researchers (OECD/Eurostat, 2015). Several countries also undertook significant work on their own initiatives in the 1970s and 1980s; the US National Science Foundation published the first report on science and technology (S&T) indicators in 1973. Other countries that released science and technology reports around this time included Australia, Canada, France, Denmark, Germany, Japan, and the United Kingdom, among others.

The OECD led the next push to measure innovation through a consistent set of concepts and tools, culminating in 1992 with the first edition of the aforementioned *Oslo Manual* (OECD, 1992), which took other indicators into account beyond simply assessing R&D. Since its second edition in 1997, the *Oslo Manual* has been published jointly with the European Commission as the *Oslo Manual: Guidelines for Collecting and Interpreting Innovation Data*. Subsequent editions have incorporated the progress made in understanding innovation processes, for example, adding services in the third edition in 2005 and new information technologies and their influence on new business models in the fourth edition in 2018. This latter edition also follows a more inclusive approach, including innovation at the household level. The *Oslo Manual* plays a crucial role in innovation measurement, as it is used by the vast majority of countries that publish innovation indicators.

Recent efforts to establish composite innovation indices that consider a variety of metrics have tried to give a more comprehensive picture of innovation efforts and innovation performance in an economy. These include the Global Innovation Index (GII) published by Cornell University, INSEAD, and WIPO (Dutta, Lanvin, & Wunsch-Vincent, 2019), which emphasizes assessing the climate and infrastructure for innovation in addition to its outcomes. We refer to the GII in Chapter 13 to illustrate innovation performance in emerging economies.

Countries have also sought guidance and assessment of their science, technology, and innovation policies. Since 2006, the OECD has published a biyearly report on science, technology, and innovation; it reviews policies in the OECD countries and beyond (https://stip.oecd.org). In its 2018 edition, the report looks at how the United Nations Sustainable Development Goals (UNSDG) led to new science, technology, and innovation (STI) policies, as well as how digitalization could allow governments to better target, implement, and monitor their policies. The OECD also regularly undertakes science, technology, and innovation policy (STIP) reviews of individual countries.

In what follows, we introduce a framework that builds on the efforts described above and that will structure much of the ensuing chapters.

1.2   AN INNOVATION FRAMEWORK FOR EMERGING MARKETS

Drawing on the NSI approach (see above and Chapter 10), case studies (see Table I.1 in the Introduction), and academic literature, we have developed the analytical framework depicted in Figure 1.1. It comprises three broad components.

First, it shows the main drivers of innovation (Part I) at the institutional and governmental level, at the industry and firm level, and at the social level. These drivers lead to different types of innovations, which are captured in Part II: product innovation, process innovation, business model innovation, organizational innovation, frugal innovation, reverse innovation, and social innovation. While many of these types are also applicable to developed markets, others, such as frugal innovation and reverse innovation, are particularly relevant to emerging markets. Last, in Part III, we consider the innovation outcomes: economic performance at the macro level, competitive advantages at the firm level, and social development.

This framework covers the characteristics of innovation in emerging markets, from the key and encompassing role of the government in state-owned enterprises (SOEs) and private firms, to the role of society to promote inclusive growth in economies with low purchasing power. Together, the framework attempts to define an integrative perspective that captures the leadership of particular emerging

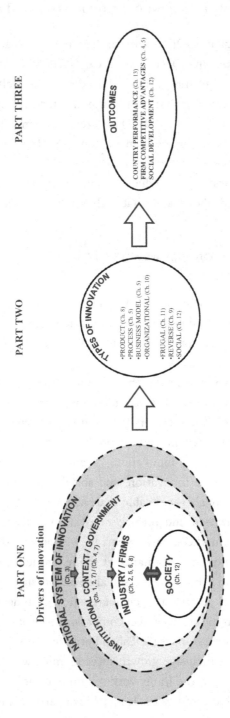

FIGURE I.I An innovation framework for emerging markets

Sources: Lourdes Casanova, Anne Miroux, and Fernanda Cahen with the contribution of Rafael Escalona, Lead Researcher, Global Innovation Index (www.globalinnovationindex.org).

markets (EMs) and their emerging market multinationals (EMNCs), which we detail in each chapter.

The picture of innovation in emerging markets is complex, reflecting the wide diversity of emerging countries in gross domestic product (GDP), population, and level of development. Argentina, Brazil, China, Colombia, India, Korea, Nigeria, and some countries in the Balkans – all examined in this book – reflect diverse political and economic contexts.

In the following sections, we map out the literature and provide more detail on the different components of the framework. In our review (see Box 1.1), we found that most studies focused on China, followed by India, and less on Latin America. The least frequently studied regions are Africa and the Middle East.

We now turn to the different elements of the framework; Part I focuses on the drivers and institutional context of innovation, Part II covers the different types of innovation, and Part III analyzes the outcomes.

I.3   PART I: DRIVERS OF INNOVATION IN EMERGING MARKETS

I.3.I   Institutional Contexts and Governments

Within the national system of innovation (see Chapter 3), institutions and local governments lay the groundwork for innovation. They play a key role in investments and promotion of innovation in emerging markets. Likewise, SOEs, more prevalent in emerging markets, champion innovation (see, e.g., State Grid Corporation of China (SGCC) and Argentina's INVAP in Chapter 4; Wan, Williamson, & Yin, 2019; Wang, Jin, & Banister, 2019).

Efficient policies, regulatory framework, and a good education system are key elements of innovation. In addition to establishing a conducive environment, the government can also act as a direct driver of innovation through advantageous procurement processes and by directing funding for R&D. State involvement in the economy is

---

BOX I.I Literature review on innovation from emerging markets

We mapped out and organized the literature in two steps.
First, we performed a systematic review. In the Web of Science
database, we searched the keywords "emerging market(s),"
"innovation," "R&D," "low-cost innovation," "frugal innovation,"
"social innovation," "reverse innovation," and "business model
innovation." We supplemented our search by manually going through
long-established studies of innovation in EMs, journal issues not
indexed in Web of Science, and country-specific studies. We
disregarded working papers, dissertations, conference articles, and
articles not directly related to innovation from EMs. This procedure
yielded a final list of 139 articles.

Second, we considered five books: Amann and Cantwell (2012),
Williamson, Ramamurti, Fleury, and Fleury (2013), Haar and Ernst
(2016), Casanova, Cornelius, and Dutta (2017), and Zhou, Lazonick,
and Sun (2016). Although other books related to EMs and EMNCs
exist, we focused on those related to innovation.

Using content analysis, we classified the material according to:
definition of innovation, geographic focus, research focus, data and
method, either empirical (quantitative or qualitative) or theoretical
(conceptual), and implications for innovation in emerging markets.
This analysis revealed a complex context with studies of varying
degrees of quality, types of analyses, and empirical settings.

---

substantial in many emerging markets, enhancing the government's
direct role in innovation (Finchelstein, 2017). Indeed, technology and
R&D-based innovation are often undertaken by SOEs or state-owned
research institutions such as the Brazilian corporation Embrapa,
which is largely responsible for the country's agricultural revolution;
the state also acts as a strategic investor in public labs and private
firms. While the private sector accounts for a large portion of R&D-
based innovation in developed countries (as much as 40–60 percent),

in emerging markets governments lead research efforts at about the same rate.

China is a prime example of a country where technology and R&D-based innovations are shaped by strong government involvement (as shown by Thun, 2018; Casanova & Miroux, 2020). This is also the case (albeit to a lesser extent) in emerging economies such as India (Krishnan & Prashantham, 2019) and Brazil (Fleury, Fleury, & Borini, 2013; Cuervo-Cazurra, Inkpen, Musacchio, & Ramaswamy, 2014). Today, China and Korea have become world leaders in innovation thanks to industrial policies promoting advancements in science and technology (Casanova & Miroux, 2018; Chapter 3).

1.3.2   Industry- and Firm-Level Drivers

Firms are at the center of the innovation process, but their ability to innovate depends, on the one hand, on industry characteristics (including the intensity of competition and foreign presence) and, on the other, on firm-level R&D investment. The latter investment includes both internal efforts to enhance the skills of their workforce and relationships with other actors in the system, such as supporting institutions, public and private R&D centers, universities, investors, and incubators.

This book highlights EMNCs' innovation capabilities in a variety of categories to illustrate the transformation of emerging markets from innovation copycats to leaders. Analyzing industry characteristics and capability formation at the firm level is therefore essential to understanding technological upgrading and innovation in emerging markets.

The level of competition within an industry influences its level of innovation, leading scholars who study innovation in EMs to pay particular attention to the relationship between competition, pro-market reform, and innovation. For example, Fleury et al. (2013), in the case of Brazilian companies, and Amann and Cantwell (2012) emphasize the role of pro-market reforms for several EMs. Such reforms stimulated competition, which in turn incentivized local companies to innovate and internationalize to adapt to the new business dynamic.

The presence of subsidiaries of developed-country MNCs in an industry is also often considered a driver of innovation in the host economy because it can foster competition and enhance local capabilities by facilitating access to foreign knowledge or through technology transfers (Narula & Zanfei 2004; UNCTAD 2005; Li, Chen, & Shapiro, 2010; McDermott & Corredoira, 2010; Sartor & Beamish, 2014). Chapter 2 illustrates one instance of this phenomenon, describing the types, industries, and regional structure of China's corporate innovation and showing how Chinese companies are increasingly involved in R&D-related activities. At the firm level, drivers include firms' innovation capabilities, R&D investments, technological knowledge, absorptive capacity, degree of internationalization, corporate governance, and type of ownership. Among these drivers, innovation capability, R&D investments, and technological knowledge are the most frequently examined (Wan, Williamson, & Yin, 2015, Wang, Libaers, & Park, 2017).

We examine the influence of internationalization on innovation in Chapter 7. In order to compete with foreign firms both at home and in the international markets, firms need to enhance their product and process development capabilities (Park, Meglio, Bauer, & Tarba, 2018). Second, international companies learn from competitors in the host country and may form technology alliances and partnerships with local firms and institutions as well as gain access to research centers. Third, the international firm may be able to reduce R&D costs by acquiring inputs from cheaper sources, and finally, when expanding abroad, EMNCs often favor acquisitions, as these provide quick access to a range of assets, including R&D capabilities (Ramamurti, 2012; Kafouros & Wang, 2015). Some studies have also shown how EMNCs specifically enhance product innovation by accessing knowledge from their R&D subsidiaries located in developed countries (Di Minin, Zhang, & Gammeltoft, 2012; Awate, Larsen, & Mudambi, 2015).

As described in Chapter 5 on e-commerce, technology has provided an opportunity for EMNCs to leapfrog and, in the case of mobile payments, has allowed China to lead a rapid expansion into other regions like Latin America or Africa. Digital technologies, Internet connectivity, mobile devices, and data analytics are triggering fast change and innovation in firms in EMs and all over the world (Cahen & Borini, 2020).

1.3.3 Society and Social Demands

In addition to the Schumpeterian approach to innovation, this book also considers society and social needs as important drivers of innovation in EMs. The social side of innovation has become an important and accepted element that transcends technology and product perspectives of innovation and focuses on delivery of value (Prahalad, 2012).

Social demands have driven innovation in, for instance, payment systems (see Box 1.2 on M-Pesa's engagement in mobile money transfers in Kenya), communications (see América Móvil, Box 1.3), and healthcare (Govindarajan & Ramamurti, 2018). Several examples in this book show how society and social needs can drive innovation in emerging markets (Chapters 11 and 12).

1.4 PART II: TYPES OF INNOVATION IN EMERGING MARKETS

In Part II of the book, we move to the different types of innovation: product, process, business model, organizational, social, frugal, and reverse, which will be defined in the following sections, providing examples of leadership across them (Chapters 5, 8, 9, 10, 11, and 12). Emerging markets have often been portrayed as focusing on business model, frugal, or reverse innovation, while Western or Japanese multinationals were the "real" innovators, producing innovative products and processes. In multiple cases, EMNCs have leapfrogged their competitors from developed countries, and they are now innovators on their own in such varied industries as facial recognition, electric

---

BOX I.2 **M-Pesa**

M-Pesa was established in 2007 by Vodafone's Kenyan associate, Safaricom. M-Pesa is Africa's largest mobile payment and money service with thirty-seven million customers in over seven countries. M-Pesa offers several products and services, including mobile payments, money transfer services, tax collection, and branchless banking services. M-Pesa allows users to deposit, withdraw, and pay for products via their mobile phones. M-Pesa customers first register for the service via authorized agents such as small phone stores, deposit cash in exchange for "mobile money," and conduct transactions by entering their PINs.

M-Pesa has an innovative business model that allows customers to manage money on a digital platform and sellers to receive payments via mobile networks. The company has benefited from traditional banks' difficulty in accessing low-income populations. The company's innovation was to create a branchless banking model, giving access to financial services to millions of people who did not have access to formal financial systems. The company has reduced robbery, burglary, and corruption, which is common in typical cash-based societies. M-Pesa conducted over 11 billion transactions in 2018, averaging over 500 transactions per second. M-Pesa, initially used in Africa, has expanded to Afghanistan, India, and Eastern Europe.

Sources: The authors, based on www.vodafone.com/what-we-do/services/ m-pesa and data from Capital IQ and 2019 Fortune Global 500, accessed November 2019.

---

vehicles, major infrastructure projects, solar panels, mobile payments, logistics, or insurance.

1.4.1 *Product and Process Innovation*

Product and process innovation are commonly associated with technology-driven and R&D-based innovation. The *Oslo Manual* defines product innovation as a new product or a significant

---

BOX 1.3   **América Móvil**

América Móvil, a multinational telecommunications company headquartered in Mexico City, offers numerous telecommunications equipment, products, and services, including fixed and wireless networks, network connection services, data and Internet services, interactive applications, cybersecurity, broadband, IT solutions, and others. América Móvil is the fourth-largest company worldwide in terms of wireless subscribers and the largest company outside China or India, with over 277 million subscribers.

The company offers products and services in over 25 countries with more than 360 million access lines, 241,990 base stations, and 6 satellites. América Móvil primarily distributes products and services via its extensive network of retailers and service centers. The company has 450,000 points of sale and over 2,800 customer service centers. América Móvil has subsidiaries in different geographic regions to expand its customer base. América Móvil acquired Telcel, the largest mobile operator in Mexico; Claro, which operates in Central and South America; and Tracfone, which provides services to customers in the United States.

América Móvil was a pioneer in expanding prepaid mobile telephones all over Latin America, which allowed the rapid expansion of mobile phones in the region. The company then exported this business model to the United States.

Sources: The authors, based on www.americamovil.com and data from Capital IQ and 2019 Fortune Global 500, accessed November 2019.

---

improvement to an existing one in technical specifications, components and materials, software used, user-friendliness, or other functional features. Process innovation is defined as a new or significantly improved method of production or delivery.

In product and process innovation, EM firms often begin by imitating more sophisticated competitors, then progressively building capabilities, and eventually innovating on their own. The literature reports a number of cases of EMNCs in private and public sectors that have evolved from a copycat stage to become market leaders (Dong & Flowers, 2016). Some EMNCs have been able to leapfrog developed-country firms in the type of services they provide without ever imitating them, especially in IT-based technologies such as mobile payments.

One part of EMNCs' competitive strategy related to product and process innovation involves accessing knowledge from R&D subsidiaries in developed countries (Awate et al., 2015). The behavior of EMNCs indicates that R&D internationalization is driven predominantly by gaining access to technology, securing R&D skills, and acquiring international brands. Chapter 7 explores this issue, focusing on Chinese R&D internationalization.

Although the highly R&D-intensive pharmaceutical industry is dominated by Western MNCs, Chapter 8 presents the evolution of the pharmaceutical industries in China, India, and Brazil and explains how local companies' capabilities have evolved. Good examples of product and process innovation are the Chinese insurance firm Ping An (Box 1.4), the cosmetics company Natura from Brazil (Chapter 11), bakery manufacturer Grupo Bimbo (Box 1.5), and the Chinese company Huawei (Chapter 13). In a single decade, each has emerged as a global innovation leader.

1.4.2   Business Model Innovation

New business models allow companies to create value by introducing novelty in the way they do business, while improving, adapting, or changing their organizational functions, structures, and process (Chesbrough, 2007). While the business changes, the product can stay the same. Business models need to adjust to local needs and demands during globalization, and firms that fail to adapt have often failed in EMs due to those markets' volatility. Because of their background in these markets, EMNCs need to be more flexible (see América Móvil in Box 1.3) and may be faster to adapt to local demands when they enter a new market. On the other hand, American companies may feel that they have perfected their business models and turned them into a

---

BOX 1.4 **Ping An**

Ping An is a Chinese conglomerate that operates in the financial services, healthcare and insurance, automobile, real estate, and smart cities sectors. Ping An offers numerous products and services ranging from life, annuity, healthcare, medical, automobile, and corporate insurance; wealth management, banking, and credit card services for individual and corporate clients; financial leasing, consulting, and IT development services; and production and distribution of chemicals.

The company derives its innovation and business expansion via technology, by incorporating consumer data analytics, artificial intelligence, and research and development in technology within its products and services. Ping An has also established an international presence through diversification efforts including investments in companies in the fintech, healthcare, real estate, and automobile sectors. To date, the company has over 700 million customers across all its segments and subsidiaries, with global networks and contact points in over 150 countries worldwide.

Sources: The authors, based on www.pingan.com and data from Capital IQ and 2019 Fortune Global 500, accessed November 2019.

---

competitive advantage, leading them to be more rigid in the same situation.

One of the sectors in which emerging market firms have become innovation leaders is e-commerce, and more broadly speaking Internet-related business, thanks to their formidable progress in digital technologies. Firms such as Alibaba, Flipkart, Jumia, and Mercado Libre have developed new payment methods as well as new logistics and modes of delivery to fit the needs of their markets (Chapter 5; M-Pesa in Box 1.2).

1.4.3 Organizational Innovation

Chapter 10 analyzes organizational innovation through the innovations in human resource management of one of the largest IT

BOX 1.5   **Grupo Bimbo**

Grupo Bimbo, headquartered in Mexico City, is a Mexican multinational baking products company that offers a variety of products, including fresh and frozen sliced bread, cookies, snacks, rolls/buns, bagels, confectioneries, pastries, prepackaged foods, and more. Grupo Bimbo is the largest baking company in the world. The company owns over 100 brands and produces 13,000 products in 32 countries worldwide. Grupo Bimbo has one of the widest distribution networks, with over 57,000 routes and 3.1 million points of sale. It has 197 production plants located across 14 countries in North, Central, and South America and Europe.

Grupo Bimbo began expanding its portfolio and product distribution in 1984, when the company first exported its products to the United States. In 1989, it opened a plant in Guatemala, expanding its distribution network into Central America. In the following years, Group Bimbo acquired numerous baking companies and chains, including American bakery Mrs. Baird's, Brazilian bakeries Plus Vita and Pullman, Chinese bakery Panrico, and Spain and Portugal's Sara Lee, among others.

Bimbo's innovations have been based on upgrading competencies in production and operations through process innovation, enhancing commercial competencies, and improving marketing and the capacity to manage mergers and acquisitions.

Sources: The authors, based on www.grupobimbo.com and data from Capital IQ and 2019 Fortune Global 500, accessed November 2019.

consulting Indian multinationals, HCL Technologies. Organizational innovation is defined by the *Oslo Manual* as a new organizational method in business practices, workplace organization, or external relations. Birkinshaw et al. (2008) apply a narrower perspective and define "management innovation" related to the creation and implementation of a management practice, process, structure, or technique that is new, state of the art, and intended to further organization goals.

Examples of management innovation include total quality management (TQM), just-in-time production, quality circle, cost accounting, 360-degree feedback, and divisional (M-form) structure. Organizational innovation is often considered a precondition for the efficient implementation of technological innovation (Damanpour & Aravind, 2012).

1.4.4 Frugal Innovation

Frugal innovation provides significant cost benefits compared to existing solutions while responding to resource constraints (Zeschky, Widenmayer, & Gassmann, 2011). Similar terms such as low-cost innovation, bottom of the pyramid innovation, trickle-up innovation, good-enough innovation, and resource-constrained innovation all describe innovations, typically triggered by the realities of emerging markets, that are less demanding in resources. Frugal innovations often have a social dimension.

Frugal innovations can include organizational and business model innovation as well as product innovations. Frugal innovation may leverage frontier science and technology. Indian healthcare organizations, for example, have taken advantage of scale to develop innovations that enable substantial cost reductions without compromising quality. This frugal approach has been replicated in obstetrics and cardiac care in India (Krishnan & Prashantham, 2019). Aravind Eye Care, for example, famously developed a new model for cataract surgeries that enabled one doctor to do twenty-five to thirty surgeries per day instead of only five to six by implementing an "assembly line" type process, using paramedical staff to perform the parts of the process that did not require more sophisticated skills. Other examples are Tata's Nano, a car that comes without convenience and safety features, but is priced at around $2,200; Haier's Mini Magical Child, a washing machine designed for small daily loads, and much cheaper than large traditional washing machines; Tata's high-tech portable water filter; and Agatsa's pocket-sized twelve-lead electrocardiogram or no-frills ultrasound machine for use in rural Chinese

---

BOX 1.6   **Bharti Airtel**

Bharti Airtel, India's largest telecom company, benefited from partnerships with equipment firms such as Ericsson that invested up front in the network infrastructure. This enabled Bharti Airtel to conserve capital and expand its network rapidly, thereby paving the way for a low-cost model that has resulted in some of the lowest mobile services prices in the world.

The company extended the low-cost logic to other domains such as information technology and even transmission towers. It is a frugal innovation that resulted from a radical rethinking of the firm's relationships with both customers and suppliers. Bharti Airtel's approach drastically cut the cost of mobile phone calls in India.

Strategic alliances, contractual arrangements, and collaboration were essential for the company to achieve growth and frugal innovation. For example, by outsourcing IT services to IBM and promising to pay a minimum monthly payment, Bharti tied IBM's revenue into its own growth, thus incentivizing performance.

Sources: The authors, based on www.airtel.in/ and on "Our frugal future: Lessons from India's innovation system." Available at: https://media.nesta.org .uk/documents/our_frugal_future.pdf, accessed November 2019.

---

areas. Chapter 11 in this book examines frugal innovation in Brazilian multinationals, and Box 1.6 highlights Bharti Airtel's experience.

1.4.5   Reverse Innovation

Reverse innovation describes new products or technological processes developed by subsidiaries of MNCs located in EMs, typically to meet local needs, and later adopted at headquarters (usually located in developed countries) or in other subsidiaries in different regions (Govindarajan & Ramamurti, 2011). The literature presents distinct explanations for reverse innovation. In one scenario, the advantages of low-cost innovations can become features suitable not just for emerging countries, but also for developed ones (Zeschky, Winterhalter, & Gassmann, 2014; Wan et al., 2019). Second, there may also be market niches in developed economies with needs similar to those in emerging economies, though typically these niches are too small to be profitable in developed country markets. Third, reverse innovation can create new consumer markets in developed economies (Govindarajan & Trimble, 2012). Chapter 9 analyzes this concept in the context of Brazil.

1.4.6 Social Innovation

Social innovation refers to innovation activities and services that are motivated by the goal of meeting a social need, thereby creating value for the whole society or for a particular community (Mulgan, 2006). Though social innovation can also create value for a company or entrepreneur, its motivation is primarily social change (Cajaiba-Santana, 2014). These innovations are predominantly diffused through organizations whose primary purposes are social, although private and profit-oriented companies may play a role as well (Phills, Deiglmeier, & Miller, 2008).

Chapter 12 examines innovation in places where social demands create opportunities for deep societal transformations. Using Colombia as a case study, the chapter explains how companies operate in territories riddled with conflicts and how they create social innovation in local communities. CEMEX's Patrimonio Hoy is another example of a firm doing social innovation in Mexico (see Box 1.7).

1.5 PART III: INNOVATION OUTCOMES IN EMERGING MARKETS

In Chapter 13, we examine the third pillar of the framework, the outcomes of innovations: (1) at the country level, in terms of country performance; (2) at the firm, in terms of level of competitive advantages, based on firm-level analyses of innovation capabilities; and

BOX 1.7 **CEMEX**

CEMEX is a construction materials company that produces, distributes, and sells concrete, clinker, aggregates, and construction products such as asphalt tiles, cement blocks, etc. CEMEX offers solutions for housing, pavement, and commercial development projects. CEMEX's products include ready-mix concrete, oil-well cement, blended cement, gravel, asphalt, sand, concrete pipes for sewer systems, architectural products, and others.

CEMEX operates in over fifty countries and is the world's second-largest building materials company. It has 92.6 million tons of installed capacity across plants, terminals, and quarries in Mexico, the United States, Europe, South and Central America, Africa, and Asia. It first expanded internationally in the 1990s with the acquisition of cement companies in Spain and Venezuela.

The company emphasizes innovation and sustainable development by offering consulting services to firms to develop sustainable housing and commercial projects. CEMEX has also helped with financing and constructing homes to reduce homelessness in Mexico and has provided over 150,000 Mexican families with homes. CEMEX's social innovation is reflected in the "Patrimonio Hoy" project that was originally launched in Mexico and has since expanded to several other low-income communities in Latin American countries. Within this scheme, emigrants in the United States can send their remittances directly to a CEMEX retail shop, and families receive construction materials instead of cash, thereby enabling the emigrant to better control the recipient's use of the remittance.

Sources: The authors, based on www.cemex.com and data from Capital IQ and 2019 Fortune Global 500, accessed November 2019.

(3) in terms of social development that transcends economic growth to encompass social stability, prosperity, and equality.

At the macroeconomic level, a large body of literature has tried to assess the specific impact of innovation on growth and economic development. This book provides case studies of EMNCs and country progress in innovation without attempting to construct broad theories of how innovation can help economic development.

Throughout the book, the firm-level experiences of EMNCs illustrate how innovation has boosted firms, catapulting many of them to leadership positions.

1.6   FROM COPYCATS TO LEADERS

Emerging markets were once seen as merely producers of cheap products; today, many of them are moving up the value chain in terms of efficiency, quality, and increasingly innovation. No longer are they simply copying advanced economies, but leading the way in categories as varied and sophisticated as e-commerce, electric cars, mobile payments, electricity technology, and specific health services. Some emerging market firms are among the largest R&D spenders in the world, creating new high-technology goods and services; Korea's Samsung and China's Huawei, discussed in Chapter 13, are notable examples. Other firms have introduced new business models or organizational processes that enable them to respond to less-affluent consumer markets than those in developed economies. A number of these successes are based on disruptive innovations that not only impact emerging economies but also influence markets and firms in developed countries. We are witnessing a radical change in the geography of global innovation, with far-reaching economic, social, and political consequences that may not yet be fully understood.

This book does not intend to provide an exhaustive picture of this evolution, but rather takes the reader through a number of experiences at both country and firm levels to illustrate the ongoing changes. The innovation framework introduced in this chapter gives an indication of the mechanisms through which this change has been possible. There are a number of reasons for this approach. For one, innovation capabilities and performance are uneven among emerging economies, and the magnitude of the changes might be lost in an overbroad view. Even if only a few emerging economies are in the lead group of innovative nations, their position challenging incumbents from developed markets represents a paradigm shift in the global landscape. In addition, a number of innovations taking place in the emerging world do not involve large R&D budgets. Both EMNC firm leadership and unique approaches to innovation from other firms demonstrate the extent to which emerging markets have changed the game on innovation.

REFERENCES

Amann, E., & Cantwell, J. (Eds.). (2012). *Innovative firms in emerging market countries.* Oxford: Oxford University Press.

Awate, S., Larsen, M. M., & Mudambi, R. (2015). Accessing vs sourcing knowledge: A comparative study of R&D internationalization between emerging and advanced economy firms. *Journal of International Business Studies, 46*(1), 63–86.

Birkinshaw, J., Hamel, G., & Mol, M. (2008). Management Innovation. *Academy of Management Review, 33*(4), 825–845.

Cahen, F., & Borini, F. (2020). International digital competence. *Journal of International Management, 26*(1), https://doi.org/10.1016/j.intman.2019 .100691.

Cajaiba-Santana, G. (2014). Social innovation: Moving the field forward. A conceptual framework. *Technological Forecasting and Social Change, 82,* 42–51.

Casanova, L., Cahen, F., Miroux, A., Finchelstein, D., Davila, A., García, J., Andonova, V., & Oliveira, M. M., Jr. (2019). Innovation in emerging markets: The case of Latin America. *AIB Insights, 19*(2), 8–12. Retrieved September 2019, from: https://aib.msu.edu/publications/insights/volume/19/issue/2.

Casanova, L., Cornelius, P. K., & Dutta, S. (2017). *Financing entrepreneurship and innovation in emerging markets.* San Diego, CA: Academic Press.

Casanova, L., & Miroux, A. (2018). *Emerging markets reshaping globalization.* Ithaca, NY: Emerging Markets Institute, S.C. Johnson College of Business, Cornell University. https://ecommons.cornell.edu/handle/1813/66953.

(2020). *The era of Chinese multinationals: How Chinese companies are conquering the world.* San Diego, CA: Academic Press. Elsevier.

Chesbrough, H. (2007). Business model innovation: It's not just about technology anymore. *Strategy and Leadership, 35*(6), 12–17.

Cuervo-Cazurra, A., Inkpen, A., Musacchio, A., & Ramaswamy, K. (2014). Governments as owners: State-owned multinational companies. *Journal of International Business Studies, 45*(8), 919–942.

Damanpour, F., & Aravind, D. (2012). Managerial innovation: Conceptions, processes and antecedents. *Management and Organization Review, 8*(2), 423–454.

Di Minin, A., Zhang, J., & Gammeltoft, P. (2012). Chinese foreign direct investment in R&D in Europe: A new model of R&D internationalization? *European Management Journal, 30*(3), 189–203.

Dong, M., & Flowers, S. (2016). Exploring innovation in Shanzhai: The case of mobile phones. *Asian Journal of Technology Innovation, 24*(2), 234–253.

Dutta, B., Lanvin, B., & Wunsch-Vincent, S. (Eds.). (2019). *Global innovation index 2019: Creating healthy lives – The future of medical innovation.* Ithaca, Fontainebleau, and Geneva: Cornell, INSEAD, and WIPO.

Edquist, C. (Ed.). (1997). *Systems of Innovation: Technologies, Institutions and Organisations.* London: Pinter Publishers.

Edquist, C. (2005). Systems of Innovation: Perspectives and Challenges. In J. Fagerberg, D. C. Mowery, & R. R. Nelson (Eds.), *The Oxford Handbook of Innovation* (pp. 181–208). Oxford: Oxford University Press.

Finchelstein, D. (2017). The role of the state in the internationalization of Latin American firms. *Journal of World Business, 52*(4), 578–590.

Fleury, A., Fleury, M. T. L., & Borini, F. M. (2013). The Brazilian multinationals' approaches to innovation. *Journal of International Management, 19*(3), 260–275.

Freeman, C. (1987). *Technology policy and economic performance: Lessons from Japan.* London: Pinter.

(1995). The "National System of Innovation" in historical perspective. *Cambridge Journal of Economics, 19*, 5–24.

Gallouj, F., & Weinstein, O. (1997). Innovation in services. *Research Policy, 26*(4–5), 537–556. Retrieved from https://halshs.archives-ouvertes.fr/halshs-01133098.

Govindarajan, V., & Ramamurti, R. (2011). Reverse innovation, emerging markets, and global strategy. *Global Strategy Journal, 1*(3–4), 191–205.

(2018). *Reverse innovation in health care: How to make value-based delivery work.* Boston, MA: Harvard Business Review Press.

Govindarajan, V., & Trimble, C. (2012). *Reverse innovation: Create far from home, win everywhere.* Boston, MA: Harvard Business Review Press.

Haar, J., & Ernst, R. (Eds.). (2016). *Innovation in emerging markets.* New York: Springer.

Johnson, B., Edquist, C., & Lundvall, B. Å. (2003). Economic development and the national system of innovation approach. In *Proceedings of the First Globelics Conference, Rio de Janeiro*, Brazil. Retrieved September 2019, from https://smartech.gatech.edu/bitstream/handle/1853/43154/BengtAkeLundvall_2.pdf.

Kafouros, M., & Wang, E. Y. (2015). Technology transfer within China and the role of location choices. *International Business Review, 24*(3), 353–366.

Krishnan, R. T., & Prashantham, S. (2019). Innovation in and from India: The who, where, what, and when. *Global Strategy Journal, 9*(3), 357–377.

Li, J., Chen, D., & Shapiro, D. M. (2010). Product innovations in emerging economies: The role of foreign knowledge access channels and internal efforts in Chinese firms. *Management and Organization Review, 6*(2), 243–266.

Lundvall, B. Å., Joseph, K. J., Chaminade, C., & Vang, J. (Eds.). (2011). *Handbook of innovation systems and developing countries: Building domestic capabilities in a global setting*. Cheltenham: Edward Elgar Publishing.

McDermott, G. A., & Corredoira, R. A. (2010). Network composition, collaborative ties, and upgrading in emerging-market firms: Lessons from the Argentine auto parts sector. *Journal of International Business Studies, 41*(2), 308–329.

Mulgan, G. (2006). The process of social innovation. *Innovations: Technology, Governance, Globalization, 1*(2), 145–162. Retrieved September 2019, from www.mitpressjournals.org/doi/pdf/10.1162/itgg.2006.1.2.145.

Narula, R., & Zanfei, A. (2004). *Globalization of Innovation: The Role of Multinational Enterprises*. Oxford Handbooks of Innovation. Oxford: Oxford University Press.

Organisation for Economic Co-operation and Development [OECD]. (1992). *The Measurement of Scientific and Technological Activities. Proposed Guidelines for Collecting and Interpreting Technological Innovation Data – The Oslo Manual*. Paris: OECD Publishing. Retrieved from www.oecd.org/science/inno/2367614.pdf.

OECD/Eurostat. (2005). *Oslo manual: Guidelines for collecting and interpreting innovation data* (3rd ed.). Paris: OECD Publishing. https://doi.org/10.1787/9789264013100-en.

(2015). *Frascati manual 2015: Guidelines for collecting and reporting data on research and experimental development*. Paris: OECD Publishing. https://doi.org/10.1787/9789264239012-en.

(2018). *Oslo manual 2018: Guidelines for collecting, reporting and using data on innovation* (4th ed.). Paris: OECD Publishing. https://doi.org/10.1787/9789264304604-en.

Park, K. M., Meglio, O., Bauer, F., & Tarba, S. (2018). Managing patterns of internationalization, integration, and identity transformation: The post-acquisition metamorphosis of an Arabian Gulf EMNC. *Journal of Business Research, 93*, 122–138.

Phills, J. A., Deiglmeier, K., & Miller, D. T. (2008). Rediscovering social innovation. *Stanford Social Innovation Review, 6*(4), 34–43. Retrieved September 2019, from https://pdfs.semanticscholar.org/8387/6f6bafdcd11e0fc16c26364d3cfc82 6af2a3.pdf.

Pisano, G. P. (1996). Learning-before-doing in the development of new process technology. *Research Policy, 25*(7), 1097–1119.

Prahalad, C. K. (2012). Bottom of the pyramid as a source of breakthrough innovation. *Journal of Product Innovation Management, 29*(1), 6–12. DOI: 10.1111/j .1540-5885.2011.00874.x.

Ramamurti, R. (2012). What is really different about emerging market multinationals? *Global Strategy Journal, 2*(1), 41–47.

Sartor, M. A., & Beamish, P. W. (2014). Offshoring innovation to emerging markets: Organizational control and informal institutional distance. *Journal of International Business Studies, 45*(9), 1072–1095.

Schumpeter, J. A. (1934). *The theory of economic development: An inquiry into profits, capital, credit, interest and the business cycle.* Harvard Economic Studies, *46.* Cambridge, MA: Harvard College.

(1939). *Business cycles: A theoretical, historical and statistical analysis of the capitalist process.* New York: McGraw-Hill.

(1942). *Capitalism, socialism and democracy.* New York: Harpers.

Thun, E. (2018). Innovation at the middle of the pyramid: State policy, market segmentation, and the Chinese automotive sector. *Technovation, 70,* 7–19.

UNCTAD. (2005). *Transnational corporations and the internationalization of R&D.* World Investment Report 2005. New York and Geneva: United Nations.

(2019). *A framework for science, technology and innovation policy reviews.* Geneva: Technology and Innovation Policy Reviews.

Wan, F., Williamson, P. J., & Yin, E. (2015). Antecedents and implications of disruptive innovation: Evidence from China. *Technovation, 39,* 94–104.

Wan, F., Williamson, P., & Yin, E. (2019). Enabling cost innovation by nontraditional organizational processes: The case of Chinese firms. *Technological Forecasting and Social Change, 139,* 352–361.

Wang, L., Jin, J. L., & Banister, D. (2019). Resources, state ownership and innovation capability: Evidence from Chinese automakers. *Creativity and Innovation Management, 28*(2), 203–217.

Wang, T., Libaers, D., & Park, H. D. (2017). The paradox of openness: How product and patenting experience affect R&D sourcing in China? *Journal of Product Innovation Management, 34*(3), 250–268.

Williamson, P. J., Ramamurti, R., Fleury, A., & Fleury, M. T. L. (Eds.). (2013). *The competitive advantage of emerging market multinationals.* Cambridge: Cambridge University Press.

Zeschky, M., Widenmayer, B., & Gassmann, O. (2011). Frugal innovation in emerging markets. *Research-Technology Management, 54*(4), 38–45.

Zeschky, M. B., Winterhalter, S., & Gassmann, O. (2014). From cost to frugal and reverse innovation: Mapping the field and implications for global competitiveness. *Research-Technology Management, 57*(4), 20–27.

Zhou, Y., Lazonick, W., & Sun, Y. (Eds.). (2016). *China as an innovation nation.* Oxford: Oxford University Press.

PART I Drivers of Innovation in Emerging Markets

2 The Breadth and Extent of Chinese Innovation as Documented in the 2017 Corporate Innovation Survey

Zhaohui Xuan and Yu Chen

2.1 INTRODUCTION

Since its reform and opening-up, China's economy has grown at a rapid and continuous pace. China has become the leader among emerging economies and made significant contributions to global economic growth, as well as to scientific and technological progress. By acquiring, assimilating, and re-innovating, Chinese enterprises have significantly improved their innovation capacity, with a far-reaching impact on global innovation patterns. As new products, corporate forms, and models based on mobile Internet and the Internet of Things have flourished in the twenty-first century, China's modern manufacturing and service industries have increasingly embraced innovation and entrepreneurial activities.

Since 2015, China has conducted a national corporate innovation survey to better understand Chinese corporate innovation's progress and improve the national innovation-driven development strategy. This survey is based on the framework of the *Oslo Manual* and the experience of the national innovation surveys of the United States and the European Union (EU). In 2018, the National Bureau of Statistics of China organized and implemented the third nationwide corporate innovation survey. It covered industries with relatively intensive innovation activities, such as manufacturing, construction, wholesale and retail sales, transportation, storage and post, information transmission, software and information technology, leasing and business services, scientific research and technological services, management of water conservancy, environment, and public facilities. In order to reflect the distinctions between different industries, the questionnaire has separate parts for businesses in industry, construction, and services.

Based on the survey results, this chapter chronicles the industrial characteristics of Chinese corporate innovation activities in 2017. It analyzes the factors supporting corporate innovation, types and modes of innovation activities, and the results of corporate innovation.

2.2   CONTEXT OF CHINESE ENTERPRISES'
INNOVATION ACTIVITIES

According to *Oslo Manual* (3rd ed.), an innovation survey guide designed by the Organisation for Economic Co-operation and Development (OECD) and Eurostat, innovation refers to the implementation of a new or significantly improved product (good or service), process, marketing method, or new organizational method in business practices, workplace organization, or external relations. The manual includes four types of innovation: product innovation, process innovation, organizational innovation, and marketing innovation. Among them, product and process innovation are collectively termed technological innovation. The term "corporate innovation activities" refers to all activities carried out to achieve innovation. China's corporate innovation survey is a nationwide questionnaire designed to track corporate innovation activities in light of the previous definitions, which the authors analyze in this chapter.

The survey samples all enterprises above a designated size,[1] for a total of 748,845 organizations. Of the surveyed enterprises,

---

[1] This survey is implemented according to relevant Chinese national statistical classification standards and regulations. Among them, industrial enterprises above designated size include legal entities of industrial enterprises with sales revenue above twenty million yuan; special, first-class and second-class construction enterprises include general contractors with qualifications of super grade and grades I & II and legal entities of professional contracting construction enterprises; wholesale and retail enterprises above designated size include wholesale enterprises with sales revenue above twenty million yuan and legal entities of retail

49.8 percent (372,602) are industrial, 332,167 are service industry, accounting for 44.4 percent, and construction enterprises comprise the final 5.9 percent. Among all enterprises, 32,017 of them belong to the high-tech manufacturing industry, accounting for 4.3 percent of all enterprises surveyed.

Overall, about 40 percent of Chinese enterprises have innovation activities. In 2017, the innovation-active enterprises accounted for 39.8 percent of the total number of enterprises in China, and 37.1 percent are innovators.[2] Product innovators and process innovators comprised 17.2 percent and 18.5 percent of all enterprises, respectively, while 13.1 percent of them achieved both product and process innovation; 25.1 percent achieved organizational innovation; and 23.2 percent innovated in marketing, while 17.3 percent innovated in both areas.

By comparison to the rest of the world, China still lags developed economies (see Figure 2.1). In EU15 countries,[3] 55.7 percent of enterprises are innovation-active on average, as compared to 49 percent in Israel and 47.9 percent in Japan. The share of innovators in those countries is not far behind, averaging 53 percent in EU15 countries, 48.4 percent in Israel, and 46.2 percent in Japan.

Despite this overall lag, the proportion of enterprises implementing technological innovation (product or process innovation) in China is relatively high. According to the survey data, 16.5 percent of enterprises in China have achieved both product or process innovation and organizational or marketing innovation, and 6 percent of enterprises have achieved product or process innovation without achieving organizational or marketing innovation, for a total of 22.5 percent of Chinese enterprises achieving technological innovation.

enterprises with sales revenue above five million yuan; service enterprises above designated size include legal entities of key service enterprises with sales revenue above ten million yuan, or with fifty employees or more at the end of the year.
[2] Enterprises with innovation activities include enterprises that have achieved innovation, as well as companies that have failed and then terminated their innovation activities. Innovators are enterprises that have achieved innovation.
[3] EU15 countries: Austria, Belgium, Denmark, Finland, France, Germany, Greece, Ireland, Italy, Luxembourg, Netherlands, Portugal, Spain, Sweden, and the United Kingdom.

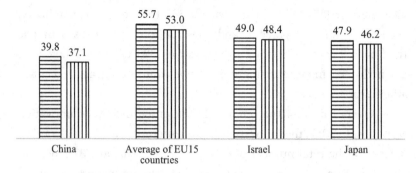

⊟ Innovation-active enterprises of total   ❏ Innovators of total

FIGURE 2.1 The proportion (%) of Chinese enterprises with innovation activities compared to other countries
Note: EU report period is 2012–2014. Israel's report period is 2010–2012. Japan's report period is 2009–2011. China's report period is 2017.
Sources: National Bureau of Statistics of China, 2018. Eurostat, https://ec.europa.eu/eurostat/data/ database.

In contrast, the proportion of Chinese enterprises with only nontechnological innovation is relatively small, and only 14.5 percent of enterprises achieved organizational or marketing innovation without product or process innovation.

The level of technological innovation activity in emerging economies, including China, Brazil, and India, is generally lower than in developed countries, and they tend to skew toward organizational and marketing innovation (see Figure 2.2). In the EU15 countries, 27.6 percent of enterprises achieved both product or process innovation and organizational or marketing innovation. Meanwhile, 14.4 percent of enterprises obtained product or process innovation without organizational or marketing innovation, yielding a total of 42 percent that achieved technological innovation, versus 13.8 percent that achieved only nontechnological innovation. We observe that developed EU countries focus heavily on technological innovation. In Brazil, 36.2 percent of companies were technological innovators, nearly equal to the 36.6 percent with solely nontechnological innovation, while Indian companies skew heavily toward nontechnological

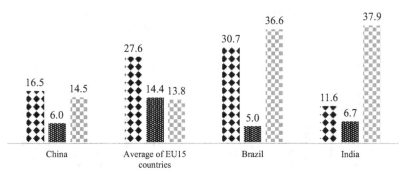

▼ Both technology, organizational or marketing innovation
▣ Technology innovation only, no organizational or marketing innovation
▱ Organizational or marketing innovation only, no technology innovation

FIGURE 2.2 The types of innovation activities achieved by enterprises in selected countries (% of total)
Source: National Bureau of Statistics of China, 2018.

innovation. Only 18.3 percent of Indian enterprises have technological innovation, while 37.9 percent of enterprises are nontechnological innovators. Chinese innovators are therefore more focused on technological innovation than those in India or Brazil, and China's innovation structure is closer to that of developed countries.

2.3 CHINESE ENTERPRISES' INNOVATION BY INDUSTRY

Each industry in the national economy has its own characteristics, innovation process, and development patterns. This section delves into these intricacies through a comparative analysis of different industries.

2.3.1 *Overall Situation*

As a whole, innovation is relatively common in industrial enterprises, while construction and service industries' innovation is mainly of the organizational or marketing varieties. Among industrial enterprises, 33.7 percent have achieved product or process innovation, and 35.6 percent have realized organizational or marketing innovation; only 12.7 percent and 11.4 percent of enterprises in the construction

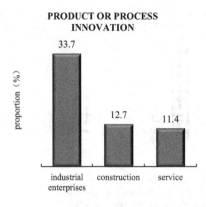
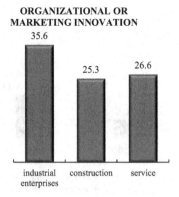

FIGURE 2.3 Proportion of innovators by industry
Source: National Bureau of Statistics of China, 2018.

and service industries, respectively, have achieved product or process innovation, and 25.3 percent and 26.6 percent of construction and service enterprises, respectively, have realized organizational or marketing innovation (Figure 2.3).

2.3.2 *Innovation in Manufacturing*

Chinese manufacturing enterprises are active in technological innovation, with a greater proportion innovating than among Chinese enterprises overall (see Table 2.1). In 2017, 52.1 percent of Chinese manufacturing enterprises carried out innovation activities, more than 10 percentage points higher than the overall total, and 47.2 percent achieved innovation. In total, 35.2 percent achieved technological innovation, more than half again as many as the overall average, while 24.6 percent achieved both technological and organizational or marketing innovation. Impressively, the proportion of enterprises achieving innovation in China's manufacturing industry (47.2 percent) has exceeded that of the manufacturing industries in developed countries such as South Korea (30.9 percent) and Spain (36.4 percent), nearing the level of Italy (48.4 percent) and Japan (47.8 percent).

This strong performance in manufacturing was led by high-tech companies carrying out technological innovation. A remarkable

Table 2.1 *Chinese enterprises' innovation by industry*

Industries	Proportions of enterprises carrying out various kinds of innovation activities (%)				
	Enterprises carrying out innovation	Enterprises achieving innovation	Enterprises achieving both product or process innovation and organizational or marketing innovation	Enterprises achieving product or process innovation without organizational or marketing innovation	Enterprises achieving organizational or marketing innovation without product or process innovation
All industries	39.8	37.1	16.5	6.0	14.5
Manufacturing	52.1	47.2	24.6	10.6	12.1
High-tech industry	74.4	68.3	44.0	15.1	9.2
Manufacture of medicines	73.5	66.3	41.1	12.2	13.0
Manufacturing of aviation, spacecraft, and equipment	83.0	75.9	51.1	18.8	6.0
Manufacture of electronic and communication equipment	73.0	67.2	43.5	15.6	8.1

Table 2.1 (*cont.*)

Industries	Proportions of enterprises carrying out various kinds of innovation activities (%)				
	Enterprises carrying out innovation	Enterprises achieving innovation	Enterprises achieving both product or process innovation and organizational or marketing innovation	Enterprises achieving product or process innovation without organizational or marketing innovation	Enterprises achieving organizational or marketing innovation without product or process innovation
Manufacture of computers and office equipment	74.2	69.1	45.7	15.9	7.5
Manufacture of medical equipment and measuring instrument and meters	78.9	73.7	48.6	16.6	8.4
Services	29.2	28.5	9.6	1.9	17.1
Wholesale and retail trades	26.5	26.3	7.1	1.0	18.2
Transport, storage, and post	21.4	21.1	5.5	1.4	14.1

Information transmission, software, and information technology	63.1	58.6	35.2	8.1	15.4
Leasing and business services	27.1	26.5	8.3	1.5	16.6
Scientific research and technical services	40.9	37.7	17.5	5.3	14.9
Management of water conservancy, environment, and public facilities	31.8	30.8	10.3	2.1	18.3

Source: National Bureau of Statistics of China, 2018.

74.4 percent of all high-tech enterprises were in manufacturing, 68.3 percent achieved innovation, and 23 percent achieved four types of innovation simultaneously. A substantial majority of high-tech enterprises, 59.1 percent, achieved technological innovation, higher than the average level of all manufacturing industries by 23.9 percent, and 2.6 times the average of all enterprises.

2.3.3   Innovation in the Service Industry

The proportion of enterprises with innovation activities in the service industry is lower than in manufacturing, and those activities mainly focus on organizational or marketing innovation. In 2017, 29.2 percent of Chinese enterprises in the service industry engaged in innovation activities, and 28.5 percent achieved innovation, roughly 10 percentage points lower than the overall average (see Table 2.1). Among them, 26.7 percent achieved organizational or marketing innovation, which was lower than the overall level of enterprises by 4.3 percent, but only 11.4 percent achieved technological innovation, which was barely half the overall average.

Within the service industry, the information transmission, software, and information technology services companies are the most active in innovation. Among information transmission, software, and information technology service enterprises, 58.6 percent achieved innovation, with 43.3 percent achieving technological innovation and 23.5 percent achieving organizational or marketing innovation. These levels noticeably exceed the average in the service industry and approach the average in manufacturing. These results highlight the deep integration and development of information technology in China in recent years, which effectively promotes the prosperity of China's network and digital economy.

2.4   CHINESE ENTERPRISES' TECHNOLOGY INNOVATION STRATEGIES

As technology innovation becomes more and more networked and systematic, the methods that enterprises deploy to achieve innovation greatly impact the efficiency and level of innovation. This section analyzes Chinese enterprises' innovation approaches based on their mode of technology development, the choice of cooperation, and the structure of innovation expenditure.

2.4.1 Independent Development of Technology Innovation Predominates among Chinese Enterprises

Among the enterprises achieving product innovation, 83.7 percent rely on independent development. In addition, 6.6 percent choose to cooperate with other enterprises in their group, though cooperative development between Chinese enterprises and external organizations remains rare, especially with overseas companies or institutions. Only 10.5 percent and 8.3 percent of enterprises choose to develop cooperatively with domestic universities and other enterprises, respectively, while 2.4 percent cooperate with overseas companies or organizations, and a mere 2 percent cooperate with overseas institutes (Figure 2.4). This pattern is increasing: In 2017, the proportion of enterprises choosing independent development increased by 3.7 percentage points compared with 2016, while the proportion of other modes mostly decreased slightly. Process innovation followed a similar pattern. In 2017, as many as 74.9 percent of those that achieved process innovation did so through independent development, an increase of 3.5 percent compared with 2016.

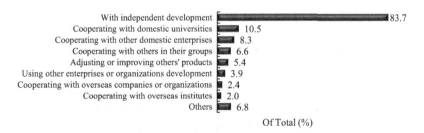

FIGURE 2.4 Innovation modes of enterprises achieving product innovation
Source: National Bureau of Statistics of China, 2018.

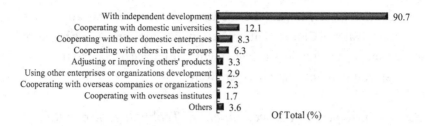

With independent development ████████████████████████ 90.7
Cooperating with domestic universities ██ 12.1
Cooperating with other domestic enterprises ██ 8.3
Cooperating with others in their groups ██ 6.3
Adjusting or improving others' products █ 3.3
Using other enterprises or organizations development █ 2.9
Cooperating with overseas companies or organizations █ 2.3
Cooperating with overseas institutes █ 1.7
Others █ 3.6

Of Total (%)

FIGURE 2.5 Innovation modes of high-technology industry enterprises achieving product innovation
Source: National Bureau of Statistics of China, 2018.

Among the high-tech industry, 90.7 percent of those that achieved product innovation developed it independently; 12.1 percent and 8.3 percent chose to cooperate with domestic universities and other enterprises, respectively, while more than 6 percent chose to cooperate with enterprises in their groups. A similar pattern held for high-tech enterprises with process innovation, as 85.7 percent independently developed it. Finally, 11.4 percent and 10.4 percent chose to cooperate with domestic universities and other enterprises, respectively, in line with the share of high-tech enterprises cooperating on product innovation (Figure 2.5).

2.4.2 The Most Important Expenditures for Corporate Innovation Are Machinery, Equipment, Software, and Internal Research and Development (R&D)

In the process of technology innovation activities, 57.3 percent of enterprises supported innovation activities by purchasing machinery, equipment, and software, and 53.3 percent carried out internal research and development (R&D) activities, the two most widely used modes of innovation activities. Training activities followed, with 37.9 percent of enterprises participating, while only 19.7 percent of businesses carried out market promotions, and 18.8 percent engaged in related designs. Last, a mere 8.7 percent of Chinese enterprises carried out external R&D, and 4.1 percent acquired related technology from outside (see Figure 2.6). Chinese enterprises invested in technology

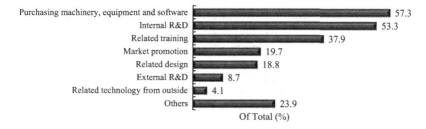

FIGURE 2.6 Types of innovation activities in enterprises with product or process innovation
Source: National Bureau of Statistics of China, 2018.

acquisition by purchasing advanced equipment and software, while enhancing their R&D and re-innovation capabilities.

2.4.3 The Main External Sources of Information for Corporate Innovation Are Clients and Intra-Industry Enterprises

Chinese enterprises report that clients are their most important source of information. Of firms with product or process innovation, 43.6 percent considered such information relevant, 38.1 percent considered internal information important, and 22.4 percent attached great importance to information from competitors or other intra-industry enterprises. Additionally, more than 18 percent considered information from suppliers and guilds significant, more than 15 percent believed that information from exhibitions and government departments had an impact, and last, information from literature and journals, market consulting institutions, and universities were regarded as less influential (Figure 2.7).

2.4.4 Upstream and Downstream Subjects Are the Main Cooperative Partners of Enterprises

Market cooperation within the value chain is the main method of cooperative innovation for Chinese enterprises. Among the enterprises surveyed, 17.5 percent carried out cooperative innovation, of which

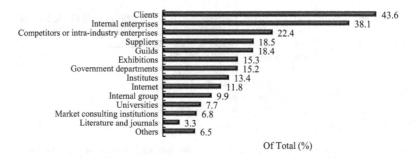

FIGURE 2.7 Information sources of enterprises with product or process innovation activities
Source: National Bureau of Statistics of China, 2018.

42.8 percent had cooperative relationships with clients and 36.4 percent with suppliers, respectively. Another 31.2 percent had cooperative relations with universities, 28.4 percent with other enterprises within the group, 20.4 percent with guilds, 18.6 percent with institutes, and 15.9 percent with competitors or intra-industry enterprises; 12 percent and 11.2 percent of enterprises had innovative cooperation with market consulting institutions and government departments, respectively, and the lowest proportion of enterprises (1.3 percent) showed cooperative innovation with venture capital institutions (Figure 2.8).

2.5   FACTORS DRIVING INNOVATION FROM THE PERSPECTIVE OF ENTREPRENEURS

Entrepreneurs' understanding of and attitude toward innovation activities have an important impact on the implementation of enterprise innovation strategy. In order to learn about entrepreneurs' understanding of innovation, three questionnaires were designed to investigate senior managers' understanding of innovation in manufacturing, construction, and service enterprises.

Overall, the vast majority of Chinese enterprises believe in promoting innovation. More than 80 percent of entrepreneurs recognize the importance of innovation for corporate development. Among them, 24.7 percent believed that innovation played an important role

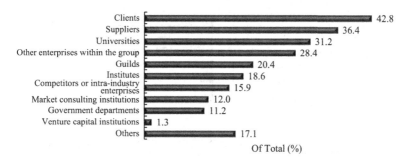

FIGURE 2.8 Partners of enterprises with cooperative innovation
Source: National Bureau of Statistics of China, 2018.

in the survival and development of enterprises, 58.8 percent thought that innovation played some role, while only 16.5 percent deemed that innovation did not play a role in the development of enterprises. Correspondingly, increasing innovation investment and enhancing the competitiveness of enterprises have become main strategic objectives of enterprises. According to the survey, 51.7 percent of the enterprises that formulated an innovation strategy focused on increasing innovation investment and enhancing the competitiveness of enterprises; 20.2 percent of the entrepreneurs set up the innovation strategy to catch up with the domestic leading enterprises in the same industry; 17.9 percent did so to maintain their existing technology level, production, and operation status; 5.7 percent defined innovation strategy as catching up with the international leading enterprises in the same industry; and 4.1 percent viewed it as key for international leadership in their field (Figure 2.9).

In the minds of entrepreneurs, product innovation is closely tied to improving product performance. Of entrepreneurs achieving product innovation, 85 percent believed that product innovation improved product performance and had a profound impact on enterprises, while more than 78 percent thought that product innovation increased product varieties and opened up new markets, 72.9 percent believed that product innovation could expand market share, and 68.7 percent stated that it could help replace outdated products (Figure 2.10).

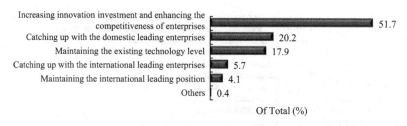

Of Total (%)

FIGURE 2.9 Strategic goals of enterprises' innovation
Source: National Bureau of Statistics of China, 2018.

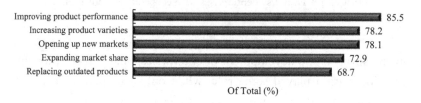

Of Total (%)

FIGURE 2.10 Entrepreneurs' understanding of the importance of product innovation
Source: National Bureau of Statistics of China, 2018.

Overall, entrepreneurs recognized that product innovation could have an impact on enterprises through a variety of channels.

Entrepreneurs similarly defined the benefit of process innovation in terms of improving efficiency and reducing costs. Over 80 percent of entrepreneurs who achieved process innovation considered it conducive to improving production efficiency, 75 percent believed that it improved production flexibility, and more than 60 percent attributed it to reductions in human costs, environmental pollution, energy consumption, and materials (Figure 2.11).

Entrepreneurs value organizational innovation for its ability to improve management efficiency. Of successful entrepreneurs, 79.6 percent deemed organizational innovation beneficial for improvements in management efficiency, 75.8 percent felt that it enhanced product quality, 75 percent appreciated improved response to customers or suppliers, and more than 60 percent cited other factors, including improved information exchange, development of new products or processes, and working conditions of employees or unit costs (Figure 2.12).

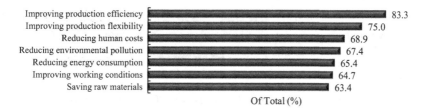

FIGURE 2.11 Entrepreneurs' understanding of the importance of process innovation
Source: National Bureau of Statistics of China, 2018.

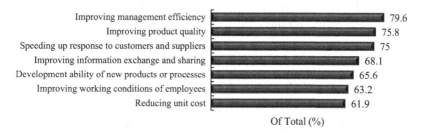

FIGURE 2.12 Entrepreneurs' understanding of the importance of organizational innovation
Source: National Bureau of Statistics of China, 2018.

Finally, marketing innovation supports the development of new customer groups. Nearly 75 percent of entrepreneurs achieving market innovation believed that it helped develop new client groups, while over 70 percent felt that it helped maintain or expand market share or viewed its utility as developing new market areas (Figure 2.13). Marketing innovation proved conducive to enhancing enterprises' market share through acquisition of new clients and expansion into new regions.

2.6   RESULTS AND IMPACT OF CHINESE ENTERPRISES' INNOVATION

China's increasingly active corporate innovation activities and innovation capabilities have achieved tremendous results. Science and technology innovation has laid the foundation for Chinese enterprises

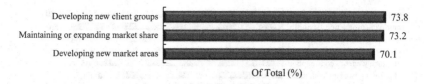

FIGURE 2.13 Entrepreneurs' understanding of the importance of marketing innovation
Source: National Bureau of Statistics of China, 2018.

to develop new products and enhance technological capabilities, supported China's economic development and social welfare, and provided high-quality product service for the world consumer market.

2.6.1   New Product Output

Enterprises have continuously developed new products through technology innovation. In 2017, 100 percent of surveyed Chinese enterprises produced products new to the firm, and more than 60 percent of them produced products that were new to the market. These new products contributed an average of 14.5 percent of total revenues to the main business (see Table 2.2). Industrial enterprises were most likely to launch new products, with 59.9 percent of enterprises generating products new to the domestic market and 20.9 percent to the international market, while the construction industry led in the share of revenue contributed by new products, with a total of 22.3 percent of revenues.

2.6.2   Technological Capabilities

Chinese enterprises have continuously strengthened their technological R&D capabilities through their innovation activities. The share of industrial enterprises with R&D activities in China has increased significantly, from 11.5 percent in 2011 to 27.4 percent in 2017 (see Table 2.3). The percentage of revenues spent on R&D has likewise grown from 0.71 percent in 2011 to 1.06 percent in 2017. This increasing frequency of spending has led Chinese enterprises to greater results as well. Chinese firms increased their patent

Table 2.2 *New product output of Chinese enterprises (2017)*

Items	Proportion in the enterprises achieving product innovation (%)		Proportion of sales revenue of new products in main business income (%)
	Enterprises with products new to the market	Enterprises with products new to the firm	
All enterprises	61.4	100	14.6
Industrial enterprises	20.9 (International market)	100	16.9 (International market)
	59.9 (Domestic market)		5.6 (Domestic market)
Construction	71.7	100	22.3
Service	65.8	100	9.3

Source: National Bureau of Statistics of China, 2018.

Table 2.3 R&D input and patent output of Chinese industrial enterprises

Indicators	2011	2012	2013	2014	2015	2016	2017
Percentage of enterprises having R&D activities to total number of enterprises (%)	11.5	13.7	14.8	16.9	19.2	23.0	27.4
Percentage of expenditure on R&D to sales revenue (%)	0.71	0.77	0.80	0.84	0.90	0.94	1.06
Inventions patent applications (number)	134,843	176,167	205,146	239,925	245,688	286,987	320,626
Patents in force (number)	201,089	277,196	335,401	448,885	573,765	769,847	933,990

Source: National Bureau of Statistics of China, 2018.

applications from 134,843 in 2011 to 320,626 in 2017, a surge of 138 percent. Total inventions reached 933,990 in 2017, 4.6 times those of 2011, with an average annual growth of 29.2 percent.

2.6.3   Promoting Economic and Social Development

Active corporate innovation effectively supported the sustained development of China's economy. From 2013 to 2018, China's economy grew rapidly with an average rate of 7 percent per year, significantly faster than the global average of 2.9 percent in the same period. New products, formats, and business models continue to emerge based on the Internet and information technology, prompting the rapid rise of e-commerce, the shared economy, and the platform economy, and supporting China's transformation and economic development.

Chinese enterprises have also made important contributions to global demand and economic development. From 2000 to 2016, China's exports of high-tech products increased more than tenfold from US$41.74 billion to US$496 billion. The proportion of high-tech products in the world's total exports increased over the same period from 4 percent to about 26 percent. Information and communications technology (ICT) services have become the largest service trade in the global economy, and from 2000 to 2016, China's ICT service exports increased eight times over, from US$9.36 billion to US$83.39 billion, with an average annual growth rate of 14.6 percent. China has become the main supplier of high-tech products and services in the world.

2.7   CONCLUSIONS

Chinese enterprises have entered an active period of innovation. Nearly 40 percent of them have innovation activities, with a higher share of technological innovation than in either India or Brazil. While the level of technology innovation activity in China remains lower than that of developed countries, and Chinese enterprises rely more on organizational and marketing innovation, innovation has become the consensus in China.

Chinese industrial enterprises are more active in innovation than any other sector, but construction and service industries show gains in organizational or marketing innovation. The proportion of enterprises achieving innovation in China's manufacturing industry exceeds that of South Korea and Spain and is near the level of developed markets Japan and Italy. The high-tech industry is particularly strong in technological innovation and leads among manufacturing sectors. The proportion of enterprises achieving technology innovation in the high-tech industry is 2.6 times that of Chinese enterprises overall. Information transmission, software, and information technology services are the best-represented sectors for innovative activities in the service industry and approach the average level of the manufacturing industry. This suggests deep integration across the information technology and traditional industries in China, a boon for the country's digital economy.

Chinese enterprises primarily innovate through independent development. Only a small share of firms cooperate with domestic universities and other enterprises, and even fewer collaborate with overseas companies and institutes. Clients and intra-industry enterprises are the main external sources of information for enterprise innovation. Generally, Chinese enterprises still learn about and apply advanced foreign technology by acquiring advanced equipment and software. For innovation, they focus on internal R&D to strengthen their absorptive capacity and enhance their R&D and re-innovation capabilities.

China's corporate innovation has paid substantial dividends. Science and technology innovation has created the conditions for Chinese enterprises to develop new product output and enhance technological capabilities, provided strong support for China's economic development and social welfare promotion, and also offered high-quality products and services for the global consumer market. As China's innovation capabilities continue to improve, it is expected to become not only the largest consumer market for the commercialization of world innovation, but also an increasingly important member of the world's technological R&D network.

REFERENCES

Chinese Academy of Science and Technology for Development et al. (2018). *The evaluation report of Chinese corporate innovation ability 2018*. Beijing: Scientific and Technical Documentation Press.

Department for Business, Energy & Industrial Strategy. (2018, October 24). *UK innovation survey 2017: Main Report*. Retrieved August 10, 2019, from www.gov.uk/government/statistics/uk-innovation-survey-2017-main-report.

Gault, F. (2016). *Measuring innovation in all sectors of the economy*. Working Paper Series, No. 2015-038. Maastricht, The Netherlands: United Nations University. www.merit.unu.edu/publications/working-papers/abstract/?id=5832.

Hall, B. H., & Jaffe, A. B. (2012). Measuring science, technology, and innovation: A review. *Annals of Science and Technology Policy, 2*(1), 1–74.

Mainyu, E. A. (2012). Community innovation survey. *Statistics in Focus Eurostat Theme, 45*(5), 332–334.

National Academies of Sciences, Engineering, and Medicine. (2017). *Advancing concepts and models for measuring innovation: Proceedings of a workshop*. Washington, DC: The National Academies Press. doi: 10.17226/23640.

National Bureau of Statistics of China. (2017). *National enterprises innovation survey yearbook 2017*. Beijing: China Statistics Press.

(2018). *National enterprises innovation survey yearbook 2018*. Beijing: China Statistics Press.

National Bureau of Statistics of China and Ministry of Science and Technology of the People's Republic of China. (2018). *China science and technology statistics yearbook 2018*. Beijing: China Statistics Press.

National Research Council. (2014). *Capturing change in science, technology, and innovation: Improving indicators to inform policy*. (Panel on Developing Science, Technology, and Innovation Indicators for the Future, R. E. Litan, A. W. Wyckoff, and K. H. Husbands Fealing, Committee on National Statistics, Division of Behavioral and Social Sciences and Education. Board on Science, Technology, and Economic Policy, Division of Policy and Global Affairs, eds.) Washington, DC: The National Academies Press.

OECD and Eurostat. (2005). *Oslo manual: Guidelines for collecting and interpreting innovation data* (3rd ed.). Paris: Author. doi.org/10.1787/19900414.

OECD. (2007). *Science, technology, and innovation indicators in a changing world: responding to policy needs*. Paris: Author. www.oecd.org/sti/inno/sciencetechnologyandinnovationindicatorsinachangingworldrespondingtopolicyneeds.htm.

OECD. (2015). *Frascati manual 2015: Guidelines for collecting and reporting data on research and experimental development, the measurement of scientific, technological and innovation activities.* Paris: Author. http://dx.doi.org/10.1787/9789264239012-en.

Whyte, J. K. (2007). Book review: *The Oxford handbook of innovation management* edited by Jan Fagerberg, David C. Mowery and Richard R. Nelson. *Organization Studies, 28*(4), 589–593.

The World Bank. (2019). World Development Indicators 2019. Retrieved July 30, 2019, from https://datacatalog.worldbank.org/dataset/world-development-indicators.

3 The Rise of an Innovation Tiger

The Catch-Up of the Indian National System of Innovation

Kristin Brandl and Ram Mudambi

3.1 INTRODUCTION

India is a leading developing country in terms of innovation output. As of May 2019, the country's total innovation output was almost 45,000 patents granted by the US Patent and Trademark Office (US PTO, 2019) and over 510,000 Indian patents recorded by the World Intellectual Property Organization (WIPO, 2019). This innovation output compares with a major developed country like Italy, one of the ten largest economies in the world in 2019. Italy's figures are just over 82,000 US patents (US PTO, 2019) and 721,000 total patents (WIPO, 2019), reflecting India's potential as an innovation hub in some industries. While India has long developed the building blocks of its innovation capabilities, the country's innovation output only took off in the twenty-first century, at least in a formalized sense.

The trend in US patent grants is by no means a complete picture. Nevertheless, the steadily increasing number of patents over time (Table 3.1) correlates very well with many other indicators of the maturity of the Indian economy and its national system of innovation (NSI). For example, the trend also relates to the integration of Indian emerging market multinational companies (eMNCs) into global automotive value chains (Kumaraswamy, Mudambi, Saranga, & Tripathy, 2012), innovative activities and market growth in the biopharmaceutical industry (Brandl, Mudambi, & Scalera, 2015; see also Figure 3.1), and the country's catch-up to world standards in wind turbine productions (Awate, Larsen, & Mudambi, 2012). Much of what has happened within the Indian NSI reflects Indian government innovation policies

Table 3.1 *Trends in US patents granted to India-based inventors*

Dates	Number of US PTO patents
1976–1989 (15 years)	247
1990–1999 (10 years)	679
2000–2009 (10 years)	5,579
2010–2018	35,321
2019*	3,067
TOTAL (1976–2019)	**44,893**

Note: * January–May
Source: US PTO (2019).

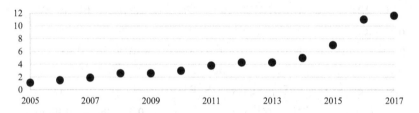

FIGURE 3.1 Indian biotech industry market size (US$ bn)
Source: ABLE (2016). Data is current as of April 2016; 2017 is a forecast.

and regulations that were implemented since India's independence in 1947.

India's NSI is a good illustration of how important innovation is for the development process of a country and how it can reflect the level of advancement of the country (Lundvall, 2010). As innovation is costly and requires advanced innovation capabilities, firms are required to develop or acquire these capabilities and bear the associated costs. Successful acquisition of these capabilities is typically indicative of firms acting as innovation leaders rather than copycats. Generally, the more innovative an emerging market and the more innovation capabilities its firms have, the better they can compete with MNCs from developed countries. Studying India's NSI and innovation output allows us to track this development. The NSI is a network structure that consists of a variety of interconnected actors. These actors include (national and international) firms, universities, and government agencies (Nelson, 1993; Freeman, 1995; Lundvall, 2010).

Each actor has its own objectives within the system, and in turn, differently influences the system. For example, the government establishes policies and regulations that support the NSI, but also participates in the system with its own public innovation. In this sense, its direct activities in institutions like national laboratories function in a manner similar to universities and mainly aim to benefit the public, with only a secondary focus on generating profits (Choudhury & Khanna, 2014). On the other hand, firms are interested in commercial innovation that can lead to competitive advantages (Motohashi, 2005). In addition to these internal actors, external actors such as foreign MNCs and supranational institutions like the World Trade Organization (WTO) and the International Monetary Fund (IMF) can also influence the NSI and innovation outputs (Brandl, Darendeli, & Mudambi, 2019).

In this chapter, we provide a process perspective of these industries and the firms within them to identify their innovation capabilities and the extent to which India has become an innovation hub. First, we discuss the literature on innovation systems and innovation progress of emerging markets. We follow this discussion with an analysis of three Indian industries that reflect different innovation systems and their efforts to catch up to their developed market counterparts. We specifically focus on the endogenous and exogenous pressures that influence this catch-up. We conclude the chapter with a discussion of possibilities for future research.

3.2 INNOVATION SYSTEMS CATCH-UP

3.2.1 *Innovation Systems*

A country's NSI covers all industries, although the most innovative industries, such as pharmaceuticals and other high-tech industries, are often overrepresented. NSI actors, such as (national and international) firms, universities, and government agencies (Nelson, 1993; Freeman, 1995; Lundvall, 2010), work closely together to encourage innovation and promote an environment to support new innovations. However, the innovation objectives of NSI actors differ. Domestic firms and MNCs aim to achieve commercial innovations that can lead to competitive advantages. In contrast, universities and governmental laboratories or innovation centers predominantly focus on innovation that enhances public welfare, with a secondary focus on profits (Choudhury & Khanna, 2014). In short, private firms most often view innovation as a private good, whereas public bodies view it as a public good (McCann & Mudambi, 2005).

Innovation can be distinguished along two generic dimensions: nature and scale. In terms of nature, scholars often distinguish between product and process innovation. Similarly, in terms of scale, they often differentiate between radical and incremental innovation. Within the implied 2x2 matrix, most innovation tends to fall into two cells: radical/product and incremental/process (Asheim & Coenen, 2005).

Product innovation is typically costlier and riskier, as well as more challenging to create, but provides more revenue (Mudambi & Swift, 2014). Process innovation is often based on extant knowledge and therefore is less costly but has less profit potential. Emerging markets often move from a focus on process innovation to a focus on product/service innovation as they develop. When categorizing the development of NSIs and emerging markets, their capabilities must progress from producing output (copying best practices) to producing innovation (novel, next-generation products).

Aside from studying innovation output type, it is important to understand the NSI as a whole and examine the roles of the various actors. It could be that a government supports process innovation and hinders product innovation, or that foreign MNCs in the country support product innovations (Brandl et al., 2019). Thus, it is imperative to understand what pressures influence an NSI. These pressures can be internal to the country or external. Endogenous and country internal pressures stem from national actors, such as domestic firms, universities, and the government. Exogenous and country external pressures stem from foreign MNCs and foreign supranational institutions.

For example, endogenous pressures often result from governmental regulations and policies that establish the "rules of the game" (North, 1991). However, these policies are influenced by other system actors, i.e., domestic firms and universities, as each actor has its own innovation objectives for which it lobbies. Universities and government activities encourage the local development of basic science and technology, which form the foundation for applied commercial innovation.

Exogenous pressures often stem from foreign firms or foreign supranational institutions that pressure the government to implement certain innovation policies. For example, foreign firms consider locating R&D activities in countries with well-established and functioning NSIs and country-specific advantages related to innovation. One of their main considerations is the protection of intellectual property (IP) in order to avoid innovation appropriation by others, especially domestic firms. Strict IP regulations and policies have been shown to attract foreign firms even to developing countries, which often have institutional voids (Nicholson, 2007). Moreover, supranational institutions also try to influence governmental policies related to IP protection; for example, the WTO's Agreement on Trade-Related Aspects of Intellectual Property Rights (TRIPS) and the IMF's influence pushed policies toward stronger protection of IP (Brandl et al., 2019).

3.2.2 Innovation Systems in Developing Countries and Their Catch-Up

Effective NSIs often exist in developed economies where policies and regulations are fully functional and strictly implemented. In developing countries, NSIs are often more disorganized and not fully functional due to large institutional voids and ineffective policy and regulation implementation (Guennif & Ramani, 2012; Beugelsdijk & Mudambi, 2013). The business environments in these countries are therefore not supportive of innovation, leading to weak performance.

Developing countries catch up to mature market standards in several distinct phases (Abramovitz, 1986). Kumaraswamy et al. (2012) developed a three-phase model to outline these processes. The authors distinguish the development into transition, consolidation, and global integration phases. The transition phase focuses on the development of process innovation. The foundation for innovation outputs at this stage of development is imitation of world-class products/services and their production processes. For example, reverse engineering in the pharmaceutical industry has led to innovations in generic drug production. Firms in this phase face challenges to develop output or production capabilities to copy existing products and services.

The consolidation phase requires the liberalization of the domestic market, which leads to foreign firms entering the developing country. This incoming foreign direct investment (FDI) brings investments into the economy – foreign firm knowledge can spill over to domestic firms (Blomstrom & Kokko, 1998) – and enhances competition, which can lead to more innovation outputs (Brandl et al., 2019). In this phase, firms have basic innovation capabilities, which are often related to process innovation rather than new product development.

Last, in the global integration phase, domestic firms gain knowledge to innovate products/services and collaborate globally, i.e., they show signs of catching up to developed country standards, transforming from copycats to leaders in their own right. Thus, the NSI has moved from learning to innovating, learning to innovate efficiently and improve innovations, and finally learning to develop leading innovations (Kale, 2010); see Figure 3.2 for an illustration of these phases.

NSI policy regime changes

Transition phase	Consolidation phase	Global integration phase
Copying existing innovations	Creation of basic innovations	Innovation leadership
Developing basic innovation capabilities	Development of process innovation capabilities	Development of advanced innovation capabilities

FIGURE 3.2 Policy regime and NSI catch-up alignment
Source: Adapted from Kumaraswamy et al. (2012).

3.3 THE INDIAN NSI

In order to illustrate the shift of India's firms from copycats to leaders in the global economy, we study three industries that have made a significant contribution to the county's NSI: wind turbines, pharmaceuticals, and auto components. These three industries are emblematic of India's development and provide a template to understand the country's development process. We base our analysis on Kumaraswamy et al.'s (2012) three development phases of transition, consolidation, and global integration. We start this discussion with a general overview of India's NSI and related policies.

3.3.1 India's Policy Changes and Innovation

After India gained independence in 1947, the country's economy was strongly influenced by a widespread system of regulations and policies, the most important being the Industrial Licensing Act of 1951. This policy restricted the expansion of existing domestic businesses and challenged new start-up firms with bureaucratic hurdles. The government focused on state-owned firms and institutions, mandating government approval to start or expand businesses. This approval required extensive interaction with regulators or politicians (Panagriya, 2008). The "commanding heights of the economy" were reserved for state-owned enterprises (SOEs), restricting domestic firms to operating and innovating in restricted sectors of the economy.

The domestic economy was sheltered by trade barriers through the 1980s, and both the import and export shares of GDP were below 10 percent. While these barriers protected domestic firms from foreign competition, they also limited the capacity of local firms to access current technologies and innovation catch-up processes (Mudambi, 2008). Radical economic reforms implemented in 1991 lowered or removed many of these barriers: Exchange rate controls were eased, many tariffs and duties were reduced, and most capital and intermediate goods were no longer subject to restrictive import licensing.

Moreover, reacting to the economic conditions after independence and the virtual nonexistence of many Indian industries, the government also invited foreign firms to operate in India and produce both intermediate and finished products for the local and international market (Haakonsson, Jensen, & Mudambi, 2012). Foreign firms brought change into the country and led to the first knowledge spillovers. However, domestic firms did not yet have the capabilities to incorporate this knowledge and use it for their own innovation outputs.

As a consequence, the government reacted and implemented various changes, such as extensive efforts to create a scientific workforce and leverage government organizations, such as the Council of Scientific and Industrial Research (CSIR) (Kale & Little, 2007). The government also increased R&D expenditures and financially supported the NSI. These changes led the import and export shares to increase to around 15 percent of GDP by the mid-2000s. The reform process continued in the new century; between 2004 and 2008 additional reforms, including further cuts to tariffs, were implemented, so that by 2009 the import and export shares of GDP had increased to levels similar to those of many advanced economies (Cagliarini & Baker, 2010). This increased international exposure also encouraged innovation in the country. R&D spending as a percentage of GDP increased, and the NSI showed an increase in innovation outputs. Last, policy changes to comply with WTO and TRIPS regulations were implemented on January 1, 2010.

India acknowledged the need to further advance and update the NSI and implemented new policies for the organization of investments in science, technology, and innovation (STI) and established the National Innovation Council (NInC) (Government of India, 2013). STI activities were announced in January 2013 with the objective of steering and coordinating investments in the NSI by both the government and the private sector. The collective work on improving the NSI is the first attempt in India to coordinate the efforts of the public and the private sectors (Abrol, 2013). The government objective with the STI policies are "to create the necessary framework for enabling this integration in identified priority areas by exploiting endogenous resources, strengths and capacities. New structural mechanisms and models are needed to address the pressing challenges of energy and environment, food and nutrition, water and sanitation, habitat, affordable health care and skill building and unemployment" (Government of India, 2013, p. 3).

Thus, the key elements of STI policies are the promotion of scientific temper and enhancement of skills and capabilities, the push to be a world leader, and to connect the NSI with economic and socioeconomic benefits. The objective is to foster resource-optimization and cost-effectiveness in the use of innovation in order to create a robust NSI. The government vowed to increase R&D spending and provide the financial as well as infrastructural support to achieve the set goals and successfully implement the policies (Government of India, 2013).

In the following years, the government enacted further policies to encourage a national innovation ecosystem. For example, in 2016 the government launched the Atal Innovation Mission, a flagship innovation program to promote innovation cultures among schoolchildren by providing them with hands-on experience in high-tech Internet-based industries, such as 3D printing and robotics (Pachouri, 2018). The government's NSI activities have since focused on investments and cooperation, and the current prime minister, Narendra Modi, has actively supported these objectives.

For example, going beyond the national borders and following a strategy of "innovation diplomacy," the government established the India–Israel Industrial R&D Technological Innovation Fund and hosts the Global Entrepreneurship Summit (Pachouri, 2018). The strong focus on innovation has improved India's recent rankings in the Global Innovation Index from the eighty-first spot in 2015 to fifty-seventh in 2018 (Cornell University, INSEAD, & WIPO, 2019). Despite this improvement, the country still ranks below the OECD countries in its innovation inputs with low inputs in university and public research and low R&D and innovation in the private sector. India's innovation by entrepreneurs significantly lags OECD counterparts (OECD, 2014).

As noted above, three industries that exemplify the successes of India's NSI are wind turbines, pharmaceuticals, and auto components (see Table 3.2). All three industries are highly innovative and have a central role in India's NSI. The wind turbine industry is a novel industry requiring high technology and engineering skills. The pharmaceutical industry depends on scientific knowledge and skills. It has developed into one of the most important industries in India since independence. The auto components industry is highly engineering based and has developed in tandem with the country's development as a whole. We use secondary data to describe, analyze, and discuss each industry. We single out firms in each industry that demonstrate the innovation capabilities of domestic firms in more detail.

3.3.2   The Indian Wind Turbine Industry

Transition Phase. The Indian government has supported the wind energy sector[1] and tried to increase public awareness with a nationwide program in the 1990s. This program included wind resource assessments and demonstrations to industry and state electricity boards. To encourage foreign entry into the market, and in line with market liberalization, the government implemented favorable

---

[1] Parts of this section are taken with permission from Brandl & Mudambi (2014).

Table 3.2 *The three industries and the NSI*

Innovation system components	Wind turbine	Pharmaceutical	Auto components
Technology level	High	High	Medium/high
Technology basis	Engineering	Science	Engineering
Industry establishment	Novel	Established	Traditional
Education level	Tertiary	Tertiary	Secondary/ tertiary
Labor skills	Electronics, mechanics, hydraulics, advanced materials, aerodynamics	Chemistry, statistics	Car/engine mechanics, advanced materials
Innovation capabilities	Energy generating turbines and energy transport	Drug development and testing	Car component design (engine components, exterior and interior components)

Source: The authors, based on research.

policies such as five-year tax holidays, customs relief, and soft loans (Rajsekhar, Van Hulle, & Jansen, 1999).

The dominant global players at the time were mostly European firms such as Vestas (Denmark) and Enercon (Germany), which also became major players in the Indian wind turbine market. Foreign firms often produced the wind turbines in India and then either installed them in the country or exported them. The Indian government's early policies included the 1995 National Guidelines for Clearance of Wind Power Projects. The policy required each Indian state electricity board to make domestic energy grids compatible with the newest developments in wind power technology. Projects were financially incentivized, with 100 percent depreciation of wind equipment in the first year after installation or five-year tax holidays (Rajsekhar et al., 1999).

Consolidation Phase. In the consolidation phase, the government understood the need to build a domestic industry and implemented policies to encourage local wind turbine manufacturing. For example, it incentivized the import of wind turbine components rather than finished wind turbines. The government also created a national certification program for wind turbines, requiring extensive tests and following international standards, in order to support domestic turbine manufacturing. Furthermore, the government introduced policies to increase wind energy usage and make the industry more attractive, such as specified minimum energy distributions from renewable energy sources. These policies resulted in states setting aggressive renewable energy targets (GWEC, 2016).

For example, in the state of Karnataka, the local state energy regulatory commission stipulated that a minimum of 5 percent of energy produced come from renewable sources by 2007, while the state of Maharashtra implemented feed-in tariffs for wind electricity, thereby providing them with long-term contracts and subsidized prices. Other states teamed up with wind turbine firms, such as Suzlon, to develop wind farms on a build-operate-transfer basis (Awate et al., 2012). As a result of these changes, by 2006 the country had installed wind turbines with a rated capacity of 6,228 MW, already higher than the 2012 target of 5,000 MW. In 2009, the government established the Generation Based Incentive (GBI) scheme for grid-connected wind power projects. The scheme facilitated the entry of large independent power producers, increasing the attractiveness of the wind power sector to FDI and to investors (Lewis, 2011).

Global Integration Phase. In the global integration phase, government policies encouraged the industry to grow, foreign wind turbine firms entered the country, and domestic firms established a stronger presence in the local and global wind turbine industry. Moreover, foreign and domestic firms began forming alliances in

R&D that led to cost-effective technologies and improvement in the quality of power generation systems (GWEC, 2016).

With the government's commitment to renewable energy, the Indian government introduced further policies to advance the industry, such as the 2015 Offshore Wind Policy. These policies are also linked to various global organizations; for example, the Facilitating Offshore Wind in India (FOWIND) is connected to a European Union cofinanced project to measure wind resources. Suzlon Energy Inc. (see Box 3.1) holds 35.4 percent of installed capacity and is the most advanced wind energy company in India (GWEC, 2016). By 2018, India ranked fourth in the global wind turbine industry after China, the United States, and Germany, with installations of over 31 gigawatts (GWs) and a market share of 5.9 percent. The Indian industry has provided leading innovations and is well integrated in global value chains. About 75 percent of its production is within India, manufacturing approximately 10 GWs annually (Arora, 2019).

3.3.3   The Indian Pharmaceutical Industry

Transition phase. The Indian pharmaceutical industry[2] developed in several stages, influenced by government policies. These policies addressed diverse objectives, such as improving the country's healthcare sector and complying with global IP protection regulations to secure access to the industry's global innovation system (Scherer, 1993). Due to economic conditions after independence and the virtual nonexistence of a local Indian pharmaceutical industry, foreign firms and imports dominated the country's domestic market in this sector for many years. However, their products were often expensive relative to local purchasing power. With government investments in the domestic science and engineering-oriented education system and improved scientific infrastructure, the domestic scientific workforce began to expand.

[2] Parts of this section are taken with permission from Brandl, Mudambi, & Scalera (2015).

BOX 3.1   **Suzlon Energy LTD**

Suzlon Energy LTD made its appearance in the global business
environment in 1995 and immediately began challenging foreign
players in the Indian wind turbine market. At the time of Suzlon's
founding, foreign firms dominated global innovation and turbine
production and sold final products in the Indian market. The turbines
sold in India were often smaller than world standards at the time.
Suzlon's catch-up strategy was to manufacture turbines of comparable
technological sophistication locally in India at a lower price than
its competitors.

   The firm did not have the necessary engineering know-how to
operate in this highly knowledge-intensive industry, which requires
expertise in electronics, mechanics, hydraulics, advanced materials,
and aerodynamics. In order to gain the necessary engineering
knowledge quickly and efficiently, Suzlon partnered with German firm
Südwind, a global player in the industry. Initially, Suzlon sold
Südwind's turbines in India and used this "apprenticeship" to gain
further technological knowledge. After Südwind went bankrupt in
1997, Suzlon hired the German firm's engineers, finally internalizing
the appropriate engineering skills to start producing their own
turbines. The firm's catch-up strategy of partnering with an established
firm to gain the necessary knowledge – also referred to as a fast-
follower strategy – was very successful. Suzlon leveraged this strategy
to rapidly dominate the Indian market and soon generated local
revenues comparable to those of other global industry leaders.

   The next step in Suzlon's catch-up strategy was to go beyond the
Indian market and start operating and selling turbines internationally,
especially in northern Europe, which had developed into the most
important wind power market from the late 1990s onward. Like other
firms in the industry, Suzlon started to undertake acquisitions, form
alliances, and sign licensing agreements with various MNCs from the
region. The aim was to gain state-of-the-art technology in the industry
and be at the forefront of new developments. Thus, Suzlon started a
wave of acquisitions, such as that of Dutch AE-Rotor Techniek BV,
which provided specialized knowledge in the design and manufacture

BOX 3.1   (cont.)

of rotor blades. Suzlon also acquired the German AX
215 Verwaltungsgesellschaft GmbH to establish an R&D unit in
Germany (close to all the important Northern European target
markets). It also bought the marketing and manufacturing rights of
Enron Wind, a bankrupt American turbine manufacturer.

Instead of building up R&D capabilities internally, Suzlon
acquired capabilities externally through corporate acquisitions and
then began the process of internalizing the acquired knowledge and
developing its own innovation capabilities to broaden the firm's
R&D and product portfolio. In 2000, Suzlon became the leader in the
Indian wind energy sector, as well as an important global player in
terms of both productivity and kilowatt output. It was listed on the
Bombay Stock Exchange and the National Stock Exchange in the
following years.

By 2005, the company crossed the 1 GW installed capacity mark in
India and continued its focus on innovations. For example, it developed
the 2.1 megawatt (MW) generator, which facilitates better and more
efficient harnessing of wind power; the S9X suite of wind turbines,
launched in 2011 at the AWEA Wind Power global conference; and the
S97 2.1 MW wind turbine generator (WTG), launched in 2012 and built
with a hybrid tower (lattice/tubular combination) and a hub-height of
120 meters. These innovations were needed to comply with global
industry standards, not just Indian standards, and Suzlon spent a
significant amount of money to certify its innovation. For example, the
S111 2.1MW WTG suite, part of the S9X series, received the German
TÜV NORD certificate in 2015 for conforming to standards and
regulations for design, testing, and manufacturing of the WTG.

In order to finance the expensive R&D and comply with the many
international wind energy standards, Suzlon needed new investors and
signed agreements with investment firms, such as Dilip Shanghvi
Family and Associates. It used the funds to enhance training and
learning facilities to educate wind turbine engineers in India and in
North America. However, the expenses for innovation and strong
global competition challenged the company, leading to increased debt

---

BOX 3.1   **(cont.)**

and sales of subsidiaries, such as the German subsidiary Senvion SE in 2015.

In its 2018 annual report, the company revealed an INR 83 billion revenue, a slight decrease from previous years. R&D spending is at 3.91 percent of the total turnover, which is a significant increase over time. The company has 17.9 GW cumulative wind installations and an additional 14.8 GW service portfolios allocated in seventeen countries in six continents. In 2019, Suzlon was among the top ten leading vendors in the global wind turbine industry, reported by Technavio.

Sources: Awate et al. (2012); Meyer, Mudambi, and Narula (2011); Suzlon (2019); Kumar, Mohaparta, and Chandraskhar (2009); Technavio (2019).

Despite these changes, the domestic innovation system did not produce breakthrough pharmaceutical innovations, as the individual components – the educational institutions, the government labs, and the private sector – did not work together as a system. The 1970 Patent Act significantly changed and strengthened the domestic pharmaceutical industry (Kale & Little, 2007; Nair, 2008). The Act enabled Indian firms to access international intellectual property (Kale & Little, 2007) and allowed firms to patent manufacturing processes instead of only complete end-products. It also allowed the development of generic equivalents to innovative products through the local development of new processes and methods (Nair, 2008).

Thus, Indian firms developed reverse-engineering capabilities and produced products that were patented in other countries, using new and locally developed production processes. Consequently, the firms could produce foreign drugs at more cost-effective prices and take market share from foreign MNCs by selling nonbranded generics (Nair, 2008). This adaptation centered on process innovations, which focused on learning through the duplication and imitation of foreign drugs (Kale & Little, 2007). Furthermore, the weak IP protection fostered by the Patent Act and the low drug prices through developed generic drugs forced foreign pharmaceutical MNCs to reduce operations in India. This provided domestic firms with expansion opportunities in the local market. Although the Indian market became large in volume, it remained comparatively low in value (Kale & Little, 2007).

Consolidation phase. Indian pharmaceutical firms also started to export their "imitated" generic drugs to emerging as well as advanced economies, supported by regulations such as the 1984 Waxman-Hatch Act in the United States. The Act allowed firms to sell generic drugs tested with less expensive and simpler "bioequivalent" and "bioavailability tests" rather than full-blown clinical trials in the US market (Kale & Little, 2007, p. 600). Not surprisingly, they were opposed by the firms that owned the IP underlying the original drugs that were imitated by the generics. Some firms chose the aggressive and high-risk/high-return route of challenging the validity of existing patents and taking on the dominant global patent holder. Others chose a more conservative approach of filing cases based on expired patents, or developing alliances and strategic ties with their larger, better resourced global rivals (Kale & Little, 2007).

A significant change in the industry was caused by India's ratification of the WTO's TRIPS in 1994. The country agreed to change its extant patent regime, previously with loose copy and reverse engineering regulations and a focus on processes, to a more rigorous product patent regime. Due to India's classification as a developing country without an existing product patent regime, the WTO granted a ten-year transition period. In return, the government agreed to legal protection for product patents and for trade-related intellectual property rights protection (Nair, 2008).

Three amendments to the Patent Act of 1970 in 1999, 2002, and 2005 applied the TRIPS regulation in practice (Nair, 2008). These regulatory changes significantly affected the Indian market. The regulations provided more security for MNCs and led to more market entrances, with new and improved products and knowledge introduced into the domestic market. Furthermore, local firms' capabilities in process developments and generic drugs increased their awareness of opportunities in new drug delivery systems and NCE research (Kale & Little, 2007). Additionally, Indian firms, such as Dr. Reddy (see Box 3.2) started to acquire foreign firms in order to enter foreign markets.

Global integration phase. The Indian pharmaceutical industry shifted from primarily process innovation to the more challenging and expensive product innovation after the full TRIPS ratification in 2005 (IBEF, 2018). The total market for healthcare products and services has markedly grown. The rise in income, enhanced medical infrastructure, and greater health insurance coverage all resulted in the need for more and better products, in turn leading to more pharmaceutical innovations and patent output. In addition, the Indian government supported local market innovation with incentives and subsidies.

More recently, the government implemented the National Pharmaceutical Pricing Policy in 2012 (NPPP-2012), with the aim of reducing drug prices for the local market, making them more accessible to the population. This policy was supported by the New Drug Pricing Control Order, which hoped to slash the prices of drugs by 80 percent (IBEF, 2018). The government also amended the 2002 Patent Act in 2015 to benefit foreign and domestic firms' innovation activities in the country.

Foreign firms positively perceived these developments. In 2014, the Indian government began to incrementally open the economy to these firms. New policies allow 100 percent foreign ownership for foreign firms in the medical devices sector (in 2014) and 74 percent foreign ownership for already-established foreign pharmaceutical companies (in 2016). In order to remain competitive and capitalize on these changes, Indian firms aggressively tried to raise funds to acquire these foreign firms or to internationalize themselves. More and more Indian firms such as Sun Pharma, Lupin, or Dr. Reddy's Laboratories invested in internationalization activities.

The country also continued to export generic drugs, resulting in a 20 percent share of the global generics market in 2016–2017 worth

BOX 3.2   **Dr. Reddy's Laboratories**

Dr. Reddy's Laboratories (hereafter referred to as Dr. Reddy's) was founded in 1984 as a supplier to many local drug manufacturers. Rather than focusing on innovation activities, the company focused on supplying local firms and firms in other developing countries with raw and semiraw material. Building on these successes, the firm continued to expand with exports to more advanced countries. The company's first international expansion in 1992, a joint venture with Russian company Biomed, lasted for two years. From then on, its focus was on the US and European markets.

Beginning in the 1990s, the company prioritized innovations and the discovery of new drugs. The company started its Research Foundation in 1992 to create generic specialty drugs and analogues. The Foundation discovered several molecules, such as the insulin sensitizer balaglitazone, used for the treatment of diabetes. To produce a final drug, Dr. Reddy's patented the molecule at the US Patent and Trademark Office and then licensed it for clinical developments in 1997 to Novo Nordisk, a Danish MNC operating in India. The innovation and resulting collaboration with Novo Nordisk were important for the development of the company but also impacted the development process of the NSI, as more foreign firms started to acknowledge the benefits of entering the country and collaborating with Indian pharmaceutical firms.

Dr. Reddy's started to acquire firms abroad, like American Remedies Ltd., to gain access to new international markets and knowledge while maintaining a focus on generic drugs. In 1999, Dr. Reddy's became one of the few Indian pharmaceutical firms that were internationally active with the launch of the generic drug fluoxetine in 2001, a version of US firm Eli Lilly's Prozac. A range of other generic drugs followed these successes. Dr. Reddy's aggressive approach drew lawsuits from US and European firms, such as the litigation case with American firm Pfizer over its drug Norvasc, which Dr. Reddy's lost. Despite these setbacks, Dr. Reddy's continued to innovate and acquire foreign firms, such as German Betapharma Arzneimittel GmbH in 2006. The company's

BOX 3.2 **(cont.)**

innovation pipeline continued to strengthen, leading to the attempt to separate R&D activities from production activities by splitting the firm. This organizational change was unsuccessful, and the firm eventually reverted to its integrated form. Continuing its acquisition of foreign firms, Dr. Reddy's acquired the Dutch firm OctoPlus N.V. in 2012.

In its 2019 annual report, the company revealed a revenue of 154 billion INR (an increase of 8 percent), mostly from the global generics market (123 billion INRs), with the dominant share coming from North America (60 billion INRs), followed by emerging markets (28.9 billion INRs) and the local Indian market (26.6 billion INRs). R&D spending is at 11.29 percent of the total turnover, a slight drop from previous years. Dr. Reddy's sells approximately 350 types of generic drugs worldwide and is a significant global player in active pharmaceutical ingredients (APIs) for drug manufacture, diagnostic kits, critical care, and biotechnology products.

Sources: Dr. Reddy Laboratory (2019); Dr. Reddy's Annual Report (2019); Renic (2009).

US$16.84 billion (IBEF, 2018). India's government launched Pharma Vision 2020, which aims to make the country a global leader in end-to-end drug manufacturing, capitalizing on the local pharmaceutical industry's global momentum (IBEF, 2018). However, most of this push is toward generic drug production rather than patented and innovative new products.

3.3.4 *The Indian Auto Components Industry*

Transition phase. Due to the mature nature of the auto components industry[3] and its technological sophistication, the competitiveness and

---

[3] Parts of this section are taken with permission from Brandl & Mudambi (2014).

survival of its firms are often dependent on cost considerations (Mudambi & Helper, 1998). Although the dominant players of the global automobile industry are traditionally from Europe, North America, and Japan, the auto components industry has been very international almost since its inception. Early on, the industry understood the benefits of dispersing a firm's value chain and sourcing components abroad. Instead of being domestically vertically integrated, firms internationalized and established long-term relationships abroad (Sturgeon, van Biesebroeck, & Gereffi, 2008). Many firms quickly understood the benefits of operating in developing countries such as India, even though market liberalization in the local auto components industry has developed far more gradually in this country than in most of the other developing countries. Local regulations largely drove the innovation capabilities of domestic auto component firms.

Consolidation phase. Three major policy changes transformed the Indian automotive industry: economic liberalization in the early 1990s, a clarification of an earlier automotive policy in 1997, and a new automotive policy in 2002. Before Indian liberalization (pre-1991), the economy consisted of a large centralized private sector. The industry reflected several characteristics of a market economy, so that most domestic firms were already familiar with the market institutions under which foreign MNCs operated. This provided these firms with operational advantages when liberalization presented new opportunities (Kumaraswamy et al., 2012). (See Bharat Forge as a case example, Box 3.3.)

During the first phase of liberalization, the Indian government adopted policies aimed to attract MNCs through reduced regulatory constraints and modified incentives for business groups (Mahmood & Mitchell, 2004; Kumaraswamy et al., 2012). Consequently, the government allowed foreign firms to maintain full or majority ownership in their local operations in India, which increased the extent of local market competition. In order to compete with the technologically advanced MNCs, local firms urgently needed to upgrade their technological competencies. At the time Indian firms' dominant strategy

---

BOX 3.3   **Bharat Forge Limited**

Bharat Forge Limited (BFL) was established in 1961 and supplies forged components to auto manufacturers. In the early years of its operations, the company focused on the local market. BFL recorded its first exports in 1985 to European countries, such as Germany. The company added more and more innovation-oriented activities to develop state-of-the-art forging technology and subsequently extended its exports to the United States and Japan. The company formed two technical knowledge and assistance agreements with MetalArt Corp. (Japan) and Lemmerze-Were (Germany) during this phase. The knowledge it gained enabled the firm to secure ISO 9002 accreditation and allowed it to implement new quality management systems to comply with global regulations.

Bharat Forge invested heavily (approx. US$80 million) in R&D, testing, and validation activities and implemented lean and more efficient manufacturing, for instance, building a new state-of-the-art heavy-duty truck crankshaft machining facility. The company continued to establish strong relationships with various suppliers, including some in China, and became a preferred supplier to major global auto companies like Toyota, Ford, and Daimler. In 2003, it also acquired the innovative German company Carl Dan Peddinghaus GmbH, Federal Forge in the United States, Imatra Forging Group in Sweden, and Scottish Stampings in the United Kingdom. With these acquisitions, BFL hoped to gain innovative skills and capabilities and strengthen its presence in foreign markets.

The firm further advanced its production operation by developing new machining capabilities, such as installing India's largest commercial open forging press, commissioned in 2008. It enhanced its innovation activities by establishing the Kalyani Centre for Technology and Innovation. While the company increasingly branched out with products for the energy, mining, and even military sectors, its main operations remained in the auto components industry, especially forges. Nonetheless, the new streams of business were closely connected and allowed cross-sectional efficiencies in innovation and

BOX 3.3 (cont.)

R&D activities. For example, in 2014 Safran and BFL formed a partnership to address opportunities in the Indian civil and military aerospace sector; in 2016, BFL started supplying Boeing with titanium flap-track forgings for several of its airplanes. In 2018, BFL also announced another R&D facility in the UK's leading automotive technology park. The facility focuses on electric vehicles and components and complements the capabilities and knowledge at the Kalyani Centre for Technology and Innovation and the Kalyani Centre for Manufacturing Innovation that was established in 2017. BFL expects future upcoming growth to be based on its aggressive innovation activities.

In its 2017–2018 annual report, the company revealed a revenue of INR fifty-three billion (an increase of 37.5 percent) with INR twenty-nine billion from export revenues. R&D spending has increased to 0.68 percent of the total turnover.

Sources: Bharat Forge (2019); Business Standard (2019); Kalyani Group (2012).

was the formation of technology/licensing agreements with incoming MNCs. This transition phase allowed local firms to gain technological knowledge and develop absorptive capacity (Kumaraswamy et al., 2012).

In phase two of the liberalization from 1997 to 2002, the Indian government sought to upgrade and grow the domestic industry by restricting imports of components and completely knocked down (CKD) kits, with the aim of strengthening foreign MNCs' commitment to local suppliers. The evolving institutional environment within the industry – allowing greater foreign ownership and control and increasingly fierce competition – ensured that strong customer relationships became more and more important. Consequently, both automotive and component companies in India teamed up with local or global suppliers or auto component firms to improve quality and productivity as well as rationalize supply chains. This consolidation phase resulted in many Indian firms entering the industry's global value chain (Kumaraswamy et al., 2012).

Global integration phase. In 2002, the Indian government started to further ease the pressure on domestic firms by reducing restrictions and custom duties, mainly to facilitate the integration of domestic firms into the global industry (Kumaraswamy et al., 2012). Moreover, in order to support foreign firms entering the country and enhance knowledge spillovers, the government changed FDI regulations and allowed 100 percent ownership for foreign auto component firms. This led to the entry of Bosch Chassis Systems (Germany), Tenneco (United States), and Fauracia (France), all of which set up R&D facilities. Although these policies under the Auto Policy 2002 Act liberalized the industry, they predominantly supported sector growth and only secondarily aimed at improving innovation and R&D (IBEF, 2016). The goal was to advance the Indian industry to become a global hub for small cars and an Asian hub for auto components. In 2015, an Automotive Mission Plan for 2016–2026 was added onto the 2002 policy to supplement growth-enhancing measures for industry production.

The government quickly recognized the importance of R&D and began to invest in innovation activities. For example, a National Automotive Testing and R&D Infrastructure Project (NATRiP) was implemented in 2016, including government laboratories (IBEF, 2016). The project conducted analysis, simulations, and engineering animation activities connected with new technologies and IT, aligned with the global trends in the industry that have been moving toward new, advanced technology and IT. The government's objective is to connect India's strong IT sector with the automotive sectors, which would allow the generation of further competitive advantages and leadership in the global market.

However, local firms need knowledge resources to capitalize on these investments and policies. Thus, the country has seen an increasing amount of acquisitions and alliances between local and foreign firms, such as Italian Magneti Marelli's JV with Indian Maruti Suzuki, and Indian Vishnu Vaibhav Industry's technical collaboration with German ZF TRW Global Body Control Systems (IBEF, 2016).

3.4   CONCLUDING DISCUSSION

We use the three phases from Kumaraswamy et al. (2012) – transition, consolidation, and global integration – to outline the development processes of three Indian industries and their contribution to the country's NSI (see Table 3.3). Each industry reflects a different development process with different concentrations in the three phases. For example, in the comparably young and very global wind turbine industry, the transition and consolidation phases were relatively short in India. The global reach of the wind turbine industry and the novelty of the industry meant that firms had to be globally active and innovative from inception. Global pressures significantly influenced the industry's development in India and led to the rise of very innovative and international Indian wind turbine firms. Innovation and the industry's contribution to NSI development is thus influenced by the international activities of local Indian firms.

The Indian government attempted to increase the industry's attractiveness for new entrants. However, this was a challenging task given the newness of the industry and the government's restricted policy practice (Nicholson, 2007). Nonetheless, the Indian wind turbine industry and its firms, such as Suzlon, are leading innovators in the global industry and reflect a clear movement from copycat to leadership innovations.

The pharmaceutical industry, on the other hand, reflected a very different development process. The industry is comparably mature and strongly connected to a country's healthcare system. In the transition phase, the Indian government sought to enact policy increasing the availability and affordability of drugs, which at the time were predominantly produced by foreign firms. In order to develop the local economy and allow the local production of drugs, the government supported the production of generic drugs and process innovations through reverse engineering. Drugs could then be sold in

Table 3.3 *India's innovation phases*

Phase	Wind turbine	Pharmaceutical	Auto components
Transition	Novel industry challenges requiring early innovation activities	Connection to healthcare system leads to focus on generic drugs (reverse engineering)	Focus on production with restricted global activities
Consolidation	Strong global competition furthers innovation	Supranational organizations/ TRIPS encourage more advanced innovations	Focus on production improvement
Global integration/ leadership	Strong global leadership role due to innovative industry	Not yet reached global leadership role, due to long focus on generic drugs	Slow movement to global leadership role based on recent links to the IT sector

Source: The authors, based on research.

the domestic market or exported to other developing countries. The pharmaceutical industry's activities in the consolidation phase were also heavily influenced by IP protection regulations enforced by supranational institutions, such as the WTO's TRIPS regulations. As NSIs often suffer from disorganization as a result of regulations that are not fully functional (Guennif & Ramani, 2012), TRIPS helped the Indian NSI achieve the stability and security to support innovative activities. With the gradual implementation of these IP protection standards, the industry liberalized and started focusing more on advanced product innovations. This gradual process allowed domestic firms to gain the required innovation capabilities and move from the consolidation phase to the global integration phase (Kumaraswamy et al., 2012). However, the process has been slow, and novel product innovations are not yet widespread, as seen in Box 3.2. In addition, the industry has not reached a global leadership role due to its continued focus on generic drugs and process innovation rather than novel product innovations.

Finally, the auto components industry is often influenced by countries with strong car manufacturers (Kumaraswamy et al., 2012). In order to be successful in this industry, especially a developing country such as India, innovations are based on cost-efficient production and qualitatively better auto components. The NSI is, thus, dependent on process improvements (Asheim & Coenen, 2005) as well as new product developments that are globally attractive. However, the Indian auto component industry has mainly focused on production activities and efficient production improvements rather than on novel innovations in the transition phase. Only in the consolidation phase have the government and firms slowly started to understand the benefits of innovation activities and global interactions. This led to various knowledge and capability-based acquisitions and alliances.

The global integration phase saw a drastic push toward R&D and innovation, especially connected to new technology and IT-based innovations. The connection of the strong and globally recognized Indian IT sector could provide a competitive advantage for Indian firms to become leaders in the auto components industry. The example of Bharat Forge encapsulates the advances of the industry, as well as its current limitations. Only recently has the company started to branch into more technologically advanced industries and recognized the need for IT, high-technology upgrades, and innovations.

3.4.1 Implications for Policy and Practice

Our chapter highlights three key realities for policymakers in emerging economies. The first is the importance of industry context for catch-up processes. Emerging economies that seek to develop from imitation-based processes upward into true innovation-centric systems need to incorporate industry specifics into their policymaking and implementation. Our research demonstrates that the nature of innovation in wind turbines, pharmaceuticals, and auto components differs markedly. The wind turbine industry is relatively young, so one of the keys to its success has been integrating technologies from underlying driver industries – electromechanical systems, aerodynamics, and IT-based control systems. The pharmaceutical industry is mature but bifurcated into two clear arenas of innovative branded drugs and imitative generics that produce imperfect substitutes. This dichotomy underlies much of the competitive dynamics in the industry. The auto components industry is also mature, but success is largely a matter of integrating into the global value chains of auto assemblers that orchestrate the industry's global profile.

The second reality for policymakers to recognize and incorporate into their decision making is the relevance of country context. India's country context has unique characteristics: a highly successful IT sector, a long history of tertiary education, and a population of managers familiar with the workings of a market economy. The country's large science and technology workforce made it possible for supportive government policies to propel a relatively rapid move into innovation-based processes in numerous industries. Similar policies in a different country without such a workforce may not have been as successful.

The third reality that emerges from our chapter is the importance of industry history and path dependency. A long history of adversarial confrontation is likely to impede the rise of cooperation, despite the best efforts of the transacting parties (Mudambi & Helper, 1998). We can see this most clearly in the Indian pharmaceutical industry. Collaboration has been sluggish between MNCs and domestic firms aided and abetted by the government even after the formal implementation of TRIPS.

The insights from our chapter buttress those from Chapters 4 and 8. Putting these chapters together, the reader can obtain both a more holistic view of the Indian context as well as a comparative view relative to its giant neighbor, China.

REFERENCES

ABLE. (2016). ABLE – Biospectrum industry survey, Make in India, Ministry of External Affairs, TechSci Research, Global Industry Analysts Report (GIA).

Abramovitz, M. (1986). Catching up, forging ahead, and falling behind. *Journal of Economic History, 46*(2), 385–406.

Abrol, D. (2013). Where is India's innovation policy headed? *Social Scientist, 41* (3/4), 65–80.

Arora, B. (2019). Why India's wind turbine makers are under stress. Bloomberg Quit. Retrieved September 2019, from www.bloombergquint.com/business/why-indias-wind-turbine-makers-are-under-stress.

Asheim, B. T., & Coenen, L. (2005). Knowledge bases and regional innovation systems: Comparing Nordic clusters. *Research Policy, 34*(8), 1173–1190.

Awate, S., Larsen, M. M., & Mudambi, R. (2012). EMNE catch-up strategies in the wind turbine industry: Is there a trade-off between output and innovation capabilities? *Global Strategy Journal, 2*(3), 205–223.

Beugelsdijk, S., & Mudambi, R. (2013). MNEs as border corssing multi-location enterprises: The role of discontinuities in geographic space. *Journal of International Business Studies, 44*(5), 413–426.

Bharat Forge Limited. (2019). Bharat Forge annual report 2017–2018. Retrieved September 2019, from www.bharatforge.com/AR2018/pdf/00-bharat-forge-annual-report-2017-18.pdf.

Blomström, M., & Kokko, A. (1998). Multinational corporations and spillovers. *Journal of Economic Surveys, 12*(3), 247–277.

Brandl, K., Darendeli, I., & Mudambi, R. (2019). Foreign actors and intellectual property protection regulations in developing countries. *Journal of International Business Studies, 50*(5), 826–846.

Brandl, K., & Mudambi, R. (2014). EMNCs and catch-up processes: The case of four Indian industries. In A. Cuervo-Cazurra & R. Ramamurti (Eds.), *Understanding multinationals from emerging markets* (pp. 129–152). Cambridge: Cambridge University Press.

Brandl, K., Mudambi, R., & Scalera, V. G. (2015, December). The spectacular rise of the Indian pharmaceutical industry. *Entrepreneur & Innovation Exchange.*

Business Standard. (2019). Bharat Forge Ltd. Retrieved September 2019, from www.business-standard.com/company/bharat-forge-69/information/company-history.

Cagliarini, A., & Baker, M. (2010, September 19–24). Economic change in India. *RBA Bulletin.*

Choudhury, P., & Khanna, T. (2014). Toward resource independence – Why state-owned entities become multinationals: An empirical study of India's public R&D laboratories. *Journal of International Business Studies, 45*(8), 943–960.

Cornell University, INSEAD, and WIPO. (2019). *The global innovation index 2019: Creating healthy lives – The future of medical innovation.* Ithaca, Fontainebleau, and Geneva: Author. www.wipo.int/edocs/pubdocs/en/wipo_pub_gii_2019.pdf.

Dr. Reddy Laboratories. (2019). Dr. Reddy Laboratories Ltd. website. Retrieved September 2019, from www.drreddys.com/.

(2019). Dr. Reddy Laboratories Ltd. annual report 2018. Retrieved September 2019, from www.drreddys.com/media/904463/annualreport2019forwebsite.pdf.

Freeman, C. (1995). The "National System of Innovation" in historical perspective. *Cambridge Journal of Economics, 19*(1), 5–24.

Global Wind Energy Council [GWEC]. (2016). Indian wind energy. A brief outlook. Retrieved September 2019, from www.gwec.net/wp-content/uploads/vip/GWEC_IWEO_2016_LR.pdf.

Government of India. (2013). *Social, technology and innovation policy 2013.* New Delhi: Government of India, Ministry of Science and Technology. Retrieved September 2019, from http://dst.gov.in/sites/default/files/STI%20Policy%202013-English.pdf.

Guennif, S., & Ramani, S. V. (2012). Explaining divergence in catching-up in pharma between India and Brazil using the NSI framework. *Research Policy, 41*(2), 430–444.

Haakonsson, S. J., Jensen, P. D. Ø., & Mudambi, S. M. (2012). A co-evolutionary perspective on the drivers of international sourcing of pharmaceutical R&D to India. *Journal of Economic Geography, 13*(4), 677–700.

India Brand Equity Foundation [IBEF]. (2016). Auto components industry in India. Retrieved September 2019, from www.ibef.org/industry/autocomponents-india.aspx.

India Brand Equity Foundation [IBEF]. (2018). Indian pharmaceutical industry. Retrieved September 2019, from www.ibef.org/industry/pharmaceutical-india.aspx.

Kale, D. (2010). The distinctive patterns of dynamic learning and inter-firm differences in the Indian pharmaceutical industry. *British Journal of Management, 21*(1), 223–238.

Kale, D., & Little, S. (2007). From imitation to innovation: The evolution of R&D capabilities and learning processes in the Indian pharmaceutical industry. *Technology Analysis and Strategic Management, 19*(5), 589–609.

Kalyani Group. (2012). About us. Company website. Retrieved September 2019, from www.bharatforge.com/company/about-us.

Kumar, N., Mohapatra, P. K., & Chandrasekhar, S. (2009). *India's global powerhouses.* Boston, MA: Harvard Business School Press.

Kumaraswamy, A., Mudambi, R., Saranga, H., & Tripathy, A. (2012). Catch-up strategies in the Indian auto components industry: Domestic firms' responses to market liberalization. *Journal of International Business Studies*, 43(4), 368–395.

Lewis, J. I. (2011). Building a national wind turbine industry: Experiences from China, India and South Korea. *International Journal of Technology and Globalisation*, 5(3–4), 281–305.

Lundvall, B. Å. (Ed.). (2010). *National systems of innovation: Toward a theory of innovation and interactive learning* (Vol. 2). New York: Anthem Press.

Mahmood, I., & Mitchell, W. (2004). Two faces: Effects of business groups on innovation in emerging economies. *Management Science, 50*(10), 1348–1365.

McCann, P., & Mudambi, R. (2005). Analytical differences in the economics of geography: The case of the multinational firm. *Environment and Planning A, 37*(10), 1857–1876.

Meyer, K. E., Mudambi, R., & Narula, R. (2011). Multinational enterprises and local contexts: The opportunities and challenges of multiple embeddedness. *Journal of Management Studies,* 48(2), 235–252.

Motohashi, K. (2005). University–industry collaborations in Japan: The role of new technology-based firms in transforming the National Innovation System. *Research Policy, 34*(5), 583–594.

Mudambi, R. (2008). Location, control and innovation in knowledge intensive industries. *Journal of Economic Geography,* 8(5), 699–725.

Mudambi, R., & Helper, S. (1998). The "close but adversarial" model of supplier relations in the US auto industry. *Strategic Management Journal, 19*(8), 775–792.

Mudambi, R., & Swift, T. (2014). Knowing when to leap: Transitioning between exploitative and explorative R&D. *Strategic Management Journal,* 35(1), 126–145.

Nair, G. G. (2008). Impact of TRIPS on Indian pharmaceutical industry. *Journal of Intellectual Property Rights, 13,* 432–441.

Nelson, R. R. (Ed.). (1993). *National innovation systems: A comparative analysis.* Oxford: Oxford University Press on Demand.

Nicholson, M. W. (2007). The impact of industry characteristics and IPR policy on foreign direct investment. *Review of World Economics, 43*(1), 27–54.

North, D. C. (1991). Institutions. *Journal of Economic Perspectives,* 5(1), 97–112.

Organisation for Economic Co-operation and Development [OECD]. (2014). OECD better policies series: India policy brief. OECD. Retrieved September 2019, from www.oecd.org/policy-briefs/India-Addressing-Economic-and-Social-Challenges-through-Innovation.pdf.

Pachouri, A. (2018). How innovation is playing an increasingly central role in Indian diplomacy. *World Economic Forum*. Retrieved September 2019, from www.weforum.org/agenda/2018/08/innovation-new-pillar-india-diplomacy-joint-israel/.

Panagariya, A. (2008). *India: The emerging giant*. Oxford: Oxford University Press.

Rajsekhar, B., Van Hulle, F., & Jansen, J. C. (1999). Indian wind energy programme: Performance and future directions. *Energy Policy, 27*(11), 669–678.

Renic, S. (2009). Pfizer sues Dr. Reddy's over cholesterol drug Lipitor. *Stock Watch*.

Scherer, F. M. (1993). Pricing, profits, and technological progress in the pharmaceutical industry. *Journal of Economic Perspectives, 7*(3), 97–115.

Sturgeon, T., Van Biesebroeck, J., & Gereffi, G. (2008). Value chains, networks and clusters: Reframing the global automotive industry. *Journal of Economic Geography, 8*(3), 297–321.

Suzlon. (2019). Suzlon annual report 2017–2018 Retrieved September 2019, from www.suzlon.com/pdf/investor/annual-report-2017-18.pdf.

Technovia. (2019). Winds of change in the power sector: The top 10 global wind turbine companies. Retrieved September 2019, from https://blog.technavio.com/blog/top-10-global-wind-turbine-companies.

United States Patent and Trademark Office [US PTO]. (2019). Patent search. India assignee country. Retrieved September 15, 2019, from http://patft.uspto.gov/netahtml/PTO/search-bool.html.

World Intellectual Property Organization [WIPO]. (2019). PCT – The International Patent System. Patent search. India assignee country. Retrieved September 2019, from https://patentscope.wipo.int/search/en/search.jsf.

4 Exploring the Role of Government Involvement in Innovation

The Case of State Grid Corporation of China (SGCC) and INVAP

Lourdes Casanova, Anne Miroux,
and Diego Finchelstein

4.1 INTRODUCTION

While great attention is paid to publicly traded companies, states can also play an important role in the economy through companies in which they have either partial or total ownership. The latter are the so-called state-owned enterprises (SOEs). While there is interesting recent literature on state capitalism, which distinguishes between minor, major, and complete state ownership (Cuervo-Cazurra, 2018; Musacchio & Lazzarini, 2014; Musacchio, Lazzarini, & Aguilera, 2015), in this chapter we look at SOEs that are fully controlled by the state. Thus, implicitly, we are focusing mainly on those companies in which a large part or all the shares are owned by the state. In these cases, decisions regarding strategy and corporate governance are directly or indirectly defined by the state, which is ultimately responsible for SOEs' behaviors.

SOEs exist in nearly all the world's economies. Although generally associated with socialist or more state interventionist regimes, these companies are also present, and many times occupy a key position, in the economies of capitalist systems, too. In western Europe, the state controls several companies in some crucial economic areas such as oil or public services, such as the French railway Société nationale des chemins de fer français (SNCF). Even in the United States, there are some interesting cases in the financial sector, for example, the Federal Home Loan Mortgage Corporation (Freddie Mac) and the Federal National Mortgage Association (Fannie Mae).

From a systemic perspective, SOEs play a crucial role in some countries' economies and are central players in the most dynamic industries. Still, China is the most emblematic case with SOEs as leaders in key industries such as banking, energy, transportation, steel, and telecommunications. There are countries in the West where the state has traditionally had an important intervention role. In a number of European countries, public services such as electricity, water, and in some cases transportation, are either partially controlled by SOEs like Electricité de France (EDF) or Deutsche Telecom, or the state/province or municipality owns a major stake. These companies are also instrumental for a broader set of economic policies. In Latin America, most energy companies have traditionally been in the hands of the state. This is the case for PDVSA (Venezuela), Pemex (Mexico), Ecopetrol (Colombia), and Petrobras (Brazil). Clearly, SOEs are not unique to socialist regimes but are a common operation in most countries around the globe.

From a corporate perspective, SOEs are more prevalent than some experts may realize. More than 20 percent of the companies on the Fortune Global 500 list of 2018 – which ranks the world's 500 largest companies – are completely or partially owned by the state (Figure 4.1). This subgroup of the ranking contains many firms in China, but it also includes companies in the Middle East, Latin America, Europe, and even the United States. The SOEs from this ranking operate in commodities like oil and steel and in services such as banking, insurance, and engineering.

A common misconception is that SOEs are not competitive or are inefficient. Some argue that SOEs are bad allocators of resources, given that their management is not qualified enough, especially in emerging economies where the institutional enforcement is low (Megginson & Netter, 2001). However, state jobs are in demand and competitive in several Asian countries. In these cases, SOEs are able to attract the best talent. Additionally, some SOEs in emerging

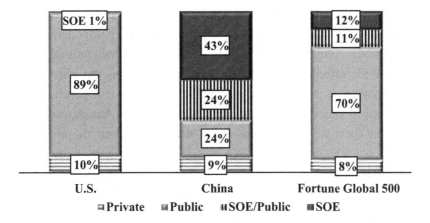

FIGURE 4.1   Share of each ownership type of company from the United States, China, and the Fortune Global 500, 2019
Sources: Fortune Global 500 (https://fortune.com/global500/), accessed August 2019, and Capital IQ (www.capitaliq.com), accessed October 2019.

economies are islands of embedded autonomy within a broader set of institutional weaknesses (Evans, 1995).

Though some studies have signaled that SOEs may have disadvantages when expanding abroad (Kornai, 1990), we believe the international exposure can actually catalyze efficiency in SOEs (Benito, Rygh, & Lunnan, 2016; Choudhoury & Khanna, 2014). By doing that, SOEs may find key resources that are unavailable in their local markets. In these cases, SOEs have an early internationalization experience that, if used wisely, can become an asset, as they must improve their efficiency and ability to compete beyond the particular advantages they have in their local market. As a result, these firms are pushed to be competitive and develop state-of-the-art operational and technological capacity and, as in the case of the State Grid Corporation of China (SGCC), become innovative global players.

Another common critique of SOEs is that they prioritize political agendas over competitive business goals (Shleifer & Vishny, 1998). While some studies show that state ownership and politics have a strong effect on a firm's strategy (Tihanyi et. al., 2019), this does not mean that these two factors are negatively correlated.

Several SOEs are competitive while following political goals, but SOEs do not necessarily have to compromise their competitiveness for politics. Actually, as the Argentine nuclear reactor manufacturer INVAP (described in this chapter) shows, sometimes the state does not interfere with the SOE's operations. Moreover, it is possible for the firm to benefit from being state-owned without having interference in their daily operations, as is demonstrated in the analysis of SGCC.

The state can actually create more opportunities for SOEs' innovation and growth. As it has been assessed, SOEs usually have a flexible budget in comparison to private firms (Cuervo-Cazurra, Inkpen, Musacchio, & Ramaswamy, 2014; Kornai, 1979). In fact, what some call a "soft" budget is a "patient" capital provided by the state without the pressures of short-term profits placed on public firms. The *helping hand* of the state can benefit SOEs, as they have extraordinary resources (Chen, Musacchio, & Li, 2019) beyond just financial ones. For instance, access to research agencies or unique knowledge and technology can create a unique competitive advantage for an SOE, as illustrated in our two case studies.

All these factors should be considered as we define the different taxonomies of SOEs. Table 4.1 summarizes the key dimensions that this chapter has identified and some potential effects.

It is important to understand that these different variables can be combined. For instance, INVAP is fully owned by the Argentine government, but at the same time, it has a unique type of ownership, as it is owned by a subnational level of authority. We will further highlight the innovation capabilities of the Chinese firm SGCC and Argentine firm INVAP in the following case studies.

4.2 STATE GRID CORPORATION OF CHINA (SGCC)

The energy sector is at a critical juncture. With the growth of the middle class in emerging markets, energy demand has increased. The initial power shortages, fragmented transmission networks, and low levels of investment in transmission and distribution networks

Table 4.1 *Taxonomy of SOEs*

Variables defining taxonomy of SOEs		Value	Example	Effects
Type of country	Development stage	Developed vs. emerging country	Statoil (Norway) vs. ONGC (India)	Defines the access to resources, the potential markets to expand abroad, and the innovation strategy
	Size	Large vs. midsize vs. small	Sinopec (China) vs. Pemex (Mexico) vs. KPC (Kuwait)	Defines the access to resources and the speed in internationalization (due to speed in market saturation)
Sector		Industrial vs. commodities // technologically intensive vs. basic	POSCO (Korea) vs. Debswana (Botswana) // Rafael (Israel) vs. OCP (Morocco)	Influences type of innovation and internationalization path
Firm size		Large vs. midsize vs. small	Eskom (South Africa) vs. Petrotrin (Trinidad & Tobago) vs. ANCAP (Uruguay)	Defines the access to resources, internationalization type due to these resources (i.e., capacity to do acquisitions), and economies of scale
Level of state ownership		Full ownership vs. minor shareholder	Aramco (Saudi Arabia) vs. Vale (Brazil)	Defines degrees of freedom to develop strategy and influences corporate governance

Table 4.1 (cont.)

Variables defining taxonomy of SOEs		Value	Example	Effects
Type of state ownership		Central vs. subnational ownership	SNH (Cameroon) vs. CEMIG (Brazil)	Defines access to resources to innovate and internationalization path
Autonomy	Financial	Subsidies//profit transfers vs. reinvest profits	ENAP (Chile) // EPM (Colombia) vs. INVAP (Argentina)	Defines access to resources influencing capacity to innovate and internationalize and the sustenance of a strategy
	Managerial	Independent from politics vs. influenced by politics // technically qualified	INVAP (Argentina) vs. PDVSA (Venezuela)// Embraer (Brazil)	Defines competitiveness levels, the capacity to innovate, and the potential to expand abroad
Relation with the state		Strong vs. weak	SGCC (China) vs. YPF (Argentina)	Defines the capacity to share knowledge and other resources; allows international support and endorsement

Source: The authors.

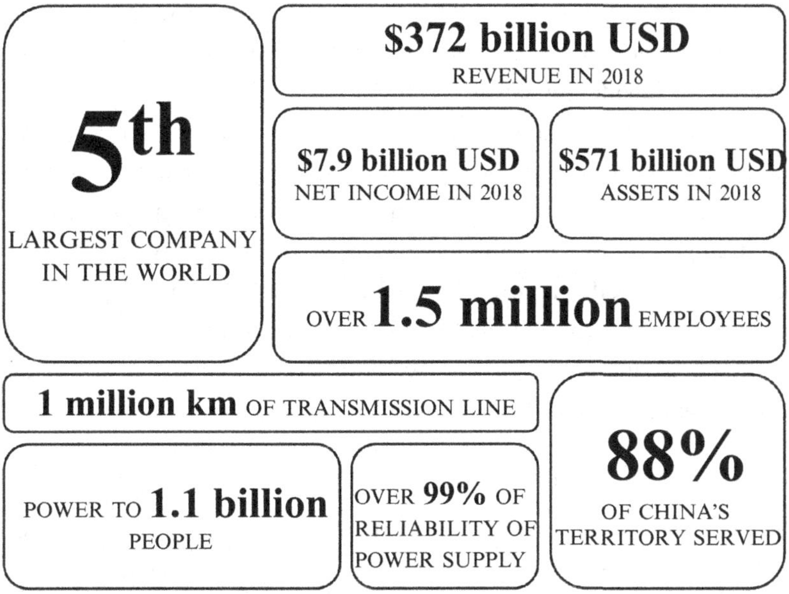

5th

LARGEST COMPANY
IN THE WORLD

$372 billion USD
REVENUE IN 2018

$7.9 billion USD
NET INCOME IN 2018

$571 billion USD
ASSETS IN 2018

OVER **1.5 million** EMPLOYEES

1 million km OF TRANSMISSION LINE

POWER TO **1.1 billion** PEOPLE

OVER **99%** OF RELIABILITY OF POWER SUPPLY

88%
OF CHINA'S
TERRITORY SERVED

FIGURE 4.2 SGCC facts and figures, 2018
Sources: Standard & Poor's Capital IQ, accessed March 2019; SGCC, 2017.
Conversion RMB to USD 6.8 (Capital IQ May 2019).

needed to be addressed. Hence, China undertook a major reform of its energy sector in 2002 by creating SGCC and tasking it with the construction, operation, management, and maintenance of the electricity transmission and distribution (T&D) networks over most of China, covering close to 90 percent of its territory.

Since then, SGCC has seen tremendous growth, both financially and technologically. By 2018, more than 1.1 billion people had benefited from the company's energy production. SGCC also reported US$372 billion in revenues and employed more than 1.6 million people (see Figure 4.2). SGCC quickly became the world's largest energy and utility company, and in the 2019 Fortune Global 500 list, it ranked as the fifth-largest company in the world by revenues. It owns and operates assets in the Philippines, Brazil, Portugal, Australia, Italy, Greece, and Hong Kong, a reflection of its growing commitment to the Global Energy Interconnection (GEI) – an initiative that envisions a global smart grid with ultra-high-voltage (UHV) technology that would generate, transmit, and distribute energy worldwide (see later).

SGCC has cemented itself as a technology innovator with a clear goal – to champion global energy interconnection in the twenty-first century. It owes its success to a convergence of factors, including the size and dramatic growth of electricity demand in China; the specific relationship that, as an SOE, it developed with the Chinese government; and its technology and innovation strategy centered around UHV technology. The latter in particular has made SGCC a global leader in the electricity sector.

4.2.1   SGCC, a Major Chinese State-Owned Company

SGCC was founded in 2002 as part of the answer to a number of problems China was facing in its energy sector. China's rapid economic growth in the 1970s was powered by coal, which had taken a toll on the environment. It was also facing power shortages and a rising demand for energy. In response, the government founded SGCC after the "plant–grid separation" reform that divided the main functions of the sector – generation, transmission, distribution, and retail. The former State Electric Power Corporation was unbundled, and its functions and assets were distributed between five generation companies, two T&D companies, and four service companies. SGCC was one of the T&D firms.

SGCC was created as 100 percent state-owned. Its chief executive is jointly appointed by the Standing Committee of the Central Political Bureau of the Communist Party of China (CPC) and the State Council. Since its constitution as an SOE, SGCC has actively promoted and implemented reform efforts through coordination with related state-level departments as well as local party committees and officials. Yet the company maintains a degree of autonomy from the CPC, which has enabled SGCC to centralize most of its subsidiaries under common governance. It was empowered to diversify, including for financial services (banks, securities, insurance, etc.), which expanded its financing sources and lowered costs.

Several central government agencies were given the responsibility to oversee certain areas of SGCC, a situation the company took advantage of by exploiting the rivalries and differences among those agencies as well as their difficulties with coordination. From its inception, SGCC was given autonomy of its operation under the country's macroeconomic control, management, and supervision (Yi-chong, 2017), and over the years it developed a range of managerial discretion while supporting government policies. Thus, the company could decide its own strategy and pursue interests as it saw fit.

The vision and determination of SGCC's leadership played a key role in its transformation into a global electricity leader and innovator (Yi-chong, 2017). SGCC's skilled leadership team was able to convince authorities to implement innovative energy projects in UHV – a highly efficient technology that enables large-capacity, long-distance power transmission – to address widespread power shortages and the country's lack of interconnectivity. The push for UHV did not follow a top-down approach, and in that sense SGCC acted more like an independent firm than a traditional SOE (Yi-chong, 2017). Yet, the UHV project fell in line with the broad priorities of the government from universal electricity supply to "indigenous Chinese innovation" and environmental objectives such as reducing air pollution, enabling SGCC to strongly move ahead. Indeed, SGCC's strategic goal had been to build a modern electricity system with a strong and smart grid. At the center of this grid are UHV transmission networks. As time went on, SGCC's pioneering in UHV was framed as part of the government's policies, enhancing China's manufacturing capacity, innovating, and leading the world in its transformation toward a low-carbon economy. Replacing coal and oil with electricity and using electricity from faraway nuclear, hydro, or solar plants through UHV transmission lines became SGCC's new ambition.

4.2.2 Electricity as a Technology and Innovation Enabler

SGCC boldly chose to pursue UHV at a time when the technology was in its infancy. There was no commercial operation, there were no commercial suppliers of equipment, and the technology was not deployed on a large scale by any other major electricity firm. But UHV would become SGCC's passport to expansion and global leadership.

The firm launched major research and development (R&D) programs in UHV technologies as well as electric equipment manufacturing and made strides in grid technology. SGCC opened the world's first 1100-kV UHV alternating current transmission line in January 2009,[1] and though other companies used UHV technologies, SGCC was the first company to implement the technology on a large scale. As a leader and pioneer, SGCC has also contributed to the development of new global industry standards.

SGCC's efforts in technology innovation took place in the broader context of China's evolving technology and innovation policies, which helped the country to build up its innovation capabilities over the past four decades. These policies evolved in five phases: experimental (1979–1985), systemic reform (1985–1995), deepening reform (1996–2006), long-term plan and optimization (2007–2014), and recent reforms for further improvements (2015–present) (Casanova & Miroux, 2020, chapter 7).

The first phases were not really successful, partly because only a minority of Chinese enterprises took advantage of the support policies and partly because most policies were still very much of a top-down nature. In addition, China continued to depend heavily on technology transfer from multinational companies (MNCs). However, with China's entry into the World Trade Organization (WTO) in 2001, the pressure for change increased. Indeed, it was becoming clear that to become a serious contender in an open global economy, China had to develop its own technologies and innovations. In 2006, China adopted a key instrument, the National Medium- and Long-Term Program for

---

[1] China was not the only country to build a UHV line at the time. Japan and Russia had actually implemented a few UHV projects, but these were operated at +550 kV (www .globaltransmission.info/archive.php?id=1434).

Science and Technology Development (2006–2020), the objective of which was to transform China into an "innovative society" that enshrined the principle of "indigenous innovation." It included among its priorities energy-related technology innovation, in particular, high-voltage transmission technology. This and other industrial policies and measures created an overall incentive structure for technology and innovation that SGCC knew how to take advantage of. We can then see that, although operationally independent, the relationship between the state and the firm was key for SGCC to become innovative. SGCC prioritized investments in cutting-edge scientific research in UHV technology, technical innovation, and green energy development, streamlining its allocation of resources toward teams of experts focused on these areas.

Since 2004, SGCC has achieved breakthroughs in UHV technology. With cables enabling UHV to be commercially transported over vast distances at lower costs than traditional transmission lines, major power projects have become increasingly feasible, such as the construction of dams in remote areas and transmission of their electricity to faraway cities. The result of large-scale adoption of UHV is culminating in a "supergrid" that would connect China's six regional grids and distribute clean energy (wind, water, and solar) produced mainly in the northern and western parts of China. This innovation capability can be replicated in other large countries, as SGCC is doing in Brazil.

In 2017, SGCC invested over US$1.1 billion in R&D, a sum intended to underwrite the sector's transformative innovation into sustainability. In particular, the firm invested in the electric vehicles industry, electrical charging stations, renewable energy, new-generation power systems, and smart grids with UHV technology. The latter innovation reduced the line loss percentage each year up to 6.7 percent.

For instance, given that pollution is one of China's perennial challenges, SGCC implemented an ambitious electricity replacement program to decrease gas emissions. According to the company's

2017 corporate responsibility report, SGCC has generated over 900 terawatt-hours (TWh) from sustainable sources. In doing so, SGCC has eliminated 820 million tons of carbon dioxide (CO_2), 1.4 million tons of sulfur dioxide, 1.41 million tons of nitrogen oxide, or atmospheric pollutants, and 220,000 tons of smoke and dust. By 2018, SGCC had integrated 280 gigawatts (GW) of renewable energy capacity, which represented 19 percent of the total installed capacity.

SGCC ranked first among central government–owned SOEs for patent ownership and invention patent applications for seven consecutive years. As of 2017, it had filed 73,350 patents, of which 16,064 are invention patents, becoming one of the most innovative companies in China.

4.2.3   Beyond China, Global Energy Interconnection (GEI)

With UHV technology, one could envision a global grid network that would transmit energy from one continent to another. SGCC has captured that vision in its proposed Global Energy Interconnection (GEI) strategy, which is based on UHV transmission technologies. The GEI strategy, which has an estimated cost of US$50 trillion, is designed to connect global electricity systems across country lines and oceans, in alignment with the Belt and Road Initiative (BRI). The strategy is designed to address global energy security and climate change, as it would replace 80 percent of carbon-based global energy with renewable sources, eliminating an estimated 66.7 billion tons of CO_2 emissions (SGCC, 2014).

The GEI plan has three phases, starting from within China's borders but, by 2050, stretching across the globe. The phases include (1) domestic interconnection (present–2020), to consolidate the development of renewable energies and smart grids within China; (2) intracontinental interconnection (2020–2030), during which SGCC plans to connect different grids across Asian countries and within other continents through efficient clean energy allocation; and (3) intercontinental interconnection (2030–2050), which will boost wind power production in the Arctic and solar power at the Equator.

SGCC created the Global Energy Interconnection Development and Cooperation Organization (GEIDCO) in cooperation with the United Nations "Sustainable Energy for All" program in 2016 to help meet its goals. GEIDCO is made up of 100 organizations, including government entities, firms, civil society entities, and universities from more than thirty countries. Its purpose is to build technical standards and coordinate the efforts of different actors in research and international cooperation, as well as provide consulting services.

To date, SGCC has built up ten cross-border power transmission lines between China and countries such as Russia, Mongolia, and Kyrgyzstan with a total power trade volume of more than 20 TWh. The company is engaged in the construction of quite a few grid interconnection projects across different countries like China–Mongolia, China–Russia, China–Nepal, and China–Pakistan and is now able to export electricity to those countries through the interconnection grids.

Looking forward, a number of areas offer opportunities for SGCC to build upon its experience and expertise in the electricity sector. Beyond further development in UHV technologies, it has been working, for instance, on charging services for electric vehicles and is enabling consumers to install their own charging stations. It has also been investing in R&D in smart network control, developing software to control the voltage and frequency at destination points throughout the network, to enable the system to react rapidly and automatically to shifting levels of supply and demand. The firm is also committed to its global expansion.

4.3 INVAP: THE ARGENTINE JEWEL

Although relatively small, the Argentine state-owned company INVAP, which specializes in the production of nuclear reactors to generate energy, is a major innovator. The company started in 1976 and has shown a clear export orientation almost from its inception. In 1978, INVAP sold its first nuclear reactor to Peru. Throughout its history, INVAP has sold nuclear reactors to emerging and

$20 million USD GROSS OPERATING MARGIN	$135 million USD SALES
	$289 million USD ASSETS	1 365 EMPLOYEES

FIGURE 4.3 INVAP facts and figures
Source: The authors, based on INVAP website (www.invap.com.ar/en/), accessed November 1, 2018.

developed countries such as Australia, India, Algeria, and the Netherlands. Currently, INVAP exports to Brazil, Saudi Arabia, Algeria, the Netherlands, and India, among others. Additionally, INVAP has opened business units in areas such as aerospace (i.e., satellites), industry (i.e., medical equipment), and technological services. Thus, in addition to nuclear reactors, INVAP also develops products such as radar, satellites, medical equipment, and wind and solar energy plants, among others. Figure 4.3 illustrates INVAP's 2018 financial data.

4.3.1 INVAP Innovation

INVAP has succeeded in the industry of manufacturing nuclear reactors, though it requires highly advanced technology and a great deal of innovation. INVAP has proven to be highly competitive abroad, even winning bids to build these reactors in developed countries. Argentina is an emerging economy characterized by the production of commodities and a few heavy industries (i.e., steel and petrochemicals) but is less known in knowledge-intensive activities. Therefore, it is quite interesting to study an Argentine state-owned firm excelling in such a high-tech industry. This has been possible in part thanks to Argentina's government and particular conditions in the area of nuclear reactors that have positively shaped the evolution of INVAP. In the late 1940s, the Argentine government of President Juan Perón launched an initiative to develop nuclear technology. It recruited an Austrian scientist, Ronald Richter, who promised to develop the technology in the short term. To this end, the government built facilities outside Bariloche in Patagonia near the Andes mountain range, very close to where INVAP now has its headquarters. However, the promised outcomes (including the capacity to create atomic bombs) were never achieved. Richter was finally caught in his deception, and the project was canceled.

Though Richter's work did not come to fruition, his attempts in nuclear science did leave a physical and nuclear-related knowledge impact that has since been built upon. A group of buildings was constructed in the area, and an atomic center with scientists who specialized in nuclear-related fields was founded. It was here in this cluster, which includes a national research and education center, the Instituto Balseiro, that the founders of INVAP received their training. The Institute and INVAP are in close proximity, and today, there is still a lot of synergy between the institute's scholars and INVAP. For example, INVAP has concluded several agreements with the Instituto Balseiro to develop and implement applied research in collaboration with the institute's scientists. In addition, the national atomic energy commission (CNEA) also works in close collaboration with INVAP, reinforcing the company's capabilities in nuclear energy.

INVAP is quite aware that its specialized expertise in the nuclear field is one of its main competitive advantages. Over the years, besides developing nuclear reactors to sell abroad, it has also found other products/services linked to nuclear technology. The first experience beyond nuclear reactors took place in South Korea in 1988, with the atomization of quality controls for an appliance factory. As illustrated by Finchelstein, Gonzalez-Perez, and Salvaj (2019), INVAP has sold medical devices that use nuclear technology, such as radiotherapy-based equipment, to Bolivia, Egypt, and Venezuela; a lyophilization plant for the treatment of food products in Mexico; and services connected to satellite technology to Brazil. Similarly, it has assisted in the recycling of radioactive residues in Saudi Arabia. In many of these operations, the buyer was not only interested in the product but also in the training and transfer of key technology that

INVAP could offer. Though INVAP is mainly an exporter, it has also opened offices in Egypt, Brazil, the United States, Algeria, Australia, and Venezuela to continue training and adjusting the nuclear facilities that it has built and to perform commercial operations. This is especially relevant for emerging economies interested in developing their own knowledge in the field. INVAP offers products and services that are open and flexible to maximize the opportunity of sharing key knowledge while continuing to generate revenue through training and permanent assistance.

INVAP's research has expanded far beyond nuclear energy research. For instance, Conrado Varotto, the founder and CEO of the company for the first fifteen years, was named director of the national aerospace activities (CONAE) soon after leaving INVAP. The firm developed a close and dynamic relationship with CONAE that helped them consolidate the aerospace business unit, which, after nuclear reactors, is one of their most dynamic business units due to the production of satellites and radar.

In short, two of the main competitive advantages that have enabled INVAP to compete in highly sophisticated technology areas are (1) its access to a unique source of human capital based on a unique cluster of nuclear research in Argentina and (2) its flexibility and capacity to adapt its knowledge to other industries and respond to the specific requirements of customers such as knowledge transfer and postsale assistance.

4.3.2 Governance

Another peculiarity of INVAP is that this SOE has thrived in a country in which state-owned firms have had very poor results. Most Argentine state-owned companies, being highly indebted, were privatized during the 1990s. Today, the universe of state-owned companies is relatively small in Argentina, especially compared to other emerging economies such as Brazil or China. Most of the Argentine SOEs that survived have continued to not perform well and must rely on state subsidies and/or are deeply in debt.

INVAP does not follow this pattern. The company has never received subsidies, and its key source of income is sales. Another distinctive feature of INVAP is that it is not owned by the central government but by a subnational level of authority: the province of Rio Negro, which has never politically interfered in the company.

INVAP has also shown continuity at the managerial level, with only three general managers since its foundation. Such steady leadership allows for long-term planning and continuity in the strategic decision-making process, which are crucial for a firm's innovation and internationalization (Bruton, Ahlstrom, & Li, 2010; Finchelstein, 2017; Yamakawa, Peng, & Deeds, 2008), as both activities require long-term thinking to succeed. This continuity stands out in a country like Argentina, where most SOEs and public agencies see a great deal of turnover in key positions (Rougier, 2007; Sikkink, 1993).

Most of the board members of INVAP are representatives of the province. The board also includes a staff representative, which improves the alignment between those responsible for daily operations and the firm's owner and leadership. The national atomic energy agency also has representatives on the board of INVAP, creating a way for the central government and the province to better align their goals with the company. Yet, INVAP's operations are mainly decided at the firm level, and the board has not had a disruptive role with politically influenced decisions.

Financial autonomy also distinguishes INVAP (Finchelstein et al., 2019). The company is funded by its own savings and revenues and has never received any subsidy to operate or to finance international activities. INVAP has used its expertise and knowledge in the nuclear field to innovate in other business opportunities and sectors abroad. In this way, INVAP follows a market-driven expansion that resembles private companies (Finchelstein et al., 2019).

Another important characteristic of INVAP is that it has the autonomy to use its savings. Given that INVAP is state owned, the state could access these benefits for its own budget. This is particularly relevant in Argentina because both the central state and other levels of state authority usually face budgetary deficits. Nevertheless, INVAP has always been able to use its profits as it sees fit.

In short, while INVAP benefits from an intense collaboration with other public agencies such as public universities, research institutions, regulatory agencies, and diplomatic delegations, the company has a very high level of financial independence. INVAP does not receive special subsidies from the state, and its profits have remained with the company. Thus, INVAP shows a unique level of autonomy at both the operational and financial levels. This integral autonomy is a crucial feature that distinguishes INVAP from other Argentine state-owned companies that have not had such a positive outcome in terms of expansion, internationalization, and innovation.

4.4 INVAP, SGCC, AND BEYOND

The two cases examined in this chapter are interesting examples of SOEs that have grown and innovated in competitive and demanding industries in two completely different regions and contexts. In addition to showing that SOEs can perform satisfactorily beyond their domestic markets, INVAP and SGCC illustrate how state ownership can actually encourage innovation and growth through different mechanisms. These mechanisms present themselves in a variety of ways that go from state financial aid, to commercial and diplomatic support abroad, and to the enhancement of key knowledge-related resources.

Despite several common characteristics, it is also important to acknowledge the particularities and differences between these two cases. We recognize several differences between INVAP and SGCC, which confirm that we need to go beyond a homogenous perception of SOEs. Size, managerial autonomy, and type and level of ownership are only a few of the key features that distinguish SOEs. The first significant distinction relates to size. The two companies have very different economic indicators confirming this assertion. INVAP has had revenues of only US$135 million in 2018, while SGCC had sales of US$387 billion in 2018. The number of employees between these two companies also presents some large contrasts: INVAP has approximately 1,400 workers, while SGCC has about one million employees working inside the company.

The size of each SOE's home country is another important difference that might indirectly affect the overall behavior of these companies. While China is the second-largest economy in the world with the highest GDP growth rate in the last decades, Argentina is a midsize country that has suffered several economic crises during the same period of time. The opportunities for growth in their respective domestic markets, as well as local access to financial and technological resources, are significantly different.

Their internationalization path also shows significant contrasts. On the one hand, INVAP's early internationalization in 1978 was more gradual, based on the company's need to increase revenues and search for new business opportunities. INVAP's expansion abroad has followed a more market-oriented path to the extent that it responded to other states' needs for nuclear reactors. After obtaining these contracts, INVAP opened offices abroad to continue assisting their clients with these complex services and equipment. Comparatively, SGCC's international expansion is more recent but also more extensive. The company initiated its first overseas project in Russia in 2007 and soon expanded into Asia (2009), Latin America (2010), Europe and Oceania (2012), Africa (2013), and North America (2014). In just seven years, SGCC developed a large presence on five continents. Another important distinction between these SOEs' internationalization is that SGCC has expanded mainly through acquisitions, while INVAP has only opened offices in other countries after obtaining a contract. INVAP has not done any international acquisition since its creation. This fact is probably largely due to the first difference highlighted here, namely size, because of its direct impact on the financial resources of each company. INVAP financial resources are clearly smaller than those of SGCC.

As several scholars have pointed out, the type of state ownership can have an important impact on the behavior of SOEs in several dimensions such as internationalization, business strategy, financial performance, etc. (Finchelstein et al., 2019; Kalasin, Cuervo Cazurra, & Ramamurti, 2020; Li, Cui, & Lu, 2014; Musacchio & Lazzarini, 2014). Thus, it is important to signal the differences in terms of type of state ownership between the two studied cases: central government ownership in the case of SGCC and a local government/provincial government ownership in the case of INVAP. Again, this has an impact on financial resources: the province of Rio Negro, INVAP's owner, is a middle-size province of a middle-size country, Argentina. Another relevant feature that needs to be considered when studying SOEs is the strength of the relationship between the government and the firm. Does the state influence the strategic decisions of the company? Is the management relatively independent from political influence? Does the state assist the company with extraordinary resources? In this respect, there are some differences between INVAP and SGCC. There seems to be a more symbiotic relationship between state and company for the case of SGCC. This company's international expansion into areas like Africa and Latin America is in line with China's foreign policy to increase its influence and relations with these regions (Child & Rodriguez, 2005; *Financial Times*, 2019; Perez Ludueña, 2017). Being one of the largest Chinese companies and having a large international presence increases the relevance of the company for the government and thus reinforces this symbiotic relationship. While SGCC had a lot of autonomy in its operation and strategic choices, the firm has also benefited from the fact that it could count on the support of state research agencies and resources for its innovations.

INVAP has a different relationship with the state. As mentioned, this company was quite independent financially from the government, as it has never received subsidies because it operates with its own profits. Its profits have never been transferred to the state. The company could manage its revenues and profits with autonomy and reinvest them within the firm. INVAP's management has also been politically independent. However, this does not mean that

INVAP is isolated from the state. INVAP had a strong collaboration with other public agencies, sharing knowledge with agencies such as the national atomic energy commission, collaborating closely with Instituto Balseiro, as mentioned above, and benefiting from the support of government's representations overseas such as diplomatic missions that assisted the company in developing business opportunities.

Both firms' technological and innovative leadership have also been related to their high level of expertise at both the technical and managerial levels. In the case of INVAP, the company has some of the most skilled engineers and scientists in the country. SGCC could count on highly competent teams of researchers as well as a management team with strong technical and managerial skills and has received several national awards for its scientific achievements.

4.5 CAN EMERGING-MARKET SOES BE LEADING INNOVATORS?

In this chapter, we have analyzed two distinct SOEs that have been able to innovate and grow in highly competitive sectors. These firms are just single examples of a broader set of SOEs that have performed very well and are global leaders within their respective sectors. Both INVAP and SGCC operate mainly in areas connected to the energy sector. Due to regulations, national politics, and economies of scale, energy is an area in which SOEs have thrived. The cases of Pemex (Mexico), PDVSA (Venezuela), Aramco (Saudi Arabia), Sinopec (China), NNPC (Nigeria), and Rosneft (Russia) are just a few examples of SOEs in emerging countries. There are also very relevant cases from the developed world, such as Norwegian company Statoil, and also very interesting examples from other industries such as the Brazilian Banco do Brasil or the Chinese ICBC in banking or even the Israeli RAFAEL defense system in weapons development.

Within emerging countries, most of the SOEs focus on commodities. The cases of the Chilean copper producer Codelco, Morocco's phosphate producer OCP, or Botswana's diamond producer Debswana are just a few examples of a broader set of emerging countries' SOEs. This majority of commodity-based SOEs increases the relevance of unique cases like INVAP. Not only does INVAP operate successfully, but it has also managed to do so in a very competitive sector. Although it has recently been acquired by Boeing, Embraer had been another interesting disruptive example. The Brazilian firm Embraer became the largest short-distance airplane manufacturer in an industry dominated by developed-country MNCs such as Airbus and Boeing.

The case of SGCC is from the electricity sector, in which other SOEs also successfully operate. Nonetheless, the relevance of this case is explained by their innovations in the electricity transmission that provides the firm with a unique competitive advantage that has been used to grow in new markets in five continents. The list of countries where SGCC operates includes some developed countries in which the competitiveness and technological demands might be higher. The success of the Korean steel manufacturer POSCO also follows this pattern. This company became one of the leading steel producers in the world, surpassing several developed-country competitors, by developing technologically superior factories and techniques (Belloc, 2013).

All the differences observed in these examples, as well as the comparative analysis between INVAP and SGCC, prove that we need to pay deeper attention to the universe of SOEs. Taking into account their capacity to innovate and good financial performances, SOEs need to be studied in depth. SOEs are not a homogenous set of companies. Quite the contrary, there is a vast heterogeneity based on key dimensions that define the particular composition of an SOE. We have mentioned how sector might play a role and how commodities are the predominant – but not exclusive – area in which SOEs proliferate. The distinction between developed countries' SOEs and those from emerging economies can also be relevant, as the former may have additional resources to innovate, invest, or expand abroad. A similar logic can be applied to the size of the SOE. Through the cases, we have also identified other key variables. The financial and political autonomy of SOEs might determine their operative efficiency, their ability to sustain long-term investments, and their access to resources. By the same token, the type of ownership can also be a determinant. As we have seen, the subnational ownership of INVAP encourages a more market-driven international expansion (Finchelstein et al., 2019), while the central ownership of SGCC has pushed for more rapid growth through acquisitions.

Another relevant distinction could be made in regard to the level of state ownership. While some SOEs are fully controlled by the state, the level of ownership can vary. There are SOEs like INVAP owned by the state; others also have a part that is publicly traded like the Indian company ONGC and the Norwegian firm Statoil. In these cases, the behavior and strategies of these SOEs is constrained by stock market regulations as well, and usually their corporate governance is more tightly controlled. There are other cases in which the government has some golden share, even when they do not have the majority of the shares, which is crucial during important decisions. This is the case of the Brazilian company Vale, which is one of the largest mining companies in the world. Even without a golden share, the government can be a minor investor and constrain or amplify the strategic policies of a company through state-exclusive aid. For instance, during the 2000s, the Argentine government used its minor shareholder status at one of the largest Argentine multinationals, Techint, to question the board's composition and the decisions they were trying to make (Finchelstein, 2013).

This chapter has examined two interesting firms that are similar in ownership but different with respect to the variables that shape the taxonomy of SOEs. In both cases, the collaboration between the state and the firm has encouraged internationalization and innovation. There might be other combinations of variables that push for a concentration in the domestic market (see Table 4.1). Not all SOEs have had good performances that could sustain competition with private firms. Nevertheless, the goal of this chapter is twofold. First, it is to depict the particular dynamics involved in the functioning of SOEs. These dynamics include corporate governance characteristics, investment capacity, access to resources, and domestic and international strategies, as well as their capacity to innovate. All these features have been examined in the cases of INVAP and SGCC. Second, by studying these thriving cases, we also show that SOEs can successfully compete in knowledge-intensive sectors. We believe that the statement that SOEs usually underperform relative to private companies and that they cannot innovate under competitive circumstances is not always true. INVAP and SGCC are just two examples of a greater universe of highly competitive SOEs that have the capabilities to innovate and grow. Both cases illustrate the role that the state, through its SOEs, can play in fostering innovation in emerging markets.

REFERENCES

Belloc, F. (2013). Innovation in state-owned enterprises: Reconsidering the conventional wisdom. *Journal of Economic Issues, 48*(3), 821–848.

Benito, G., Rygh, A., & Lunnan, R. (2016). The benefits of internationalization for state-owned enterprises. *Global Strategy Journal, 6*, 269–288.

Bloomberg L.P. (2018) Retrieved July 1, 2018, from Bloomberg database.

Brazilian Ministry of Planning. (2018). Development and management. *Bimonthly Newsletter on Chinese Investment in Brazil - nº 5*. Retrieved July 2018, from bit.ly/3jp7J7Ubi.

Bruton, G. D., Ahlstrom, D., & Li, H. (2010). Institutional theory and entrepreneurship: Where are we now and where do we need to move in the future? *Entrepreneurship Theory and Practice, 34*(3), 421–440.

BusinessWorld. (2018) NGCP now expects unified power grid by 2020. Retrieved July 2018, from http://bworldonline.com/ngcp-now-expects-unified-power-grid-by-2020/.

Casanova, L., & Miroux, A. (2019). *Emerging Markets* Multinationals *Report 2019: Building constructive engagement*. Ithaca, NY: Cornell University.

(2020). *The era of Chinese multinationals: How Chinese companies are conquering the world*. San Diego, CA: Academic Press Elsevier.

Chen, V. Z., Musacchio, A., & Li, S. (2019). A principals-principals perspective of hybrid leviathans: Cross-border acquisitions by state-owned MNEs. *Journal of Management, 45*(7), 2751–2778.

Child, J., & Rodrigues, S. (2005). The internationalization of Chinese firms: A case for theoretical extension? *Management and Organization Review, 1*(3), 381–418.

Choudhury, P., & Khanna, T. (2014). Toward resource independence – Why state-owned entities become multinationals: An empirical study of India's public R&D laboratories. *Journal of International Business Studies, 45*(8), 943–960.

Cuervo-Cazurra, A. (2018). *State owned multinationals: Governments in global business.* London: Palgrave Macmillan.

Cuervo-Cazurra, A., Inkpen, A., Musacchio, A., & Ramaswamy, K. (2014). Governments as owners: State-owned multinational companies. *Journal of International Business Studies, 45*(8), 919–942.

Evans, P. B. (1995). *Embedded autonomy: States and industrial transformation.* Princeton, NJ: Princeton University Press.

Financial Times. (2019). The other side of Chinese investments in Africa. Retrieved December 2020, from www.ft.com/content/9f5736d8-14e1-11e9-a581-4ff78404524e.

Finchelstein, D. (2013). Estado e internacionalización de empresas: los casos de Argentina, Brasil y Chile. *Desarrollo Económico, 209–210*, 113–142.

(2017). The role of the state in the internationalization of Latin American firms. *Journal of World Business, 52*(4), 578–590.

Finchelstein, D., Gonzalez-Perez, M. A., & Salvaj, E. (2019). The role of subnational governments on the internationalization of state owned enterprises. Paper presented at the 79th Academy of Management Conference, August 12, Boston, MA.

Gee, R. W., Zhu, S., & Li, X. (2007). China's power sector: Global economic and environmental implications. *Energy LJ, 28*, 421.

HK Electric Investments. (n.d.). About us. Retrieved July 2018, from www .hkelectric.com/en/about-us.

Independent Power Transmission Operator (ADMIE SA). (n.d.). Company. Retrieved July 2018, from www.admie.gr/en/company/.

Jemena. (n.d.). About us: Who we are. Retrieved July 2017, from http://jemena.com .au/about/about-us/who-we-are

Kalasin, K., Cuervo-Cazurra, A., & Ramamurti, R. (2020). State ownership and international expansion: The S-Curve relationship. *Global Strategy Journal, 10*(2), 386–418.

Kornai, J. (1979). Resource-constrained versus demand-constrained systems. *Econometrica, 47*(4), 801–819.

(1990). The affinity between ownership forms and coordination mechanisms: The common experience of reform in socialist countries. *Journal of Economic Perspectives, 4*(3), 131–47.

Li, M. H., Cui, L., & Lu, J. Y. (2014). Varieties in state capitalism: Outward FDI strategies of central and local state-owned enterprises from emerging economy countries. *Journal of International Business Studies, 45*(1), 1–25.

Megginson, W. L., & Netter, J. M. (2001). From state to market: A survey of empirical studies on privatization. *Journal of Economic Literature, 39*(2), 321–389.

Musacchio, A., & Lazzarini, S. (2014). *Reinventing state capitalism*. Cambridge, MA: Harvard University Press.

Musacchio, A., Lazzarini, S., & Aguilera, R. (2015). New varieties of state capitalism: Strategic and governance implications. *Academy of Management Perspectives, 29*(1), 1–17.

Ni, C. C. (2008). The Xinfeng Power Plant Incident and Challenges for China's Electric Power Industry. The Institute of Energy Economics, Tokyo, Working Paper (February 2007). Retrieved May 2019, from https://eneken.ieej.or.jp/en/data/pdf/382.pdf.

National Grid Corporation of the Philippines (NGCP). (n.d.). Corporate profile. Retrieved July 2018, from www.ngcp.ph/corporate-profile.asp.

Patel, S. (2016, February 25). China rolls out proposal for worldwide grid. *Power Magazine.* Retrieved May 2019, from www.powermag.com/china-rolls-out-pro posal-for-worldwide-grid/?pagenum=1.

Perez Ludueña, M. (2017). Chinese investments in Latin America: Opportunities for growth and diversification, ECLAC Working Papers, N. 208. Santiago: United Nations.

REN. (n.d.). About REN: Company profile. Retrieved July 2018, from www.ren.pt/en-GB/quem_somos/perfil_da_empresa/.

Rougier, M. (2007). Instituciones y crecimiento económico. La experiencia del Banco Nacional de Desarrollo, Nación – Región – Provincia. *Desarrollo Económico, N° 1.*

Shleifer, A., & Vishny, R. W. (1998). *The grabbing hand: Government pathologies and their cures.* Cambridge, MA: Harvard University Press.

Sikkink, K. (1993). Nuevo Institucionalismo y Política Desarrollista: Capacidad y Autonomía del Estado en Brasil y la Argentina. *Desarrollo Económico, 128*(32), 501–531.

Standard & Poor's Capital IQ. (2018) Retrieved July 1, 2018, from Capital IQ database.

State Grid Brazil Holding SA [SGBH]. (n.d.). About us. Retrieved July 2018, from www.stategridbr.com/about-us-en.html.

State Grid Corporation of China [SGCC]. (2013). Corporate social responsibility report 2013. Retrieved July 2018, from www.sgcc.com.cn/images/ywlm/social responsiility/brief/2014/10/23/2FE46B3DA8D748AF3A0F1854CD73F75D.pdf.

(2014). Corporate social responsibility report 2014. Retrieved May 2019, from www.sgcc.com.cn/html/files/2019-04/08/20190408100223322793249.pdf.

Corporate Social Responsibility Report 2016. (2016). Retrieved May 2019, from www.sgcc.com.cn/html/files/2018-07/28/20180728130448830583544.pdf.

(2017). Corporate social responsibility report 2017. Retrieved May 2019, from http://www.sgcc.com.cn/html/files/2018-08/29/20180829165036376453337 .pdf.

(n.d. a). Power grid: Clean energy. Retrieved May 2019, from www.sgcc.com.cn/ html/sgcc_main_en/col2017112619/column_2017112619_1.shtml?childColumnId =2017112619.

(n.d. b). State Grid Corporation of China completed the acquisition of equity stake in CDP RETI. Retrieved July 2018, from www.sgcc.com.cn/ywlm/media center/corporatenews/11/311305.shtml.

Tihanyi, L., Aguilera, R., Heugens, P., van Essen, M., Sauerwald, S., Duran, P., & Turturea, R. (2019). State ownership and political connections. *Journal of Management*, 45(6), 2293–2321.

Uhlmann, C. (2016). ABC News: Chinese investment in Australia's power grid explained. Retrieved July 2018, from www.abc.net.au/news/2016-08-21/chi nese-investment-in-the-australian-power-grid/7766086.

United Energy. (n.d.). Company information. Retrieved July 2018, from www .unitedenergy.com.au/our-story-and-vision/company-ownership/.

U.S. Energy Information Administration (EIA). (2017). International energy outlook 2017. Retrieved September 2019, from www.eia.gov/outlooks/ieo/pdf/0484 (2017).pdf.

(n.d.). International energy statics. Retrieved November 2020, from https://bit.ly/ 2Z34ECX.

Yamakawa, Y., Peng, M. W., & Deeds, D. (2008). What drives new ventures to internationalize from emerging to developed economies? *Entrepreneurship Theory and Practice*, 32(1), 59–82.

Yi-chong, X. (2017). *Sinews of power: The politics of the State Grid Corporation of China*. New York: Oxford University Press.

Zinfra. (n.d.). About us. Retrieved July 2018, from www.zinfra.com.au/About-Us.

5 Digital Companies Driving Business Model Innovation in Emerging Markets

The Cases of Alibaba, Flipkart, Jumia, and Mercado Libre

Lourdes Casanova, Anne Miroux, and Diego Finchelstein

5.1 A LOOK AT THE WORLD OF RETAIL E-COMMERCE

More than ever, consumers are turning to e-commerce websites to purchase goods throughout the world. Though the American company Amazon and the Chinese retailer Alibaba are powerful players in this space, other e-commerce businesses in emerging markets have risen as strong, competitive players. These companies are growing differently from the likes of Amazon. As we shall see, the most relevant players from emerging markets – Alibaba, Flipkart, Jumia, and Mercado Libre – share several similar features: innovative mobile payment systems, adaptability to emerging markets customers, business model innovation with cash payments on delivery, and partnerships with small- and medium-sized companies. Such an increase is reinforced by large regional markets for e-commerce (see Table 5.1).

In the United States, Amazon was able to grow quickly due to the efficiency of the US Postal Service (USPS) and credit-card networks. Emerging markets, however, cannot always count on having such robust systems in place and have had to create their own delivery methods. While this might limit growth at first, e-commerce sites in key emerging markets are looking at tremendous growth ahead with better infrastructure and more customers turning to online retail.

Table 5.1 *Facts and figures of the largest emerging-market retail e-commerce companies compared to Amazon, 2019 (US$ billion)*

Company	Country of origin	Gross merchandise volume	Market cap/ valuation	Revenue	Net income	Number of countries[b]	Employees (thousands)	Mobile payment brand
Amazon	USA	427.20	858.68	252.06	12.10	14	647.50	Amazon Pay
Alibaba	China	833.36	435.40	59.83	14.65	18	103.70	Alipay
Flipkart	India	6.20[a]	20.78[II]	3.76[a]	(0.60)[a]	1	3.30	PhonePe
Jumia	Nigeria	0.94	0.62	0.17	(0.24)	14	5.13	JumiaPay
Mercado Libre	Argentina	12.49	27.40	1.80	0.02	18	7.24	Mercado Pago

[a] Data from fiscal year ended in March 2018.

[b] Number of countries with different platforms, including the country of origin.

Sources: The authors and EMI team, based on FactSet database, Barclays Capital Live, Retail Without Borders [https://rwb .global/], and https://services.amazon.com/global-selling/overview.html, https://group.jumia.com/, www.Mercado Libre .com/, and www.alibaba.com/ all accessed October 2019.

Though Amazon was late to adopt a mobile payment platform, several emerging market multinational companies (EMNCs) have pioneered their own payment systems, including Alibaba in China with Alipay, Jumia in Nigeria with JumiaPay, and Mercado Libre in Argentina with Mercado Pago. These platforms have become a core part of their business, offering more features than Amazon, such as money transfers and even loans.

E-commerce retail sales are expected to reach US$6.542 trillion by 2023, according to emarketer.com. In 2019 alone, these sales are slated to grow by 17.9 percent, making up a greater portion of overall retail sales, from 12.2 percent of total retail sales in 2018 to 22 percent in 2023 (emarketer, 2019). Such an increase is reinforced by large regional markets for e-commerce.

As Statista shows, Asia enjoys the world's largest e-commerce market with US$831.7 billion, and China makes up most of that market at US$740 billion. The United States follows with a US$501 billion market. Europe touts the third-largest market at US$346.5 billion, with the rest of the world holding an e-commerce market of US$54.9 billion. Despite strong regional e-commerce markets in Asia, North America, and Europe, the largest e-commerce markets are located in a select few countries. China, in particular, is set to boast the world's fastest-growing e-commerce market, with a projected 2023 market size of US$1 trillion.

Nine E-20 countries are listed among the top ten fastest-growing e-commerce markets, according to Shopify, an indication of the promising opportunities in the emerging world in this sector (Shopify, 2020). Critically, e-commerce sales are concentrated among a few online retailers. Indeed, the top ten global online retailers generated US$427.28 billion in 2018, a 22.5 percent increase from the previous year. With the rise of e-commerce globally, and in specific regional markets, there is a subsequent rise in the popularity of digital payment methods (whether in-app or browser-based payments), with 43 percent of consumers preferring digital payment systems, second only to credit cards, according to Shopify.

In the following sections, we study China's Alibaba, India's Flipkart, Nigeria's e-commerce leader Jumia, and Argentina's Mercado Libre as the vanguards of the e-commerce world both in emerging markets and beyond.

5.2 ALIBABA'S RISE TO BECOME THE WORLD'S LARGEST RETAIL AND E-COMMERCE COMPANY

Alibaba Group Holdings, one of Fortune's World's Most Admired Companies in 2018, is a multinational conglomerate that operates in e-commerce, retail, mobile payments, artificial intelligence, digital media, entertainment, and other areas. Headquartered in Hangzhou, China, Alibaba was founded in 1999 by Jack Ma with seventeen employees. The firm became profitable in 2002 and in 2003 launched Taobao Marketplace, a consumer-to-consumer marketplace like Amazon and eBay. By 2005, Jack Ma decided to partner with Yahoo! Inc. as its search engine. Yahoo bought a 40 percent stake in Alibaba for US$1 billion. Alibaba went on to acquire numerous companies, including China's leading Internet provider, HiChina, and logistics firms such as Vendio and One-Touch, along with several new ventures. By 2014, Alibaba had ushered in the largest initial public offering (IPO) in world history (US$25 billion).

In the first quarter of 2019, Alibaba had over 654 million annual active customers, a large user base that it would convert to its new ventures. In line with the vision of Jack Ma to create a global marketplace, Alibaba spread its reach across the world soon after their IPO, spending over 2014–2017 almost US$34 billion in equity in the American companies Snapdeal and Lyft, the Indian company One97 Communications, the online e-commerce company Lazada Group in Singapore, and the Indonesian online marketplace Tokopedia, among others. The company strengthened its portfolio of mobile payments, e-commerce, and retail with the goal to link online with offline, encompassing retail in brick-and-mortar stores in the service of a "shopping economy." Alibaba pushed this vision by investing over US$4.5 billion in eleven e-commerce and online retail ventures, one-third of which furthered the digitalization of the grocery market by linking e-commerce, food, and mobile payments.

Meanwhile, Alibaba's research division, AliResearch, led the company to innovate with its technology, using artificial intelligence (AI) to power customer sales and marketing. By 2017, the firm launched an augmented reality project in collaboration with Starbucks in Shanghai, China, making it a leader in innovation in AI, tech, and cloud services.

Today, 56 percent of company's shares are held by noninstitutional holders. As of 2019, the company touted revenues of US$53 billion and gross profits of US$24 billion with almost 104,000 employees. It would become the second Chinese company after Tencent to reach a US$500 billion market cap, joining an exclusive group of companies (e.g., Apple, Microsoft, Facebook, Alphabet, and Amazon). Although Alibaba remains the leader of the e-commerce market with 55 percent of market share, JD.com is a formidable competitor with 25 percent of the Chinese e-commerce market.

Alibaba has become a global leader in mobile payments with Alipay, founded in 2004. As with other e-commerce leaders in emerging markets, the company resorted to cash on delivery (COD), a time-consuming process. Now, based on an escrow model, consumers avail themselves of Alipay, which, once the customer receives the product, releases the cash to the supplier on a periodic basis. Alipay first differed from mobile payment service competitors as it was free for small users, simply acting as a "middleman." It revolutionized the transaction market in China by making use of QR codes, which were popularized by most merchants in China. Since 2013, payments could also be made by sound waves from the merchant's phone to the vending machine.

In 2013, Alipay beat PayPal as the world's largest mobile payment service with more than one billion users. Alipay and its rival service, Tencent's WeChat, dominate nearly 93 percent of the Chinese market, with mobile payments of US$41.51 trillion in 2018.

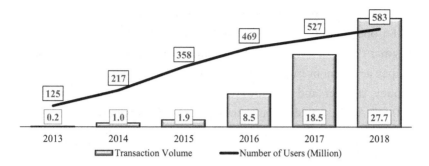

FIGURE 5.1 China's mobile payments in transactions (US$ trillion) and the number of users (at least once in the year), excluding virtual products,* from 2013 to 2018.
* Excluded products like e-papers, downloads of images, ringtones, or games.
Source: The authors and EMI team, based on iResearch reports' information (http://iresearchchina.com), accessed September 2019.

Figure 5.1 gives a window into the annual size of the mobile payments in China, showing the increasing value transacted and the number of users. The number of users quadrupled from 125 to 583 million from 2013–2018, and the transaction volume increased by 15,775 percent.

Alibaba's Alipay and Tencent's WeChat are the two most used mobile payment applications in China, holding a total market share of more than 90 percent (53.7 percent for Alipay; 33.8 percent for WeChat Pay) as of 2018.

Alibaba has done an exceptional job of creating its own ecosystem, in which e-commerce, mobile payments, retail, and other services are all interconnected and dependent. Mobile payments in China are used for everything from purchasing street food to donating spare cash to beggars. But with the market in China largely saturated, both Alipay and its rival WeChat Pay are working to capture the international market. Alipay was the first to establish cross-border payments and rapidly expanded into Europe, North America, Southeast Asia, and Australia, establishing services in fifty-four countries and regions, compared to WeChat's forty-nine.

By 2016, Alibaba partnered with banks and payment companies in Europe, including BNP Paribas, Barclay's PLC, UniCredit, and SIX Payment Services to increase the number of merchants that accept Alipay as payment methods. Additionally, Ant Financial acquired UK money transfer and currency exchange firm WorldFirst with over 400,000 users based mostly in the United Kingdom and Europe. WorldFirst specializes in international money transfers and now operates as a wholly owned subsidiary.

Similarly, in the United States, Alibaba has partnered with Walgreens to bring its mobile payment service to more than 9,500 Walgreens stores. In 2019, Alipay announced that it would be teaming up with Atlanta-based credit card processing service First Data to expand its services for Chinese tourists and US customers in over four million stores nationwide.

If we compare Alibaba with Amazon, almost 70 percent of Amazon's revenue was still attributed to the United States in 2018. And yet, even as the gross merchandise value (GMV) of Alibaba doubles Amazon's, its market capitalization as of November 2019 is only half of its counterpart's. However, Figure 5.3 shows an increase in Alibaba's market capitalization, which has nearly doubled from US$231.4 billion to US$435.4 billion since the IPO in 2014 but still trails the American giant (see Tables 5.1 and 5.2 and Figure 5.2).

Another milestone indicating Alibaba's e-commerce might was Alibaba's Singles Day revenues in 2019, which reached US$38 billion versus Amazon's equivalent Black Friday and Cyber Monday, which reached US$16.6 billion.

Alipay's success and market domination in China can be attributed mainly to its innovation in the mobile payment space and the rapid incorporation of new technology. For instance, as of 2019, Alipay launched a new technology called "Smile and Pay," which utilizes AI and facial recognition technology to verify the customer's identity. Furthermore, Ant Financial, Alipay's parent company, launched the world's first cross-border remittance payment network in 2018. In partnership with Alipay and mobile payments service GCash in the

Table 5.2 *Alibaba facts and figures (US$ million) in June 2019;
and Fortune Global 500 ranking, 2019*

Alibaba Group Holding Limited (NYSE: BABA)	
Balance sheet	
Total assets	148,361
Full-time employees	103,699
Key stats	
Total revenue	59,826
Net income	14,651
Fortune Global 500	
Ranking	182
Last year changing	+118
Years presented	3

Sources: The authors and EMI team based on Capital IQ database (www
.capitaliq.com/) and Fortune Global 500 (https://fortune.com/global500/),
accessed September 2019.

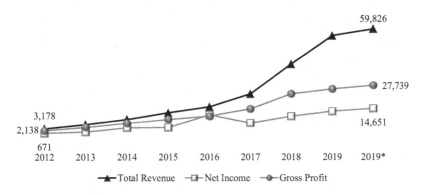

FIGURE 5.2 Alibaba's annual total revenue, gross profit, and net income
Source: The authors and EMI team, based on Capital IQ database
(www.capitaliq.com/), accessed September 2019.

Philippines, remittances can be transferred from Hong Kong to the
Philippines with much lower fees than standard money transfers.

Alipay was also one of the first mobile payment services to
make a variety of financial services readily accessible to people, such

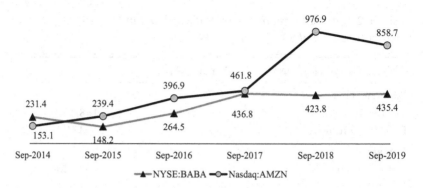

FIGURE 5.3 Alibaba's and Amazon's market capitalization value
(US$ billion) since Alibaba's IPO
Source: The authors and EMI team, based on Capital IQ (www.capitaliq.com/),
accessed November 2019.

as loans for small businesses and money market accounts, and the
first one to launch payments for rent, tickets, and other commodities/
services. This front-end experience distinguishes Alipay from overseas mobile payment technology such as Google Pay or Apple Pay.
Through the years, Alibaba's business model has shifted from
following eBay to becoming a leader at the forefront of innovation in
mobile payments and using AI.

5.3   FLIPKART AND THE RACE TO THE TOP
OF INDIAN E-COMMERCE

Flipkart's journey to becoming a market leader in Indian e-commerce is
enlightening. The company was founded in 2007 by engineers Sachin
Bansal and Binny Bansal, and its success can be attributed in part to
consistent access to funding and an Amazon-like philosophy to be
customer-centric, leading to a solid brand reputation. Flipkart stands
out in an emerging country like India, where service orientation and
customer experiences did not yet match those in the developed world.
By 2009, Flipkart began raising two rounds of angel funding of
US$40,000 and US$100,000 followed by the first round of venture
funding with Accel Partners. This validation of the business model lent

the founders the confidence needed to aggressively pursue their growth ambitions. By 2013, Flipkart became the first Indian unicorn.

5.3.1 Flipkart Innovates with Payment Methods

When Flipkart was founded, credit card penetration in India was less than 1 percent, and online shopping was still a new concept. As such, customers were not quick to trust this payment method. As in other emerging markets, Flipkart's solution was to innovate its business model and allow customers to pay with COD.

Flipkart faced poor infrastructure across India paired with a lack of shipping capabilities and suppliers. The focus on its own value chain was important. In response, the company set up a hub with five main fulfillment centers across the country in Delhi, Mumbai, Kolkata, Bangalore, and Hyderabad, which would receive, sort, and package products and then ship packages across different regions.

In 2012, Flipkart further expanded its portfolio to fashion and lifestyle products, one of the most profitable categories for e-commerce companies, with profit margins as high as 40–45 percent, with the acquisition of online fashion players such as Myntra (in 2014) and Jabong (in 2016), thus securing as much as 70 percent of market share.

5.3.2 E-Commerce Competitors Come to India

Flipkart is not alone in the e-commerce space in India. It has faced competition from India-based Snapdeal, as well as Amazon. In 2013, Amazon announced a US$2 billion investment in its Indian subsidiary (which had opened in 2004) and launched its retail operations, and as a result, the competitive landscape changed overnight. Regulations in India do not allow foreign companies to sell directly to customers, so when Amazon entered the market in June 2013, it devised a platform that small merchants could use to sell their products to online shoppers.

Until 2018, Flipkart had benefited from a regulation loophole to sell products to customers with an entity called WS Retail, owned by

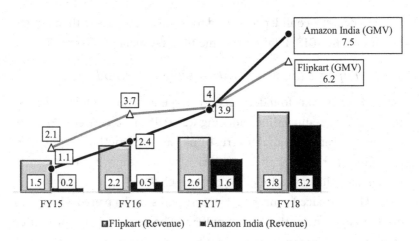

FIGURE 5.4 Flipkart and Amazon India's GMV and revenue, 2015–2018
Source: The authors and EMI team, based on Barclays Capital Live (https://live
.barcap.com/), accessed October 2019.

Flipkart's cofounders, Sachin Bansal and Binny Bansal. As part of a
complex arrangement, WS Retail bought goods at a discount from
Flipkart India Pvt. Ltd, the arm of the main group holding company,
and sold them to customers on Flipkart's site. WS Retail also owned
and ran Flipkart's key logistics business, called Ekart, that delivers
products to customers.

The race in the e-commerce industry generally boils down to a
competition of who sells the most GMV. Since 2017, Amazon has
managed to cross and maintain its lead GMV (see Figure 5.4), with
respect to Flipkart, though, in revenues, Flipkart outrivals Amazon in
India with US$3.8 billion versus US$3.2 billion for its main competitor.

Besides Amazon, Alibaba.com (the business-to-business arm) is
also active in India with 4.5 million registered users, the second-most-
important country for the company after China, and it intends to go to
the retail space as of 2019.

5.3.3 Bumps on the Road: The Need for More Customization

With 100 million registered users by 2018, Flipkart offered an attractive marketplace for third-party sellers. This, combined with the

resources and funds invested by Flipkart, enabled it to rapidly add sellers to its marketplace. Its number of active sellers (those having sold at least one product in the previous month) was estimated at between 30,000 and 50,000 in 2018. However, as it grew, Flipkart wielded less control over product quality, consistency, and replacement policies. With every incident of poor service or even downright cheating by sellers, Flipkart's reputation suffered. Meanwhile, Amazon was investing in technology and new supply chains to implement its "customer-obsessed" philosophy in India. Amazon even offered refunds and replacements in the event of problems with the products or service.

To address quality issues, and as the local leader, Flipkart was fast to adjust its business model. The firm found that it needed to move past a one-size-fits-all approach and create a customized model that suited the needs of the Indian market. For categories such as books, mobile phones, large appliances, etc., in which the number of stock-keeping units (SKUs) was not high, Flipkart worked directly with up to 100 sellers to manage all their needs and even stored their products in Flipkart's warehouses. For other categories such as accessories, home furnishings, and women's fashion, among others with personalization and a large number of SKUs, Flipkart worked with the few thousand sellers who managed their own inventory. This helped ensure product and service quality even as the company offered customers a wide selection of products and categories, a strategy that empowered Flipkart to hold onto its leadership position despite fierce competition, particularly from Amazon.

5.3.4 *Moving Forward: Pressure from Amazon Will Lead to More Consolidation*

As Flipkart exhausted its cash, Walmart announced its acquisition, which the Competition Commission of India approved in August 2018. Around the same time, a new local player was entering the competitive space: The powerful Reliance group announced its launch of an online-offline retail model. The innovative idea was to rely on 350 million customers from its Reliance stores and 307 million mobile Jio customers to reach the far edges of its e-commerce platform.

Walmart bought a 77 percent stake of Flipkart for US$16 billion, securing a significant share in Indian e-commerce with the assumption that the landscape would keep growing in the ensuing years. Minority stakeholders like founder Binny Bansal, the Chinese company Tencent Holdings Limited, and the American firms Tiger Global Management LLC and Microsoft Corp. kept some stake in the company.

Flipkart's customer-centric approach set the foundation for the company's business model innovation (e.g., COD and mobile payments) within a customer-centric approach, which was central to the emergence of India's first unicorn (see Figure 5.5). And yet, amid so many competing variables, one thing is certain: Consistent pressure from Amazon and Alibaba will hasten the process of further consolidation in the Indian e-commerce industry. With the entrance of Walmart, India has become one of the most competitive places with all the world leaders present: Amazon, Alibaba, Walmart/Flipkart, and the powerful new Reliance hybrid model.

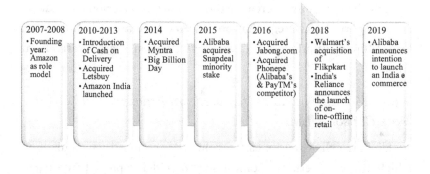

2007-2008	2010-2013	2014	2015	2016	2018	2019
• Founding year: Amazon as role model	• Introduction of Cash on Delivery • Acquired Letsbuy • Amazon India launched	• Acquired Myntra • Big Billion Day	• Alibaba acquires Snapdeal minority stake	• Acquired Jabong.com • Acquired Phonepe (Alibaba's & PayTM's competitor)	• Walmart's acquisition of Flikpkart • India's Reliance announces the launch of on-line-offline retail	• Alibaba announces intention to launch an India e commerce

FIGURE 5.5 Flipkart and Indian e-commerce landscape timeline
Source: The authors and EMI team.

5.4 AFRICA'S FIRST UNICORN, JUMIA

Jumia, which controls 70 percent of the African e-commerce market, was crowned the first African unicorn in 2016. As of September 2019, it was the continent's largest e-commerce platform with a presence in fourteen countries – Cameroon, Nigeria, Kenya, Morocco, Senegal, Tunisia, Algeria, Ivory Coast, Uganda, Rwanda, Egypt, Tanzania, Ghana, and South Africa – and had 4.3 million customers. Having risen at a remarkable speed, it was viewed as the most prominent African web-based business and start-up.

The company was founded in 2012 by Tunde Kehinde from Nigeria and Raphael Afaedor from Ghana, who originally merged their individual start-ups into one called Kasuwa ("marketplace" in Hausa, spoken in Nigeria), along with two Frenchmen, Jeremy Hodara and Sacha Poignonnec. By 2013, Jumia secured US$26 million for its Series A round of funding. The German Venture Capital Fund Rocket Internet invested significantly in Jumia's first round through the Africa Internet Group (AIG), a subsidiary of Millicom International, a Luxembourg-based company providing digital services, which would become the lead investor for Jumia's Series B round.

Jumia reached a US$500 million valuation at the end of its Series C round of funding in 2016. With buy-in from established venture capitalists and investors such as the French insurance AXA Group, South African MTN Group, Summit Partners, and Goldman Sachs, the executive board felt confident about the future success of the company, even as certain voices in Africa, as well as African media, criticized the fact that Jumia sells itself as an African company while its investors and owners are European.

Jumia was often referred to as the golden star within the AIG portfolio, and on closing the US$326 million round in Series C, AIG quietly rebranded itself as Jumia Group, absorbing all the individual start-ups into ten different lines of service embedded under the Jumia name – Mall, Market, Travel, Deals, Food, House, Car, Services, Jobs, and Pay. By 2016, Jumia reached a prominent valuation of US$1 billion and the coveted title of first unicorn in Africa.

5.4.1   E-Commerce Challenges in Africa

Nigeria is Jumia's primary market, but the company has also expanded in a number of African countries. E-commerce firms face an array of challenges in low-income markets, with a difficult infrastructure and lack of services, which are particularly acute in Africa. First, according to the International Telecommunication Union (ITU), Internet access in Africa is still very limited at about 28 percent of the population in 2019, the lowest in the world, compared to about two-thirds in Latin America, for instance. The context varies substantially across countries, with South Africa, Nigeria, and Kenya accounting for about half of African Internet users. In addition, in many regions, there is no proper system for mailing addresses. The quality of transportation infrastructure is another serious issue. Finally, payment proves an obstacle given that only 24 percent of the population in sub-Saharan Africa holds a bank account.

To grow, Jumia adapted to these market conditions by opening up customer adoption centers, enabling users to place orders on Wi-Fi-connected laptops and tablets, and helping them become familiar with online shopping. It set up its own logistics network based on a fleet of motorcycles and maintained a network of warehouses as Flipkart had done in India. Initially, deliverymen were often accompanied by aides who knew the terrain. Today, 80 percent of delivery is outsourced to small independent businesses with their own fleet of vehicles, mainly motorbikes.

Meanwhile, to address the payment challenge, Jumia first relied on the COD model, which rewarded Jumia with customer loyalty. Then, in 2016, following the example of the Chinese juggernaut Alibaba, Jumia set up its own payment system, Jumia Pay, in Nigeria, Egypt, Ivory Coast, Ghana, Morocco, and Kenya. While facilitating safe and fast payments, Jumia Pay bypasses the need for bank accounts.

Today, Jumia, and the African e-commerce industry as a whole, remain relatively nascent, and numerous challenges still persist. Lack of consumer confidence in online purchases, low literacy rates, and the prevalence of informal markets with many buyers and sellers, as well as disparate economies and a variety of regulations that differ among countries, are significant obstacles to reaching customers across the continent. Such high barriers to entry keep out short-term international players but provide an opportunity for a local unicorn to monopolize the market, should they find solutions.

The African online retail market was expected to hit US$18.6 billion by 2019, compared to just over US$8 billion in 2013. Numerous online retailers were vying to be the dominant player in the African continent (Jumia, Konga, Takealot, Afrimarket, and Kilimall, among others), while Amazon and eBay await cautiously from the outside. Alibaba through Aliexpress, however, has followed an aggressive strategy and has 4.2 million customers. All competitors were engaged in similar verticals – electronics, fashion, home appliances, and children's items. Recently, however, the competitive landscape cleared up for Jumia (see below).

Fundraising is critical to the success of any e-commerce business in Africa, given the need to expand the market. Profitability in this space is a long-term objective, as start-ups require the injection of cash into their businesses to scale teams, operations, and logistics. By the end of 2018, Jumia had raised the most among African e-commerce businesses and had established the largest operation base. While some of Jumia's competitors, such as Konga and Takealot, raised smaller rounds or failed in fundraising, Jumia was backed by high-profile global investors, an advantage for rapid expansion. Jumia embraced the mantle of "Amazon for Africa," as it did not face major competitors with similar scale and access to funds.

Over the years, Jumia has accumulated multiple business models. While sourcing its own inventory, they also partner with over 500,000 merchants on the Jumia marketplace. Konga (until its closure, see below) and Kilimall eventually moved away from managing their own inventory toward merchant marketplace models.

5.4.2   Customer-Focused Model Helps Jumia Grow

In just a few short years, Jumia has been able to target increasing middle-class consumers in areas like Lagos and Abuja in Nigeria and to scale up to become the largest e-commerce company in Africa. As was the case for Flipkart, focusing on customer satisfaction has been a key part of the company's success. For example, once an order is placed through the site, customers receive a confirmation call within 30 minutes. This reduces the risk of mistakes and breeds trust for the consumer. By incorporating a mobile app into its digital products, as well as a chatbot functionality, Jumia has given customers the ability to continually stay connected within its ecosystem. This agile strategy enabled the company to aggressively expand into marketplaces, travel services, and more, which has attracted the attention of investors and media alike.

Jumia also incorporated a social consciousness component to its mission. In October 2016, the company announced an initiative to promote local products and entrepreneurs through its Jumia Local feature. To that end, consumers would be empowered to buy locally made goods and leverage e-commerce platforms to boost manufacturing. In Nigeria, Jumia Local vendors were able to quadruple their sales in just six months using the platform, supporting the economy and small business owners. Jumia charges a 1 percent commission for the first three months, then implements a tiered rate based on demand. Small businesses can significantly increase their reach by utilizing Jumia's platform, which receives around a million visits to its website daily.

While Jumia's expansion has been extremely fast, it has not been without setbacks. In October 2015, in a downsizing and restructuring effort, it laid off about 300 workers in Nigeria, about 30 percent of its workforce. More recently in November and December of 2019, it suspended activities in Cameroon, Rwanda, and Tanzania, reflecting the difficulties to run and scale up an e-commerce business in an environment with poor infrastructure, underdeveloped logistics, and a lack of trust in online shopping.

Among Jumia's perennial problems is the struggle to generate profits. This situation tends to be relatively common for start-ups, and achieving profitability is even more challenging in the e-commerce sector in Africa because margins are low while operating expenses are high, given the challenges mentioned above. Yet, for some observers, eight years – to date, the time since Jumia was created – is quite a long time. The company's operating losses keep rising, reaching US$188 million in 2018. Altogether, Jumia has lost more than US$1 billion since being founded in 2012 (Munshi, 2019). As of December 2019, Jumia declared about US$346 million in cash, barely enough for two years of service at the rate the firm is currently burning through cash.

5.4.3 Moving Ahead in Africa

Jumia has contributed to an increasing acceptance of online shopping by African consumers through, for instance, its customer adoption centers and its Jumia Pay system. It launched Black Friday sales on the continent in 2014, touting discounts on coveted items like PS4s, cell phones, and tablets. While originally faced with operational problems as the site was not equipped to handle the influx of traffic, Black Friday sales later became successful.

Like all e-commerce platforms that have reached a critical size, Jumia began to diversify into a wide range of activities, such as food and meal delivery (Jumia Food), hotel and flight booking (Jumia Travel), classified ads, and real estate. In doing so, it has followed the examples of Amazon, Alibaba, and Mercado Libre, which have expanded into a variety of areas. For CEO Sacha Poignonnec, diversification is indeed the next step; Jumia, like Alibaba and Amazon, will have the possibility to diversify precisely because the firm was conceived as an evolving platform (Veysset, 2019).

Jumia Pay is a key innovative element in this diversification strategy. Besides facilitating transactions, Jumia Pay enables the firm to introduce additional online services such as cellular data recharging (an important item in countries where a large part of the population favors prepaid models versus more expensive monthly subscriptions) and payments of bills, for instance. Furthermore, given the widespread use of cash on the continent, there is little basis for assessing consumer credit capabilities. With its expanding activities in payment-related services, Jumia may plan to enter this area and provide an e-commerce-based credit scoring infrastructure as Alibaba does in China.

In line with the search for increasing revenues, the firm's strategy was largely focused on expanding its customer base and increasing the use of its platform. Its sales have been constantly on the rise, registering significant growth over the years. During the second quarter of 2019, for instance, they rose again significantly (by 58 percent), and the number of its clients increased from 3.2 to 4.8 million compared to the same period the year before (*Financial Afrik*, 2019). The aforementioned retreat from Cameroon, Tanzania, and Rwanda may indicate a pause in a strategy centered around scale and a shift toward a search for profitability and a stronger focus on the JumiaPay platform. The transaction volume on that platform nearly doubled to €32m (about US$36 million) in the third quarter of 2019 compared to a year earlier.

Jumia currently benefits from a favorable competitive environment in Africa with few competitors. Konga, one of its main contenders, fired most of its workforce in early 2019 and was bought back by local firms, while AfrikaMarket, also a significant competitor, went bankrupt in September 2019. The two global giants in the industry, Alibaba and Amazon, have not yet really deployed their financial and technological firepower to the continent, except for some ventures in Rwanda for Alibaba and in Egypt for Amazon, through a local company Souq.com., though Alibaba is eyeing the African market. Yet, Jumia still enjoys the first-comer advantage.

A milestone in Jumia's trajectory was its IPO in April 2019 in the New York Stock Exchange through Jumia Technologies AG. The

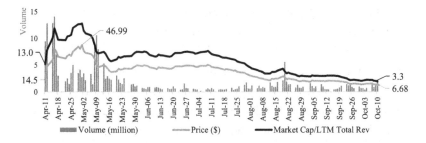

FIGURE 5.6 NYSE: JMIA's volume negotiated, close price, and market capitalization over revenue index since the IPO on April 12, 2019
Sources: The authors and EMI team, based on data from New York Stock Exchange (www.nyse.com/), accessed October 2019, and Capital IQ (www.capitaliq.com/), accessed October 2019.

IPO was successful, raising US$196 million, opening at US$18.95 and closing at US$25.46. Since then, however, the firm has faced a few headwinds, including accusations of not having provided proper information at the time of the IPO and lower-than-expected financial results: The company's operating losses for the first three quarters of 2019 reached US$61.3 million, a 35 percent increase compared to the same period the year before (Jumia, 2019). Jumia's share price had tripled in value in the first few weeks of trading, only to fall dramatically in the months that followed. As of October 10, 2019, it had lost about 70 percent since the IPO (Figure 5.6).

Despite this fluctuation in the stock market, Jumia's management remains confident, stressing that what matters is the firm's strategy and its long-term valuation (Clemencot, 2019), referring to the example of Mercado Libre (see next case study). When it was first listed twelve years ago, Mercado Libre's share went through major ups and downs, from US$20 at its initial price offering to US$70 a few months later and falling to less than US$10 a few months later. As of September 2019, however, its share is worth more than US$500.

Jumia is betting on the potential for e-commerce in Africa, a continent with a population of 700 million people. Today, it is estimated that e-commerce accounts for about 1 percent of all sales in Africa, while in China the ratio is estimated at 20 percent.

By 2025 that figure may reach 10 percent in the continent's largest economies. The population of Nigeria alone is expected to grow 44 percent by 2030, which would make it one of the top five most populous countries in the world. With an increasing population in its home market, the company remains well positioned to test new methods and break new records. Against this background, whether financiers will continue giving Jumia more time to fulfill its potential and turn out profits remains to be seen. A possibility could be for the firm to develop key partnerships with global leaders of e-commerce, including from China – as hinted by some observers.

5.5   MERCADO LIBRE, THE LATIN AMERICAN LEADER

Founded in 1999 in Argentina by Marcos Galperin, Mercado Libre was created to bring e-commerce to Latin American consumers. The company has become one of the largest firms by market capitalization in Latin America, operating as the e-commerce leader in eighteen countries. In 2018, Mercado Libre touted US$1.8 billion in revenue (Table 5.3) and US$30 billion in market capitalization.

To date, more than half of Mercado Libre's revenue comes from Brazil, though Mexico is increasing its share relative to Argentina and Venezuela, which have decreased their value partly due to the devaluations of their currencies (see Figures 5.7, 5.8, and 5.9).

While the e-commerce model was already very successful in the United States by 1999 with eBay, the sector had not been fully developed in Latin America. Thus, several start-ups attempted to replicate eBay's model in the region. Successfully implementing an e-commerce business in Latin America comes with several challenges, given the different cultural characteristics and infrastructure constraints in the region.

First, its post office system is not as efficient. While eBay sellers and buyers could reliably use the postal service in the United States to send and receive their products, this option could not be replicated in Latin America. In Argentina, for instance, the company could not

Table 5.3 *Mercado Libre financial data (US$ million) as of June 2019*

Mercado Libre, Inc. (NasdaqGS: MELI)	
Balance sheet	
Total assets	4,595
Full-time employees	7,239
Key stats	
Total revenue	1,802
Net income	15.7

Source: The authors and EMI team, based on Capital IQ database (www.capitaliq.com/).

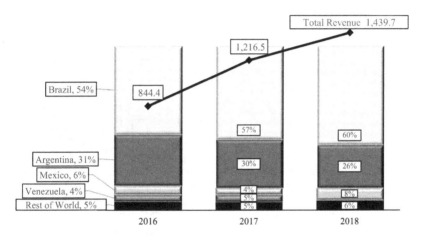

FIGURE 5.7 Mercado Libre's revenue per country, 2016–2018 (US$ million)
Source: Mercado Libre's 2018 Annual Report.

send valuable packages through the postal service. Instead, Mercado Libre would connect buyers and sellers.

Second, Mercado Libre engineered an innovative payment system to address the security needs of its marketplace. This new system, Mercado Pago, emulated the PayPal model and guaranteed mediation in the marketplace while also providing a safer tool for its users. This would become a full-fledged money-management

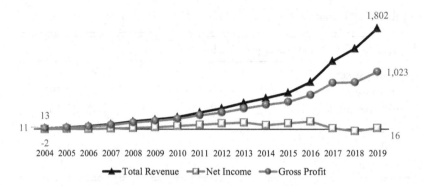

FIGURE 5.8 Mercado Libre's revenue, gross profit, and net income 2004–2018

Source: The authors and EMI team, based on Capital IQ database (www.capitaliq .com/), accessed September 2019.

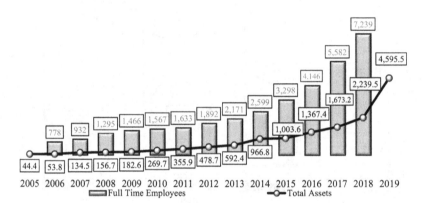

FIGURE 5.9 Mercado Libre's employment and total assets (US$ billion) annual performance since 2005*.

* Data on full-time employees were not found for 2005 and for Jun 2019.

Source: The authors and EMI team, based on Capital IQ database (www.capitaliq .com/), accessed September 2019.

system, complete with payments to friends, investment options, and small loans. The challenge with this system is the high level of informality that exists in Latin America affected by low levels of bancarization. As in other emerging markets, in the early 2000s, credit cards and bank accounts were not the primary way of trade

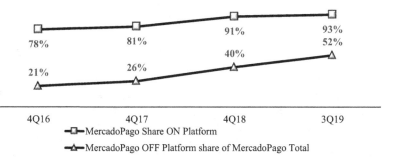

4Q16   4Q17   4Q18   3Q19
—□—MercadoPago Share ON Platform
—▲—MercadoPago OFF Platform share of MercadoPago Total

FIGURE 5.10 Mercado Pago's share of on-platform transactions and share of off-platform in all Mercado Pago's transactions
Sources: The authors and EMI team, based on Mercado Libre's Results (http://investor.Mercado Libre.com/financial-information/quarterly-results), accessed November 2019.

for Latin Americans. Thus, Mercado Libre partnered with agencies to collect the money deposited by users and send it to buyers, once the transaction had been confirmed, for an additional fee. This initial model was later modified, but Mercado Pago continues to be the main source of payment and a significant part of its revenue. Currently, Mercado Pago is one of the pillars of the company, and this payment method has expanded beyond the marketplace platform and is used in brick-and-mortar stores and other online marketplaces. Mercado Libre wants to be something close to a full-fledged digital bank. Having built its own infrastructure, it is on the path to becoming one.

As Figure 5.10 confirms, the volume transacted through Mercado Pago increased since 2013, reaching US$6.52 billion in the second quarter of 2019.

Another distinctive feature of Mercado Libre's origin was the decision to create its own technological platform to gain full proprietary control of its technology (Barnett & Mekikian, 2013). Conversely, DeRemate, a dynamic competitor for Mercado Libre at first, opted to acquire licensed technology to speed the launch of the company in the region. However, this strategy generated technical

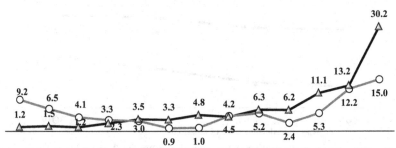

FIGURE 5.11 Mercado Libre's market capitalization value (NASDAQ: MELI) since its IPO in August 2007, compared to Brazilian B2W Digital (BOVESPA: BTOW3), US$ billion
Source: The authors and EMI team, based on data from Capital IQ database (www .capitaliq.com/), accessed November 2019.

issues for DeRemate, which was acquired by Mercado Libre in 2008, as the scalability grew (Barnett & Mekikian, 2013).

Figure 5.11 presents Mercado Libre's market capitalization, which doubled from June 2018 to June 2019.

One challenge Mercado Libre had to overcome was some customers' hesitation to buy and sell on a virtual market, due to institutional voids existing in Latin America. The company worked to build a reputation system on its platform that rewarded well-established and well-ranked buyers. Mercado Libre put a team in place to review the message board to prevent buyers and sellers from offering additional information or using dubious methods.

5.5.1   Adjusting and Seeking New Business Opportunities

After becoming the main e-commerce company in the region, Mercado Libre continued to improve and innovate its business model, transforming from an auction platform like eBay to a more integrated sales and logistics platform similar to the current Amazon or Alibaba model. The firm is heavily investing in technologically advanced facilities and distribution centers, where it has been able to fend off Amazon competition without major turbulence. Mercado Libre continues to be the largest player in the business both in Mexico and Brazil, two countries in which it is facing competition from Amazon.

Mercado Libre started to expand into financial services using its marketplace platform as well as its payment services to create a solid consumer base. These financial services grew at a fast pace, creating a potentially unique source of revenue for the company. Fintech services are still an immature market in Latin America, and Mercado Libre possesses a unique set of resources, which positions it at a clear competitive advantage. The firm's size, technology, and customer base are strong advantages in comparison to other regional players or local start-ups.

The institutional and cultural particularities of Latin America also fueled Mercado Libre's expansion into financial technology. In comparison to developed regions, the region has low levels of bancarization, between 30 and 50 percent, depending on the country, and high levels of informality. An important, and increasing, part of this population makes use of Mercado Libre's marketplace and payment tools. In addition, the population in Latin America typically has little to no access to credit. The company thus developed a system of offering small short-term loans, with high potential growth and margin opportunities.

5.5.2 Current Challenges and Perspectives Ahead

Mercado Libre continues to be the largest Latin American unicorn and the regional leader in e-commerce. The company boasted a record of operative and technological prowess within its industry while developing innovative solutions that adjusted well to the Latin American environment. This behavior catapulted the company ahead of other local competitors. However, Mercado Libre faces a strong challenge with the entrance of Amazon in Mexico and Brazil.

This may be the first time Mercado Libre will compete with companies that have more financial and technical capabilities. Thus far, Amazon's entrance into Latin America has not displaced Mercado Libre, which has leaned on an aggressive strategy toward its competitors, with increasing investments in logistics and new business solutions (i.e., credit services).

Mercado Libre now shows two distinctive features and advantages. First, the company has built a vast knowledge of business know-how in Latin America and was able to deal with the institutional weaknesses as well as political and economic instability. Even under severe economic crises like in Venezuela and Argentina, Mercado Libre managed to continue expanding and growing. Finally, the company shows a first-mover advantage. It is the most well-known e-commerce company in the region, and it touts solid technology and a well-developed base of buyers and sellers. As long as Mercado Libre continues to offer state-of-the-art services and innovative business opportunities, Amazon's attempt to conquer these markets could prove a difficult task.

5.6 THE NEW E-COMMERCE LEADERS FROM EMERGING MARKETS

As shown in the case studies above, e-commerce leaders in emerging markets should not be dismissed as copycats because they have emerged as regional leaders, in some cases fending off competition from even top global competitors. Even if lagging in market valuation, Alibaba stands out in this respect, as it has double the volume of sales as Amazon, and it is a world leader in mobile payments.

Although some of the e-commerce leaders in EMs are still losing money, their business model innovations and product innovations have allowed them to transform some challenges in their home countries into opportunities to innovate. Allowing COD (Flipkart and Jumia) or calling customers to confirm their deliveries (Jumia) has turned out to be a big advantage for homegrown companies in emerging markets. Lack of credit card penetration was the trigger to start mobile payments in the case of Alibaba.

In the process, these companies with homegrown innovative business models and products like aggressive online payment platforms have been successfully building trust for online marketplaces, paving the way for formidable growth.

REFERENCES

Barnett, W., & Mekikian, G. (2013). Mercado Libre. Stanford GSB, Case IB105.

Clemencot, J. (2019, September 24). E-commerce: Jumia sur la corde raide. *Jeune Afrique*. Retrieved September 2019, from www.jeuneafrique.com/mag/ 832202/economie/e-commerce-jumia-sur-la-corde-raide/.

emarketer. (2020). Global ecommerce 2019. https://www.emarketer.com/content/ global-ecommerce-2019.

Financial Afrik. (2019). Jumia "l'africaine" face au retour de bâton de la Bourse de New York. *Financial Afrik*. Retrieved September 2019, from www .financialafrik.com/2019/11/04/jumia-lafricaine-face-au-retour-de-baton-de-la- bourse-de-new-york/.

ITU, (2020). Measuring digital development - Facts and figures 2019. Retrieved from https://www.itu.int/en/ITU-D/Statistics/Documents/facts/FactsFigures2019.pdf.

Jumia. (2019). Company website, Jumia reports third quarter results. Retrieved December 2019, from https://investor.jumia.com/Cache/1001258825.PDF? O=PDF&T=&Y=&D=&FID=1001258825&iid=14406054.

Munshi, N. (2019, December 10). Africa's Amazon hopeful Jumia retreats from big expansion. *Financial Times*. Retrieved September 2019, from www.ft.com/ content/a4f6ee1e-182b-11ea-9ee4-11f260415385.

Shopify. (2020). https://www.shopify.com/enterprise/the-future-of-ecommerce.

Veysset, T. (2019, November 2). « Jumia sera-t-il l'Amazon Africain ». *Entreprendre*. Retrieved September 2019, from www.entreprendre.fr/jumia-sera-il-amazon- africain/.

6 Entrepreneurial Ecosystems and Innovation in the Balkans

Veneta Andonova

6.1 INTRODUCTION

Balkan nations score comparatively high on measures of innovation. In the 2019 Global Innovation Index (GII), all Balkan countries scored above or in line with expectations for their level of development (GII, 2019: table A). Moreover, countries like Bulgaria and Slovenia surpassed large emerging economies such as India, Mexico, and Brazil in the efficiency metric of the innovation index, demonstrating their ability to achieve higher innovation output per unit of input (see Figure 6.1). This marked positive performance in innovation rankings contrasts with the general perception of the region's historical performance.

Winston Churchill once said that "the Balkans produce more history than they can consume." He was highlighting the disruptive and occasionally destructive power of this part of the continent in its own history and the history of the world, which has adversely affected the region's economic prosperity and social progress. In economic terms, the Balkans remain an emerging part of Europe, despite the fact that some of these countries have been part of the European Union (EU) for more than a decade. The characteristics that make the region somewhat similar to other emerging economies include institutional weaknesses, brain drain, social inequality, and poverty (Andonova, Pérez, & Schmutzler, 2020). We included Greece in this study because it belongs to the Balkans geographically and culturally, even though its status as an emerging market is debated (Sizemore, 2013).

Despite the challenges that characterize emerging economies, Bulgaria, Croatia, and Montenegro are repeated high achievers in innovation on par with other emerging middle-income countries and

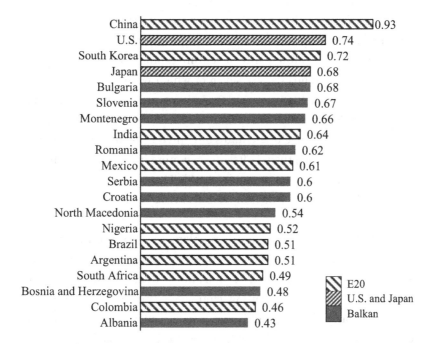

FIGURE 6.1 Efficiency innovation index (GII's efficiency ratio)
Source: The authors, based on Global Innovation Index Report 2019,
www.globalinnovationindex.org/gii-2019-report, accessed July 2019.

even alongside China (GII, 2018). Of course, the degree of innovation varies significantly between Balkan countries. For example, Albania ranks 83rd and Slovenia ranks 31st in the 2019 GII, while most other Balkan countries rank in the first half of the 129 countries assessed in the index. We argue that understanding the Balkan economies' innovation performance can provide actionable insights for other emerging countries. In particular, we argue that the young entrepreneurial ecosystems in the Balkans have nourished innovation-driven entrepreneurship, improving the innovation performance of the region as a whole. Many of the transformational effects that entrepreneurial ecosystems have produced on the region cannot be captured by traditional measures of entrepreneurial dynamics, which are better suited for more mature entrepreneurial ecosystems. As a result, those unacquainted with the region are surprised by the fact that between 2010 and 2017, Central and Eastern Europe generated some €5 billion of investor wealth through fifteen venture capital (VC)-backed exits of technology-driven businesses, seven of which were from the Balkans (Ezekiev, 2017). In 2018, a record €0.7 billion was invested in Central and Eastern Europe start-ups. When we include start-ups that subsequently moved to the United States or United Kingdom to be closer to clients and investors, the results are even more impressive, reaching a total of €1.3 billion (Dealroom.co, 2019). These numbers are indicative of the interest that innovation-driven ventures stir among investors.

Despite pervasive structural problems such as brain drain, deficient legal frameworks for technology transfer, and poorly managed and financed public research organizations, there are signs that the Balkan region has been maturing genuine entrepreneurial ecosystems that contribute to the region's status as a leader in innovation efficiency. We believe that the Balkans have the potential to produce a large-scale impact on both the productive base and the social and political realities of the region (see Figure 6.1). We explore the factors that led to the creation of the Balkan entrepreneurial ecosystems as part of the research and innovation dynamics in the Balkans. We argue that the enterprise sector – especially innovation-driven entrepreneurial ventures – are at the core of the region's entrepreneurial ecosystems and act as key players that will propel the region to the forefront of innovation efficiency.

6.2 HOW ENTREPRENEURIAL ECOSYSTEMS RELATE TO NATIONAL SYSTEMS OF INNOVATION

We understand the concept of an ecosystem as a metaphor, according to which business organizations can operate not only as components of industries but also as interlinked nodes of a network that traverses industry boundaries (Neumeyer & Corbett, 2017). From this perspective, entrepreneurial success is not the result of isolated individual effort but is a consequence of the coordination and collective work of various stakeholders (Isenberg, 2016; Spigel & Harrison, 2018). For example, pivotal stakeholders for innovation-driven entrepreneurial ventures include the participants in the national system of innovation (NSI) (Andonova et al., 2020). Both entrepreneurial ecosystems and innovation systems are seen as drivers of economic growth (Malecki, 1997), but they are distinct concepts, and we do consider them synonymous (Tsvetkova, Schmutzler, & Pugh, 2020). For the purpose of our argument, we highlight the most significant differences between entrepreneurial ecosystems and NSIs. Our work closely follows the approach of Andonova et al. (2020), and we summarize their key insights below.

The literature on NSIs takes a systems view of the innovation process and recognizes that learning and innovation are socially embedded and interactive phenomena (Smits & Kuhlmann, 2004; Lundvall, 2008) to which the ecosystem metaphor can be applied. Innovation systems are presented as systemic interconnections of firms, institutions, and socioeconomic structures that shape the process of "science-based and experience-based learning" (Lundvall, Vang, Joseph, & Chaminade, 2009, p. 7), which determines the rate of innovation and competence-building (Lundvall, 1992; Nelson, 1993). More recently, in the systemic analysis of entrepreneurship (e.g., Van der Ven, 1993), the concept of entrepreneurial ecosystems has emerged to reflect "a set of interdependent actors and factors coordinated in such a way that they enable productive entrepreneurship within a particular territory" (Isenberg, 2010, p. 3). Well-defined territoriality and interdependency among actors are common features of both entrepreneurial ecosystems and NSIs. Entrepreneurial ecosystems, however, place the entrepreneurial agency at the center of the system (Acs, Autio, & Szerb, 2014) and focus on the micro foundations of firm dynamics, paying special attention to entrepreneurial motivations, venture financing, and support (Brown & Mason, 2017), as well as incubators, mentor institutions, universities, and research centers (Alvedalen & Boschma, 2017), which are seen as generators and facilitators of entrepreneurial culture (Mason & Brown, 2014).

While extant research has framed entrepreneurial ecosystems as emergent, fast-paced, self-organizing, and self-sustaining arrangements, NSIs are seen as more slow-paced and formal systemic designs that revolve around the research sector's R&D activities and technology transfer systems toward companies. In this environment, institutional and policy frameworks encompass the policies that foster ideas and knowledge creation for the economy. Of course, NSIs include both start-ups and well-established businesses, as well as public and private business organizations that introduce innovations in the economy. We argue that the entrepreneurial initiative and ambition nourished by the local entrepreneurial ecosystems play a greater role in the performance of Balkan countries in innovation rankings than the strength of the research sector and the technology transfer systems.

We identify and analyze the interactions between six different components of the entrepreneurial ecosystem and their associated actors. In that, we subscribe to the parsimonious version of entrepreneurial ecosystems proposed by Isenberg (2011) and adapted by Andonova, Nikolova, and Dimitrov (2019), emphasizing the following components: (1) government programs and public sector, (2) academic and research institutions and R&D transfer, (3) market functioning and private-sector sophistication, (4) infrastructure, (5) culture, and (6) entrepreneurial finance. The discussion of how these building blocks come to interact with the innovation capabilities of countries in the Balkans is structured at three levels following the conceptual model presented in the Introduction of this book.

6.2.1 Institutions, Infrastructure, and Government Programs

From the perspective of entrepreneurial ecosystems, these include physical, legal, and human infrastructures, government programs, and agencies that support and shelter entrepreneurs against volatile market trends. Public funds frequently back entrepreneurial finance – never the most important ingredient of an entrepreneurial ecosystem, but a necessary contributor to experimentation, scaling, and ultimately positive economic outcomes and exits that matter for long-term entrepreneurial dynamics.

6.2.2 R&D Capabilities, Transfer Capabilities, and Universities

Within entrepreneurial ecosystems, academic and research institutions as well as R&D transfer capabilities deliver marketable innovations into the product–market fit phase of start-ups and corporations engaged with intrapreneurship.

6.2.3 Business Sophistication and Entrepreneurial Culture

Market-supporting institutions, the private sector's business processes and level of competitive sophistication, and the presence of multinational corporations all contribute to innovation-driven entrepreneurship. Entrepreneurial mind-set and communities shape the venture creation process and give rise to entrepreneurial culture. It is both the proximate environment, comprising family members and role models, and the distal cultural environment reflecting social norms and values (Schmutzler, Andonova, & Díaz-Serrano, 2018) that mold the entrepreneurial dynamics of innovation-driven ventures.

6.3 DATA AND METHOD: WHY THE BALKANS?

This chapter is set in the context of the Balkan Peninsula and relies on quantitative and qualitative data from Albania, Bosnia and Herzegovina, Bulgaria, Croatia, Greece, Kosovo, the Republic of North Macedonia, Montenegro, Romania, Serbia, and Slovenia. It also builds on our previous research describing the emergence of entrepreneurial ecosystems in South Eastern Europe (Andonova et al., 2019) and some of their specific features (Andonova et al., 2020). The extensive data collection process included more than seventy face-to-face interviews with entrepreneurs, start-up experts, public officials, and researchers across the region to provide the rich context behind the essential elements of the Balkan entrepreneurial ecosystems that gave rise to innovation-driven ventures. In the process, we realized that our insights spanned both entrepreneurial ecosystems and innovation, and we validated the hard data that we use in the rest of this chapter through our interviews. While this research is original, it draws on some of our previous arguments in Andonova et al. (2019) and Andonova et al. (2020).

In essence, the innovation-driven entrepreneurial ventures from the Balkans represent a significant share of both the number of such ventures and their value created in Central and Eastern Europe (see Table 6.1). Moreover, these ventures appear to be spread across industry and technology verticals, invariably relying on knowledge and idea creation. The Greek company Workable, for example, produces a global hiring software available on mobile and desktop devices that allows small and medium-sized companies to recruit by sourcing candidates, tracking applicants, and advertising jobs (TNH, 2018). Rimac from Croatia produces a high-performance electric car that outperforms its more renowned competitors in both speed and acceleration (Clarkson, 2017). The Slovenian firm Outfit7 created the mobile pet game Talking Tom, which reached eight billion downloads before being acquired by Chinese investors. Transmetrics, a Bulgarian company, offers big data predictive analytics software for the cargo transport industry (Tanev, 2019). UiPath is a Romanian software company that develops platforms for robotic process automation and has a valuation above US$1 billion.

It is clear that innovation is at the core of these entrepreneurial ventures. Therefore, understanding the entrepreneurial ecosystems in the Balkans could shed light on the forces at work behind the region's high innovation efficiency rankings that many emerging economies also strive to achieve.

6.4 BRIEF OVERVIEW OF THE ENTREPRENEURIAL ECOSYSTEMS IN THE BALKANS

6.4.1 Institutions, Infrastructure, and Government Programs

Infrastructure, government programs, and policies, as well as a functioning public sector, are important factors in entrepreneurial

Table 6.1 *Selected innovation-driven entrepreneurial ventures from Central and Eastern Europe (Balkan companies/countries bold)*

Valuation (US$ billions)	Company	Country	Valuation (US$ billions)	Company	Country
5–10	Skype	Estonia	2–5	TransferWise	Estonia
	UiPath	**Romania**		avast	Czech Republic
1–2	kiwi.com	Czech Republic		LogMein	Hungary
	SiteGround	**Bulgaria**		Allegro	Poland
	Playtech	Estonia	1–2	Taxify	Estonia
	CD Projekt	Poland		**eMag**	**Romania**
<1	Tresorit	Hungary		**Outfit7**	**Slovenia**
	Softomotive	**Greece**	<1	alza.cz	Czech Republic
	DCS+	**Romania**		socialbakers	Czech Republic
	Brainly	Poland		Mintos	Latvia
	tecnologies	Estonia		**Software Group**	**Bulgaria**
	Flo	Belarus		**Zemanta**	**Slovenia**
	elefant.ro	**Romania**		Docplanner	Poland
	Frosfit	**Bulgaria**		NordVNP	Lithuania
	Atlas dynamics	Latvia		Tesonet	Lithuania
	Geneplanet	**Slovenia**		**Workable**	**Greece**

Table 6.1 (cont.)

Valuation (US$ billions)	Company	Country	Valuation (US$ billions)	Company	Country
	Sonarworks	Latvia		**Transmetrics**	**Bulgaria**
	Grupa Pracuj	Poland		**Bellabeat**	**Croatia**
	Almotive	Hungary		Banuba	Belarus
	Huuuge	Poland		Pipedrive	Estonia
	Vinted	Lithuania		WANNABE	Belarus
	Infobip	**Croatia**		Citybee	Lithuania
	Rimac	**Croatia**		Prezi	Hungary
	Blueground	**Greece**		pilulka.cz	Czech Republic
	Skeleton	Estonia		Monese	Estonia

Source: The authors, based on Dealroom.co, 2019.

ecosystems. Even though governments do not start new businesses in modern market economies, government policies, programs, and initiatives indirectly shape innovation-driven entrepreneurial endeavors. Following the Global Entrepreneurship Monitor's (GEM, n.d.) methodology, Balkan national experts rated the sufficiency of the framework conditions under which government programs, infrastructure, and institutions operate (see Table 6.2).

In Greece and Croatia, taxes and bureaucracy are a much bigger problem than in Bulgaria and Slovenia, for example. Greece and Slovenia, on the other hand, report more government support and more relevant government programs. At the same time, among the four Balkan countries that participated in the Global Entrepreneurship Monitor Report 2018/2019, physical infrastructure is rated as adequate, while commercial and legal infrastructure exhibits a greater lag in comparison with the US score. Remarkably, government entrepreneurship programs in Slovenia appear to be particularly sufficient.

The number of government programs for start-ups and entrepreneurial ventures has increased since 2012, when the European Investment Fund enabled the creation of regional accelerator venture funds. In Bulgaria's case, the country's president even led initiatives supporting the creation of science parks and business incubators. There are, however, multiple ways that infrastructure management might be improved and transformed into more effective support mechanisms for the entrepreneurial and scientific communities.

Despite these encouraging initiatives, a significant number of diverse stakeholders in the Balkan entrepreneurial ecosystem express concerns about the ability of state officials to carry out even the most thoughtfully designed programs for entrepreneurial support. The most extreme example in this regard is that of Bosnia and Herzegovina, which incorporated multiple levels of government to guarantee the transition from war to peace in a multiethnic setting. The multilevel government is a major problem for the development of a more vibrant entrepreneurial community because of the high opportunity cost that

Table 6.2 *Entrepreneurship framework conditions for four Balkan countries and the United States*

Framework conditions	Bulgaria	Croatia	Greece	Slovenia	USA
Entrepreneurial finance	5.24	3.97	3.99	4.97	5.95
Government policies: support and relevance	3.16	2.82	3.30	4.39	4.17
Government policies: taxes and bureaucracy	4.51	2.10	2.57	3.33	4.68
Government entrepreneurship programs	3.48	3.29	3.34	4.96	4.38
Entrepreneurial education at school stage	2.82	2.45	2.76	3.12	4.33
Entrepreneurial education at postschool stage	4.05	3.71	3.99	4.77	5.49
R&D transfer	3.35	2.97	3.94	4.29	4.39
Commercial and legal infrastructure	5.19	3.76	4.45	4.98	5.92
Internal market dynamics	4.67	5.13	4.49	5.33	5.49
Internal market burdens	3.9	3.01	3.73	4.78	4.74
Physical infrastructure	6.93	5.61	6.34	6.91	7.08
Cultural and social norms	3.49	2.74	4.19	3.72	7.27

Source: Data from the National Experts Survey of the Global Entrepreneurship Monitor Report, 2018/19.
Note: 1 = highly insufficient; 9 = highly sufficient.

abundant and well-paid government jobs impose on young potential entrepreneurs. On the other hand, in Bulgaria, the fact that many public servants are incapable of understanding the business models of some young innovation-driven ventures is presented as a fortunate circumstance! Innovation-driven entrepreneurs share that they are protected from extortion by government officials' ignorance rather than by the institutions for law enforcement in the country. In other countries, such as Serbia, where only private-sector money fuels the entrepreneurial ecosystem, corruption is only a marginal problem for the entrepreneurial community because of the lack of public funds distributed. As a result, the absence of government financing is perceived as a shelter against corruption in a number of non-EU Balkan countries. In relatively adverse circumstances with insufficient financing opportunities, entrepreneurial ventures emerge under harsh conditions, making them remarkably resilient.

In places with more abundant EU-backed entrepreneurial finance such as Bulgaria, market-based incentives built into the management of the public funds made them very effective. Better coordination with the private sector and the entrepreneurial community improve the talent pool and the efficiency of government programs designed to stimulate entrepreneurial endeavors in the Balkans. Not surprisingly, experts are increasingly recognizing the efforts of Balkan governments to establish programs for new and growing businesses as better than most of the other government initiatives. On the other hand, when programs for stimulating entrepreneurship lack market-based incentives and stimulate bureaucratic procedures and centralized decision making and control (as in Romania), the results are less satisfactory.

Serious reservations about the capacity of government officials to effectively and competently stimulate both entrepreneurship and R&D activities are pervasive across the region. Policy coordination and institution building remain key challenges in the Balkans at all levels, but countries have begun to improve the governance of R&D institutions. For example, North Macedonia has a national council in charge of coordinating innovation policy and a national innovation strategy. Albania has a coordinating agency under the Council of Ministers to support, monitor, and evaluate science, technology, and innovation initiatives, while Montenegro created a Council for Scientific and Research Activity with the participation of the public and private sectors, research institutes, and academics (WB Technical Assistance Project P123211, 2013).

Among the best-rated aspects of government entrepreneurship programs in the Balkans is the support offered by science parks and incubators, where there is significant involvement by the private sector and successful entrepreneurs, who participate as mentors, role models, and investors. Nevertheless, more dynamic developments are hindered by the need for restructuring and consolidation of the predominantly public research organizations. In Croatia (population of four million), for example, there are more than thirty research institutes. In many of these research institutes, especially in the Western Balkans, a command-and-control type of regulation persists along with a lack of performance-based evaluation systems and vague distribution of responsibilities (WB Technical Assistance Project P123211, 2013).

Budgets in the Balkans are modest; Bulgaria, Croatia, Greece, and Serbia spent around 0.9 percent of their GDP on R&D in 2017 (see Figure 6.2). In contrast, EU countries on average spent 2.05 percent of their GDP on R&D, while Baltic and Central European countries such as the Czech Republic, Hungary, and Estonia spent around 1.5–2 percent on R&D. Romania's public spending on R&D lagged that year, hovering at around 0.5 percent of GDP. In the Balkans, the positive outlier is Slovenia, with 1.9 percent of GDP spent on R&D, higher than the average rate of the EU. Despite this gap in spending, a number of Balkan countries have better-than-predicted (based on their GDP per capita) capabilities for knowledge creation and innovation. We see the creation and consolidation of entrepreneurial ecosystems in the Balkans as one of the main factors behind this performance.

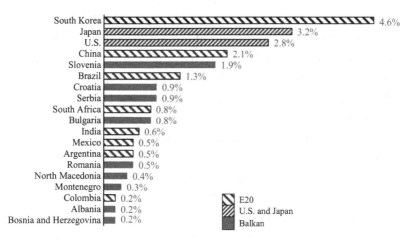

FIGURE 6.2 Gross R&D expenditure (% of GDP)
Source: The authors, based on Global Innovation Index Report 2019,
www.globalinnovationindex.org/gii-2019-report, accessed July 2019.

At supra-national levels, EU institutions have made a big difference in entrepreneurial finance. Since 2012, the EU has funded
innovation-driven start-ups in this region through seed and venture
capital. The Joint European Resources for Micro to Medium
Enterprises (JEREMIE) program of the EU, for example, invested about
US$1.5 billion in Bulgaria. Four funds were selected to manage a total
amount of €350 million, conditional on raising additional private
funds, which focused on innovation-driven start-ups and small-to-
medium enterprises (SMEs). These initial public investments
achieved a 2.57 multiplier effect that by 2017 attracted €875 million
in private financing (Angelov, 2017). As a result, cities like Sofia,
Bulgaria, became important growth hubs for the tech sector in the
Balkans, creating incentives for firms to set up there. Arguably these
investments have enhanced the competitiveness of 9,476 SMEs and
180 start-ups, helping to support more than 25,550 jobs in the region
(Angelov, 2017). Growth since then has been continuous: In 2016, 210
start-ups from the Balkan region raised US$74 million (O'Brien, 2018).

Successful VC players are active in the region, and many of
them are homegrown. For instance, Romanian company Gecad

Ventures successfully backed Vector Watch and RAV Antivirus, the latter of which was sold to Microsoft in 2003. Still, the overall level of VC investments in Romania, the largest Balkan country by population, is just 0.001 percent of GDP, compared to the EU average of 0.027 percent, according to Invest Europe (MacDowall, 2017). In Croatia, there is only a single fund, South Central Ventures, that also covers the West Balkans. Angel investors exist, but are not very active. In Romania, for example, start-up ventures lack access to capital, leading the most promising start-ups to relocate their core management operations to the United Kingdom or the United States in search of venture financing.

On average, however, regional financing needs have remained comparatively low. Most of the start-ups are in the information and communication technologies (ICT), digital, engineering, and mid-tech sectors. The regional ecosystem promotes these types of start-ups, given the tradition of successful innovations and the presence of corporations, education, and community organizations with such focuses. The entry cost and capital requirements in these industries are low to moderate, and the region already has adequate infrastructure for start-ups to leverage complementary resources, limiting their capital requirements and the need for entrepreneurial finance.

Two accelerator venture funds, Eleven and Launchub, were instrumental in these developments – both are located in Sofia, but have a mandate to invest in the whole region. Eleven was a US$15 million start-up accelerator and seed fund, while Launchub started as a $12 million preseed fund. Both funds were focused on investment in innovation-driven start-ups that had the potential to benefit from exponential growth, rather than in SMEs. Much of the entrepreneurial finance that kick-started the entrepreneurial ecosystems in the Balkans came from the EU, which invites policy discussions on the role of national governments as an arm's-length limited partner investor, rather than the leading decision maker and manager in innovation-driven ventures.

According to the application data between November 2012 and December 2015 obtained from Eleven, 81 percent of start-ups in the region reported they had invested their own funds in their start-up ventures, with the average amount equal to US$20,210. The average amount sought by ventures to grow their operations between 2014 and 2015, according to Launchub data, was a modest US$645,730.

The experiences of the Balkan countries show that governments need to focus on creating a broad context for a functioning entrepreneurial ecosystem, but probably cannot be an active manager of the funds, as the correct incentives lie with the funds' partners and managers, not bureaucrats. Unresolved challenges remain in the region, such as market gaps in both equity and debt instruments and a marked scarcity of investment funds beyond the seed level. It is undisputed, however, that the availability and management of entrepreneurial finance in the Balkans after 2012 has produced a deep effect on the local entrepreneurial ecosystems. The region faces a lack of late-stage funding opportunities, which creates incentives for promising local entrepreneurial ventures to sell prematurely, as they do not expect to be able to access funds to fuel their aggressive international growth. Though this is a problem, it also indicates that the base of the Balkan entrepreneurial ecosystems is solid and set for expansion.

6.4.2 R&D Capabilities, Transfer Capabilities, and Universities

Universities are key players in the start-up ecosystem because they attract and develop young talent, shape and influence students' mindsets, and create and serve as a repository of knowledge and expertise in learning and education, all of which nurture entrepreneurial ecosystems. At their best, universities can support entrepreneurial ecosystems if they inspire proactiveness and promote a culture of innovation. They can help students strengthen the required skills and knowledge they need as entrepreneurs and act as a safe space for experimentation and early failure, a platform for research in support of the ecosystem, and a place for sharing knowledge and best practices. In sum, universities engage in lasting relationships with ecosystem partners to build synergies for continuous improvement and act as an indispensable part of the most developed entrepreneurial ecosystems in the world (Andonova & Nikolova, 2015).

In the Balkans, universities have contributed little to local entrepreneurial ecosystems. Although science, technology, engineering, and mathematics (STEM)-related departments occasionally receive credit for their ability to provide large-scale basic training, the majority of entrepreneurs, government agency officials, and investors in the Balkan entrepreneurial ecosystems perceive university processes and their knowledge base as antiquated and out of sync with today's requirements. The introduction of new and innovative programs to state-owned universities is often perceived as a threat to the long-lasting status quo of faculty members, who are government employees. The incentives for universities and their staff to be entrepreneurial are largely absent or very weak. Not surprisingly, investors, entrepreneurs, managers of established companies, and NGOs are calling for ambitious and thorough educational reform that would transform the university and research sectors to support the Balkan entrepreneurial ecosystem.

Historically, however, universities have been very important for research and development in the region. Universities, more than governmental institutions or hospitals, have been the primary authors of scientific publications (WB Technical Assistance Project P123211, 2013). The number of scientific and technical articles from the Balkans looks impressive, but these numbers must be interpreted with an understanding of the local context (see Figure 6.3). In particular, there is a notorious absence of knowledge and processes for technology transfer and a lack of well-established industry–science collaborations. The ability to create economic value from scientific knowledge is also low. For example, analyzing the ratio of R&D expenditures and patents reveals that a single US-registered patent from Serbia or Croatia requires about four times more R&D

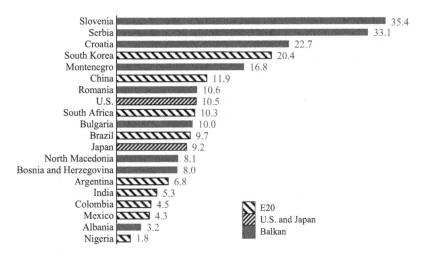

FIGURE 6.3 Scientific and technical publications (per billion US$ PPP GDP)

Source: The authors, based on Global Innovation Index Report 2019, www.globalinnovationindex.org/gii-2019-report, accessed July 2019.

expenditures than a German patent (WB Technical Assistance Project P123211, 2013).

As a general rule, Balkan innovation systems have emphasized knowledge and competence building over financing and economic impact. However, our case study shows that key stakeholders in the Balkans believe that the root cause of issues in their NSI is the broken linkage between the academic and research entities on the one hand, and the markets and market participants on the other. In fact, R&D expenditures not only tend to be low in the Balkans, but they are also perceived as generating limited scientific and economic results.

One important reason for optimism is that local talent is very competitive (Andonova et al., 2019). The Balkans regional programming talent is recognized worldwide mostly due to the tradition of technical education that dates back to the socialist period of most Balkan countries. According to data from Stack Overflow – the most dominant Q&A platform for coders, with about 3.5 million users – the best coders are from the Balkans (Salkever, 2015). Stack Overflow ranks the skill level of coders around the world by considering the "up or down" votes to answers for previously posted questions about coding and systems, as well as peer user ranking. As such, the result is entirely crowd-driven. Using the average country rankings of 14,898 Stack Overflow users with a reputation score of 5,000 or more, Bulgarian coders scored the highest average reputation in the world. Bulgaria is also home to forty top-performing users of Stack Overflow, and their impressively high scores make Bulgaria the country with the highest average reputation in the world. Croatia and Greece, the other Balkan countries in the top twenty, appear in sixth and nineteenth places, respectively.

This top-performing talent in coding comes at a rather modest price when we consider the average wages, salaries, and benefits paid by entrepreneurial ventures in the Balkans. Table 6.3 compares the average yearly personnel expenses of Balkan and Baltic early-stage ventures, pointing to a huge gap in the average cost of labor, although top spenders in both regions report comparable maximum expenditures (US$266,505 vs. US$250,000). On average, entrepreneurial ventures from the Balkans operate at a 50 percent discount when compared to labor costs in the Baltic states. However, entrepreneurial

Table 6.3 *Average yearly wages, salaries, and benefits paid to workers, in US$ (2013–2017)*

	Average	Standard deviation	Minimum	Maximum	Sample size
Balkan countries	$12,518	$43,759	$0	$266,505	48
Baltic countries	$23,784	$68,521	$0	$250,000	12

Note: The Balkan countries represented are Albania, Bulgaria, Romania, Serbia, Greece, Croatia, Macedonia, and Slovenia. The Baltic countries represented are Estonia, Latvia, and Lithuania.
Sources: Data available from the Entrepreneurship Database Program at Emory University, supported by the Global Accelerator Learning Initiative, 2013–2017. Data from Andonova et al. (2019).

ventures from the Balkans have a higher share of founders with technical degrees as their highest educational achievement.

The educational profiles of new venture founders in the Balkans and in the Baltics are comparable (Andonova et al., 2019). The most highly educated founders among Balkan entrepreneurial ventures completed an average number of seventeen years of education compared to eighteen years for Baltic ventures, with a maximum of twenty-one years in both cases. The percentage of founders who have PhD degrees as their highest level of education is twice as high for Baltic entrepreneurial ventures when compared with Balkan entrepreneurial ventures, whose founders more frequently have bachelor's or technical degrees as the highest level of education, as shown in Table 6.4.

The difference in labor cost in comparison with other geographies has encouraged talented workers to leave Balkan nations for work elsewhere. According to Andonova et al. (2020), the end of communist regimes in the Balkan countries triggered a huge "brain drain,"

Table 6.4 *Highest level of education completed by the venture founders with the most education (2013–2017) (%)*

Level of education	Balkan countries	Baltic countries
PhD	10	20
Master's	41	40
Bachelor's	15	30
Technical degree	23	0
High school	10.30	10
Middle school	0	0

Note: Balkan countries are Albania, Bulgaria, Romania, Serbia, Greece, Croatia, Macedonia, and Slovenia. Baltic countries are Estonia, Latvia, and Lithuania.
Sources: Data available from the Entrepreneurship Database Program at Emory University, Global Accelerator Learning Initiative, 2013–2017. Data from Andonova et al. (2019)

understood as the emigration of engineers, physicians, scientists, and other very highly skilled professionals with university training. This brain drain is still an important phenomenon for the region. According to the Gallup Potential Net Migration Index, the share of highly skilled population that is willing to emigrate from Albania is 50 percent, 16 percent from Bulgaria, 40 percent from Bosnia and Herzegovina, 14 percent from Croatia, 11 percent from Greece, 43 percent from Kosovo, 39 percent from Macedonia, and 22 percent from Romania (Gallup, 2018).

However, this phenomenon has had a somewhat positive effect on the regional entrepreneurial ecosystems (Andonova et al., 2020). Connectedness to the Balkans diaspora became one external resource that created advantages for the region's entrepreneurial ventures beyond the physical co-location of actors in the local entrepreneurial ecosystems. Those ties contained networks of knowledge sharing and spillovers, constituted social capital, and acted as gateways to investors and clients from geographically distant but economically important regions.

The scientific diaspora from the Balkans has not had a similar effect on the region's entrepreneurial ecosystem, despite a massive brain drain in the research sector. North Macedonia saw a 70 percent decline in the number of researchers and scientists between 1995 and 2000 (Mustafa, Kotorri, Gashi, Gashi, & Demukaj, 2007). According to a survey, in Albania, more than 50 percent of all research workers and lecturers in ten public universities and forty research institutions emigrated between 1991 and 2005 (UNDP, 2006). Similar dynamics affected the rest of the Balkan countries, in particular Romania, Bulgaria, Serbia, Kosovo, and Bosnia and Herzegovina. According to Andonova et al. (2020), the Balkan diaspora of researchers and developers has been deterred from closer involvement by the bureaucratic top-down governance structures that still characterize most of the research and innovation sector in the region. However, there have been attempts to reverse the brain drain dynamics. Croatia, for example, created a program to finance joint research between the local scientific community and the scientific diaspora, the Unity through Knowledge fund (www.ukf.hr/). Still, more remains to be done.

6.4.3 Business Sophistication and Entrepreneurial Culture

The entrepreneurial landscape in the Balkans is mostly defined by its success in creating hubs for innovation-driven start-ups, mainly in the domain of digital technology. Some aspects of the region's business landscape have played an important role in this process.

Within the Comecon system of Soviet bloc countries, Romania and Bulgaria experienced economic specialization in information technology (IT). This IT tradition, coupled with strong STEM-focused education, gave both countries a head start in the digital economy when they became EU members in 2007. Bulgaria rapidly became a competitive outsourcing destination for leading incumbents in the digital economy, such as Cisco Systems, Hewlett-Packard, VMWare, Microsoft, Oracle, SAP, and IBM. The presence of IT leaders and the availability of advanced IT professionals laid the groundwork for IT-based entrepreneurial development. According to the president of the Bulgarian Venture Capital Association, the export of IT-related products and services has grown more than fourfold since 2008. The presence of leading global companies with R&D operations in the Balkans has unquestionably improved the knowledge and relevant experience available in the region's labor markets.

The region also has some important regulatory advantages, such as low tax rates. In Bulgaria, for example, there is a 10 percent flat tax on profits and 5 percent on dividends. This, plus the growing number of well-run coworking places, accelerators, and VCs, is setting the scene for the Balkans to be one of the most dynamic young entrepreneurial ecosystems.

There are some unquestionable challenges too: The fragmentation and variety of the small markets within the region is frequently perceived as one of the biggest obstacles for start-ups (Guerrini, 2017). Nevertheless, small national markets have helped innovation-driven start-ups to strive for regional and global reach since their inception, a factor that has energized the local entrepreneurial ecosystems, attracting the attention of diverse foreign stakeholders.

Regional buyers are not very sophisticated, and often there is no local demand for the products that the advanced regional engineering talent creates. This fact pushes entrepreneurial ventures into early-stage internationalization, adding another layer of complexity to their operations. Two significant challenges arise from the fact that local markets are small and unsophisticated. First, Balkan innovation-driven ventures experience a shortage of business skills because the large majority of them lack proper business training, despite possessing world-class technical and engineering talent. Second, in the not-too-distant past, the mostly negative image of Balkan countries produced a damaging spillover effect, even for the most innovative entrepreneurial ventures. Some of the region's most successful business-to-business (B2B) ventures were explicitly asked to keep the names of their world-renowned clients confidential for fear that the Balkan origin of their suppliers might invite suspicion and mistrust about their operations. This outlook has changed gradually, largely because some of the most successful entrepreneurs made substantial efforts to educate their clients and show pride in their country as part of their business strategy.

Improving the region's branding is very important for the future of Balkan entrepreneurial ecosystems. Recognition as an attractive place to live and work by foreigners is essential for these young regional ecosystems to mature and reverse the brain drain into brain gain. Regional governments, especially those of Balkan EU-member countries, are taking cautious steps to encourage the immigration of high-skilled workers and attract talent from non-EU-member neighbors. More frequently, there are voices in favor of aggressive government programs to attract high-skilled immigrants from outside the region. Actors within the ecosystem overwhelmingly agree that attracting diverse talent is the most important thing to encourage a vibrant entrepreneurial and innovation ecosystem.

Bitdefender from Romania is an excellent case in point. In 2017, PricewaterhouseCoopers ranked Bitdefender as the seventeenth-largest emerging market software company. The company claims to serve more than 500 million users. This global cybersecurity firm began as an entrepreneurial effort between Florin Talpes and his wife, Mariuca, just after the end of the Communist regime. Early entrepreneurs and other businesses in the region were threatened by cyber-criminals and computer viruses. This situation led Talpes to design antivirus programs to protect his start-up, which focused on outsourcing software to the French market due to the political and economic proximity of these two countries. France was one of the first countries to invest in and trade with Romania in the technology and car components sectors, establishing several assembly lines for computers and cars in the country. Bitdefender's successful products were then requested by other clients starting new businesses, which led to a global expansion in 2001, quickly reaching other big markets such as the United States, Germany, the United Kingdom, Canada, and Australia. The company's innovations in fighting cyberattacks were an industry breakthrough, launching a novel technological solution that rapidly became embedded in security software globally. Led by Bitdefender, Romanian cybersecurity solutions became a byword in cybersecurity innovation. As the sector developed and Romania joined the EU in 2007, the business climate and opportunities in Romania greatly improved. This Romanian brand became recognized internationally, creating a sense of trust and reliability that encouraged venture capital firms to invest in the country.

Ongoing structural challenges still affect the functioning of the Balkans' market. Most of the economies in the Balkans are small and open. There has been some progress, with the transition to working market institutions, beginning in the 2000s, that introduced structural reforms and market stabilization, which improved the attractiveness of Balkan economies to foreign investors. The European Bank for Reconstruction and Development (EBRD) transition index for the region – a measure of a country's progress toward a free-market economy – rose from an average of 2.3 in 2000 to 3.2 in 2008 on a scale of 1 to 4 (Izvorski, 2015). More Balkan economies joining the EU are also expected to radically improve the region's markets. As of 2018, Albania, Macedonia, Serbia, and Montenegro were candidates for admission to the EU, but there is no firm commitment as to their accession date. While the general business environment is improving, it is unlikely that the desired entrepreneurial culture develops and permeates Balkan societies due to positive macroeconomic indicators and political achievements alone. Entrepreneurial attitudes take time to propagate.

The accelerator venture funds that started operations in 2012 were instrumental for building a Balkan entrepreneurial community and responsible for a culture shift. Accelerators catalyzed this process by channeling new financial resources, attracting substantial private capital. Private money brought discipline to companies and investments, increasing expertise and know-how. The newly built community that formed around the loci of the Balkan entrepreneurial landscape provided essential support to keep the ventures and their portfolios on track. They also capitalized on relationships with Balkan diaspora members to provide support as mentors, business partners, and occasionally investors. Thus, the creation of a community and establishing a culture of belonging was nearly as important as funding itself.

The hugely important educational role of Balkans accelerator venture funds can be better understood using data available from the Entrepreneurship Database Program at Emory University (n.d.). Tables 6.5 and 6.6 show the relative importance of the benefits that the Balkan and the Baltic entrepreneurs sought in their participation in 178 accelerator and support programs around the world. As of February 2018, the database surveyed a total of 13,495 ventures. According to this data, Balkan and Baltic entrepreneurs sought mostly network development. However, Baltic entrepreneurs recognized business skill development and mentorship as essential elements of the accelerator experience, in contrast to the Balkan entrepreneurs,

Table 6.5 *Relative importance of accelerator benefits as perceived by entrepreneurs in Balkan states (2013–2017) (%)*

			Benefit of accelerators as perceived by Balkan entrepreneurs				
Rank	Network development	Business skills development	Mentorship	Connection to potential investors	Secure direct funding	Access to a group of entrepreneurs	Awareness and credibility
1	34	19	11	11	19	4	2
2	17	11	11	36	13	6	6
3	11	17	30	11	23	9	0
4	19	15	15	19	11	6	15
5	11	17	17	17	15	17	6
6	6	9	15	2	13	36	19
7	2	13	2	4	6	21	51

Note: Balkan states are Albania, Bulgaria, Romania, Serbia, Greece, Croatia, Macedonia, and Slovenia.
Sources: Data available from the Entrepreneurship Database Program at Emory University supported by the Global Accelerator Learning Initiative. Data from Andonova et al. (2019).

Table 6.6 *Relative importance of accelerator benefits as perceived by entrepreneurs in Baltic states (2013–2017) (%)*

	Benefit of accelerators as perceived by Baltic entrepreneurs						
Rank	Network development	Business skills development	Mentorship	Connection to potential investors	Secure direct funding	Access to a group of entrepreneurs	Awareness and credibility
1	36	27	18	9	0	0	9
2	36	9	18	9	18	0	9
3	9	27	27	18	9	9	0
4	9	9	9	27	9	27	9
5	9	27	0	18	36	9	0
6	0	0	9	18	18	27	27
7	0	0	18	0	9	27	45

Note: Baltic countries are Estonia, Latvia, and Lithuania.

Sources: Data available from the Entrepreneurship Database Program at Emory University supported by the Global Accelerator Learning Initiative. Data from Andonova et al. (2019).

who gave a higher priority to securing direct funding and connections to potential investors (Table 6.5). This evidence may indicate two things: the relative scarcity of venture capital in the Balkan region and a marked overconfidence among Balkan entrepreneurs in their business skills and abilities. Entrepreneurship needs optimism, and the region has not been traditionally known for the optimistic views of its inhabitants. It is much more problematic that Balkan entrepreneurs underestimate the importance of business skills and dismiss them as minor or unimportant. Certainly, the process of crystallizing a local entrepreneurial culture will require this attitude to change.

6.5 CONCLUSIONS

In this chapter, we argue that the young entrepreneurial ecosystems in the Balkan countries have played a pivotal role in the region's impressive performance in international rankings of innovation excellence. We contend that the entrepreneurial ecosystems have supported the better-than-expected positions of many Balkan countries in terms of innovation output and efficiency.

The Balkan countries provide a very interesting case for emerging economies in their search for innovation excellence, given their relatively modest investment in R&D and less-than-perfect institutions. We provide evidence that the interactions facilitated by entrepreneurial ecosystems can create economic value, even when the research sector per se and technology transfer systems are somewhat deficient.

In particular, we find evidence that well-structured schemes for entrepreneurial finance that rely on performance-based market incentives, rather than on slow-paced bureaucratic procedures, stimulate the development of entrepreneurial ecosystems. Financing opportunities attract the attention of local and regional talent, and participants in turn engage with a globally minded entrepreneurial community that thrives on a culture of sharing and knowledge exchange. This creates an ecosystem with a level of connectedness that supports the emergence and scaling of innovation-driven ventures, while much of the innovation happens outside specialized research centers. These dynamics are particularly relevant for industries that have relatively low entry costs, mostly related to digital technologies. In essence, from a copycat approach that relied on software development, the region is emerging as a bubbling entrepreneurial playground that mobilizes local talent and stimulates innovation. There are many remaining challenges, but the positive impact that innovation-driven entrepreneurship is having in the region is undeniable.

Future research shall focus on better understanding the differential effect that the Balkan entrepreneurial ecosystem has on different verticals that stir investor interest. The insights of this research can have a profound impact on government policies supporting innovation-driven ventures. The implications of this research potentially span beyond the context of the Balkan and emerging economies.

REFERENCES

Acs, Z. J., Autio, E., & Szerb, L. (2014). National systems of entrepreneurship: Measurement issues and policy implications. *Research Policy, 43*(3), 476–494.
Alvedalen, J., & Boschma, R. (2017). A critical review of entrepreneurial ecosystems research: Towards a future research agenda. *European Planning Studies, 25*(6), 887–903.
Andonova, V., & Nikolova, M. (2015). Universities & entrepreneurship. Why universities are important members of the start-up ecosystem. Presentation delivered at start-up community meetings, Sofia, Bulgaria.
Andonova, V., Nikolova, M., & Dimitrov, D. (2019). *Entrepreneurial ecosystems in unexpected places examining the success factors of regional entrepreneurship.* London: Palgrave Macmillan.
Andonova, V., Pérez, J., & Schmutzler, J. (2020). The role of diaspora in entrepreneurial ecosystems and national innovation systems. In A. Tsvetkova, J. Schmutzler, & R. Pugh (Eds.), *Entrepreneurial ecosystems meet innovation systems: Synergies, policy lessons and overlooked dimensions* (pp. 61–83). Cheltenham: Edward Elgar.
Angelov, E. (2017). Funding entrepreneurs. Bulgarian Venture Capital Association, Presentation, Vienna. Private communication with the author, May 31, 2017.

Brown, R., & Mason, C. (2017). Looking inside the spiky bits: A critical review and conceptualization of entrepreneurial ecosystems. *Small Business Economics*, 49(1), 11–30.

Clarkson, J. (2017). Jeremy Clarkson: Well, we did tell Richard Hammond to fire it up. *The Sunday Times Magazine, UK*. Retrieved September 2019, from https://www.thetimes.co.uk/article/jeremy-clarkson-richard-hammond-s-crash-and-the-new-range-rover-qrsbdwlft.

Dealroom.co. (2019). Central & Eastern Europe: Startup & investment landscape. Retrieved September 2019, from https://blog.dealroom.co/wp-content/uploads/2019/03/Google-CEE-v25.pdf.

Entrepreneurship Database Program at Emory University. (n.d.). Retrieved September 2019, from https://docs.wixstatic.com/ugd/4d837d_797f386156d042128e88da78cb5ad30c.pdf.

Ezekiev, P. (2017). The $5 billion CEE exits lead table. Neo Ventures. [Blog Post]. Retrieved February 2018, from https://neoventures.net/2017/08/06/5-bn-lead-table-cee-rising-in-technology/.

Gallup. (2018). Potential Net Migration Index.

Global Entrepreneurship Monitor (GEM). (n.d.). Annual reports various years. Retrieved June 2018, from www.gemconsortium.org/report.

Guerrini, F. (2017). Is Sofia the real digital capital of the new markets? *Forbes*. Retrieved February 2018, from www.forbes.com/sites/federicoguerrini/2016/04/14/is-sofia-bulgaria-the-real-digital-capital-of-the-new-markets/print/.

GII. (2018). Global innovation index report. Retrieved September 2019, from www.globalinnovationindex.org/gii-2018-report.

(2019). Global innovation index report. Retrieved September 2019, from www.globalinnovationindex.org/gii-2019-report.

Isenberg, D. (2010, June). The big idea: How to start an entrepreneurial revolution. *Harvard Business Review*, 2–11.

Isenberg, D (2011). *The entrepreneurship ecosystem strategy as a new paradigm for economy policy: Principles for cultivating entrepreneurship, Babson Entrepreneurship Ecosystem Project*. Babson Park, MA: Babson College.

(2016). Applying the ecosystem metaphor to entrepreneurship: Uses and abuses. *The Antitrust Bulletin, 61*(4), 564–573.

Izvorski, I. (2015). The three transitions of the western Balkans. The World Bank Blog. Retrieved April 2017, from http://blogs.worldbank.org/developmenttalk/three-transitions-western-balkans.

Lundvall, B.-Å. (Ed.). (1992). *National systems of innovation: Towards a theory of innovation and interactive learning*. London: Printer.

Lundvall, B.-Å. (2008). *Innovation system research: Where it came from and where it might go.* Atlanta: Georgia Institute of Technology.

Lundvall, B.-Å., Vang, J., Joseph, K. J., & Chaminade, C. (2009). Innovation system research and developing countries. In B.-Å. Lundvall, K. J. Joseph, C. Chaminade, & J. Vang (Eds.), *Handbook of innovation systems and developing countries: Building domestic capabilities in a global setting* (pp. 1–30). Cheltenham: Edward Elgar.

MacDowall, A. (2017). How Romania became a popular tech destination. *Financial Times.* Retrieved January 2018, from www.ft.com/content/a0652dba-632f-11e7-8814-0ac7eb84e5f1.

Malecki, E. J. (1997). *Technology and economic development: The dynamics of local, regional, and national change* (2nd ed.). London and Boston: Addison Wesley Longman.

Mason, C., & Brown, R. (2014). *Entrepreneurial ecosystems and growth oriented entrepreneurship.* Paris: OECD.

Mustafa, M., Kotorri, M., Gashi, P., Gashi, A., & Demukaj, V. (2007). *Diaspora and migration policies.* Prishina: Riinvest Institute.

Nelson, R. R. (1993). *National innovation systems: A comparative analysis.* New York: Oxford University Press.

Neumeyer, X., & Corbett, A. (2017). Entrepreneurial ecosystems: Weak metaphor or genuine concept? The great debates in entrepreneurship (Advances in the study of entrepreneurship, innovation and economic growth, Vol. 27). In D. F. Kuratko & S. Hoskinson (Eds.), *The great debates in entrepreneurship* (pp. 35–45). Bingley: Emerald Publishing Limited. https://doi.org/10.1108/S1048-473620170000027005.

O'Brien, C. (2018). Bulgaria rising: Can a growing startup movement reinvent the country's economy? *VentureBeat.* Retrieved May 2018, from https://venturebeat.com/2018/03/23/bulgaria-rising-can-a-growing-startup-movement-reinvent-the-countrys-economy/.

Salkever, A. (2015). Data: Best programming talent in the world is not in California. *VentureBeat.* Retrieved May 2018, from https://venturebeat.com/2015/04/05/data-best-programming-talent-in-the-world-is-not-in-california/.

Schmutzler, J., Andonova, V., & Diaz-Serrano, L. (2018). How context shapes entrepreneurial self-efficacy as a driver of entrepreneurial intentions: A multilevel approach. *Entrepreneurship Theory and Practice, 43*(5), 880–920.

Sizemore, C. (2013). Greece downgraded to "emerging market," but will it ever emerge? *Forbes.* Retrieved November 2019, from www.forbes.com/sites/moneybuilder/2013/06/20/greece-downgraded-to-emerging-market-but-will-it-ever-emerge/#383e15b7361b.

Smits, R., & Kuhlmann, S. (2004). The rise of systemic instruments in innovation policy. *International Journal of Foresight and Innovation Policy*, 1(1–2), 4–32.

Spigel, B., & Harrison, R. (2018). Toward a process theory of entrepreneurial ecosystems. *Strategic Entrepreneurship Journal*, 12(1), 151–168.

Tanev, M. (2019). Bulgarian software startup Transmetrics plans cap hike, bond conversion. *SeeNews*. Retrieved September 2019, from https://seenews.com/news/bulgarian-software-startup-transmetrics-plans-155-mln-euro-cap-hike-644340.

TNH. (2018). The Greek-American startup workable raised $50M in additional funds. Available at Retrieved September 2019, from www.thenationalherald.com/221723/the-greek-american-startup-workable-raised-50m-in-additional-funds/.

Tsvetkova, A., Schmutzler, J., & Pugh, R. (2020). *Entrepreneurial ecosystems meet innovation systems: Synergies, policy lessons and overlooked dimensions.* Cheltenham: Edward Elgar.

UNDP. (2006). From brain drain to brain gain: Mobilizing Albania's skilled diaspora. Policy paper for the Government of Albania prepared by the Center for Social and Economic Studies in collaboration with the Development Research Center on Migration, Globalization and Poverty, University of Sussex, Tirana. Retrieved September 2019, from https://assets.publishing.service.gov.uk/media/57a08c46ed915d3cfd0012ac/Brain_Gain.pdf.

Van de Ven, H. (1993). The development of an infrastructure for entrepreneurship. *Journal of Business Venturing*, 8(3), 211–230.

WB Technical Assistance Project P123211. (2013). Western Balkans regional R&D strategy for innovation, Overview of the research and innovation sector in the Western Balkans.

PART II Types of Innovation in Emerging Markets

7 The Political Economy of China's R&D Internationalization

Policy-Led Innovation and Changes in China's Growth Model

Peter Gammeltoft and Max von Zedtwitz

The extent and speed with which China has captured gains from R&D internationalization sets the country apart from other emerging economies and has furthered its aspirations to upgrade from innovation follower to innovation leader. In this chapter, we discuss how the internationalization of China's industrial R&D has evolved in the interplay between firm strategies, domestic government policies and international policies and regimes. First, we outline the development of China's R&D internationalization, identifying its major drivers and motives. Second, we link this to China's broader domestic and international political economy: its growth model, domestic S&T upgrading (e.g., the Made in China 2025 plan), firm-level internationalization (e.g., in the Belt and Road Initiative), and the emergence of more restrictive inward FDI regimes in Western countries. Finally, we comment on the likely future trajectory of Chinese R&D internationalization against a global backdrop characterized by increasing economic nationalism, trade frictions, and geopolitical security concerns.

7.1 INTRODUCTION: POLICIES MATTER IN CHINA'S DEVELOPMENT OF GLOBAL INNOVATION

This chapter, which opens Part II, considers a core aspect of innovation and asks how emerging market multinational corporations (EMNCs) access and leverage knowledge from R&D internationalization. China serves as a key example in recent history of a country that

185

has successfully attracted foreign firms to engage in R&D, formulated policies to stimulate domestic innovation, and redirected its own domestic firms to establish a global R&D presence. It is a case study on how a country can accelerate its evolution from copycat to innovation leader by creating conducive economic and policy conditions. As such, China is an example of how innovation in emerging markets differs from innovation in more established and mature markets.

China's R&D internationalization has grown quickly in recent years and expanded at a relatively early stage relative to Western countries. Another distinguishing feature is the strong support the Chinese government provides for R&D internationalization through both domestic and foreign policies. R&D internationalization has been a characteristic feature of China's highly successful growth recipe, a modality for learning from abroad, and a contributor to advancing the Chinese economy. It is set to become even more important in China's drive to become an innovation leader.

China's historically unprecedented growth spurt over the past four decades has been the subject of intense investigation, and countless attempts have been made to identify the most important ingredients in China's approach to economic development. While efforts to formulate frameworks of the distinct development models of the preceding successful latecomer nations in Asia have merit and value (Lall, 1996), it makes little sense to identify a single development model in China's case: The sheer size and diversity of the country makes it meaningless to invoke a single specific model. Furthermore, deliberate institutional and technological experimentation has been a pronounced feature in the country's approach to development. Across time, geography, and activities, China has applied and experimented with most policies applied by preceding successful developers.

Above all, China's rapid development has been accomplished through the skillful and disciplined combination of foreign sources of technology and knowledge with the upgrading of domestic capabilities and institutions. While South Korea and Japan have relied more on arm's-length modes of accessing technology from abroad, Singapore more on MNCs, Taiwan more on internationally linked clusters of local small to medium enterprises (SMEs), and Hong Kong more on a laissez-faire approach, China has relied on a wide array of instruments, including foreign direct investment (FDI), technology licensing, equipment purchase, foreign experts and consultants, and recruitment of foreign talent. Yet, an element applied systematically and fruitfully by China, especially over the last decade and a half, was not a pronounced feature in preceding development models, namely outward foreign direct investment (Gammeltoft & Kokko, 2013). By investing abroad in knowledge-intensive activities and setting up foreign R&D laboratories, China extended the portfolio of techniques from mainly behind-the-border processes to reach across borders.

Chinese firms have thus internationalized their R&D as part of a larger process of intensified national development at a critical juncture in China's development trajectory dominated by avoiding the middle-income trap. Given that the Chinese national innovation system is still comparatively weak, more attention has been paid to the coevolution of firms' technology acquisition and the development of a more comprehensive innovation system through supporting firms' internationalization as well as the absorption into the domestic system of the resources acquired abroad.

In what follows, we give a short account of the evolution of R&D internationalization by Chinese firms. We discuss the unsustainability of the growth model, which China has pursued so successfully in the past, and how the emergence of a new model has intensified both domestic technological upgrading and internationalization. The subsequent two sections focus on each of these two dimensions and the recent policy initiatives driving them, viz. "indigenous innovation" and "Made in China 2025," where domestic upgrading is concerned, and "Going Out" and "Belt and Road Initiative," where internationalization is concerned. We scrutinize and discuss available evidence on Chinese firms' R&D internationalization. Finally, we end with the recent policy response from Western countries to the more assertive Chinese policies.

7.2   A HISTORICAL REVIEW OF GLOBAL CHINESE
R&D PRACTICES

While the internationalization of R&D by Western MNCs started in the mid-twentieth century (e.g., IBM's establishment of a research center in Switzerland in the 1950s), Chinese firms only ventured abroad to any significant extent after the political reforms in the early 1980s. Moreover, their primary focus was production, not R&D, and most of the internationalization concerned the establishment of joint ventures with foreign investors in China and developing the technological foundations of Chinese industrial firms.

The 1990s saw the maturation of private firms into technological enterprises that ventured beyond Chinese national borders. Founder was one of the earliest Chinese MNCs to establish an R&D office in Hong Kong when the city was still under British jurisdiction in 1992, and Huawei followed with a research center in Silicon Valley in 1993. Galanz opened an R&D center in Seattle in 1997. These investments took place at a time when R&D internationalization was at a relatively early stage even among Western firms: The United States averaged approximately 10 percent R&D internationalization in the mid-1990s, Japan less than half of that, and only Europe, with its relative ease of investing in nearby and small-market European Union (EU) member states, reached a 35 percent level by then (von Zedtwitz & Gassmann, 2002).

The 2000s were dominated by the post-Internet-bubble revival and the reorientation of MNCs in the United States, Europe, and Japan on the one hand, leading to a strengthening of decentralized R&D and reduction of central research organization, as well as by the rise of China as the new location for global R&D investment. Ironically, this led Western observers to overlook the emerging R&D efforts of Chinese firms during the same period. As mentioned elsewhere, the new "Going Out" and "indigenous innovation" policies of 2000 and 2006 permitted Chinese efforts and resources for more significant R&D investments abroad. Pioneers such as Huawei and Haier had long established global R&D centers in major markets and technology hotbeds by then, but now also smaller and lesser-known MNCs followed suit. By and large, however, the first decade of the 2000s was focused on inbound R&D internationalization toward China rather than on China's own such investments abroad.

This would change with the economic recession of 2008–2009 and the rise of Chinese brands globally. Weakening foreign (i.e., non-Chinese) technology investment into China, even if only in relative terms, and the greater assertiveness of Chinese MNCs in developing their own markets and operations far from China brought about the need to establish local R&D centers and local firms with their own R&D. This led to a dramatic expansion of the Chinese R&D footprint, which was not always easy to manage for the generally centralized management patterns of young entrepreneur-led firms or local bureaucratic organizations of large-scale resource firms in China.

Many R&D centers survived only for a few years before they were closed down or merged with other domestic operations, R&D related or not. These examples constituted the learning stages of most Chinese technology firms in their first foray into international R&D, amplified by relatively cheap money and high growth rates both at home and overseas. For instance, even state-owned enterprises (SOEs) such as national railroad companies managed to develop technical competences in several key fields, merge into a single champion called CRRC, and establish R&D centers in the United Kingdom, Germany, Czech Republic, Bulgaria, the United States, Russia, Switzerland, Denmark, Thailand, and Australia.

Toward the end of the 2010s, Chinese foreign investment had lost some if not all of its innocence and experienced less welcome and more resistance even for setting up new R&D centers, as argued in a later section. As Chinese MNCs have caught up in many technologies, they have become strong competitors in overseas markets, and several countries have pressed for reciprocity and tried to impose restrictions on Chinese MNCs abroad similar to what they perceive Western firms have faced in China already for some time. The consequences for continued Chinese R&D globalization are difficult to predict and depend not only on China's own efforts but also on the policy response in host countries.

7.3   THE NECESSITY OF TRANSFORMING CHINA'S GROWTH MODEL

Both domestic upgrading through R&D activities and firm internationalization are structurally influenced by the underlying growth model, particularly in a state capitalist economy, and the growth model pursued by China is undergoing considerable change: From being based primarily on very high investment rates and export-oriented manufacturing, the focus has shifted to upgrading and diversifying further the domestic economy on the one hand and strengthening China's international engagement on the other. China's shift of growth model provides a strong impetus to further internationalize R&D as it contributes to both of these agendas.

7.3.1   *The Shift of Growth Model*

Even though China's economic growth model has been effective beyond historical precedent, the country is at a major impasse. First, the extant growth model has resulted in major imbalances that cannot be sustained. Second, emerging economies often grow quickly in the earlier stages but then stagnate and fail to progress beyond a certain level of economic development, and Chinese policymakers are concerned to avoid this "middle-Income trap" (Das & N'Diaye, 2013; Lee & Li, 2014). Graduating from innovation follower to innovation leader, from learning to invention, requires shifting from extensive to intensive growth, i.e., from comparatively easy quantitative mobilization of resources to more difficult productivity improvements through technological, organizational, and institutional innovations.

It is well documented that learning from abroad is crucial for economic and technological development. It is equally well documented that effective utilization of foreign technology is not an automatic process but contingent on deliberate domestic technological efforts (Bell & Pavitt, 1995; Ernst, 2008; Fu, Pietrobelli, & Soete, 2011). A careful combination of learning from abroad with domestic technological upgrading has been a part of China's growth model since 1978 but has intensified considerably in the 2000s.

Furthermore, the two agendas are very much complementary: To engage effectively and credibly internationally requires strong domestic capabilities, which in turn demands tapping into and leveraging international flows of technology and knowledge.

Even though growth rates have remained comparatively high, the limits of China's investment and export-driven growth model have become clear, fueling concerns about its sustainability not only in terms of growth rates, but also in terms of its social and environmental costs and its ability to maintain structural and technological upgrading. Resource- and labor-intensive manufacturing might not ensure sustained growth and upgrading; inward FDI no longer produces sufficient spillovers of knowledge and technology or develops service and knowledge-intensive sectors, and overinvestment along with income and regional disparities might not be alleviated.

Despite the aggregate effects on economic growth, there were concerns that the market-for-technology strategy did not generate the technology transfer expected, while enabling foreign MNCs to take large market shares. Decreasing reliance on foreign technology would reduce commercial and security vulnerabilities and diminish Chinese producers' liabilities on foreign royalties. Developing Chinese technologies based on Chinese intellectual property and standards were pursued as core pillars of a more sustainable and quality growth path that is expected to propel China beyond the middle-income trap toward becoming a leading economic and technological power.

7.3.2 *"Becoming Strong," Domestically and Internationally*

These concerns led then-President Hu Jintao to declare "indigenous innovation" and a "harmonious society" as national goals in a January 2006 speech to the National Conference on Science and Technology; they were incorporated into the 2006–2020 National Medium- and Long-Term Science and Technology Development Plan and the Eleventh Five-Year National Economic and Social Development Program. The new development strategy emphasized economizing on material inputs; upgrading the economic structure; enhancing indigenous innovation capability; protecting the environment; balancing urban and rural development and development in the east, middle, and west regions; job creation; and improving social equality (Gu, Lundvall, Liu, Malerba, & Schwaag Serger, 2009).

The second dimension of reform of China's growth model focuses on growing China's international engagement. Through most of its history, China had been inward oriented and passive in its international relations. Foreign affairs were subordinate to internal affairs, and the foreign ministry was relatively weak. Painted with a broad brush, modern China's development can be divided into three periods (Wang, 2012): the first period from 1949 to 1978, the second from 1979 to about 2001, and the third period since 2001. The first period was concerned with ensuring survival and basic living conditions for the population, applying centralized Soviet-style planning systems. Where international relations were concerned, Mao Zedong declared that "China was not and would never be a super-power in the future" (Ministry of Foreign Affairs, 2019). Under Deng Xiaoping's "Reform and Opening-up" in the second period, China invited foreign investment and accelerated growth through shifting public toward private ownership to achieve a "moderately prosperous society" and a middle class. Firms' access to technology and knowledge from abroad was vastly improved through both purchases in international technology markets and technology spillovers associated with inward FDI. Deng Xiaoping prescribed the foreign policy strategy of "bide our time, hide our capabilities": China was to focus internally on developing its economy rather than seeking international leadership. For years, China avoided getting involved in international issues not closely related to its national interests.

In the third phase from the early 2000s onward, China recognized that prioritizing economic growth had generated a number of adverse effects, e.g., in economic, social, and regional inequality; the environment; and public health. Hence, the focus now shifted to achieving a "harmonious society" and on more strategic international engagement to establish for China an international position commensurate with its economic power and technological capabilities. The old development model was seen as overly reliant on foreign technology. "Indigenous Innovation" would restore and revise competitiveness in Chinese industries, along with programs to strengthen firms' internationalization to create internationally competitive "champions." China's foreign policy became more assertive, with heavy investments in Africa, the South China Sea, and elsewhere. China also stepped up efforts in global governance with the Asian Infrastructure Investment Bank, the Shanghai Cooperation Organization, the BRICS summits, the New Development Bank, the 16+1 initiative, and increased influence in international standard-setting bodies.

In his address to the Nineteenth National Congress of the Communist Party of China in October 2017, President Xi Jinping suggested a similar periodization in his account of the first 100 years of modern China's development and referred to the three periods as "standing up," "getting rich," and "becoming strong," respectively. The final period is to last until 2049, guided by Xi Jinping's own thoughts on a new development philosophy and roadmap, dubbed "Xi Jinping Thought on Socialism with Chinese Characteristics for a New Era." By 2049, the 100th anniversary of the People's Republic of China (PRC), it should be a completely modernized nation with an advanced and innovative economy and a modern system of governance. Figure 7.1 displays the evolution of China's GDP per capita throughout the three periods.

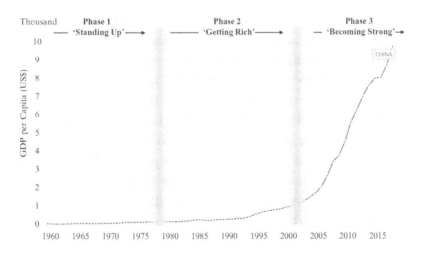

FIGURE 7.1 China's growth per capita shifting gears over time
Source: By the authors. GDP data from the World Bank.

These fundamental strategies aimed at realigning the Chinese economy provided new and stronger framework conditions for China's firms to commit to innovation and engage in greater outward internationalization.

7.4 DOMESTIC UPGRADING: "INDIGENOUS INNOVATION" AND "MADE IN CHINA 2025"

To reduce dependence on foreign technology and to capture gains from innovation, China has intensified domestic technological upgrading efforts. Meanwhile, technology was increasingly acquired by way of new ventures abroad. This has been motivated in part by a perception that technology transfer from joint ventures within China has been unsatisfactory. In the policy domain, these aspirations were manifested particularly through "indigenous innovation" and the more recent "Made in China 2025" program.

7.4.1 The "Indigenous Innovation" Drive

The Chinese government put "indigenous," i.e., domestically - driven, innovation center stage at the aforementioned 2006 National Conference on Science and Technology (see also Chapter 2). On this occasion, then-Premier Wen Jiabao endorsed the new policy to overcome "an irrational economic structure, the overproduction of low-quality goods, low rates of return, and increasingly severe constraints resulting from energy and other resource scarcity and severe environmental degradation" (quoted in Suttmeier, Cao, & Simon, 2006, p. 78). China was to become an innovation-oriented and "well-off" country by 2020 and a world leader in the long term. With this plan, innovation policy was upgraded to the status of national economic policy, and the focus shifted from the acquisition of foreign technology to the development of domestic innovation capability (Liu & Cheng, 2011).

The new policy stipulated R&D funding to increase to 2.5 percent of GDP by 2020; to make science, technology, and innovation the key drivers of GDP growth and contribute 60 percent to this growth; to decrease dependence on foreign technology to less than 30 percent; and to be among the top five nations globally in annual number of invention patents and of international citations of scientific papers (State Council, 2006a). Among many other measures, the policy called for financial and tax incentives, government procurement, integrating government programs with domestic enterprises, intellectual property rights and standards activities, and expanding international exchanges. The plan also proposed to "support our country's enterprises in their 'going out' efforts ... and helping them to establish R&D centers or industrialization bases overseas" (State Council, 2006a, p. 50).

7.4.2   The "Made in China 2025" Program

While successful in its own right, the "indigenous innovation" drive became a cornerstone in the 2015 promulgation of the comprehensive "Made in China 2025" (MIC2025) program, according to which China was to be transformed into the world leader in manufacturing by 2049. The plan rests on the observation that "the rise and fall of world powers has proven that without strong manufacturing, there is no national prosperity" and that China can only become a world power by "building internationally competitive manufacturing" (State Council, 2015, p. 1).

Through government direction and support, the goal of the program is to upgrade the industrial and technological strength of China's economy, upgrade China's position in international value chains, and increase national self-sufficiency. This is to be accomplished by strengthening indigenous innovation, substituting imports, building domestic brands, acquiring technology from abroad, developing secure and controllable standards, localizing production and data, and enhancing overall competitiveness. The program targets ten priority sectors, which include next-generation information technology, automated machine tools and robotics, aerospace technology, new energy vehicles, and biopharmaceuticals and medical devices. Local content of core components and materials is to be increased to 40 percent in 2020 and 70 percent in 2025. Forty percent of mobile phone chips are supposed to be produced in China by 2025, as well as 70 percent of industrial robots and 80 percent of renewable energy equipment.

Even though the program does mention SOE reform, industrial overcapacity reduction, and reliance on markets, MIC2025 is predominantly a top-down strategy, reinforcing the role of the state in the economy. It is supported by massive government funds and subsidies provided preferentially to domestic companies such as the Advanced Manufacturing Fund (US$3.0 billion), the National IC Fund (US$21.2 billion), and the Emerging Industries Investment Fund (US$6.0 billion). This is complemented by numerous provincial-level financing vehicles (Wübbeke, Meissner, Zenglein, Ives, & Conrad, 2016). MIC2025 builds on themes and goals of several past plans such as the Medium to Long Term Science and Technology Plan, Project 863, China Mega Projects, the National Informatization Development Strategy, and the Strategic and Emerging Industries Plan. It is also heavily inspired by a similar strategy launched by Germany in 2013, "Industrie 4.0," which, however, does not discriminate between domestic and foreign companies and was only supported with US$223 million. The United States and Germany tend to see MIC2025 as distorting to competition and trade.

While MIC2025 primarily concerns domestic initiatives and reforms, the acquisition and absorption of technology from abroad is also an important element, and it supports the internationalization of R&D of Chinese companies in several ways. Overall, the program aims to strengthen "internationalization design" by "formulating a strategy for manufacturing to go abroad and building a planning and coordination system." This includes relatively easy credit and financial support for Chinese firms pursuing foreign technology, particularly in high-speed rail, electric power equipment, automotives, and engineering equipment. This policy gives new support to R&D internationalization also by otherwise mostly domestically oriented and resource exploration-heavy SOEs. They too now pursue technology acquisitions, set up research centers, and engage in international standard-setting. Many SOEs are also frontline in furthering the Belt and Road Initiative (BRI), and their technology must be internationally competitive to deliver Beijing's ambitious goals abroad.

The forceful Chinese rhetoric surrounding MIC2025 has fueled concerns over China's increasing economic and technological strength and the role acquisitions in the West may play in this process, which has contributed to the tightening of investment screening regimes in the West, as will be discussed later.

7.5 OUTWARD DRIVE: "GOING OUT" AND THE "BELT AND ROAD INITIATIVE"

In terms of recent policies, the increasing outward orientation of China's firms and industries have especially been expressed in the "Going Out" strategy and the "Belt and Road Initiative" (BRI).

7.5.1 The "Going Out" Strategy

The "Going Out" strategy was initiated in February 1999 when the State Council authorized government agencies to encourage enterprises to develop overseas processing and assembly operations (State Council, 2006b, 2006c; Gu & Reed, 2013). The strategy was formally proposed in March 2000 and approved at the CCP Congress in October 2000. It was consolidated by inclusion in the Tenth Five-Year Plan (2001–2005), further expanded in the eleventh, and again reinforced in the twelfth and the current thirteenth one (2016–2020). In later years, it has been somewhat subsumed under the BRI and its activities reinterpreted into this latter framework.

The "Going Out" strategy is part of China's overall strategy of economic openness and has played an important role in China's outward foreign direct investment (OFDI) boom. Its primary focus is to promote overseas investment by Chinese firms, but it also covers overseas construction projects and service provision. Among the provisions of the program have been information about investment opportunities, granting of incentives, relaxation of foreign exchange controls, and forging of international investment agreements (UNCTAD, 2006). Incentives have included direct grants, tax benefits, low- or no-interest loans, and access to foreign exchange. Rather than being a single uniform policy statement, it is a series of regulations issued by various agencies and has evolved over the years.[1] For instance, in October 2004 the government issued a circular to promise preferential credit and other financial incentives for resource exploration projects; projects that promote exports; overseas R&D centers to internationally utilize advanced technologies, managerial skills, and professionals; and mergers and acquisitions (M&As) that enhance competitiveness and market access (Zhang, 2009).

In their totality, the various "Going Out" policies serve multiple purposes: enhancing international experience and competitiveness of Chinese firms, accessing natural resources abroad, strengthening exports of goods and services, and acquiring foreign technology and advanced business practices. It serves as a noninflationary outlet of China's foreign exchange reserves (much of which is held in US dollar securities) and reduces appreciation pressures on the RMB. Countervailing investment flows help appease concerns with major trading partners over Chinese surpluses and strengthens China's political and diplomatic relations with recipient countries (Gu & Reed, 2013; Jiang, 2013). Hence, the program also alleviates several of the imbalances created by the extant growth model.

7.5.2   The Belt and Road Initiative (BRI)

The BRI[2] is a grand economic and diplomatic strategy to develop a China-centered international transport and trading system, including a vast network of infrastructure, roads, railways, ports, pipelines,

---

[1] Among the regulations are the 2003 Notice on Simplifying Foreign Exchange Administration Relating to OFDI, 2004 Interim Administrative Measures on the Approval of Overseas Investment Projects, 2004 Circular on the Supportive Credit Policy on Key Overseas Investment Projects Encouraged by the State, 2005 Provisions on Issues Concerning the Approval of Overseas Investment and Establishment of Enterprises, and various other regulations and circulars on, e.g., foreign currency management, statistics, performance assessment, and state-owned asset management (UNCTAD, 2006; Luo, Xue, & Han, 2010).

[2] When BRI was first launched, it was called "One Belt, One Road" (OBOR), but concerns that this term might signal a China-centered and exclusive program rather than a collaborative and open one led to the relabeling to "BRI" in 2016.

telecommunications, and energy systems, along with political and institutional arrangements supporting it. It is a timely yet controversial response to the many economic and diplomatic challenges that China faces at its current development juncture. Together with MIC2025, the BRI policy builds on and combines earlier initiatives and attempts to extend China's aspirations for sustained yet qualitatively different growth.

As systematic and inclusive as BRI looks today, its origin appears to be a sequence of individual developments that become more comprehensive only over time. It was initially cast in terms of the huge infrastructure deficit in Asia, offering a solution beyond what existing international development banks are able to do.[3] The land-based part of BRI, the "Silk Road Economic Belt," was first announced by Xi Jinping on a visit to Kazakhstan in September 2013, and the sea-based part, the "Maritime Silk Road," on a visit to Indonesia in October of the same year. A third leg, the "Digital Silk Road," was announced in 2015 and focuses not only on enhancing digital connectivity abroad but equally on strengthening capabilities with advanced technologies at home, including through establishment of R&D labs and technology transfer centers abroad (NDRC, 2015a).

China has not only ample experience and credibility in building infrastructure, but it also looks to connect its remote central and western provinces to efficient markets of nearby Asian neighbors, i.e., future BRI partners, offering growth opportunities for both parties. China thus seeks to build markets for exporting manufactured goods as much as it is an outlet for its industrial overcapacity in nontradable sectors, especially construction. All this constitutes a welcome opportunity for many ailing SOEs, deploying Chinese management, labor, materials, and equipment in projects abroad and further strengthening technological capabilities of participating

---

[3] According to an estimate by the Asian Development Bank in 2017, there is a US$459 billion yearly financing gap in physical infrastructure in 2018 (Ra & Li, 2018).

Chinese companies. In the process, Chinese standards and systems are internationally promoted and adopted, e.g., in telecommunications, railways, and satellite navigation. The Chinese renminbi (RMB) becomes a de facto trade currency (at the expense of the US dollar), and there are plans to establish special arbitration courts for Belt and Road Initiative projects, promoting a legal system underpinned by Chinese rules (Economy, 2018). While the economics of the BRI initiative are appealing to many of the targeted countries, China certainly also sees the geopolitical advantages that come with such a web of partnerships with itself at the center. At the national level, BRI also helps to refocus the narrative legitimizing state and party power from one based on economic growth to one based on international engagement: That BRI is more than just an infrastructure project is reflected in the fact that it was written into the constitution of the Communist Party of China (CPC). Among the primary beneficiaries are private and state-owned Chinese technology companies that already have international experience in operations, innovation, and R&D.

In two domains in particular, the BRI may be set to impact the future framework conditions for internationalization of R&D and innovation: standards and digitization. The Digital Silk Road, the third leg of the BRI mentioned above, is formally focused on enhancing digital connectivity by building physical digital infrastructure and digital free trade zones abroad (Cheney, 2019). At the same time, it also bolsters the domestic development of high-tech industries, such as telecom (5G), satellite navigation, AI, cybersecurity, and digital commerce. Finally, it leverages Chinese influence on the governance of presently thinly regulated digital spaces in terms of both institutions and standards in alignment with Chinese preferences on issues such as cybersecurity and digital sovereignty.

Where standards are concerned, the BRI propagates Chinese systems and standards in several different ways: Chinese firms' BRI-related projects abroad are direct conduits. The Addis Ababa to Djibouti railway project is a recent example of the use of Chinese standards. Further, China provides free engineering and science training programs for BRI partner countries, and participants subsequently bring home Chinese standards and practices (Li & Liu, 2019). Finally, an explicit policy program associated with BRI aims to promote Chinese standards abroad: In October 2015, the government issued an "Action Plan for Harmonization of Standards along the Belt and Road (2015–2017)" (NDRC, 2015b),[4] detailing development, diffusion, and harmonization of standards in association with the BRI.

In addition to facilitating internationalization, applying Chinese standards can reduce BRI project costs.[5] More generally, adoption of Chinese standards can cut expenses on royalty fees, of which China is one of the top global spenders with US$36 billion in 2018. More generally still, for China, historically a standard taker, graduating to a standard maker has become a strategic ambition with wide-ranging economic, technological, and even geopolitical dimensions. Hence, the Chinese government and firms are pushing forcefully for representation and influence in key international standards-settings bodies. This includes, for example, the International Telecommunication Union (ITU, which now has a Chinese Head), the International Organisation for Standardisation (ISO, e.g., standards committee SC42 on artificial intelligence),[6] the Institute of Electrical and Electronics Engineers (IEEE), and the Third Generation Partnership Project (3GPP).

"Going Out" and BRI have provided a strong impetus for Chinese firms to internationalize their activities, including R&D. Today, these policies have such pervasiveness that most large firms

---

[4] Later succeeded by a "2018–2020" action plan.
[5] China National Petroleum Corporation saved an estimated 15 percent on a gas field project in Turkmenistan by using Chinese standards (Feng, 2019).
[6] As of May 2016, China had 189 proposals accepted by ISO as international standards, especially in high-speed railway, nuclear power, communications, and automobiles (Feng, 2019).

employ them for their overseas investment rationales, even if they are not directly benefiting from their incentives.

7.6 CHINESE R&D INTERNATIONALIZATION AT THE FIRM LEVEL

Having suggested that especially in the case of China it is important to understand R&D internationalization in terms of underlying government policies and strategies, we return now to the issue of R&D internationalization at the firm level. In this section, we briefly review the literature on firm-level internationalization of Chinese R&D and present a recent review of Chinese overseas R&D locations.

7.6.1   A Review of Pertinent Literature

Research on the general phenomenon of R&D internationalization emerged in the 1980s and became a mainstream pursuit only in the late 1990s (with, e.g., a dedicated special issue in *Research Policy*). Fueled by research conducted by scientists based in the West, the literature in the 2000s took note of China mostly as a destination of global R&D flows rather than a source (e.g., special issues on the topic in *R&D Management* and *Technological Analysis and Strategic Management*). Research on Chinese R&D internationalization did, by and large, not exist, in part due to the scarcity of Chinese firms engaging in R&D outside their home country (with IP infringement cynics scoffing at the notion of China conducting real R&D anywhere at all) and in part due to the inaccessibility of Chinese MNC R&D practice even to Chinese researchers.

Some of the earliest works on the topic are thus case studies based on the fortunate openness of a few Chinese firms to management research, e.g., the Haier case by Liu and Li (2002) that covered some of that company's R&D efforts. Chinese MNCs also became popular subjects for teaching cases (e.g., the Haier case by Fischer, 2000, or the Midea case by Dawar & Yuan, 2000), but any aspects of R&D and innovation were confined to China, if covered at all. Lenovo's high-profile acquisition of IBM's PC division in 2005 jolted the international R&D community as well, as this was the first time that a Chinese firm took advantage of a significant and technologically powerful global R&D footprint. While still quite small in comparison to global R&D elsewhere, Chinese R&D internationalization became a subject of research, with the first publications still mostly descriptive rather than explanatory in nature (e.g., von Zedtwitz, 2005). The China literature took momentum from the emerging literature on EMNCs (Mathews, 2006; Luo & Tung, 2007; Gammeltoft, 2008; Yamakawa, Peng, & Deeds, 2008), which, however, was not specialized to R&D internationalization. Historical parallels to the internationalization of R&D in Japan were insightful, yet, due to the substantial contextual differences, not easily applicable (e.g., Asakawa, 2001; Cantwell & Zhang, 2006; Dunning, Kim, & Park, 2008).

While case studies continued to abound (von Zedtwitz, 2008; Duysters, Jacobs, Lemmens, & Yu, 2009; Ester, Assimakopoulos, von Zedtwitz, & Yu, 2010; Fan, 2011; Prange & Bruyaka, 2016), first research appeared on putting the internationalization of Chinese MNCs in a wider context. This literature was initially not R&D specific (Child & Rodrigues, 2005; Ernst, 2008; Athreye & Kapur, 2009; Deng, 2012); later research started to consider innovation (e.g., Wu, Wang, Hong, Piperopoulos, & Zhuo, 2016) and R&D aspects of Chinese MNCs (Li & Kozhikode, 2009; Awate, Larsen, & Mudambi, 2012; Di Minin, Quan, & Zhang, 2012). This research was initially also still heavily based on describing patterns and locations of Chinese R&D, but gave rise to research, if only by demonstrating the empirical need, aimed at the theoretical fundamentals of the phenomenon.

Expanding on these early building blocks, recent research has become more sophisticated, better embedded, and more insightful regarding the theory of international business. Chen, Zhao, and Tong's (2011) paper is a good example of an early concept-development paper. Although still inspired by a case study (Huawei), the authors analyzed twenty-eight Chinese MNCs to propose a three-stage model of R&D internationalization: start-up, development, and maturity. In this model, the driver for R&D internationalization (of Chinese firms) changes from technology acquisition to market development.

As an example of more recent research, Jiang, Branzei, and Xia (2016) demonstrate how and why Chinese firms internalize R&D problem-solving capabilities and thus shift the locus of indigenous innovation within the global R&D network. Wang, Xie, Li, and Liu (2018) investigated the antecedents of individual center missions of Chinese R&D units, suggesting what context factors contribute to stronger innovation performance of Chinese firms. He et al. (2017) use two firms (Huawei and CSR) to illustrate how strategic coupling, decoupling, and recoupling may have contributed to the internationalization of innovation in Chinese firms. Di Minin, Quan, and Zhang (2017) examine differences in strategies of Chinese firms based on their R&D internationalization in Europe and the United States. Ervits's (2018) study on the patenting behavior of Chinese MNCs domestically and abroad allows interesting implications for the internal organization of Chinese MNC R&D organization and their underlying strategies. Fu, Hou, and Liu (2018) showed that having FDI in developed countries positively affected Chinese firms' innovation performance by acting as an external learning channel; however, they also found that FDI in developed countries acted as a substitute for in-house R&D in these Chinese firms, suggesting that FDI replaced in-house R&D and served an innovation-seeking strategy through acquiring external knowledge in advanced host countries.

Concluding this short review of firm-level R&D internationalization of Chinese MNCs, it appears that research becomes both more focused and resourceful in its quest to understand Chinese R&D and, at the same time, also more embedded and integrated in the big picture of international business theory and innovation, thus diluting some of the sharpness and precision a singular focus sometimes permits. Nevertheless, research and the literature have become richer

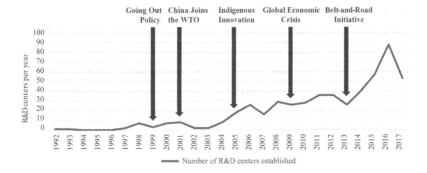

FIGURE 7.2   Growth of overseas R&D investments by Chinese MNCs
1992–2017
Source: The authors' analysis based on GLORAD data.

and provide more sophisticated analysis of the international R&D of Chinese firms.

7.6.2   Scale and Extent of Chinese R&D Internationalization

Chinese R&D internationalization did not start until the mid-1990s and became commonplace only in the early 2010s (see Figure 7.2), i.e., it trailed Western MNCs by thirty years and Japanese MNCs by twenty. Chinese firms did not internationalize other operations, including sales, until the late 1980s and early 1990s, in part because most of the Chinese firms of sufficient scale at the time were SOEs with a strong national service focus (e.g., power distribution, railroad, telecommunications) and in part because most of the market and market growth for Chinese firms was in China itself. After all, many non-Chinese MNCs were attracted to China for its exceptional market growth rates in the 1990s and 2000s, thus why engage in faraway business when most of the business was taking place at home?

This changed as some Chinese firms developed or acquired more internal competencies and diversified their value chain activities to supply increasingly sophisticated, integrated, and customized products and components to their customers overseas. Once Chinese firms started to sell directly to overseas consumers, R&D on these geographically distant needs and necessities became more important. The global economic crisis of 2008–2009 provided a window of opportunity for many Chinese firms to occupy territory less well served by Western MNCs, and once China's own growth rates declined, foreign markets became more attractive to serve, a development supported by state-level policies. Another strong driver was the increasing competition in the domestic market, both between Chinese companies and from MNCs, which enticed firms to seek technology abroad to remain competitive. The greatest overseas push thus started in about 2014 and is presently still ongoing; the dip in 2017 (see Figure 7.2) is likely a combination of two effects: (1) increasing scrutiny of Chinese technology-oriented acquisitions and R&D investments overseas, and (2) latency in disclosing the most recent R&D units and our own research's failure to cover those.

The first overseas R&D investments predominantly went to the United States, and they were mostly greenfield establishments. Between 1992 and 1998, eight R&D centers were established in the United States and one each in Chile, Russia, and Hong Kong. Huawei, Galanz, Konka, and ZTE all set up their first R&D centers in Silicon Valley, Texas, Washington, and New Jersey. Most of these centers had a relatively limited scope of activities, usually related to technology scouting.

This changed with the first "Going Out" policy in 2000, when the Chinese government more actively supported international technology ventures. This led to the establishment of R&D centers in other Western countries, Japan, and India. Between 1999 and 2005, forty-eight more R&D centers were established, and by the end of 2005, twenty-five Chinese MNCs had established at least one foreign R&D unit. Huawei and ZTE alone (both in telecom) increased their global R&D footprint with a combined twenty-four R&D locations in thirteen countries. Most of the new R&D sites were greenfield investments (81 percent), but this time period also witnessed the first large acquisitions of foreign companies and their R&D sites: Lenovo's acquisition of IBM's PC division with R&D sites in the United States and Japan, and TCL's acquisitions of Alcatel and Thomson,

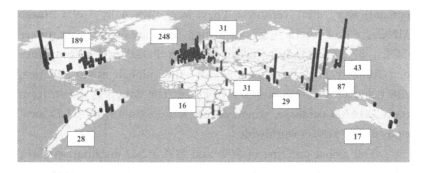

FIGURE 7.3 China's overseas R&D footprint, total numbers of R&D
centers per region
Source: GLORAD database.

creating a global R&D organization with R&D units in the United
States, Germany, France, and India.

The two key policies of "indigenous innovation" and "Going Out"
launched a period of global technology seeking for Chinese MNCs. Since
2006, 159 Chinese MNCs have opened up an average of 38 international
R&D centers or R&D JVs per year, with a peak of 88 such R&D units in
2016. By the end of 2017, 113 Chinese companies had an R&D presence
in 58 countries. The top 3 companies (Huawei, ChemChina, Haier) alone
accounted for nearly 200 global R&D centers. With a total of 111 R&D
units, the United States was the most attractive destination overall,
followed by Germany with 56 R&D units and the United Kingdom
and Japan with 28 and 27 R&D units, respectively. The United States
led also among almost all sectors, except for industrials, where Germany
was more attractive, and it is a tie between Germany, France, and the
United States in the materials sector. At the wider regional scope,
Europe led with 194 R&D units between 2006 and 2017, followed by
North America (116) and the Asia-Pacific region (106). See Figure 7.3 for
a snapshot of China's global R&D footprint.

7.6.3   SOE versus POE Internationalization

Of the 719 overseas Chinese R&D units identified, 188 (27 percent)
were acquired, 484 (68 percent) were greenfield investments, and 37 (5

percent) were joint ventures. They were owned by 159 Chinese MNCs, 68 of them were identified as state-owned enterprises (SOEs), 87 as privately owned enterprises (POEs), and 4 companies had unidentifiable ownership. Of the global R&D centers, 238 belonged to SOEs and 471 to POEs. The data was drawn from the GLORAD database, which covers more than 10,000 R&D locations of 500 MNCs worldwide.[7]

The global patterns of SOE and POE R&D distribution show differences in geography, mode-of-entry, and sectoral dimensions. Some of these patterns are correlated, as some countries (e.g., Germany) attracted more investment in the industrial sector, which may be more SOE than POE driven. Overall, 39 percent of the Chinese R&D centers in Europe were SOE-owned, compared to 28 percent in North America and 27 percent in the Asia-Pacific region. Europe also has seen a higher share of R&D acquisitions, as of the 186 R&D units acquired in total, 53 percent were located in Europe, only 23 percent in North America, and 16 percent in Asia-Pacific. For the entire dataset, two-thirds of the POEs chose to start R&D internationalization via a greenfield establishment, as opposed to only one-third of the SOEs. Analyzing the mode-of-entry over time, POEs always favored greenfield over M&A R&D establishments, approaching a 50–50 balance for their fifth or sixth R&D establishment, whereas the share dropped to zero greenfield establishments for SOEs, eventually resorting to acquisitions as their own R&D internationalization matured. This is a significant difference in R&D internationalization for Chinese SOEs and POEs. This may be explained in part by the more market-driven orientation of POEs and the relevance of the three stages as documented by Chen et al. (2011), and also by the subsidized lines of credit available to SOEs facilitating outright R&D acquisitions (Bruche & Hong, 2016). As the data for long-term

---

[7] The Chinese data was expanded and analyzed by G. Heusser in his 2019 bachelor's thesis at the University of St. Gallen, under the supervision of one of the coauthors of this chapter.

R&D internationalization of Chinese SOEs is still limited, the analysis of its long-term evolution is very sensitive to the relatively few SOEs engaging in large-scale R&D globalization, requiring further research before allowing definite conclusions.

Europe, and especially Germany, has been a very attractive target for the acquisition of R&D capabilities. Thirty-five percent of all R&D units of industrial SOEs have been acquired and 82 percent of them in Europe. The share of acquired R&D units is lower in POE industrials (21 percent), consumer discretionary (20 percent), and particularly IT (11 percent). The most important source of R&D units in Europe was Germany, with 33 percent of the acquired R&D facilities, followed by the United Kingdom (14 percent), France (12 percent), and Italy (8 percent). Thus, Germany seemed to have been particularly interesting and has contributed a disproportionate amount of R&D units. As for greenfield R&D investments, there is no such asymmetry between North America, Europe, and Asia-Pacific, which account for roughly 30 percent each, and Africa, South America, and the Middle East, accounting for 3–4 percent each.

7.7   COUNTERREACTION: INVESTMENT SCREENING REFORM IN THE EU AND THE UNITED STATES

Chinese R&D internationalization is shaped by the strategies of Chinese firms, under the influence of the incentives, direction, and sometimes command of Chinese government policies. But in addition to home-country factors, Chinese R&D internationalization is also shaped by policies and institutions of the countries hosting the R&D activities. Initially perceived as a welcome injection to ailing firms and governments in the wake of the 2008 financial crisis, the discourse today surrounding Chinese investments has changed into one of skepticism and concern, and policies have followed suit.

The concern is not caused so much by the volume of Chinese investment. Even though Chinese investment flows to the EU and the United States have increased significantly over the last decade, they remain minuscule in terms of aggregate stock. An analysis by the

European Commission estimates that while a total of 35 percent of all company assets in the EU are under foreign ownership, investors from China, Hong Kong, and Macao own only 1.6 percent (European Commission, 2019).

Rather, concerns are over the character and modalities of Chinese investments and how they may relate to national security. In addition to more mundane types of investments, Chinese companies are buying into strategic industries and critical infrastructures, and concerns have been mounting on how these investments could potentially be exploited in adverse ways. This has been compounded by the fact that some acquisitions are made by Chinese entities with opaque ownership structures and deep connections to the Chinese state. Other concerns relate to the possible long-term effects on Western companies' competitiveness when Chinese firms acquire key technological inputs and the possible competition-distorting effects if such acquisitions are subsidized by the Chinese state.

Along with the increasing economic and technological strength of China, Western governments are growing less tolerant given the lack of reciprocity in trade and investment affairs in China, where Western companies are subject to restrictive rules and practices while Chinese companies benefit from liberal regimes in the West. Furthermore, in recent years, particular concern has been associated with the fact that Chinese companies under the 2017 National Intelligence Law and the 2014 Counter-Espionage Law are required to cooperate with and hand over data to the state at its request. In China, all large companies have extensive linkages to the state and the CPC, including a party committee within the company, and would not be able to resist any such demands.

In a joint letter to the European Commission in February 2017, the economy ministers of France, Germany, and Italy requested to rethink EU rules on foreign investment to address the "possible sell-out of European expertise" and the "lack of reciprocity" (Guernigou & Thomas, 2017). At the time, some twelve out of the twenty-eight EU countries had investment review mechanisms of varying natures. In

September, the European Commission started drafting a framework for a pan-EU investment screening mechanism, and an EU investment screening framework was endorsed by the EU Council on March 5, 2019, to be implemented over an eighteen-month period (European Parliament, 2019).

The EU framework is not a tight and comprehensive mechanism that allows the EU to screen and block investments into member states, as is the case in the United States and some other OECD countries. The EU does not force individual countries to introduce screening legislation, and one EU member country cannot block Chinese investments in another. Rather, it is a coordination and cooperation mechanism under which member states and the Commission can exchange information and raise concerns. Reviews of investments only concern "security and public order" and not economic criteria, and only acquisitions are covered, not greenfield, venture capital, or other portfolio investments (Hanemann, Huotari, & Kratz, 2019). The framework facilitates sharing of information on non-EU investments in a number of sensitive areas, e.g., strategic industries, critical infrastructures, critical and dual-use technology, and investments related to state-controlled entities or state-led programs. An analysis by Rhodium Group and MERICS suggests that more than 80 percent of Chinese acquisitions in the EU in 2018 would likely be subject to investment-screening reviews (Hanemann et al., 2019).

In the United States, investment screening is undertaken by an inter-agency body, the Committee on Foreign Investment in the United States (CFIUS). CFIUS was established in 1975, initially to address concerns over OPEC countries' portfolio investments in the United States and later further formalized over concerns with acquisitions of US defense-related firms by Japanese investors. CFIUS is mandated to focus on national security alone (not on other national interests) and considers twelve specific factors in its reviews, including domestic production needed for national defense; the control of domestic industries and commercial activity by foreign citizens; US technological leadership in areas affecting US national security; and critical infrastructure, major energy assets, and critical technologies (Jackson, 2019). From 2008 to 2015, 333 investment projects were screened. During the lifetime of CFIUS, only 5 transactions have been blocked (Jackson, 2019). However, in addition, in a number of instances, investment plans have been abandoned preemptively over concerns that CFIUS might intervene (e.g., Unocal, Micron, and Fairchild Semiconductors).

Similar to the EU, US investment regulation did not previously target any specific nations. However, with the increasing economic and technological frictions between the United States and China, US investment law was recently revised with the Foreign Investment Risk Review Modernization Act (FIRRMA), which specifically targets China along with Russia (Rose, 2018). FIRRMA took effect in November 2018 and extended the scope and jurisdiction of CFIUS to include also smaller noncontrolling investments in critical technology or critical infrastructure, joint venture investments, and transactions where a foreign government has a substantial interest; to allow discrimination among investors by country of origin; and to require mandatory reviews of certain transactions.

While overall Chinese investment into the United States has dropped drastically in the last two years due to both increasing US scrutiny and tighter controls in China, small noncontrolling stakes in US start-ups by Chinese venture capitalists have grown quickly over the last three years in sectors such as biotechnology, nanotechnology, and wireless communication equipment. This type of investment was not previously subject to CFIUS review but will be scrutinized under FIRRMA. In 2018, Chinese venture capital investment in the United States reached a record US$3.6 billion, while FDI flows were only US$5 billion (Hanemann, Rosen, Gao, & Lysenko, 2019).[8]

The appetite of Chinese companies for establishing R&D and technology-related activities in the West is not likely to diminish,

---

[8] In 2017, venture capital investments were US$2.1 billion, and FDI flows were US$29 billion (Fannin, 2019).

rather the opposite given the activist policy initiatives in China discussed above. But Chinese investments in sensitive activities are likely to be affected by the tightening of investment regimes and practices. Even though the exact impact is difficult to assess, under the tighter regimes and practices Chinese firms are likely to seek out less contentious or conspicuous operating modes. For example, a shift is likely to occur from acquisitions toward greenfield investments and toward arrangements with minority rather than majority ownership, as is a shift from FDI toward venture capital financing.

7.8 CONCLUSION

This chapter reviewed the rise of the internationalization of R&D by Chinese firms in the context of China's own rise as a technology and economic superpower. China is no longer the copycat it used to be in the 1980s and 1990s and now shows clear signs that it is reaching the leading edge of technology development, at least in selected fields. In conclusion, we conjecture a number of propositions that synthesize the observations.

The timing of the scale and nature of outward R&D investment correlates with the introduction of several innovation-related national policies. This, per se, should not be surprising. However, what is interesting is how deliberate and instrumental these policies affected Chinese MNCs' overseas R&D expansion. Not only is China's innovation greatly policy driven, but its internationalization of R&D is as well, and to a much greater degree than we have so far witnessed in any other country. Among recent historic examples, neither Korea, Japan, Taiwan, nor Singapore could trade a large domestic market for inbound technology transfer upon which domestic champions could be built. Their own domestic MNCs may have received financial support in going global, but only Korea and Japan succeeded at any scale in this effort, and their MNCs are far more limited and focused on their own R&D globalization patterns. China, however, not only supported but very much masterminded international technology activities of its own MNCs, as might have been suspected by the pervasive influence the Chinese Communist Party has had in the domestic economy and is evident in the rise of SOE internationalization after consequential events in the late 2000s. The key difference is that the Chinese government anticipated the need for a strong international Chinese R&D presence well before most Chinese MNCs were willing (or capable) to pursue it on their own, and thus nudged its MNCs with the promulgation and enforcement of such policies through a web of financial, legal, and other means to go global.

We make no value statement with this observation; if anything, China seems to have been remarkably successful in achieving its goals so far. We merely point out that China has been more deliberate and strategic in crafting a global R&D presence than other countries, the United States, Germany, and Japan in particular. This was perhaps more important given the relative weakness of China's national innovation system compared to most Western countries when they started to internationalize R&D. China came from a long period of inward orientation and lack of technological sophistication. Germany had its infrastructure destroyed in the Second World War but benefited from Western-led worldwide industrialization. Japan joined later, but it is worth noting that Japan had opened up and internationalized as early as the Meiji-Restoration era in the 1870s and thus had more than 100 years of successful catch-up when it internationalized its own R&D in the 1980s. China, in comparison, opened up much later and forced internationalization much sooner. Of course, the big difference is that China had market access to trade and a crafty national leadership that had analyzed and learned from the mistakes made by Japan and other R&D followers. Also, the overall global context in the 2000s was a different one from the 1970s and 1980s.

Still, China had, and still has, plenty of hurdles to overcome. A fundamental one is the top-heavy centralization of Chinese decision making, leading to global R&D structures akin to the hub-and-spoke model that are considered somewhat introductory and cautious forms of R&D internationalization (Gassmann & von Zedtwitz,

1999). This will make it difficult for Chinese MNCs to balance between home-base augmenting and home-base exploiting organizations. Chinese firms also face a form of "liability of Chineseness," e.g., at the product level in markets that historically considered Chinese products of inferior quality (often in advanced industrialized nations), or in markets that feel that Chinese firms squeeze out national products and firms due to unfair business practices (often in markets of other developing countries).

More recently, Western countries that were initially welcoming Chinese investment have become apprehensive, and local R&D establishments of Chinese MNCs have been scrutinized for their presumed role in transferring national technology back to China, undermining their host country's competitiveness in the process. This could very well become a litmus test for China: If Chinese R&D centers abroad really serve primarily a one-sided role, they will likely be restricted under the new geopolitical climate; if they deliver benefits also to their hosts, they are likely to survive the tougher scrutiny. So far, the general tendency has been that Chinese investors have nurtured and developed their assets in the West to the benefit also of the hosts.

In sum, while Chinese R&D internationalization took shape more quickly than expected, fueled also by strong policy support, it appears it may also be disrupted more effectively, in part due to political responses from host countries. Chinese MNCs share the responsibility to make clear that their global R&D serves not only Chinese national purposes, but also, and more importantly, common business interests and thus the interests of global customers and markets.

REFERENCES

Asakawa, K. (2001). Organizational tension in international R&D management: The case of Japanese firms. *Research Policy*, 30(5), 735–757.

Athreye, S., & Kapur, S. (2009). Introduction: The internationalization of Chinese and Indian firms – trends, motivations and strategy. *Industrial and Corporate Change*, 18(2), 209–221.

Awate, S., Larsen, M., & Mudambi, R. (2012). EMNE catch-up strategies in the wind turbine industry: Is there a trade-off between output and innovation capabilities? *Global Strategy Journal, 2*(3), 205–223.

Bell, M., & Pavitt, K. (1995). The development of technological capabilities. In I. ul Haque (Ed.), *Trade, technology and international competitiveness* (pp. 69–101). Washington, DC: World Bank.

Bruche, G., & Hong, Y. (2016). Resource acquisition, internationalization, and the catch-up path of Chinese construction machinery champions – The case of Sany, XCMG, and Zoomlion. *Frontiers of Business Research in China, 10*(2), 290–323.

Cantwell, J., & Zhang, Y. (2006). Why is R&D internationalization in Japanese firms so low? A path-dependent explanation. *Asian Business Management, 5*(2), 249–269.

Chen, J., Zhao, X., & Tong, L. (2011). China's R&D internationalization and reform of science and technology system. *Journal of Science and Technology Policy in China, 2*(2), 100–121.

Cheney, C. (2019). China's Digital Silk Road: Strategic technological competition and exporting political illiberalism. *Issues & Insights, 19*, Working Paper 8. Honolulu: Pacific Forum.

Child, J., & Rodrigues, S. B. (2005). The internationalization of Chinese firms: A case for theoretical extension? *Management and Organization Review, 1* (3), 381–410.

Das, M., & N'Diaye, P. (2013). Chronicle of a decline foretold: Has China reached the Lewis turning point? (IMF Working Paper. WP/13/26). Retrieved September 2019, from www.imf.org/external/pubs/ft/wp/2013/wp1326.pdf.

Dawar, N., & Yuan, P. (2000). Midea: Globalization challenge for a leading Chinese home appliance manufacturer. Ivey Case Study # 9B00A031.

Deng, P. (2012). The Internationalization of Chinese firms: A critical review and future research. *International Journal of Management Reviews, 14*, 408–427.

Di Minin, A., Quan, X., & Zhang, J. (2017). A comparison of international R&D strategies of Chinese companies in Europe and the USA. *International Journal of Technology Management, 74*(1–4), 185–213.

Di Minin, A., Zhang, J., & Gammeltoft, P. (2012). Chinese foreign direct investment in R&D in Europe: A new model of R&D internationalization. *European Management Journal, 30*(3), 189–203.

Dunning, J. H., Kim, C., & Park, D. (2008). Old wine in new bottles: A comparison of emerging-market TNCs today and developed-country TNCs thirty years ago. In K. P. Sauvant (Ed.), *The rise of transnational corporations from emerging markets: Threat or opportunity?* (pp. 158–180). Cheltenham: Edward Elgar.

Duysters, G., Jacobs, J., Lemmens, C., & Yu, J. (2009). Internationalization and technological catching up of emerging multinationals: A case study of China's Haier Group. *Industrial and Corporate Change*, 18(2), 325–349.

Economy, E. C. (2018, May/June). China's new revolution: The reign of Xi Jinping. *Foreign Affairs*, 97(3), 60.

Ernst, D. (2008). Asia's "upgrading through innovation" strategies and global innovation networks: An extension of Sanjaya Lall's research agenda. *Transnational Corporations*, 17(3), 31–57.

Ervits, I. (2018). Geography of corporate innovation. *Multinational Business Review*, 26(1), 25–49.

Ester, R. M., Assimakopoulos, D., von Zedtwitz, M., & Yu, X. B. (2010). Global R&D organization and the development of dynamic capabilities: Literature review and case study of a Chinese high-tech firm. *Journal of Knowledge-Based Innovation in China*, 2(1), 25–45.

European Commission. (2019), *Foreign direct investment in the EU, commission staff working document SWD (2019) 108 final*. Brussels: European Commission.

European Parliament. (2019). Regulation (EU) 2019/452 of the European Parliament and of the Council of 19 March 2019 establishing a framework for the screening of foreign direct investments into the Union. Retrieved September 2019, from https://eur-lex.europa.eu/legal-content/EN/TXT/?uri=CELEX:32019R0452.

Fan, P. (2011). Innovation, globalization and catch-up of latecomers: Cases of Chinese telecom firms. *Environment and Planning A*, 43(4), 830–849.

Fannin, R. (2019, January 14). China rises to 38% of global venture spending in 2018, nears US levels. *Forbes*.

Feng, T. (2019). Standard setting and institutional building for international infrastructure. In C. Fang & P. Nolan (Eds.), *Routledge Handbook of the Belt and Road* (pp. 341–345). London: Routledge.

Fischer, W. A. (2000). Building market chains at Haier. IMD Case Study GM 939.

Fu, X., Hou, J., & Liu, X. (2018). Unpacking the relationship between outward direct investment and innovation performance: Evidence from Chinese firms. *World Development*, 102, 111–123.

Fu, X., Pietrobelli, C., & Soete, L. (2011). The role of foreign technology and indigenous innovation in the emerging economies: Technological change and catching-up. *World Development*, 39(7), 1204–1212.

Gammeltoft, P. (2008). Emerging multinationals: Outward FDI from the BRICS countries. *International Journal of Technology and Globalisation*, 4(1), 5–22.

Gammeltoft, P., & Kokko, A. (2013). Outward foreign direct investment from emerging economies and national development strategies: Three regimes.

International Journal of Technological Learning, Innovation and Development, 6(1–2), 1–20.

Gassmann, O., & von Zedtwitz, M. (1999). New concepts and trends in international R&D organization. *Research Policy, 28*(2–3), 231–250.

Gu, L., & Reed, W. R. (2013). Chinese overseas M&A performance and the Go Global policy. *Economics of Transition, 21*(1), 157–192.

Gu, S., Lundvall, B. A., Liu, J., Malerba, F., & Schwaag Serger, S. (2009). China's system and vision of innovation: An analysis in relation to the strategic adjustment and the medium- to long-term S&T development plan (2006–2020). *Industry and Innovation, 16*(4–5), 369–388.

Guernigou, Y. L., & Thomas, L. (2017, February 14). France, Germany, Italy urge rethink of foreign investment in EU. Reuters. Retrieved September 2019, from http://uk.reuters.com/article/uk-eu-trade-france/france-germany-italy-urge-rethink-of-foreign-investment-in-eu-idUKKBN15T1ND.

Hanemann, T., Huotari, M., & Kratz, A. (2019, March). *Chinese FDI in Europe: 2018 trends and impact of new screening policies.* New York: Rhodium Group.

Hanemann, T., Rosen, D. H., Gao, C., & Lysenko, A. (2019). *Two-way street: 2019 update. US–China investment trends. A report by the US–China investment project.* New York: Rhodium Group.

He, S., Fallon, G., Zaheer, K., Lew, Y. K., Kim, K.-H., & Ping, W. (2017). Towards a new wave in internationalization of innovation? The rise of China's innovative MNEs, strategic coupling and global economic organization. *Canadian Journal of Administrative Sciences, 34*(4), 343–355.

Jackson, J. K. (2019). The Committee on Foreign Investment in the United States (CFIUS). Congressional Research Service. Retrieved September 2019, from https://crsreports.congress.gov/product/pdf/RL/RL33388.

Jiang, M. S., Branzei, O., & Xia, J. (2016). DIY: How internationalization shifts the locus of indigenous innovation for Chinese firms. *Journal of World Business, 51*(5), 662–674.

Jiang, S. (2013, February 25). *Chinese investment in the EU: A win-win game – A view from China.* Brussels: European Policy Centre. Retrieved September 2, 2019, from www.epc.eu/documents/uploads/pub_3344_chinese_investment_in_the_eu.pdf.

Lall, S. (1996). *Learning from the Asian Tigers: Studies in technology and industrial policy.* London: Macmillan.

Lee, K., & Li, S. (2014). Possibility of a middle-income trap in China: Assessment in terms of the literature in innovation, big business and inequality. *Frontier of Economics in China, 9*, 370–397.

Li, J., & Kozhikode, R. K. (2009). Developing new innovation models: Shifts in the innovation landscapes in emerging economies and implications for global R & D management. *Journal of International Management, 15*(3), 328–339.

Li, L., & Liu, X. (2019, May 20). Belt and Road drawing more international students to Chinese universities. *Global Times.*

Liu, H., & Li, K. (2002). Strategic implications of emerging Chinese multinationals: The Haier case study. *European Management Journal, 20*(6), 699–706.

Liu, X., & Cheng, P. (2011). Is China's indigenous innovation strategy compatible with globalization? *Policy Studies, 61,* Honolulu: East West Center.

Luo, Y., & Tung, R. (2007). International expansion of emerging market enterprises: A springboard perspective. *Journal of International Business Studies, 38*(4), 481–498.

Luo, Y., Xue, Q., & Han, B. (2010). How emerging market governments promote outward FDI: Experience from China. *Journal of World Business, 45*(1), 68–79.

Mathews, J. A. (2006). Dragon multinationals: New players in 21st century globalization. *Asia Pacific Journal of Management, 23*(1), 5–27.

Ministry of Foreign Affairs. (2019). Chairman Mao Zedong's theory on the division of the three world and the strategy of forming an alliance against an opponent. Ministry of Foreign Affairs of the People's Republic of China. Retrieved September 6, 2019, from www.fmprc.gov.cn/mfa_eng/ziliao_665539/3602_665543/3604_665547/t18008.shtml.

NDRC. (2015a, March 28). Vision and actions on jointly building Silk Road Economic Belt and 21st-century Maritime Silk Road. National Development and Reform Commission. Retrieved September 16, 2019, from http://en.ndrc.gov.cn/newsrelease/201503/t20150330_669367.htm.

(2015b, October 22). Action plan for harmonisation of standards along the Belt and Road (2015–2017). National Development and Reform Commission. Retrieved October 24, 2019, from www.yidaiyilu.gov.cn/wcm.files/upload/CMSydylgw/201702/201702150616033.pdf.

Prange, C., & Bruyaka, O. (2016). Better at home, abroad, or both? How Chinese firms use ambidextrous internationalization strategies to drive innovation. *Cross Cultural & Strategic Management, 23*(2), 306–339.

Ra, S., & Li, Z. (2018). *Closing the financing gap in Asian infrastructure.* ADB South Asia Working Paper Series No. 57, Manila: Asian Development Bank.

Rose, P. (2018). *FIRRMA and national security.* Ohio State Public Law Working Paper No. 452. Columbus: The Ohio State University.

State Council. (2006a). The national medium- and long-term program for science and technology development (2006–2020): An outline. Retrieved September 3,

2019, from www.itu.int/en/ITU-D/Cybersecurity/Documents/National_
Strategies_Repository/China_2006.pdf.

(2006b). Better implement the "going out" strategy. Retrieved September 2,
2019, from www.gov.cn/node_11140/2006-03/15/content_227686.htm
(in Chinese).

(2006c). The General Office of the State Council forwarded the notice of the
Ministry of Foreign Trade and Economic Cooperation, the State Economic and
Trade Commission and the Ministry of Finance on encouraging enterprises to
carry out overseas processing and assembly operations. Retrieved September 2,
2019, from www.gov.cn/fwxx/bw/swb/content_449812.htm (in Chinese).

(2015, May 8). Made in China 2025. Retrieved August 23, 2018, from www.gov
.cn/zhengce/content/2015-05/19/content_9784.htm, English translation: www
.cittadellascienza.it/cina/wp-content/uploads/2017/02/IoT-ONE-Made-in-
China-2025.pdf.

Suttmeier, R. P., Cao, C., & Simon, D. F. (2006, Summer). China's innovation
challenge and the remaking of the Chinese Academy of Sciences.
Innovations: Technology, Governance, Globalization, 78–97.

UNCTAD. (2006). *World Investment Report 2006 – FDI from developing and
transition economies: Implications for development*. New York: United
Nations.

von Zedtwitz, M. (2005). International R&D strategies of TNCs from developing
countries: The case of China. In UNCTAD (Ed.), *Globalization of R&D and
developing countries* (pp. 117–140). New York: United Nations.

(2008). Huawei: Globalization through innovation. In R. Boutellier, O. Gassmann,
& M. von Zedtwitz (Eds.), *Managing Global Innovation* (3rd ed., pp. 507–522).
Heidelberg: Springer.

von Zedtwitz, M., & Gassmann, O. (2002). Market versus technology drive in R&D
internationalization: Four different patterns of managing research and development. *Research Policy, 31*(4), 569–588.

Wang, S. (2012). Chinese socialism 3.0. In M. Leonard (Ed.), *China 3.0* (pp. 60–67).
London: European Council on Foreign Relations.

Wang, Y., Xie, W., Li, J., & Liu, C. (2018). What factors determine the subsidiary
mode of overseas R&D by developing-country MNEs? Empirical evidence from
Chinese subsidiaries abroad. *R&D Management, 48*, 253–265.

Wu, J., Wang, C., Hong, J., Piperopoulos, P., & Zhuo, S. (2016).
Internationalization and innovation performance of emerging market enter-
prises: The role of host-country institutional development. *Journal of World
Business, 51*(2), 251–263.

Wübbeke, J., Meissner, M., Zenglein, M. J., Ives, J., & Conrad, B. (2016). *Made in China 2025: The making of a high-tech superpower and consequences for industrial countries*. Papers on China No. 2. Berlin: Mercator Institute for China Studies.

Yamakawa, Y., Peng, M. W., & Deeds, D. L. (2008). What drives new ventures to internationalize from emerging to developed economies? *Entrepreneurship Theory and Practice, 32*(1), 59–82.

Zhang, K. H. (2009). Rise of Chinese multinational firms. *The Chinese Economy, 42*(6), 81–96.

8 Emerging Pharmaceutical Companies from China, India, and Brazil

From Generic Drugs to Innovation Strategies

Fernanda Cahen

8.1 INTRODUCTION

A small group of large pharmaceutical multinational companies (pharma MNCs) long dominated drug discovery in advanced economies with high research and development (R&D) investments. The top ten global pharma MNCs accounted for 55 percent of global sales of patent drugs, where the revenue driver of pharma MNCs relied on the innovative drugs portfolio (Dutta, Lanvin, & Wunsch-Vincent, 2019). And yet, since the 2000s, the traditional R&D model of innovation has run its course. As costs per drug rise into the billions, the complexity of R&D projects sprawls, and breakthrough innovation diminishes (Dutta et al., 2019; Gassmann, Schuhmacher, von Zedtwitz, & Reepmeyer, 2018).

With slow growth for pharmaceutical sales in developed markets, some MNCs such as GlaxoSmithKline (UK), Sanofi (France), Merck & Co (US), and Roche (Switzerland) have now made bets in emerging markets (EMs), diversifying into generic drugs, over-the-counter (OTC) medicines, diagnostics, and other markets (Dutta et al., 2019). EMs represent a third of the global pharmaceutical market (IQVIA, 2019), with double-digit growth rates driven by generic drugs, government investment, the rise of upper-middle-class customers, and an aging population seeking long-term treatments. Since 2010, large acquisitions, international joint ventures, and new entrants have transformed the landscape (Gassmann et al., 2018).

In EMs, generic drugs account for more than half the sales and the industry growth.[1] The potential for profitable growth for local players in the sector is clear: Generics have lower barriers to entry, require little to no R&D investments, and need minimal spending on advertising. In turn, competition has intensified, and significant players from China, India, Brazil, and other EMs have risen, producing drugs no longer protected by patents and substituting products and services to MNCs.

EM pharmaceutical companies began a fortuitous cycle: from capacities for mass manufacturing, to investments in capabilities formation, to better-qualified human resources, to higher standards for local suppliers. As we shall see, this process has enabled them to become global leaders in the generic segment and to further invest in R&D innovation (Gassmann et al., 2018).

8.2 PHARMACEUTICAL INNOVATION AND THE NEW ROLE OF EMERGING MARKETS

The birth of the modern pharmaceutical industry can be traced to the mid-nineteenth century with the emergence of the synthetic dye industry in Germany and Switzerland. The industry's early years were not linked to formal science, and important innovations such as penicillin and aspartame only took place by serendipity. First movers such as Schering AG, Boehringer Ingelheim, and Merck began to produce at a large scale based on uniform standards toward the beginning of the twentieth century. The demand for antibiotics during WWII marked the transition to a science-guided industry, with large vertically integrated operations and R&D-intensive companies with global sales (Malerba & Orsenigo, 2002).

---

[1] According to the IQVIA report (2019), new products and losses of exclusivity will continue to drive similar dynamics across developed markets, while product mix will continue to shift to specialty and orphan products. The impact of losses of exclusivity should rise to US$121 billion between 2019 and 2023, with 80 percent of this impact, or US$95 billion, in the United States.

The period through to the 1980s was considered a "golden era" for the industry. Profitable pharma MNCs, especially from the United States, continuously launched new drugs for different kinds of diseases (Munos, 2009). Public funds became commonly available for academic research, and patent protection proved essential for innovative companies. Swiss and German companies remained strong, as the US pharma industry invested heavily in R&D labs. Other countries such as France, Italy, Spain, and Japan were initiating smaller and less-innovative operations.

In the late 1970s, biotechnology created a new frontier for pharmaceutical innovation, with a significant impact on the industry structure. Biotech companies created new vaccines, blood products, and biotherapeutics. However, most of these companies never managed to become fully integrated producers (Malerba & Orsenigo, 2002). Strategic alliances with large MNCs funded R&D and access to the necessary structures to control testing, production, and marketing.

Since the 2000s, pharmaceutical research has been limited by rapidly increasing costs and a decline in major drug approvals (Dutta et al., 2019).[2] The process of developing a breakthrough drug involves a commitment of at least ten years from research to use on patients and an additional four years of preclinical discovery and testing. The increasingly high costs have shown diminishing returns on drug innovation and other breakthroughs (Dutta et al., 2019).

Despite these challenges, competition still centers on new drugs. The pharmaceutical sector is a top investor in global R&D (Dutta et al., 2019; IQVIA, 2019).[3] However, incremental innovation

---

[2] In a broader context of the pharmaceutical sector, the number of new drugs approved by the US Food and Drug Administration (FDA) per billion US dollars spent on R&D has halved roughly every nine years over the past sixty years (Scannell, Blanckley, Boldon, & Warrington, 2012).

[3] The European Commission publishes data on the R&D investments by the top 2,500 companies that globally invest the most in R&D. Of this 2,500, the 15 largest pharmaceutical companies were in the top 50 group of global innovators and R&D investors in 2018 (see Chapter 13).

after patent expiration and process innovation for cost efficiency have gained salience in the industry.

This dynamic, combined with changes in EMs such as GDP growth, local promarket reforms, and institutional changes following international intellectual property (IP) regulations, has enabled a large number of pharmaceutical companies from EMs to thrive, especially in the generic segment. EMs represent a third of the global pharmaceutical market (IQVIA, 2019). This trend has afforded a new role to pharmaceutical EMNCs.

The pharmaceutical context in EMs is defined by a combination of relatively low GDP per capita (less than US$30 thousand annually) and significant market growth potential (adding at least US$1 billion of pharmaceutical market value until 2020), a highly dynamic landscape for local players and attractive to MNCs. IMS Health (2014) and IQVIA (2019) classified twenty-one pharmaceutical EMs based on economic growth levels.[4] These twenty-one countries accounted together for US$187 billion in annual sales between 2012 and 2017, two-thirds of global pharmaceutical growth. Table 8.1 summarizes the most important EMs in the pharmaceutical sector.

China, India, and Brazil have large populations, which makes them especially attractive to large pharmaceutical MNCs. Typically, the strategy for MNCs in EMs is to acquire a local successful product or a company with a strong local presence that enables fast entry in the market. Another now common strategy is adapting existing products to local habits as well as building an innovative portfolio unique to the market. For example, in China, MNCs have invested, acquired,

[4] The twenty-one pharmaceutical EMs are divided into three tiers. Tier I: China, which dominated the global pharmaceutical EM scene and receives high government funding. Tier II: Brazil, India, and Russia, all of which feature a large population that is rapidly aging and experiences a rise in consumer sophistication and favorable government policies. Countries in Tier III, which hold the least market shares among these countries, include Mexico, Argentina, Colombia, Venezuela, South Africa, Algeria, Egypt, Nigeria, Turkey, Indonesia, Thailand, Vietnam, Pakistan, Poland, Romania, Saudi Arabia, and Ukraine.

Table 8.1 *Market size and growth rate of pharmaceutical sector in emerging markets*

Country	Market size	CAGR 2012–2017	Market observations
China	US$86.8 bn in 2018	16.7%	In 2018, the value of pharma sales in China surpassed Japan and became the world's second-largest market
Brazil	US$30.7 bn in 2018	12%	In 2018, the market share for generics exceeded 33%. The improving economy, promarket reforms, and rising employment levels will boost growth in the 2019–2023 period.
India	Around US$25 bn in 2017	12.5%	India is ranked eleventh among the biggest pharmaceutical markets and projected to grow to US$55 billion by 2022.
Russia	US$20.9 bn in 2016	10.1%	Revenues are forecasted to continue to grow and could potentially total around US$38.6 billion by 2021, representing a compound annual growth rate of 13%.
Poland, Argentina, Turkey, Mexico, Venezuela, Romania, Saudi Arabia, and Colombia	Combined market size of US$82 bn in 2017	These eight countries have grown at a rate of 9%	Countries with pharma sales above US$85 per capita
Vietnam, South Africa, Algeria, Thailand, Indonesia, Egypt, Pakistan, Nigeria, and Ukraine	Combined market size of US$45 bn by 2017	These nine countries will grow at a rate of 11%	Countries with pharma sales below US$85 per capita

Sources: The author, based on IQVIA (2019); IMS Health (2014). Deloitte Global life sciences outlook, 2019.

or made partnerships to develop traditional Chinese medicines and incorporate them into their OTC portfolios (Gassmann et al., 2018).

Pharmaceutical EMs contribute to only 32 percent of the global sales of the top ten MNCs, indicating that MNCs are underrepresented in these countries and lose share to more aggressive local competitors (IQVIA, 2019). Local players have low-cost competitive advantages and also experience with local institutional contexts that in many cases can better anticipate and take advantage of changes in the economic, regulatory, and political environment, relative to other MNCs (Gassmann et al., 2018).

The pharmaceutical industry is one of the most internationalized in terms of R&D locations. Large pharmaceutical MNCs are progressively globalizing their R&D activities, which has had spillover effects on local pharma companies and other EM institutions (Gassmann et al., 2018). Similar to other industries, the global dispersion of pharmaceutical R&D is concentrated in the United States, European countries, and Japan, as well as major regional centers in South Korea, Singapore, and some emerging economies such as India (especially Mumbai and Bangalore) and China (especially Shanghai and Beijing) (Table 8.2).

8.2.1 From Copycats to Leaders in the Pharmaceutical Value Chain

The pharmaceutical value chain is composed of several sets of activities with different firm-level capabilities (Figure 8.1). The increasing technological complexity requires an increased input of original knowledge as well as stronger marketing and distribution infrastructure (Kale & Little, 2007). There is some technical-productive independence between stages, which enables firms to operate more or less cohesively, according to the competitive needs of the markets in which they operate (Gassmann et al., 2018).

Compared to large MNC standards, the R&D investments by EM companies has traditionally been low. Even EM leaders in pharmaceuticals lag behind the frontier of the industry. These

Table 8.2 Top thirty-five pharmaceutical companies in the world (US$ billion), 2019 Forbes Global 2000

Pharma rank	General rank	Company	Country	Sales	Profits	Assets	Market value	R&D intensity (%)
1	54	Pfizer	USA	53.6	11.2	159.4	218.6	14.1
2	60	Novartis	Switzerland	51.9	12.6	145.6	175.6	17.5
3	88	Roche Holding	Switzerland	58.1	10.7	79.6	222	19.5
4	114	Sanofi	France	40.7	5.1	127.4	102	15.5
5	119	Merck & Co	USA	42.3	6.2	82.6	189.1	25.3
6	147	GlaxoSmithKline	UK	41.1	4.8	74	97.6	12.8
7	167	AbbVie	USA	32.8	5.7	59.4	114.7	17.7
8	237	AstraZeneca	UK	23.9	2.2	60.7	99.2	24.1
9	238	Eli Lilly & Co	USA	24.6	3.2	43.9	119.3	18.2
10	266	Bristol-Myers Squibb	USA	22.6	5	35	74.4	28.7
11	376	Novo Nordisk	Denmark	17.7	6.1	17	116.3	12.9
12	377	Takeda Pharmaceutical	Japan	16.1	1	52.6	56.6	18.4
13	412	AmerisourceBergen	USA	172.9	1.2	39.3	15.3	–
14	566	Merck	USA	17.7	0.46	42.8	45.8	13.9
15	572	Sinopharm Group	China	51.9	0.88	34.3	11.1	10.9
16	580	McKesson	USA	213.5	–0,316	61	21.9	–
17	595	Allergan	Ireland	15.8	–5.1	101.8	46.3	12.9
18	602	Astellas Pharma	Japan	11.8	1.9	17.6	26	17.0

19	Cardinal Health	USA	141.9	-0.038	40.5	13.7	–
20	Otsuka Holding	Japan	11.7	0.747	22.6	19	14.2
21	Teva Pharmaceutical	Israel	18.8	-2.3	60.7	15.5	8.3
22	Daiichi Sankyo	Japan	8.4	0.602	17.3	28.7	24.6
23	China Res. Pharma Group	China	24.2	0.515	22.5	9.1	0.6
24	Zoetis	USA	5.8	1.4	10.8	47.5	7.3
25	IQVIA	USA	10.4	0.259	22.5	26.3	–
26	Mylan	UK	11.4	0.353	32.7	13.8	6.5
27	UCB	Belgium	5.5	0.933	12	14.9	23.4
28	Jiangsu Hengrui Medicine	China	2.7	0.642	3.5	42	10.7 [a]
29	Shionogi	Japan	3.1	1.1	6.6	17.4	17.4
30	Bausch Health Inc[b]	Canada	8.4	-4.3	32.5	8.1	4.1
31	Eisai	Japan	5.7	0.577	9.4	16.3	21.8
32	Medipal Holdings	Japan	28.8	0.311	15.4	4.9	–
33	Alfresa Holdings	Japan	23.8	0.410	12.6	5.5	–
34	Guangzhou Baiyunshan	China	6.3	0.532	7.5	9.9	1.8
35	Sun Pharma Industries	India	4.2	0.484	9.8	16	7.0

Sources: The author, based on Forbes Global 2000 – The world's largest public companies (2019 ranking), EU 2018 Industrial R&D Investment Scoreboard – R&D Intensity Eurostat (https://iri.jrc.ec.europa.eu).

[a] The 2018 Global Innovation 1000 study (PwC Strategy)

[b] Bausch Health Companies Inc. previously Valeant Pharmaceuticals

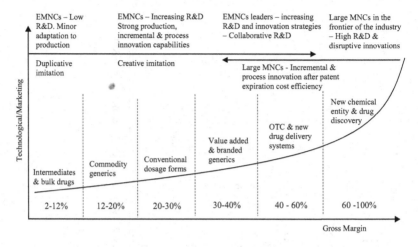

FIGURE 8.1 From copycats to leaders in the pharmaceutical value chain
Sources: The author, based on Bartlett and Ghosal (2000); Luo, Sun, and Wang (2011); Kale and Little (2007).

markets represent less than 10 percent of the global market sales for new drugs, despite the fact that R&D spending has grown since 2010. China has seen a particularly strong increase with greater R&D investments from MNCs and domestic companies. Relative to China and India, other EMs trail behind (von Zedtwitz & Gassmann, 2016).

EMNCs have typically developed less technologically and financially sophisticated products (Gassmann et al., 2018; Guennif & Ramani, 2012). In order to survive in the new institutional and competitive environment, EMNCs have faced technical challenges that have caused difficulties acquiring a set of specific capabilities required for producing generic drugs, which in turn has necessitated strengthening their own innovation capabilities.

Large MNCs are investing in the generics business themselves and becoming more aggressive in EMs (Lorenzetti, 2015). Consequently, for EMNCs, even if the generic business market opportunity is sustainable now, it might deteriorate in the future (Gassmann et al., 2018). Considering the intensification of the market's competitive environment, developing capabilities and technologies that enable incremental innovations and research capabilities will allow EMNCs to improve their technological abilities and achieve a more complex process of drug discovery.

Specific internal capabilities required to produce generic drugs and to develop research include the following.

Production capabilities: (1) Processing and packing of basic ingredients (bulk drugs) into tablets, capsules, syrup, injections, and plasters; (2) higher level of scientific and technological capabilities and the production of a bulk drug containing the therapeutic molecule in powder or liquid; and (3) active pharmaceutical ingredients (APIs) (Guennif & Ramani, 2012).

Market intelligence capabilities: Prospecting patents that are about to expire to quickly launch a product in the market. Often an active ingredient patent expires before the patents related to the medicine itself. Generic producers must take advantage of those active ingredients to accelerate their product into the market (Luo et al., 2011).

Regulation-handling capabilities: Bioequivalence data demonstrating the same effect as the original drug. For the commercialization of a new drug, extensive data on clinical trials is necessary as well as "Drug Master Files" with comprehensive details on the manufacturing and distribution process.

Combinative capabilities – collaborative R&D: Transferred knowledge from strategic alliances (with other companies or universities) modifying it with the firm's own resources and production designs for product development.

Reengineering and incremental innovation capabilities: Bringing together capabilities to gradually increase the complexity of product development.

New drug-discovery capabilities: Systematic investment in R&D activities and, in most cases, the integration of research capabilities of other firms or research institutions in one or more of the steps in the new drug discovery process (Guennif & Ramani, 2012).

8.3 PHARMACEUTICAL INDUSTRY IN CHINA, INDIA, AND BRAZIL

China, India, and Brazil lead most of the pharmaceutical market growth globally and will be among the top ten by sales value by 2020 (IQVIA, 2019). In this section, we detail the local industry, firm capabilities, and institutional conditions of these countries (see Table 8.5).

8.3.1 Chinese Pharmaceutical Market

The Chinese pharmaceutical industry is ranked second globally in terms of value, with total revenues exceeding US$86.7 billion per year. It is one of the world's fastest-growing pharma markets, even as growth slowed from a 19 percent compound annual rate (CAGR) from 2008–2013 to an 8 percent CAGR in 2013–2018. It is expected to continue declining to 3–6 percent through 2023 (IQVIA, 2019).

8.3.1.1 Players, Competition, and Capabilities in the Market

The pharmaceutical industry in China is highly fragmented. There are around 5,000 domestic pharmaceutical manufacturers in operation and around 14,000 domestic distributors (PwC, 2019). Around 3,500 domestic companies accounted for 75 percent of annual sales, of which 95 percent operate in the low-cost generics market (Gassmann et al., 2018). Over 75 percent of China's pharmaceutical needs are met by local generics, with only 6 percent to 7 percent of the market going to patent-protected innovative drugs and 11 percent to traditional Chinese medicine (Deloitte, 2019).

The "Made in China 2025" industry plan emphasizes the importance of the pharmaceutical industry, with a focus on innovation and increasing investments in R&D. The Chinese government's policy is to stimulate "national champions," providing resources to innovate and to compete internationally (Prud'homme & von Zedtwitz, 2018). Reform policies and the Eleventh (2006–2010),

Twelfth (2011–2015), and Thirteenth (2016–2020) Five-Year Plans accelerated mergers and acquisitions (M&A) activity in the pharmaceutical industry.[5]

Most of the M&A activity is from local players consolidating for scale. Consolidation via M&A will intensify concentration and limit competition in the sector. Reverse engineering of existing drugs has had a considerable learning effect for Chinese pharma companies, facilitating the adoption of new technologies and enabling transition into innovative activities (Prud'homme & von Zedtwitz, 2018). MNCs represent a small share of overall M&A activity in the market since 2010. From 2008 to 2013, 360 M&A deals involved local companies, while only 166 involved foreign companies. From 2014–2017, local companies benefited even more from M&As – 670 deals versus only 32 with foreign MNCs (PwC, 2019).

China's top four major players – Sinopharm Group, China Resource Pharma Group, Jiangsu Hengrui Medicine, and Guangzhou Baiyunshan – are among the largest companies in the world (see Table 8.2). Table 8.3 presents the top ten Chinese pharmaceutical investors in R&D according to Eurostat R&D Scoreboard.[6]

Large MNCs are interested in China's US$86.7 billion industry and its growing market in generic drugs. By the mid-2000s, the IP situation in China was better understood, and global MNCs valued the country for strategic R&D operations, as in-country research offered a general low-cost base, a large patient pool, increasing scientific capabilities, local industry knowledge in the field of generic drugs, insight into the country's growing drug markets, and access to the research on traditional Chinese medicines (Gassmann et al., 2018; Prud'homme & von Zedtwitz, 2018).

---

[5] The following number of Chinese deals were recorded according to PwC (2019): 2014 (domestic: 146; foreign: 9), 2015 (domestic: 194; foreign: 4), 2016 (domestic: 172; foreign: 8), and 2017 (domestic: 158; foreign: 11).

[6] Jiangsu Hengrui Medicine, considered one of the most innovative Chinese pharmaceutical companies, does not appear in the Eurostat ranking.

Table 8.3 *Top ten Chinese pharmaceutical investors in R&D*

World rank	Company	R&D 2017/18 (US$ mn)	R&D 1-y growth (%)	R&D intensity (%)	Net sales (US$ mn)	Employees
497	Beigene	255.4	174.8	111.8	228.5	900
535	Sino Biopharm.	237.3	22.4	10.9	2,181.5	18,649
748	Shanghai Fosun	151.1	43.6	5.6	2,702.9	28,848
812	Fosun International	138.4	48.4	1.1	12,958.1	63,000
856	China Res. Pharm. Group	129.3	45.3	0.6	21,164.8	56,000
887	Zhejiang Hisun	124.3	8.9	8.2	1,509.3	9,497
897	Sichuan Kelun	122.7	48.4	7.5	1,640.8	18,289
931	Shanghai Pharm.	116.2	24.4	0.6	19,261.8	42,236
1030	CSPC Pharmaceutical	100.1	101.0	5.3	1,896.8	11,206
1035	Joincare Pharm. Group	99.79	16.0	6.4	1,552.4	9,906

Source: The author, based on Eurostat R&D Scoreboard, 2019.
Note: 1 EUR = 1.1496 US$, December 31, 2018.

8.3.1.2 Key Institutional Changes and Innovation

China's patent law met international standards in 1993 by extending the object of patent protection from method to products. China's IP law conforms to most international IP standards such as the Trade-Related Aspects of Intellectual Property Rights (TRIPS).

However, since 2010, China's WTO commitment has influenced the drug distribution system. Foreign manufacturers can only receive regulatory authorization for products based on clinical trials done in China (Deloitte, 2019). Foreign companies have long pushed for stronger IP protection. The combination of a stronger IP regime, more capable Chinese companies, and state support for indigenous patenting poses several new challenges for how foreign companies conduct R&D. As a result, both foreign MNCs and Chinese companies have filed more patents in China.

The Chinese government is helping to build these patenting trends. A massive system of patent-related subsidies, financial awards, and tax breaks, some with relatively limited qualification requirements, was launched to help meet targets. This support boosts the patent portfolios of local companies, universities, and public research institutes. The government plays a vital role in the Chinese pharmaceutical industry. It uses its influence on market access and business rights to shape the involvement of foreign MNCs, state-owned enterprise (SOE) labs, and policies controlling prices and medical treatments (Perri, Scalera, & Mudambi, 2017).

8.3.2   Indian Pharmaceutical Market

Meanwhile, the Indian pharmaceutical market is now the eleventh largest in terms of value and third largest in terms of volume, with a market size of approximately US$26 billion in 2017.

8.3.2.1 Players, Competition, and Capabilities in the Market

The Indian pharmaceutical market includes a diverse range of companies that vary in size (IQVIA, 2019). Similar to China, the local market is highly fragmented. Intense market consolidation has become an important characteristic of the Indian pharmaceutical market, which also relies on a massive local market. In 2017, the Indian pharmaceutical sector witnessed forty-six M&A deals worth US$1.47 billion (PwC, 2019), for instance.

Local companies meet around 70 percent of the country's demand for medicines, and generic drugs form the largest segment of the Indian pharmaceutical sector. Indian pharma companies have a history of manufacturing low-cost medicines and, more recently, for developing low-cost processes for off-patent drugs. Since 2000, Indian companies have accumulated strong manufacturing capabilities in the generic segment and are more likely to collaborate with foreign firms to accumulate innovation capabilities compared to Chinese and Brazilian companies.

Since the 2000s, Indian pharma companies have procured supply contracts from international agencies supporting public health programs in developing countries (Guennif & Ramani, 2012).[7] India became the largest provider of generic medicines globally, with the United States as the key market (Pharmexcil Report, 2019).[8] India exports drugs to more than 200 countries, and generic drugs account for 20 percent of global exports in volume. The country accounts for 60 percent of global vaccine production and 25 percent of all medicine in the United Kingdom. India achieved the distinction of "world No. 1 supplier of low-cost generic drugs" and is known as the "pharmacy of the world" (IPA, 2019). The Indian government implemented "Pharma Vision 2020," which aims to make the country a global leader in drug manufacturing. Approval time for new facilities has been reduced to encourage investments from local companies and MNCs (IBEF, 2019).

---

[7] In Africa, the availability of affordable Indian drugs contributed to greater access to AIDS treatment, with around 40 percent of patients receiving treatment in 2017 compared to just 2 percent in 2003. The cost of HIV/AIDS treatment has gone down to $400 per year from $12,000. Source: Contribution to global healthcare (Pharmexcil Report, 2019).

[8] Around 30 percent (in volume) and about 10 percent (in value) of the US$70–80 billion US generics market (IPA, 2019).

In terms of R&D investments, pharmaceuticals have emerged as India's most innovative industry (Bhagavatula, Mudambi, & Murmann, 2019; Krishnan & Prashantham, 2019). Table 8.4 indicates the top ten Indian pharmaceutical investors in R&D, according to Eurostat R&D Scoreboard (see Chapter 13). Sun Pharma (detailed in this chapter) and Dr. Reddy's Laboratories (Chapter 3) are among the top two investors in R&D. Indian pharma companies have also experimented with developing new chemical entities since the 2000s but have been notably less successful (Krishnan & Prashantham, 2019).

The Indian pharmaceutical industry followed a trajectory that started with duplicative imitation followed by creative imitation, eventually progressing up the value chain of pharmaceutical R&D (Guennif & Ramani, 2012; Kale & Little, 2007; Krishnan & Prashantham, 2019). Since 2010, the country has stood out in the global scene through its innovatively engineered generic drugs and APIs.

As Chapter 3 indicates, efficient and low-cost manufacturing capabilities have enabled some Indian companies to become leaders in the global generic pharmaceutical industry.

Since the mid-1990s, the Indian market has become attractive to MNCs. Its institutional reforms provided more security for foreign companies' operations and thus led to more market entries, with new and improved products and knowledge introduced into the domestic market. India, along with China, became an attractive country for pharmaceutical R&D (Gassmann et al., 2018). MNCs are motivated to invest and start relationships with local companies due to the lower R&D costs and cheaper scientific labor (Sahasranamam, Rentala, & Rose, 2019).

8.3.2.2 Key Institutional Changes and Innovation

Chapter 3 gives a detailed description of the institutions in the Indian pharmaceutical sector, of how the new patent legislation affected the local firms, and of how the increase of patents domestically boosted the leadership of Indian companies and the support of the government

Table 8.4 *Top ten Indian pharmaceutical investors in R&D*

World rank	Company	R&D 2017/18 (US$ mn)	R&D 1-y growth (%)	R&D intensity (%)	Net sales (US$ mn)	Employees
408	Sun Pharma	315.2	−1.2	7	4,497.5	17,516
458	Dr. Reddy's Lab.	279.7	−3.5	13.1	2,129.6	–
495	Lupin	256.0	−21.7	11	2,332.0	17,042
640	Glenmark	183.7	−2.9	13.7	1,345.4	13,716
852	Cipla	129.6	0.4	5.9	2,202.3	23,610
1014	Cadila Healthcare	102.4	14.2	5.9	1,746.7	11,819
1182	Aurobindo Pharm.	84.4	19	3.5	2,428.5	17,332
1550	Biocon	57.9	−3.9	9.7	596.5	10,293
1592	Alembic	55.8	−10.1	11.9	468.5	9,526
1681	Torrent	51.6	−3.9	5.9	878.2	14,700

Source: The author, Eurostat R&D (European Innovation Scoreboard, 2019).
Note: 1 EUR = 1.1496 US$, December 31, 2018.

(Brandl, Mudambi, & Scalera, 2015; Choudhury & Khanna, 2014; Guennif & Ramani, 2012; Kale & Little, 2007).[9]

8.3.3   Brazilian Pharmaceutical Market

Brazil is the largest pharmaceutical market in Latin America and ranked sixth in the world. Economic recession has not shrunk the pharmaceutical market. Few of the world's largest pharmaceutical markets have grown at a sustained pace since 2010, and Brazil stands as one of the best performing, according to IQVIA (2019).

8.3.3.1 Players, Competition, and Capabilities in the Market

The Brazilian drug market comprises 241 pharmaceutical laboratories, of which 97 (40 percent) were MNCs and 144 (60 percent) national companies (Sindusfarma, 2018). Brazilian players in the generic sector are growing faster than MNCs in the country (IMS Health, 2014; IQVIA, 2019).

The Brazilian companies produce 75 percent of the products demanded by the market. Most Brazilian pharma companies began by producing copies of original patented drugs that MNCs were selling in the country, while the Brazilian government did not comply with international IP protection rules. In the 1990s, with major institutional reforms, local players advanced toward producing generic drugs, as patents of many relevant medicines expired, and Brazil joined TRIPs in 1994. Local players took advantage of this "training" period to learn and develop more sophisticated capabilities toward innovation strategies.

The leading domestic pharmaceutical companies in the Brazilian market are Aché, EMS, Hypera Pharma, Biolab, and Eurofarma, and together these companies hold more than 75 percent of the generics market. Generics have boosted the participation of

---

[9] Between 1950 and 1993, the Council of Scientific and Industrial Research (CSIR) produced only 27 patents registered with the US Patent and Trademark Office (USPTO). In contrast, between 1994 and 2015, it produced 540 (Bhagavatula et al., 2019).

national laboratories in the total sales of the industry. According to IQVIA (2019), among the five largest pharmaceutical companies operating in Brazil, four are Brazilian, and among the thirty largest, ten are local to the country (all of whom offer generics). Unlike their Chinese and Indian counterparts, the largest Brazilian pharmaceutical companies are not ranked internationally.

The market share of international laboratories stands 10 percent higher than domestic laboratories. In the generics market, about 88 percent are national companies, 3.6 percent Indian, 1.8 percent German, 5.1 percent Swiss, 1.1 percent American, and 0.3 percent Canadian (Fonseca, 2018). Currently, twenty-three Indian pharmaceutical companies are based in Latin American countries, fourteen of which are based in Brazil.

SOE labs have a significant presence in the Brazilian market. Currently, there are eighteen state-owned pharmaceutical laboratories and two state-owned vaccine manufacturers: They produce about 200 different drugs. They are the primary suppliers for the Brazilian public health system (SUS) and the Brazilian Program for National Immunization. Currently, about 35 percent of drugs distributed by SUS are produced by SOE labs.

Multinational companies hold approximately 25 percent of the market in sales. After promarket reforms, foreign companies began operating in Brazil, due to the high growth rates of the country's market. Today, all major pharmaceutical MNCs operate in the Brazilian market, of which the biggest are Pfizer, Novartis, Sanofi, and Roche, with R&D activities all over the country.

Large acquisitions, international joint ventures, and new entrants have reshaped the market. In 2009, French pharmaceutical company Sanofi acquired Medley, Brazil's leading generics brand. Sanofi became the leading player in the Brazilian market for a time, but in 2019 it ranked fourth. Three domestic firms outrank Sanofi – Aché, EMS, and Eurofarma. Pfizer acquired a 40 percent stake of the Brazilian generic producer Laboratorio Teuto Brasileiro in 2010.

Multilab was acquired by Japanese company Takeda two years later. Some MNCs, including Novartis and Roche, use Brazil as a production platform, exporting to Latin America, North America, and Europe.

8.3.3.2 Key Institutional Changes and Innovation

There is a history of innovation in the pharmaceutical sector in Brazil. Fiocruz and the Butantan Institute began researching and producing vaccines for tropical diseases in the early twentieth century. Large-scale industrial production began in the 1930s as Brazil became self-sufficient in vaccines, with national companies also producing serums and natural extracts from plants and vitamins. Part of this initial success was due to Brazil not complying with the international patent system. The absence of necessary infrastructure in the chemical industry, however, prevented vertical integration of these domestic firms, contrary to what occurred in the United States and Germany (Caliari & Ruiz, 2013; Guennif & Ramani, 2012).

The Brazilian government started to attract pharmaceutical multinationals after WWII, with a massive movement of companies to Brazil, especially US firms. At the same time, to protect its nascent industry, the government strengthened import substitution policies and thus changed the patent system in 1945 to allow only process patents (similar to India), excluding pharmaceuticals from patenting. These attempts were not linked with industrial policies to support domestic firms, of small scale compared to MNCs (Guennif & Ramani, 2012). Process patents were removed in 1969, but with little effect on the national industry structure.

Beginning in the 1970s, the government encouraged national companies to copy successful drugs. R&D activities were extremely concentrated at public institutions, and MNCs' subsidiaries operating in Brazil were not accomplishing R&D locally. MNCs incorporated new products and quality into the market, but added little in terms of technological innovation (Caliari & Ruiz, 2013).

By the early 1990s, major promarket reforms affected the local pharmaceutical market. Brazil joined TRIPs in 1994, and both product and process patents came to procure a twenty-year validity period.[10] The government issued the Act of Generic Drugs (1997) to improve the quality and safety of drugs and, two years later, to define the conditions for market introduction of reengineered drugs. Meanwhile, the government created the National Health Surveillance Agency (ANVISA), similar to the FDA in the United States, with the purpose of regulating both the quality of all drugs in the market and health services across the country.

Since the early 2000s, the pharmaceutical industry has become one of the strategic focuses of industrial policies in Brazil. In 2004, the Brazilian Development Bank (BNDES) began directly supporting the pharmaceutical industry with the release of the Support Program for the Development of the Pharmaceutical Productive Chain (Profarma). Profarma represented unprecedented support, with long-term credit lines at low interest rates for national companies building competitiveness in three ways: (1) expanding and modernizing of production capacities, (2) increasing R&D and innovation for national companies and MNCs operating in Brazil, and (3) scaling up companies through M&As and internationalization. Most firms adapted their factories and significantly expanded their production capacity and innovation activities.

These factors brought about changes to the industry, the country's access to drugs, and the competitive dynamics of pharmaceutical companies in Brazil.

See Table 8.5 for a summary of the pharmaceutical industry in Brazil, India, and China.

---

[10] In 1996, the Brazilian government sanctioned Act No. 9,313, enabling Brazilians' universal and free access to antiretrovirals through SUS, and began local production. Brazil issued compulsory licenses to HIV/AIDS products by turning to the World Health Organization (WTO). The Brazilian National AIDS Program is widely recognized by the WTO as the leading example of an integrated HIV/AIDS approach, including prevention, care, and treatment.

Table 8.5 *Overview of pharmaceutical industry in Brazil, India, and China*

	Brazil	India	China
Demand	Predominantly domestic, concentrated in public sector. SUS utilizes 75 percent generics.	Domestic and to large extent international. Concentrated in private sector. Low-cost generics.	Predominantly domestic, concentrated in public sector. Over 75 percent of produced drugs are generics, and 11 percent are traditional Chinese medicine.
Internationalization	Low, but increasing since 2010. The leading companies (such as EMS, Eurofarma, and Ache) are internationalizing, most are targeting neighboring countries in Latin America.	High. The poor domestic market boosted internationalization. Intense M&A abroad.	Low. The focus of the local manufacturers is the domestic market. Increasing since 2010.
Exports	Historically low, increased since 2010. Export revenue grew 73 percent, reaching US$2.3 billion in exports in 2015. Brazil became an export hub of MNEs to Latin America.*	High. Exports drugs to more than 200 countries, and generics is 20 percent of global exports in volume. "World No. 1 supplier of low-cost generic drugs" and is known as the "pharmacy of the world."	Low. Increasing since mid-2010s. Most Chinese pharma companies with foreign distribution export APIs or traditional Chinese medicine mainly to Asian countries.

Table 8.5 (cont.)

	Brazil	India	China
Market leaders	Fragmented. National companies retain 70 percent of the market.	Highly fragmented. MNEs had less than 20 percent in 2006, but around 45 percent in 2013 after M&A of local players.	Highly fragmented. "National champions" policy, consolidation via M&A with prevalence of national companies. Chinese companies have 75 percent of annual sales,
Innovative capabilities	Concentration in the public sector and SOE labs. Re-engineering skills; integration of biotechnology; focus on niches of drug discovery process. Public–private cooperation is strengthening, but public-sector firms are also leaders in innovation generation.	Concentration in the private sector. Re-engineering skills; integration of biotechnology; focus on niches of drug discovery process. International cooperation is crucial – innovation led by private firms.	Focused on low-cost generics. Big pharmas are investing in R&D facilities. Government is encouraging local companies to increase R&D investments.

Production capabilities	Skills in formulations; integration of biotechnology with focus on niches of API; focus on niches of drug discovery process.	Skills in formulations; large-scale bulk drug production; large-scale production of API; integration of biotechnology; focus on niches of drug discovery process	Large-scale bulk drug production; large-scale production of API.
Regulation	TRIPs in 1994; both product and process patents were reintroduced with a twenty-year-validity period.	India's ratification to the WTO in 1994. Full implementation of TRIPs in 2005.	Met international standards in 1993, entry into the WTO. It has strengthened patent law – WTO/TRIPS agreement.
Main regulatory agencies	1999 creation of ANVISA, similar to the US FDA, regulates both the quality of all drugs marketed and health services across the country.	Drugs Standard Control Organization (CDSCO – 2008) regulatory agency for pharmaceuticals and medical devices – similar to the US FDA.	In 2003, creation of State Food and Drug Administration (SFDA), the national supervising authority.

Sources: The author, based on * BNDES data; PwC (2019), Deloitte (2019), IPA (2019), IMS Health (2014), and IQVIA (2019).

8.4 CASES

8.4.1 Jiangsu Hengrui Medicine

Hengrui was established in 1970 in Lianyungang, Jiangsu Province, as a state-owned local medicine manufacturer of imitative drugs. In the 1980s, it started production of APIs and became one of China's largest generic producers in the 1990s. By 1997, Jiangsu Hengrui Medicine Co., Ltd. was incorporated and in three years launched its initial public offering (IPO) in the Shanghai Stock Exchange (Jiangsu Hengrui Medicine, 2019).

The company began investing in R&D in 2004, and its innovation strategies have increased significantly since then. The recent innovation strategies of Jiangsu Hengrui Medicine and other innovative pharmaceutical companies in China are the result of major government innovation policies encouraging generic producers to register products in foreign markets and to increase investments in R&D (Perri et al., 2017).

To date, around 80 percent of Jiangsu Hengrui's revenue is from generic drugs, and 20 percent of its revenue is from innovative drugs (Jiangsu Hengrui Medicine, 2019). Since 2010, the company has sustained a CAGR of 23 percent in sales revenue, which exceeded US$2.7 billion in 2018 (see Table 8.2).

> Producing generic drugs funds our R&D. – Weikang Tao, vice president and CEO of Shanghai Hengrui, the company's innovative drug subsidiary[11]

The company's R&D innovative drug strategy was gradual, utilizing a conservative approach to reduce the risk of failure. In 2004, at the beginning of its innovative investments, the company relied on developmental compounds licensed from other companies. Jiangsu initially targeted drugs with the same mechanisms of action

---

[11] Interview available at: https://cen.acs.org/articles/95/i29/Chinese-drugmaker-Hengrui-RD-plans.html. Accessed November 2019.

as others already on the market (Tremblay, 2017). Years later, the company invented compounds offering slight improvements over existing ones. With clear incremental innovations, the company's R&D strategy became more ambitious, and its scientists broadened the range of diseases and drugs to develop capabilities internally (Tremblay, 2017).

We went from me-too to me-better to now best in class, and then we will do first in class. – Weikang Tao[12]

Hengrui spends around 10 percent of its revenue on R&D each year, reflecting its dedication and advancements in innovation (Fortune, 2019; Jiangsu Hengrui Medicine, 2019). In 2018, it ranked 64th among Forbes's Top 100 World's Most Innovative Companies. The company has created 7 R&D centers, including in the United States and Japan, with 1,800 research professionals. It is currently running more than 120 clinical trials and 29 National Science and Technology Major Projects, with 4 innovative drugs (imrecoxib, apatinib, mecapegfilgrastim, and pyrotinib) launched in China, 1 product under New Drug Application (NDA) review, over 30 drug candidates in clinical development worldwide, and 50 in the preclinical stage (Jiangsu Hengrui Medicine, 2019).

Since 2014, the company has led research in cancer drugs, contrast agents, and surgical medicines. To date, the firm has seven injectable medicines approved by the US FDA and eleven products approved for oral formulations and inhalational anesthetics (Jiangsu Hengrui Medicine, 2019). Hengrui is ranked in the top thirty pharmaceutical companies worldwide with a market capitalization of over US$30 billion and more than 21,000 employees in 2018 (see Table 8.2). The company is also ranked number fourteen in Fortune's Future 50, a ranking identifying companies with the strongest long-term growth potential (Fortune, 2019).

---

[12] Interview available at: https://cen.acs.org/articles/95/i29/Chinese-drugmaker-Hengrui-RD-plans.html. Accessed November 2019.

8.4.2 Sun Pharma

Sun Pharmaceuticals (Sun Pharma) was founded in 1983 as a local provider of low-cost medicines. It started its operations by producing cheap copies of patented drugs. Local laws permitted such a copycat strategy based on a production method different from the patented process. Sun Pharma made significant improvements to its manufacturing capabilities through expertise in making ingredients for MNCs.

The changes in regulations in the local industry and India's agreement to TRIPs in 1994 shifted the company's strategy. In 1994, Sun Pharma went public through an IPO, following which it initiated an aggressive internationalization strategy. By 1996, it expanded its sales network to twenty-four countries, investing in acquisitions and expansion. The company has twenty-one manufacturing plants in India and twenty-three manufacturing sites approved by global health regulatory agencies in several EMs such as Bangladesh, Egypt, Malaysia, Nigeria, Hungary, Romania, Russia, and Israel and in developed countries such as Australia and Canada, including five plants in the United States and two in Japan (Sun Pharma, 2019).

The company first attempted innovation in the late-1980s. In 1988, it launched two products for cardiology, still used today, and in 1989 introduced gastroenterology products in India. In 1991, it established the first research center for product and process development. Its R&D investments are mainly targeted at developing complex generics and specialty products. In 2007, it created Sun Pharma Advanced Research Company (SPARC) as a separate unit, which became the first R&D company listed on the stock exchanges in India. The company has six major R&D centers, three in India associated with SPARC, Chemistry and Discovery Research in Israel, Taro Pharmaceuticals in Canada, and Ohm Laboratories in the United States. The company invests 7 percent of sales in R&D (Sun Pharma, 2019).

The acquisition of Ranbaxy Laboratories from the Japanese company Daiichi Sankyo in 2015 was a milestone for Sun Pharma.[13] In an all-stock deal of a total equity value of US$3.2 billion, Sun Pharma acquired Ranbaxy, and Daiichi Sankyo became the second-largest shareholder of Sun Pharma with an 8.9 percent stake after the merger. This acquisition made Sun Pharma the fifth-largest generic pharmaceutical company in the world in 2015.

The acquisition complemented Sun Pharma's strengths and fulfilled its ambition of being a global company, as a leader in high-growth emerging markets with a significant presence in the Indian market and in the United States (Ramachandran, Manukonda, & Awate, 2017).

Partnerships and collaborations are an essential part of Sun Pharma's international strategy. To strengthen its presence in different countries, the company does in-licensing (products that are already in the market) and out-licensing (first operation, or in late stage of clinical development) in its key therapy product areas. The company created a market intelligence area with regulatory affairs specialists experienced in timely filing of dossiers and concurrently managing the regulatory queries and timelines of regulatory local authorities (Sun Pharma, 2019).

Its specialty portfolio in dermatology, ophthalmology, and oncology represents the company's capability to move up the pharmaceutical value chain and enhance innovation. Over the years, Sun Pharma has developed a strong portfolio of specialty products, funding their clinical trials and establishing the requisite front-end capabilities for this segment. The company has a global specialty pipeline with focused R&D investments. The main market for these products is the United States. In 2019, Sun Pharma made 118 abbreviated

---

[13] Ranbaxy started operations in 1962 and grew to be one of the ten largest Indian pharma companies by the mid-1980s. The company became one of the largest manufacturers of intermediates, bulk drugs, and generics from India. Ranbaxy also led all of Indian industry in R&D expenditures in the late 1990s and had built up chemical synthesis capabilities (Ghemawat & Kothavala, 1996).

NDAs (generic drug approval for an existing licensed medication or approved drug) and 8 NDAs pending US FDA approval, including a combination of complex generics, patent challenge opportunities, and pure generics (Sun Pharma, 2019).

Sun Pharma has US$4.2 billion in global revenues and is ranked thirty-fifth in the world in the pharmaceutical sector (Forbes, 2019), see Table 8.2. Including its subsidiaries and associates, Sun Pharma is the fourth-largest generic company in the world (first in India and eighth in the United States). It is the largest Indian pharmaceutical company in the United States, which contributes 46 percent of its revenues.

8.4.3 Eurofarma

Eurofarma was founded in 1972. The company started producing drugs by copying or using known processes to manufacture medicines at lower costs. Like other Brazilian companies, Eurofarma benefited from weak patent laws to reverse-engineer drugs with minor modifications to the formulations. The company deepened its operations by developing initial innovation capabilities in the 1980s when it acquired ISA, the first Brazilian laboratory to produce penicillin. When Brazil's Generics Law came into force in 1999, the company expanded the variety of products offered.

Eurofarma took its first step toward internationalization in 2009, with an initial focus on Latin America due not only to geographical proximity, but also to similar regulatory requirements, which facilitated the approval of generic drugs. The initial strategy was to gain scale in international operations and to build competitive advantage as a regional player (Cahen & Oliveira, 2017). The company's priority was to become a top three regional player in Latin America.[14]

[14] Eurofarma's Vision 2022: "We will be one of the three largest pharmaceutical companies of regional capital in Latin America, leaders in medical prescription in Brazil, and a reference in innovation and sustainability. With increasing profitability, 30 percent of the sales will come from international operations, 40 percent from products launched since 2017, and 10 percent from the protected portfolio (drugs with some level of protection, based on incremental or radical innovation, or exclusive products)" (Eurofarma, 2019).

Eurofarma invested about US$310 million in international expansion since 2009, and in 2018 it covered 82 percent of the Latin American market. Now, Eurofarma is the third-largest pharmaceutical company in Brazil with manufacturing operations in eighteen countries in Latin America and one facility in Mozambique.

In 2015, the company turned to more strategic asset-seeking acquisitions. That year, it acquired the Argentinean factory of the French laboratory Sanofi. The deal involved an outsourced production agreement with Sanofi itself, which no longer holds manufacturing units in the country. Meanwhile, Eurofarma started a technological partnership with South Korean laboratory Dong-A. The companies agreed to codevelop and commercialize evogliptina, a drug used in diabetes patients, then valid for the Brazilian market and seventeen other countries in Latin America. The partnership with Dong-A is one of a series involving research on new molecules, with technology transfer for local production.

Partnerships with several international companies have become the main strategy for the company to absorb new technologies. Currently, Eurofarma keeps licensing agreements with twenty-five companies in Argentina, Spain, the United States, France, India, and beyond. Eurofarma signed new licensing agreements in 2018, such as for Belviq's Latin American Exclusivity Agreement, for the treatment of obesity, and the innovative Delabax, for the treatment of acute bacterial skin infections (Eurofarma, 2019).

In 2006, the company founded its "Innovation Nucleus" and since 2015 formed the Organic Synthesis Laboratory and the Innovation Center with investments of around US$42 million. With 400 professionals, including researchers and technicians, the Center is totally devoted to R&D. The company created a Vice-Presidency for Innovation, which comprises several boards: R&D, Regulatory Issues, Management of Portfolio & Licenses, and Medical. This structure is completed by management-level positions in Biotechnology, Strategic Projects of Innovation, Pre-Clinical Development, and Clinical and Pharmaceutical Research. By the end of 2018, it opened an R&D

center in Argentina to meet the specific demands of international operations.

Together with acquisitions, innovation became one of Eurofarma's main sources of growth. The company has increased investments of innovative strategies in products, processes, services, and technology. The company substantially increased its R&D investments: In 2016, it invested US$40.4 million; in 2017, US$56 million; and in 2018, US$69 million.

8.5   CONCLUSIONS

Even innovative pharmaceutical companies in EMs are not yet at the frontier of the industry, but they show unique potential. While pharmaceutical EMs are substantially behind advanced markets in terms of modern medicines' use per capita, they have progressed from drug imitators to generics leaders and are now pursuing innovation strategies in important products.

Local and regional players in the generic sector are growing faster than other MNCs in China, India, and Brazil. Indeed, generic companies from EMs have made significant gains in sales revenues, in building more sophisticated internal capabilities, and in venturing into innovative R&D activities.

Accordingly, local players are outcompeting large MNCs in these countries. With ever-growing portfolios since the 2010s, they have forged strong relationships with government and home institutions, which enable them to establish integrated distributors and accelerate decision making. As a result, large MNCs represent only a small share of overall M&A activity, with over 90 percent of deals in Brazil, India, and China conducted by local players or smaller foreign generic companies (IMS Health, 2014, IQVIA, 2019).

In short, promarket reforms in the 1990s and 2000s built a foundation on which firms could no longer rely on "reengineering" as a strategy to catch up to production of branded drugs patented by MNCs. Ultimately, local companies needed to build internal R&D

capabilities and expand the acquisition of knowledge and new technology from the inside out.

REFERENCES

Bartlett, C. A., & Ghoshal, S. (2000). Going global: Lessons from late movers. *Reading, 1*(3), 75–84.

Bhagavatula, S., Mudambi, R., & Murmann, J. P. (2019). Innovation and entrepreneurship in India: An overview. *Management and Organization Review, 15*(3), 467–493.

Brandl, K., Mudambi, R., & Scalera, V. G. (2015). The spectacular rise of the Indian pharmaceutical industry. *Entrepreneur & Innovation Exchange*. Retrieved November 2019, from https://eiexchange.com/content/111-the-spectacular-rise-of-the-indian-pharmaceutical-industry.

Cahen, F., & Oliveira, M. M., Jr. (2017). Brazilian multinationals, moving ahead. In L. Casanova & A. Miroux (Eds.), *Emerging multinationals in a changing world. Emerging Market Multinationals Report (EMR)* (pp. 90–111). Retrieved November 2019, from www.johnson.cornell.edu/Portals/32/EMI percent20Docu/EMR/Emerging percent20Multinationals percent20in per cent20a percent20Changing percent20World.pdf.

Caliari, T., & Ruiz, R. M. (2013). Brazilian pharmaceutical industry and generic drugs policy: Impacts on structure and innovation and recent developments. *Science and Public Policy, 41*(2), 245–256.

Choudhury, P., & Khanna, T. (2014). Toward resource independence: Why state-owned entities become multinationals: An empirical study of India's public R&D laboratories. *Journal of International Business Studies, 45*(8), 943–960.

Deloitte. (2019). Global life sciences outlook. Retrieved November 2019, from www2.deloitte.com/global/en/pages/life-sciences-and-healthcare/articles/global-life-sciences-sector-outlook.html.

Dutta, S., Lanvin, B., & Wunsch-Vincent, S. (Eds.). (2019). *Global innovation index 2019: Creating healthy lives – the future of medical innovation*. Ithaca, Fontainebleau, and Geneva: Cornell, INSEAD, and WIPO.

Eurofarma. (2016, 2019). Annual Reports. Retrieved November 2019, from www.eurofarma.com.br/relatorio-anual/.

European Innovation Scoreboard. (2019). Retrieved November 2019, from: https://interactivetool.eu/EIS/EIS_2.html.

Fonseca, E. M. (2018). How can a policy foster local pharmaceutical production and still protect public health? Lessons from the health–industry complex in Brazil. *Global Public Health, 13*(4), 489–502.

Forbes. (2019). Global 2000 – The world's largest public companies. Retrieved November 2019, from www.forbes.com/global2000/#5603c1ae335d.

Fortune. (2019). Jiangsu Hengrui Medicine. Retrieved November 2019, from https://fortune.com/future-50/2019/jiangsu-hengrui-medicine/.

Gassmann, O., Schuhmacher, A., von Zedtwitz, M., & Reepmeyer, G. (2018). *Leading pharmaceutical innovation: How to win the life science race.* Cham, CH: Springer.

Ghemawat, P., & Kothavala, K. (1996). *Repositioning Ranbaxy. Case Study N9-796-181.* Cambridge, MA: Harvard Business School.

Guennif, S., & Ramani, S. V. (2012). Explaining divergence in catching-up in pharma between India and Brazil using the NSI framework. *Research Policy, 41*(2), 430–441.

IBEF – India Brand Equity Foundation. (2019). Indian pharmaceutical industry. Retrieved November 2019, from www.ibef.org/industry/pharmaceutical-india.aspx.

IMS Health. (2014). Pharmerging markets – picking a pathway to success [White Paper]. Retrieved November 2019, from www.pharmatalents.es/assets/files/Pharmerging_white_paper_06_2013.pdf.

IPA – Indian Pharmaceutical Association. (2019). The Indian pharmaceutical industry – the way forward. Retrieved November 2019, from www.ipa-india.org/static-files/pdf/publications/position-papers/2019/ipa-way-forward.pdf.

IQVIA. (2019, October 21). Growth perspectives for the Pharma market. IQVIA Market Prognosis Team. Retrieved November 2019, from www.iqvia.com/blogs/2019/10/growth-perspectives-for-the-pharma-market.

Jiangsu Hengrui Medicine. (2019). Company profile. Retrieved November 2019, from www.hrs.com.cn/hren/About_hr_company.html.

Kale, D., & Little, S. (2007). From imitation to innovation: The evolution of R&D capabilities and learning processes in the Indian pharmaceutical industry. *Technology Analysis & Strategic Management, 19*(5), 589–609.

Krishnan, R. T., & Prashantham, S. (2019). Innovation in and from India: The who, where, what, and when. *Global Strategy Journal, 9*(3), 357–377.

Lorenzetti, L. (2015). Why drug companies are betting big on "pharmerging" countries. Retrieved November 2019, from https://fortune.com/2015/08/14/drug-companies-pharmerging-countries/.

Luo, Y., Sun, J., & Wang, S. L. (2011). Emerging economy copycats: Capability, environment, and strategy. *The Academy of Management Perspectives, 25*(2), 37–56.

Malerba, F., & Orsenigo, L. (2002). Innovation and market structure in the dynamics of the pharmaceutical industry and biotechnology: Towards a history-friendly model. *Industrial and Corporate Change, 11*(4), 667–703.

Munos, B. (2009). Lessons from 60 years of pharmaceutical innovation. *Nature Reviews, 8*(12), 959–968.

Perri, A., Scalera, V. G., & Mudambi, R. (2017). What are the most promising conduits for foreign knowledge inflows? Innovation networks in the Chinese pharmaceutical industry. *Industrial and Corporate Change, 26*(2), 333–355.

Pharmexcil Report. (2019). 15th Annual Report, 2018–2019. Retrieved November 2019, from https://pharmexcil.com/uploadfile/ufiles/AnnualReport05092019.pdf.

Prud'homme, D., & von Zedtwitz, M. (2018). The changing face of innovation in China. *MIT Sloan Management Review, 59*(4), 24–32.

PwC. (2019, April). M&A 2018 review for China pharmaceutical and medical device sectors. Retrieved November 2019, from www.pwccn.com/en/indus tries/pharmaceuticals-and-life-sciences/publications/ma-2018-review-for-china-pharmaceutical-and-medical-device-sector.html.

Ramachandran, J., Manukonda, S., & Awate, K. (2016). Ranbaxy Laboratories Limited: Changing aspirations. Teaching Case. Harvard Business Publishing Education. Retrieved November 2019, from https://hbsp.harvard.edu/product/IMB601-PDF-ENG.

Sahasranamam, S., Rentala, S., & Rose, E. (2019). Knowledge sources and international business activity in a changing innovation ecosystem: A study of the Indian pharmaceutical industry. *Management and Organization Review, 15* (3), 595–614.

Scannell, J. W., Blanckley, A., Boldon, H., & Warrington, B. (2012). Diagnosing the decline in pharmaceutical R&D efficiency. *Nature Reviews, 11*(3), 191–200.

Sindusfarma. (2018). Profile of the pharmaceutical industry in Brazil and relevant sector aspects. São Paulo. Retrieved November 2019, from https://sindusfarma .org.br/Perfil-IF2018-20-07-INGLES.pdf.

Sun Pharmaceutical Industries Ltd. (2019). Annual Report 2018–2019. Specialty in Progress. Retrieved November 2019, from www.sunpharma.com/sites/default/ files/annual/Complete percent20Annual percent20Report.pdf.

Tremblay, J. F. (2017). For Chinese drugmaker Hengrui, R&D plans pan out – Ambitious program to launch innovative drugs starts to pay off for generics producer. *Chemical & Engineering News, 95*(29), 24–25. Retrieved November 2019, from https://cen.acs.org/articles/95/i29/Chinese-drugmaker-Hengrui-RD-plans.html.

von Zedtwitz, M., & Gassmann, O. (2016). Global corporate R&D to and from emerging countries. In S. Dutta, B. Lanvin, & S. Wunsch-Vincent (Eds.), *The Global Innovation Index 2016* (pp. 125–131). Ithaca, NY: Cornell University.

9 Reverse Innovation and the Role of Local Partners in Emerging Markets

The Experience of Foreign Subsidiaries in Brazil

Victor Ragazzi Isaac, Felipe Borini,
and Moacir de Miranda Oliveira Jr.

9.1 INTRODUCTION

Operating in emerging markets (EMs) requires subsidiaries of multinationals to develop innovations that bear different standards than those in developed markets (Iyer, LaPlaca, & Sharma, 2006; Zeschky, Widenmayer, & Gassmann, 2011). In general, the need to develop innovations in subsidiaries in these contexts is related to a number of different institutional factors, the nature of the consumer market (which has specific demands, relative to those of developed markets), as well as to the potential for collaboration with local partners that often have their own unique resources and needs (Govindarajan & Ramamurti, 2011; Kostova & Marano, 2019). Based on these factors, Agnihotri (2014) elaborated in his study a synthesis of three types of innovation specific to EMs.

First, we have frugal innovation, characterized as meeting the scarcity of resources and technologies that these emerging markets provide (Winterhalter, Zeschky, Neumann, & Gassmann, 2017). Thus, this type of innovation is characterized by the low price charged for the service or product combined with large-scale production of the same (Kumar & Puranam, 2012). On the other hand, frugal innovation is also linked to sustainability and robustness because the products and services developed are more durable and less damaging to the ecosystem (Prabhu & Gupta, 2014; Radjou & Prabhu, 2014). As an example, we have the company Tata Motors, which developed Nano, the cheapest car model in the world, with features and technologies found in India (Soni & Krishnan, 2014).

The second innovation is jugaad innovation, which, while not seeking sophistication or perfection, is focused on the quick, inexpensive, practical, and flexible solution of temporary problems (Radjou et al., 2012). This innovation is widely found in EM, but especially in India, which has a very large consumer market with low purchasing power favoring innovations that are "good enough" to meet their needs (Radjou et al., 2012). SELCO is an example of a company that developed jugaad innovation to solve a recurring problem: the lack of electricity in rural areas. Having to develop a product at a price point similar to using a kerosene lamp throughout the year, the company developed a product that captures and stores solar energy during the day, offering residents a new way to access energy at night. As the product has a low cost, it can be purchased by rural residents (Prabhu & Jain, 2015).

This chapter will focus on analyzing reverse innovation. This third category of innovation is related not only to the peculiarities of EM innovations, but also to their geographic dimensions (Govindarajan & Ramamurti, 2011, 2014). Thus, reverse innovation consists of the development of new products, processes, and services created initially to meet the local demands of EM, but that are later understood as fundamental by the multinational for generating gains of global competitive advantage, only to be disseminated to the headquarters and applied in developed markets (Govindarajan & Euchner, 2012). This flow of innovation transfer thus differs from the conventional understandings, whereby subsidiaries in EMs replicate innovations from headquarters (Immelt, Govindarajan, & Trimble, 2009).

And yet, it is important to note that in many cases, when setting up in an EM, MNC subsidiaries face a differentiated consumer market, an institutional environment based on uncertainties, as well as competitors accustomed to working with local resources (Buckley & Tian, 2017; Rottig, 2016). Studies have shown that it is important for the subsidiary to develop relationships with local partners to gain access to knowledge and resources that will enable local innovations

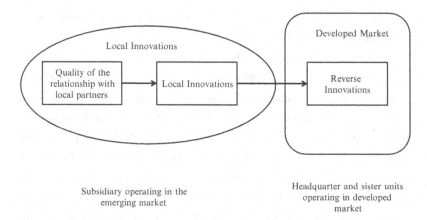

FIGURE 9.1 Relationship between local partners, subsidiaries, and
headquarters in the reverse innovation process
Source: The authors.

to emerge (Figure 9.1). However, for access to these assets to occur,
the subsidiary must first develop a quality relationship with local
partners, based on trust and mutual adaptations, favoring the emergence of local innovations that may be used by the parent company
and other sister units installed in developed markets (Isaac, Borini,
Raziq, & Benito, 2019).

As a specific purpose of this chapter, we analyze how the quality
of the relationship – relational embeddedness – that subsidiaries from
developed markets have with local partners influences the development of reverse innovations in EMs.

9.2   REVERSE INNOVATION IN EMS

Reverse innovation has been widely discussed in the literature on
international business (IB) in past years (Shan & Khan, 2016; Talaga,
2010; von Zedtwitz, Corsi, Søberg, & Frega, 2015). The seminal study
for the characterization of reverse innovation was that of
Govindarajan and Ramarmuti (2011), whose scope was to demonstrate that several product, service, and process innovations in subsidiaries of multinationals located in EMs were gaining ground and being

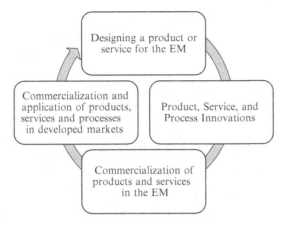

FIGURE 9.2 The four stages of reverse innovation
Sources: Adapted from Govindarajan and Ramarmuti (2011) and von Zedtwitz et al. (2014).

replicated in developed markets, contrary to the traditional view that the flow of innovation was always from developed markets to EMs (Vernon, 1966; 1979). Subsidiaries of multinationals operating in EMs have a local role, as they are important in assisting the development of EMs through the promotion of local innovations, as well as a global role, as they provide innovations to the headquarters and other sister units operating in developed markets.

Moreover, in order to clarify the understanding of the process development of reverse innovations, we will show a model based on Govindarajan and Ramarmuti (2011) and von Zedtwitz, Friesike, and Gassmann (2014), consisting of four stages, as shown in Figure 9.2.

Initially, subsidiaries operating in EMs should meet the demands of the consumer market of these countries (Ernst, Kahle, Dubiel, Prabhu, & Subramaniam, 2015; von Zedtwitz et al., 2014). When we characterize such consumer markets, we come up with two differentials compared to those of developed markets. First, the market in emerging countries is made up of a significant proportion of consumers with low purchasing power. This often causes MNC subsidiaries to lower the costs of products, processes, and services

(Agnihotri, 2014). An example is GE, which in 2009 was operating in China and needed to develop a low-cost portable ultrasound device (sold at US$15,000, while a conventional device can cost US$60,000) to meet the demands of the rural populations of that country. In addition, the consumer markets in these countries also demonstrate other needs that are not only related to their purchasing power, but also to the cultural differences of each emerging country. In this sense, PepsiCo developed a lentil-based snack in India that, despite its price, sought to meet the differentiated demand that Indians have in terms of taste (Govindarajan & Euchner, 2012). Thus, products and services are developed not only to meet the needs in relation to costs, but also the tastes and habits of consumers in these markets.

On the other hand, the second and third stages are character-ized, respectively, by the development and commercialization of the product and service in the EM. To occur in an efficient and effective manner, it is important for the subsidiary to have not only an R&D center with skilled and qualified local researchers (Meyer & Estrin, 2014), but also autonomy from the headquarters to develop new products, processes, and services (Mudambi, Mudambi, & Navarra, 2007). Moreover, the product, service, or process development phase is deemed important because it is in this phase that the idea is put to the test, thus using the resources that the subsidiary bears (von Zedtwitz et al., 2014). This phase requires significant investments of time as well as human and financial resources from the subsidiary. The third phase, commercialization, is characterized by the introduc-tion of the new product, process, or service in the EMs (von Zedtwitz et al., 2014). The successful implementation of the innovation in the EMs relates to the subsidiary's ability to capture and add value during the development process (Birkinshaw & Hood, 1998), in addition to engaging with local partners to overcome the institutional voids existing in EMs (Ernst et al., 2015).

Finally, the fourth phase is the commercialization and applica-tion of the innovation developed in products, processes, and services in the EM to the developed market. It is common to ask ourselves why a consumer from a developed market would want to consume an innovation from an EM, as this goes against the traditional logic of MNCs launching a new product. According to Govindarajan and Euchner (2012), several products and services resulting from innovations developed in EMs can be more efficient and less expensive than those already existing in developed markets, a "good enough" innovation. It is also proposed that making adaptations or developing new products and services for EMs requires the addition of new features that may be enticing to consumers of developed markets. Finally, the authors point out that technologies developed in EMs may be at the forefront of global innovations. This can be seen in the EMs' ability to develop low-cost technologies for the health and information technology areas, which are subsequently replicated globally. As a result, enterprises from EMs have emerged as leaders in various segments of the economy, especially technology, reinventing a scenario in which they are no longer supporting players but now assuming a leading role (Huang & Sharif, 2016).

Innovations of EMs can thus serve as a source of sustainable competitive advantage for multinationals operating in developed markets due to their particular characteristics. For example, in the mid-1990s in South Africa, Vodacom innovated by launching prepaid service for mobile phones and debited customer accounts in real time. This marketing and service innovation resulted from the low purchasing power of the South African consumer market. Unlike the postpaid model, where the customer signs a long-term contract with the telephone company, receiving an invoice with the current month's telephone expenses, in the prepaid model the customer credits a certain amount from which their charges are deducted. The services and calls are made without necessarily having to sign a contract with the service provider. With the success of the prepaid model in South Africa, Vodafone UK has replicated the prepaid model for the UK market, attracting millions of new consumers. It has become a widely accepted mobile phone model used by young people around the world (Akin, 2011).

In addition, it is important to emphasize that the innovation process for the subsidiary is not simple. In general, it shows many difficulties in the first three stages. Initially, the subsidiary struggles to develop ideas that meet the consumers' needs in these countries. Once it reaches the EM, it develops knowledge about the characteristics and needs of local consumers (Govindarajan & Euchner, 2012). Likewise, the institutional environments of these countries, which are often full of gaps, also affect MNC subsidiaries operating in EMs (Liu, 2011). More corrupt governments and companies (Javorcik & Wei, 2009), deficient patent legal aspects (Delios & Heinsz, 2000), unconventional technological standards (London & Hart, 2004), and infrastructure (Moe & Rheingans, 2006) are just a few of the factors that hinder the operation of subsidiaries in these markets. As a result, the subsidiary needs to resort to local partners, who generally bear a wealth of knowledge regarding the needs and characteristics of the local consumer market (Kostova, Marano, & Tallman, 2016; London & Hart, 2004).

In view of this scenario, some studies (e.g., Peng, Wang, & Jiang, 2008) seek to understand how MNC subsidiaries develop innovations in EMs (Ernst et al., 2014). The authors argued that the quality of the relational embeddedness of developed MNC subsidiaries vis-à-vis local partners could work as an alternative to not only overcome the institutional barriers of these markets, but also to assist the process of development of local and global innovations through the access and acquisition of resources, knowledge, and learning that the partners can provide (Isaac et al., 2019). The gains, however, were not only on the side of the subsidiary. Local partners in the EMs also obtain gains, as their contact with developed MNC subsidiaries enables the acquisition of new knowledge, often related to R&D, which enables the development of innovations and competitive gains in the local market (Manning, 2008).

On the other hand, it is worth noting that the access to such information, resources, and knowledge is not easy (Inkpen & Tsang, 2005). This is due to the fact that the subsidiary is foreign, which means that local partners are often unaware of their reputation and modus operandi, adopting a more cautious approach when it comes to sharing knowledge and resources (Hitt, Dacin, Levitas, Arregle, & Borza, 2000).

Initially, the subsidiary is required to develop a relationship with local partners based on trust (Chang, Cheng, & Wu, 2012). Trust between companies is defined as the willingness from an enterprise to accept vulnerability based on positive expectations about another's intentions or behaviors from the other enterprise. Thus, trust is important, as it reduces uncertainties and the risk of opportunistic behavior on both sides. Studies (Nooteboom, 2013) suggest that relationships based on trust favor a greater exchange of knowledge, information, and resources on both sides. Thus, the subsidiary manages to have access to information and knowledge of local partners in relation to their consumers and the country's institutional environment, as well as leverage access to local resources (Peng et al., 2008). Likewise, it is important for the subsidiary to adapt its routines, practices, products, services, and processes to effectively deploy the resources it has access to and to meet the needs of local partners (Ernst et al., 2015; Prahalad, 2012).

The combination of these two factors (adaptation and trust) leads to the development of local innovations, essential for both the subsidiary and local partners in acquiring competitive advantage in their market (Isaac et al., 2019).

9.3 METHODOLOGY

The purpose of this chapter is to analyze how the quality of the relationship – relational embeddedness – that subsidiaries of multinationals from developed markets have with local partners influences the development of reverse innovations in EMs. Thus, in order to conduct this study, quantitative research was performed in Brazil. Located in South America, Brazil has a population of over 200 million people. It is the ninth-largest economy in the world, with an approximate GDP of US$2 trillion in 2018. It is also the Latin American country that received the most foreign direct investment (FDI) in 2017, totaling 47 percent of all investment in the region (US$75 billion). Nevertheless, Brazil is a country of extreme social inequality, paired with corruption and poor distribution of resources by politicians. Given this scenario, the country has a consumer market with low purchasing power, but in recent decades Brazil has increasingly changed its consumer profile, seeking to consume products and services through digital platforms, thanks to the recent expansion of digital inclusion. Finally, Brazil is one of the most innovative countries in Latin America, standing out in R&D, information, and communication technology (ICT), as well as knowledge absorption and creation (Dutta, Lanvin, & Wunsch-Vincent, 2019).

Moreover, data were collected in 2014, through surveys applied on an online platform, with follow-up by phone. In total, 113 foreign multinational companies operating in Brazil, which rank among the top 600 in terms of revenue generation in the market, were analyzed. The director of the innovation area of each of these companies was responsible for answering the survey. The questions of the survey were related to the quality of the relationship that the subsidiary has with the local partners (suppliers and customers), focusing on the degree of trust and adaptations that the partners make to meet the demands of the subsidiary, and on the development of reverse innovations made by the subsidiaries. Moreover, the questions were formed on a scale of one to five, in which one represented "totally disagree" and five signified "totally agree." The statistical technique used for data analysis was hierarchical clustering. This method consists of the hierarchical clustering of data, in which the groups are divided according to the similar characteristics that the members have (Yim & Ramdeen, 2015). The research results are presented below.

9.4 RESULTS

Initially, through the responses of the sources, an average was tallied regarding the relationship of foreign subsidiaries with local partners.

Table 9.1 *Clusters*

	Cluster	
	1	2
Total subsidiaries	32	81

Source: The authors.

The results indicate that there are two clusters of companies that behave differently (see Table 9.1).

On the one hand, group one, composed of thirty-two foreign subsidiaries, is only nominally included in local business networks; they therefore do not worry about developing a relationship based on trust and adaptations to meet the needs of local partners. This is evidenced through partners that, in general, were not concerned about developing a quality relationship with the foreign MNC subsidiary, but showed a greater concern about conducting economic and commercial transactions among the partners of the network (Granovetter, 1985). On the other hand, the second group is made up of eighty-one foreign multinationals that are more included in the network of local partners. We were able to see this due to the high degree of trust and adaptations that local partners made to meet the demands of the foreign MNC subsidiary.

The trust construct is based on work done by Hallin, Holm, and Sharma (2011) and Kingshott (2006) and is composed of the following responses: (a) in the last three years, our subsidiary has a strong relationship of trust with its main suppliers, (b) in the last three years, our subsidiary frequently communicates with its major suppliers to detect and obtain counterparty information, (c) in the last three years, our subsidiary has a strong relationship of trust with its main contractors, and (d) in the last three years, our subsidiary frequently communicates with its main contractors to detect information and obtain contract information.

Table 9.2 *Clusters and reverse innovation*

		Reverse innovation?		Total subsidiaries
		No	Yes	
Cluster	1	23	9	32
	2	34	47	81
Total		57	56	113

Source: The authors.

The adaptation construct is based on Andersson, Forsgren, and Holm (2001), Andersson, Holm, and Johanson (2005), and Najafi-Tavani, Zaefarian, Naudé, and Giroud (2015) and is composed of four items: (a) in the last three years, our subsidiary has made several product and process adaptations to suit its major suppliers; (b) in the last three years, our subsidiary has made several product and process adaptations to suit its major outsourcers; (c) in the last three years, our major suppliers have made various product and process adaptations to suit our subsidiary; and (d) in the last three years, our major outsourcers have made various adaptations to products and processes to suit our subsidiary.

The local innovation and reverse innovation construct is based on Iammarino, Padilla-Pérez, and von Tunzelmann (2008) and von Zedtwitz, Gassmann, and Boutellier (2004) and is composed of two items: (a) in the last three years, its subsidiary has often created new products and processes for the local market; and (b) in the last three years, its subsidiary has often created new products and processes for the global marketplace. In addition, we analyzed how the clusters behaved in relation to the development of reverse innovations. Based on the results (chi square <0.05), it was possible to see that most of the foreign subsidiaries that developed a quality relationship with the network of local partners developed reverse innovations. Table 9.2 shows the two clusters of foreign multinationals and the reverse innovations performed.

9.5 ANALYSIS OF RESULTS

The results reinforce the importance for foreign subsidiaries to show quality relationships with the local partners in EMs. Foreign subsidiaries that place less emphasis on developing a relationship based on social aspects, such as trust and adaptation, find it more difficult to develop local and reverse innovations. According to Verbeke and Yuan (2005), as well as Andersson and Forsgren (2000), subsidiaries that do not prioritize a business relationship with local partners tend to have a headquarters with greater control over their operations, making it difficult for the subsidiary to act with autonomy.

Conversely, foreign subsidiaries that seek to develop a quality relationship (e.g., based on trust and adaptation) with the partners of EMs end up developing more local innovations that can be replicated globally (Isaac et al., 2019). Overall, these innovations arise as the subsidiary bears access to unique resources available in these countries and as it meets the specific needs of these markets. In this sense, the role of the local partner is important. Through a relationship with the suppliers, distributors, and local customers, the subsidiary is able to understand the differentiated context of the EM, in addition to demonstrating access to tangible and intangible resources that the partners hold (Ferraris, 2014). However, for local partners to be able to effectively perform these actions, the subsidiary is required to develop a quality relationship with the local partners, making relational investments, translated into one that must first be based on trust (Hallin et al., 2011), so that adaptations and adjustments are subsequently made according to the needs of partners of the local network (Andersson, Forsgren, & Holm, 2002).

And yet, partnerships with subsidiaries of multinationals are very important, as they allow access to unique knowledge, as well as technological resources that often only the multinational enjoys, once it aggregates knowledge acquired by their companies' subsidiaries in different countries. This translates into competitive advantage gains from local partners who are able to primarily develop new products and processes, enabling cost savings and value addition.

9.6 CASES

It is worth noting some cases of reverse innovation accomplished by subsidiaries that developed their relationships based on trust and adaptation with local partners. With this in mind, we present in the following section three cases of reverse innovation in the Brazilian market, pointing out how the relationship between foreign subsidiaries and local partners was fundamental for the emergence of innovations that brought competitive advantages to all partners involved in the process.

9.6.1 Case 1: 3M Brazil and Natura

The first case is about 3M Brazil, a subsidiary of the US multinational 3M, which has been operating in Brazil since the mid-1940s. A role model in innovation, 3M Brazil has made several local innovations that have subsequently been replicated in developed markets. One example is the Multipack Solution (Solução Multipack 3M, n.d.) developed by the multinational jointly with its client and partner company, Natura. Natura is a Brazilian company in the cosmetics industry. It is the largest company in the sector in the Brazilian market (sales) and the fourth largest in the world in the business (Casanova et al., 2009), with annual revenues exceeding US$10 billion. In addition, Natura stands out for seeking to develop products that are sustainable. To that end, the company invests heavily in R&D, as well as open innovation with partners. In 2016, it ranked among the ten most innovative companies in the world (Forbes, 2016).

In addition, in 2013, 3M Brazil developed a Multipack aimed at the market of promotional soap packs. Aligning sustainability with efficiency, 3M Brazil developed a Multipack device that optimized the accommodation of the bar soap packs because there is no need for traditional secondary packaging, such as cartridges or plastic shrink wrap, reducing both energy and outsourcing costs when compared to the use of cartridges and equipment from outsourced companies, and greenhouse gas emissions due to the use of a potentially recyclable material. The partnership between 3M Brazil and Natura gave way to the exchange of knowledge and information from both parties, enabling the development of the device beyond cost, to the reduction of the emission of waste to the environment and greenhouse gases. This innovation led 3M Brazil to develop customized equipment that would fit niches other than bar soaps. Currently, the Multipack device is marketed by 3M worldwide, thanks to the various economic and sustainable gains that the equipment provides to the company that uses it.

Finally, we contend that some factors eventually influenced the emergence of innovations for 3M and Natura. While both companies are recognized worldwide for being innovative, it is clear that by partnering to develop a new product, both companies were able to exchange knowledge, information, and data, enabling the emergence of a product of greater efficiency and sustainability (an increasing consumer preference).

9.6.2 Case 2: Visa and Suplicy Cafés

The second case of reverse innovation is the result of the partnership between the Brazilian company Suplicy Cafés (n.d.) and Visa, the US multinational financial services company. Suplicy Cafés is a franchise of the food and beverage segment that sells specialty coffees. Envisioning the steady growth of the sector in recent years (in 2018 alone, it grew 18 percent), the company has established a cocreation partnership with Visa for the development of an application that facilitates the payment and withdrawal of the order by customers. To this end, Suplicy Cafés has made its consumer market knowledge available, while Visa has entered with its online payment and technology expertise. Before this, there was no development of a technological app that optimizes the entire buying process for customers, to preorder and pay via app; they previously could only pick up their order at the point of sale (Visa, 2018). Meanwhile, Suplicy Cafés needed to innovate its organizational model and marketing to cope with the new ordering process. These innovations prompted the franchise to capture a growing niche of consumers in Brazil: the millennials (Caputo, 2018). The app enabled Visa not only to develop a new service/product (app), but also to acquire new knowledge, which will assist in the replication of the product/service in other markets that show similar demands.

9.6.3   Case 3: Orisol and Artecola

The third case is the partnership between the Brazilian company Artecola (adhesives sector) and the Israeli multinational Orisol (footwear sector). Artecola is a Brazilian giant that operates in the segment of adhesives for industry and construction. The company ranks among the twenty most-internationalized Brazilian companies (Casanova & Kassun, 2013). Orisol is a multinational of Israeli origin that is currently associated with the Pou Chen Taiwan group. The MNC has been operating in the Brazilian market since 1995, with the Brazilian subsidiary as its second-largest plant. To date, the company is a world leader in the development of technologies for increasing productivity and quality in the footwear sector.

Binding soles to shoes has long been done manually, which results in high rates of material waste, in line with the large-scale use of solvent-based adhesives. Thus, in 2008, Artecola saw the opportunity to innovate by developing a new type of adhesive (powder) for binding soles to shoes. Throughout, the company identified that it would be necessary to develop not only the chemical component (powder adhesive) but also all the machinery for applying the adhesive. Accordingly, the company turned to Orisol. To Artecola's delighted surprise, Orisol already had a design of powder adhesive application machinery under development, even owning a machine prototype in Taiwan. Amid efforts to develop the machine and powder adhesive, Orisol eventually brought the machine from its Taiwanese plant into Artecola's laboratory located in Brazil. The partner companies still worked together for a few years, perfecting the product formulation and the machine system. As a result, the Brazilian company was able to develop a powder adhesive that had the proper characteristics (such as particle size) to be applied by the foreign partner's machine. With the development of the new adhesive (Artepowder), Artecola has made an exploration innovation, moving past product replication, to playing a leading role in the international adhesive market. In other words, its innovation has enabled Artecola to gain a sustainable competitive advantage as the only company to dominate this technology in the world market today. This is reflected in the company's revenues, which grew more than 50 percent in just three years (2013–2016). Today, Orisol has developed a brand new machine on the world market, being the only company to master this technology.

9.7 CONCLUSION

Operating in EMs has been a challenge for many developed market multinationals. Until a few decades ago, these markets were only seen as replicators of knowledge created in developed markets. Today they are considered dynamic markets, whose local companies have increasingly sought to break patterns imposed by developed economies, realizing innovations often then replicated globally (Govindarajan & Euchner, 2012). In this area, more and more studies (e.g., Khanna, Palepu, & Sinha, 2005; London & Hart, 2004) have pointed out that it is essential that MNC subsidiaries operating in EMs perform innovations to achieve sustainable, competitive advantages.

However, in many cases, the institutional voids, low purchasing power of the consumer market, and the lack of knowledge of the emerging context end up being obstacles for the subsidiary to innovate. In this study, we have argued that subsidiaries in EMs that invest in relationships with local partners tend to develop more local innovations, and later reverse innovations.

Local companies that establish relationships with subsidiaries of foreign multinationals show competitive gains when the subsidiary provides local businesses with knowledge and technologies that often such companies cannot access. The interaction between the local company and the subsidiary enables the emergence of innovations that reduce costs and add value to the product, service, or process developed. Accordingly, we emphasize that subsidiaries in EMs must develop quality relationships with local partners to enable the emergence of local innovations that will serve as a competitive advantage for both the subsidiary and local partners.

The results obtained converge with the expected. At first glance, we observed through cluster analysis that subsidiaries that have a quality relationship with local partners perform more local and reverse innovations than those that do not develop such a quality relationship. In addition, we present three cases of innovations that were possible, thanks to the partnership between a local Brazilian partner and the subsidiary.

In the first case, it was observed that the exchange of knowledge and information between the Brazilian company Natura and the multinational 3M Brazil led to the development of a new Multipack device, which provided not only a lower cost, but also a reduction in the emission of waste to the environment and greenhouse gases. The second case featured the cocreation of an app, made by Visa and Suplicy Cafés. In this case, it was necessary for Suplicy Cafés to make its consumer market knowledge available while Visa introduced the knowledge related to online payment and technology. The third case was the partnership between MNC Orisol and the Brazilian company Artecola. With the development of a new (powder) adhesive, Artecola partnered with Orisol so that a new machine could be developed to meet their needs.

We conclude by highlighting that more and more EMs are taking a leading role on the world stage. This is due to several innovations made to meet the different needs of these markets. These innovations not only translate into new products, processes, marketing, or organizational models, but also to cost reductions, sustainability gains, and value creation for competitive advantage.

REFERENCES

Agnihotri, A. (2014). Mass-media-based corporate reputation and firms' market valuation – Evidence from emerging markets. *Corporate Reputation Review, 17*(3), 206–218.

Akın, M. (2011). Predicting preferences of university students for prepaid vs post paid cell phone service plans. *Expert Systems with Applications, 38*(8), 9207–9210.

Andersson, U., & Forsgren, M. (2000). In search of centre of excellence: Network embeddedness and subsidiary roles in multinational corporations. *MIR: Management International Review*, 329–350.

Andersson, U., Forsgren, M., & Holm, U. (2001). Subsidiary embeddedness and competence development in MNCs: A multi-level analysis. *Organization Studies, 22*(6), 1013–1034.

(2002). The strategic impact of external networks: Subsidiary performance and competence development in the multinational corporation. *Strategic Management Journal, 23*(11), 979–996.

Andersson, U., Holm, D. B., & Johanson, M. (2005). Opportunities, relational embeddedness and network structure. In P. N. Ghauri, A. Hadjikhani, & J. Johanson (Eds.), *Managing opportunity development in business networks* (pp. 27–48). London: Palgrave Macmillan.

Birkinshaw, J., & Hood, N. (1998). Multinational subsidiary evolution: Capability and charter change in foreign-owned subsidiary companies. *Academy of Management Review, 23*(4), 773–795.

Buckley, P. J., & Tian, X. (2017). Internalization theory and the performance of emerging-market multinational enterprises. *International Business Review, 26*(5), 976–990.

Caputo, V. (2018). Suplicy Cafés lança app para "furar fila" que permitirá loja sem atendente. Retrieved September 2019, from https://epocanegocios.globo.com/Tecnologia/noticia/2018/07/suplicy-cafes-lanca-app-para-furar-fila-que-permitira-loja-sem-atendente.html.

Casanova, L., Golstein, A., Almeida, A., Fraser, M., Molina, R., Hoeber, H., & Arruda, C. (2009). *From multilatinas to global Latinas: The New Latin American multinationals*. Washington, DC: Inter-American Development Bank.

Casanova, L., & Kassum, J. (2013). Brazilian emerging multinationals: In search of a second wind. *SSRN Electronic Journal*, 10.2139/ssrn.2712662.

Chang, M. L., Cheng, C. F., & Wu, W. Y. (2012). How buyer-seller relationship quality influences adaptation and innovation by foreign MNCs' subsidiaries. *Industrial Marketing Management, 41*(7), 1047–1057.

Delios, A., & Henisz, W. I. (2000). Japanese firms' investment strategies in emerging economies. *Academy of Management Journal, 43*(3), 305–323.

Dutta, S., Lanvin, B., & Wunsch-Vincent, S. (Eds.). (2019). *Global innovation index 2019: Creating healthy lives – the future of medical innovation*. Ithaca, Fontainebleau, and Geneva: Cornell, INSEAD, and WIPO.

Ernst, H., Kahle, H. N., Dubiel, A., Prabhu, J., & Subramaniam, M. (2015). The antecedents and consequences of affordable value innovations for emerging markets. *Journal of Product Innovation Management, 32*(1), 65–79.

Ferraris, A. (2014). Rethinking the literature on "multiple embeddedness" and subsidiary-specific advantages. *Multinational Business Review, 22*(1), 15–33.

Forbes. (2016). www.forbes.com/#39f10c322254.

Govindarajan, V., & Euchner, J. (2012). Reverse innovation. *Research-Technology Management, 55*(6), 13–17.

Govindarajan, V., & Ramamurti, R. (2011). Reverse innovation, emerging markets, and global strategy. *Global Strategy Journal, 1*(3–4), 191–205.

(2014). Reverse innovation, emerging markets, and global strategy. *IEEE Engineering Management Review, 42*, 79–79.

Granovetter, M. (1985). Economic action and social structure: The problem of embeddedness. *American Journal of Sociology, 91*(3), 481–510.

Hallin, C., Holm, U., & Sharma, D. D. (2011). Embeddedness of innovation receivers in the multinational corporation: Effects on business performance. *International Business Review, 20*(3), 362–373.

Hitt, M. A., Dacin, M. T., Levitas, E., Arregle, J. L., & Borza, A. (2000). Partner selection in emerging and developed market contexts: Resource-based and organizational learning perspectives. *Academy of Management Journal, 43*(3), 449–467.

Huang, C., & Sharif, N. (2015). Global technology leadership: The case of China. *Science and Public Policy, 43*(1), 62–73.

Iammarino, S., Padilla-Pérez, R., & von Tunzelmann, N. (2008). Technological capabilities and global–local interactions: The electronics industry in two Mexican regions. *World Development, 36*(10), 1980–2003.

Immelt, J. R., Govindarajan, V., & Trimble, C. (2009). How GE is disrupting itself. *Harvard Business Review, 87*(10), 56–65.

Inkpen, A. C., & Tsang, E. W. (2005). Social capital, networks, and knowledge transfer. *Academy of Management Review, 30*(1), 146–165.

Isaac, V. R., Borini, F. M., Raziq, M. M., & Benito, G. R. (2019). From local to global innovation: The role of subsidiaries' external relational embeddedness in an emerging market. *International Business Review, 28*(4), 638–646.

Iyer, G. R., LaPlaca, P. J., & Sharma, A. (2006). Innovation and new product introductions in emerging markets: Strategic recommendations for the Indian market. *Industrial Marketing Management, 35*(3), 373–382.

Javorcik, B. S., & Wei, S. J. (2009). Corruption and cross-border investment in emerging markets: Firm-level evidence. *Journal of International Money and Finance, 28*(4), 605–624.

Khanna, T., Palepu, K. G., & Sinha, J. (2005). Strategies that fit emerging markets. *Harvard Business Review, 83*(6), 4–19.

Kingshott, R. P. (2006). The impact of psychological contracts upon trust and commitment within supplier–buyer relationships: A social exchange view. *Industrial Marketing Management, 35*(6), 724–739.

Kostova, T., & Marano, V. (2019). Institutional theory perspectives on emerging markets. In R. Grosse & K. E. Meyer (Eds.), *The Oxford Handbook of Management in Emerging Markets* (pp. 99–126). Oxford: Oxford University Press.

Kostova, T., Marano, V., & Tallman, S. (2016). Headquarters–subsidiary relationships in MNCs: Fifty years of evolving research. *Journal of World Business, 51*(1), 176–184.

Kumar, N., & Puranam, P. (2012). Frugal engineering: An emerging innovation paradigm. *Ivey Business Journal, 76*(2), 14–16.

Liu, Y. (2011). High-tech ventures' innovation and influences of institutional voids: A comparative study of two high-tech parks in China. *Journal of Chinese Entrepreneurship, 3*(2), 112–133.

London, T., & Hart, S. L. (2004). Reinventing strategies for emerging markets: Beyond the transnational model. *Journal of International Business Studies, 35*(5), 350–370.

Manning, S. (2008). Customizing clusters: On the role of Western multinational corporations in the formation of science and engineering clusters in emerging economies. *Economic Development Quarterly, 22*(4), 316–323.

Meyer, K. E., & Estrin, S. (2014). Local context and global strategy: Extending the integration responsiveness framework to subsidiary strategy. *Global Strategy Journal, 4*(1), 1–19.

Moe, C. L., & Rheingans, R. D. (2006). Global challenges in water, sanitation and health. *Journal of Water and Health, 4*(S1), 41–57.

Mudambi, R., Mudambi, S. M., & Navarra, P. (2007). Global innovation in MNCs: The effects of subsidiary self-determination and teamwork. *Journal of Product Innovation Management, 24*(5), 442–455.

Najafi-Tavani, Z., Zaefarian, G., Naudé, P., & Giroud, A. (2015). Reverse knowledge transfer and subsidiary power. *Industrial Marketing Management, 48*, 103–110.

Nooteboom, B. (2013). Trust and innovation. In R. Bachmann & A. Zaheer (Eds.), *Handbook of advances in trust research* (pp. 106–122). Cheltenham: Edward Elgar.

Peng, M. W., Wang, D. Y., & Jiang, Y. (2008). An institution-based view of international business strategy: A focus on emerging economies. *Journal of International Business Studies, 39*(5), 920–936.

Prabhu, G. N., & Gupta, S. (2014, July). Heuristics of frugal service innovations. In *Proceedings of PICMET'14 Conference: Portland International Center for Management of Engineering and Technology; Infrastructure and Service Integration* (pp. 3309–3312). Piscataway, NJ: IEEE.

Prabhu, J., & Jain, S. (2015). Innovation and entrepreneurship in India: Understanding jugaad. *Asia Pacific Journal of Management, 32*(4), 843–868.

Prahalad, C. K. (2012). Bottom of the pyramid as a source of breakthrough innovations. *Journal of Product Innovation Management, 29*(1), 6–12.

Radjou, N., & Prabhu, J. (2014). What frugal innovators do. *Harvard Business Review, 10*.

Radjou, N., Prabhu, J., & Ahuja, S. (2012). *Jugaad innovation: Think frugal, be flexible, generate breakthrough growth*. San Francisco, CA: Jossey-Bass.

Rottig, D. (2016). Institutions and emerging markets: Effects and implications for multinational corporations. *International Journal of Emerging Markets, 11*(1), 2–17.

Shan, J., & Khan, M. (2016). Implications of reverse innovation for socio-economic sustainability: A case study of Philips China. *Sustainability, 8*(6), 530.

Solução Multipack 3M. (n.d.). Retrieved September 2019, from www.3m.com/intl/br/mkt/3M_Magazine/2014/julho/revista/assets/basic-html/page2.html.

Soni, P., & Krishnan, R. T. (2014). Frugal innovation: Aligning theory, practice, and public policy. *Journal of Indian Business Research, 6*(1), 29–47.

Suplicy Cafés. (n.d.). Lança APP. Retrieved September 2019, from https://epocanegocios.globo.com/Tecnologia/noticia/2018/07/suplicy-cafes-lanca-app-para-furar-fila-que-permitira-loja-sem-atendente.html.

Talaga, P. (2010). Opinion: The future of pharmaceutical R&D: Somewhere between open and reverse innovation? *Future Medicinal Chemistry, 2*(9), 1399–1403.

Verbeke, A., & Yuan, W. (2005). Subsidiary autonomous activities in multinational enterprises: A transaction cost perspective. *MIR: Management International Review*, 31–52.

Vernon, R. (1966). International trade and international investment in the product cycle. *Quarterly Journal of Economics, 80*(2), 190–207.

(1979). The product cycle hypothesis in a new international environment. *Oxford Bulletin of Economics and Statistics, 41*(4), 255–267.

Visa. (2018). Suplicy Cafés lança solução de pedido e pagamento por aplicativo. Retrieved September 2019, from www.visa.com.br/sobre-a-visa/noticias-visa/nova-sala-de-imprensa/suplicy-cafes-especiais-lanca-solucao-de-pedido-e-pagamento-por-aplicativo.html.

von Zedtwitz, M., Corsi, S., Søberg, P. V., & Frega, R. (2015). A typology of reverse innovation. *Journal of Product Innovation Management, 32*(1), 12–28.

von Zedtwitz, M., Friesike, S., & Gassmann, O. (2014). Managing R&D and new product development. In M. Dodgson, D. M. Gann, & N. Phillips (Eds.), *The Oxford Handbook of Innovation Management* (pp. 530–547). Oxford: Oxford University Press.

von Zedtwitz, M., Gassmann, O., & Boutellier, R. (2004). Organizing global R&D: challenges and dilemmas. *Journal of International Management, 10*(1), 21–49.

Winterhalter, S., Zeschky, M. B., Neumann, L., & Gassmann, O. (2017). Business models for frugal innovation in emerging markets: The case of the medical device and laboratory equipment industry. *Technovation, 66*, 3–13.

Yim, O., & Ramdeen, K. T. (2015). Hierarchical cluster analysis: Comparison of three linkage measures and application to psychological data. *The Quantitative Methods for Psychology, 11*(1), 8–21.

Zeschky, M., Widenmayer, B., & Gassmann, O. (2011). Frugal innovation in emerging markets. *Research-Technology Management, 54*(4), 38–45.

10 Innovation Based on Value Co-creation through Employees at HCL Technologies

Anabella Davila

10.1 INTRODUCTION

In 2005, Vineet Nayar, former vice chairman and CEO of HCL Technologies, introduced his modern management philosophy, "Employees First, Customers Second" (EFCS), to the business world and provoked a revolution in the way companies create value for their customers. Nayar understood that it is the employees who create real value for the customers and transformed the entire organization to empower them and ensure their well-being. Thus, the EFCS philosophy changed the nature of engagement and relationship between the company and its employees, and between the employees and customers and other stakeholders. As a result, value is created in the interface between HCL Technologies employees and the customers that think collaboratively and partner with the company on innovation. Through EFCS, HCL Technologies focuses on empowerment and internal transformation rather than external innovation for value co-creation.

When the model of value co-creation was introduced by Prahalad and Ramaswamy (2004), they placed the customer as an active and informed actor at the center of the model. The main pillar of the co-creation model is to grant the customer an influential role in the value creation process. Although the value co-creation model transformed how companies define and create value for the customer, the model pays little attention to the employees that deliver the value that the customer buys.

The purpose of this chapter is to showcase the EFCS management philosophy at HCL Technologies, a global IT consulting company that originated in India, and the supporting management and human resource systems. The analysis of the case presents an emerging model of innovation based on value co-creation through employees. The model is supported by three pillars: employee well-being, employee empowerment, and innovation based on value co-creation. In each pillar, management and human resource practices offer support to the EFCS management philosophy. Implications for innovation management in other emerging market multinationals are discussed.

10.2   THE VALUE CO-CREATION FRAMEWORK

Prahalad and Ramaswamy (2004) challenged the traditional view of value creation that is centered in the company and assumes that customers are isolated, unaware, and passive. They observed that today customers are informed, connected, and active in a way that they desire to participate in the co-creation of value. The amount of information that is accessible to customers makes them not only more knowledgeable but also capable of developing a network of customers to challenge traditional industry practices. Moreover, companies now have active customers that offer unsolicited feedback and can influence other customers about a certain product or service. In other words, customers understand their influence and seek to interact with companies to co-create value. Therefore, the more informed the customers are about a certain product and service, the stronger their bargaining power.

For Prahalad and Ramaswamy (2004) customer–company interaction is one of the building blocks of the value co-creation model and where the customer experience and engagement occurs. In the past, businesses created products and services with value granted by the market. Within the value co-creation model, customers play a central role in the process of defining and creating value. In this regard, customers need to have significant and convincing engagement experiences to co-create value (Ramaswamy, 2008). Therefore, companies   must   provide   the   appropriate   infrastructure   to   allow individuals to co-construct and personalize their experiences. Thus, it is important to place the employee close to the customer to understand not only the requirements of the customer but also their desires and motivations.

The resulting model of value co-creation is composed of four building blocks: dialogue, access, risk assessment, and transparency (Prahalad & Ramaswamy, 2004). Dialogue is about continuous interaction between the company and the customer, and the latter expects a truly honest and transparent communication. Regarding access, the company should provide appropriate infrastructure so that the customer can actively participate. When customers are active coparticipants in the creation of value, they also share responsibility, which implies that they need to be fully informed about all the risks associated with the products or services. In terms of transparency, companies that implement the value co-creation model require an honest treatment of information and transparent policies and structures of prices, costs, and profit margins to inform the customer (Prahalad & Ramaswamy, 2004).

The aforesaid key building blocks that sustain the value co-creation model require an entire reconfiguration of the company in terms of its innovation capabilities. Moreover, it is necessary to create new competencies and business practices to implement such a model (Ramaswamy, 2008). In particular, for some firms, implementing the value co-creation model has been translated into a sustainable competitive advantage (Ramaswamy, 2008).

Although the value co-creation model has attracted considerable research attention, current literature reviews have identified three theoretical perspectives that have contributed most to this body of knowledge: service science, innovation and technology management, and marketing and consumer research. Most of what we know about value co-creation has emerged from the service management literature and, to a lesser extent, from other related disciplines (Gummesson, Mele, Polese, Galvagno, & Dalli, 2014). This indicates that the value co-creation model places the customer at the center, and this might unbalance the organization–customer relationship needed for interaction, limiting its applicability. The call is to understand the complementary role of a variety of organizational actors involved in the value creation process (Saarijärvi, Kannan, & Kuusela, 2013). This is the case of organizational employees that research tends to overlook.

Therefore, this chapter extends current research on value co-creation through understanding how an IT service provider builds its management and human resource systems to grant its employees the leading role in the co-creation process. The following sections present the methods for the case study and the case of HCL Technologies.

10.3 METHODS

Annual reports have been used to trace human resource accounting (HRA) disclosures in major Indian companies to understand how HR practices contribute to the company's profits (Kaur, Raman, & Singhania, 2014). Because it is voluntary for companies to disclose HRA, the analysis not only shows the lack of an industry standard for reporting such practices, making the information unusable for auditing, but also reveals that few companies reported HRA in their annual reports (Kaur et al., 2014).

The case of sustainability reports is quite different for Indian companies such as HCL Technologies. HCL Technologies started to publish sustainability reports in 2011 based on the Global Reporting Initiative (GRI) guidelines and standards. The GRI is a well-known and legitimate independent international organization (US origin) that has pioneered sustainability reporting since 1997 (GRI, 2019a). Since its foundation, the GRI has focused on how businesses and governments worldwide communicate their impact on sustainability issues such as climate change, human rights, and social well-being. The GRI developed a reporting framework to recommend how companies could communicate their progress on sustainability issues focusing on practices. Through the Global Sustainability Standards Board, in 2016 the GRI launched the first global standards for sustainability reporting, a major accomplishment since the previous sets of guidelines for reporting. The GRI Standards are a reliable reference for policymakers and regulators and have been used for research extensively in the realm of social issues (e.g., Marquis & Qian, 2013) and in human resource management (e.g., Vuontisjärvi, 2006), among other research interests. The GRI website shows that 93 percent of the world's largest 250 corporations report on their sustainability progress according to the GRI Standards.

All standards require a management approach disclosure toward a specific issue. It is a narrative explanation of how an organization manages the particular material topic, its impacts, and stakeholders' expectations and interests. In terms of employees, the standards require that the company report on issues related to employment, labor and management relations, training and education, diversity and equal opportunity, nondiscrimination, child labor, and human rights assessment (GRI, 2019b). Thus, sustainability reports based on GRI standards provide a reliable source of data for further analysis toward the aim of this chapter.

The HCL Technologies sustainability reports analyzed in this chapter, as shown in Table 10.1, range from 2011 to 2016. Although HCL Technologies has published six sustainability reports, the company also included information according to the Business Responsibility Report (BRR) mandated by the guidelines of the Securities and Exchange Board of India (SEBI). In 2015, the requirement of publishing a BRR was made part of the Listing Regulations for the top 500 listed companies according to their market capitalization (National Stock Exchange of India [NSE], 2019). The BRR requires companies to describe initiatives from an environmental, social, and governance perspective, in the format as specified by SEBI (NSE, 2019). The purpose of having a standard format for reporting in India is to help the companies to publish their BRR in a structured manner (NSE, 2019). In this way, the information could serve for comparative analysis as it provides the same parameters for all the companies (NSE, 2019). Further, this approach to BRR also offers reliable

Table 10.1 *Inventory of the HCL Technologies sustainability and annual reports*

Year	Type of the report	Number of employees	Length of the report (pages)	GRI Guidelines	GRI Adherence level	Other guidelines or standards	Global compact	External assurance
2011	Sustainability	77,046	58	GRI G3.1	A+	ISO 26000;[a] AA 1000[b]	√	Det Norske Veritas AS
2012	Sustainability	88,817[c]	86	GRI G3.1	A+	ISO 26000; AA 1000	√	Det Norske Veritas AS
2013	Sustainability	90,574[d]	114	GRI G3.1	Undeclared	ISO 26000; AA 1000; Business Responsibility Report (BRR)[e]	√	KPMG

Table 10.1 (cont.)

Year	Type of the report	Number of employees	Length of the report (pages)	GRI Guidelines	GRI Adherence level	Other guidelines or standards	Global compact	External assurance
2014	Sustainability	91,691[f]	81	Citing GRI	None	Business Responsibility Report (BRR)	√	NA[g]
2015	Sustainability	106,107	115	GRI G3.1	Undeclared	Business Responsibility Report (BRR)	√	KPMG
2016	Sustainability	103,394	164	GRI G4	In accordance – Core	Business Responsibility Report (BRR)	√	KPMG
2017	Annual	115,973	284	Non-GRI	–	Business Responsibility Report (BRR)	NA	NA
2018	Annual	127,742[h]	268	Non-GRI	–	Business Responsibility Report (BRR)	NA	NA

| 2019 | Annual | 137,965 | 297 | Non-GRI | – | Business Responsibility Report (BRR) | NA | NA | NA |

[a] ISO 26000 provides guidance, rather than requirements, on how businesses and organizations can operate in a socially responsible way.

[b] AA1000 is a series of accountability principles-based standards and frameworks to demonstrate leadership and performance in accountability, responsibility, and sustainability.

[c] Includes 4,498 contract staff (staff for noncore activities such as operations, maintenance, security, and housekeeping services).

[d] Includes 5,069 contract staff.

[e] This report is mandated by the Securities Exchange Board of India (SEBI).

[f] Includes 7,783 contract staff.

[g] NA: Not Available

[h] Includes 7,661 contract staff.

Source: Elaborated by the author.

information for research. Thus, from 2017 to 2019, HCL Technologies published the annual report including the BRR; there is no public evidence if they published the sustainability report during that time. See Table 10.1 for the analyzed inventory of the HCL Technologies Sustainability and Annual Reports.

Finally, the case study analysis also included HCL Technologies' former CEO Nayar's public speeches, news reports, and research papers related to EFCS and HCL Technologies' management and human resource practices.

10.4 HCL TECHNOLOGIES

HCL Group, with headquarters in Noida, India, was founded in 1976 by six entrepreneurs in the computer hardware manufacturing sector in India. With a clear orientation toward the creation of new knowledge and with a strong belief in engineering and research and development, HCL started to develop its innovation capabilities through the introduction of its own microprocessor to the Indian market. Eventually, the company evolved into a more comprehensive software services organization. HCL Technologies is a division of the HCL Group, and it was originally incorporated in 1991, becoming one of the largest software development infrastructures in India.

In 1998, HCL Technologies started to target the markets of Europe and Asia Pacific. Later, in 1999, the company expanded to America through a wholly owned subsidiary. With a great heritage of knowledge in web-based technologies, the company developed the capability to work with a wide variety of computing platforms and created a strategic methodology of consulting services. By 2000, Goldman Sachs rated Infosys Technologies and HCL Technologies as market outperformers and among the best-quality names in the industry. Since the beginning of the century, the company has developed many opportunities to collaborate with different partners through joint ventures or alliances seeking to complement their technological capabilities with global experts. In 2008, it started to cover the Latin American region with Global Development Centers, and in 2012, it entered the South African market.

At the time of writing this chapter (2019), HCL Technologies said on its webpage that it aims to help global enterprises reimagine their businesses for the digital age. The company seeks to solve complex business problems for its clients through a variety of web and IT platforms. The company operates in 44 countries with over 147,000 employees from 140 nationalities and has consolidated revenues of US$9.3 billion, for the 12 months ending September 30, 2019 (HCL Technologies, 2019). In 2009, HCL Technologies was selected as the Most Admired Knowledge Enterprises (MAKE) Winner. Since then, the company has started to receive numerous global accomplishment awards.

10.4.1   The EFCS Management Philosophy

In 2010, Nayar reflected on his EFCS management philosophy that was introduced in 2005. He stated that organizational trust increased because the company granted employees more power and control over their work, and several initiatives were installed in the organization. For example, information began to flow and was shared among all the employees, making processes transparent, creating new mechanisms for answering questions, and allowing employees to request solutions from middle management. Employees were given the opportunity to decide on the resolutions and in the long run, innovation increased. For Nayar (2010), EFCS is a means to satisfy the needs of value-creating employees, and those employees were the ones to receive the corresponding resources over the non-value-creating employees.

To dissect the EFCS, the case turns to the three major pillars that the evidence points out: employee well-being, employee empowerment, and innovation based on value co-creation.

10.4.2   Employee Well-Being

The EFCS is strongly based on employee well-being. In this vein, feedback takes a primary role in developing a good working environment. The company reports various forms of feedback forums to institutionalize several communication channels through which employees can voice their options, report on grievances, and obtain support from enabling functions to resolve day-to-day problems. For example, there is a secure hotline designed to provide all employees with a work environment that is secure, fair, and free from harassment as per Indian and global regulations.

The company's human resources practices have a strong orientation toward human development. For example, the Diversity and Inclusive (D&I) Strategy derives from an equal opportunities policy, and it sustains three areas: recruiting employees from diverse backgrounds; engaging and enabling employees from diverse backgrounds, and community participation.

In terms of recruitment, the company seeks a diverse talent pool that comprises women; different nationalities, cultures, and work experiences; and people with disabilities. In particular, in India, the company recruits employees from smaller cities to facilitate inclusive growth. Additionally, in 2012 the company launched a leadership program targeting potential Gen Z employees at university-level campuses across India. The program invites students to present innovative ideas to company challenges.

To engage employees from diverse backgrounds, the company reports that it employs various initiatives. For example, there are affinity networks and Employee First Councils. The goal of the networks is to ensure that diverse perspectives are included in all business operations. There are programs that include development conferences and social media for improving awareness of both HCL Technologies and the ecosystem in which the company operates. Along with this initiative, team leaders at the company are equipped with skills to work across the globe in virtual teams. For the company, community participation means that open conversations with all employees will promote sensitivity on any matter, be it gender, ability, or generational gap. Additionally, there is an African Diaspora Employee Council and a Latino Employee

Alliance for Diversity that seek to facilitate the professional development of employees.

When recruiting internally, there are equal opportunities for competent employees to take up new roles through internal job postings. The postings are available in a career portal, and the company ensures that eligible employees undergo a transparent selection process for placement. All eligible employees receive performance and career development feedback from their managers.

The company reports a strong orientation to gender inclusion due to the CEO's commitment to this issue. Thus, the reports highlight the affinity network where women connect and advance by peer networking, advocate a gender-neutral work environment and suggest policies to the company (e.g., BlogHer platform). Moreover, a series of interactive programs are led by women at HCL Technologies and are facilitated by life coaches, business leaders, and members of academia.

Another important topic presented in the reports is how the company facilitates work–life balance. Policies and support systems include flexible hours, telecommuting, and extended maternity, paternity, and adoption leave. In some locations, daycare facilities for children are also provided, and there are family connect programs, which bring families on-site. There are also communication channels for employees to make suggestions on how to improve their work–life balance. In particular, there is a life-coach program that provides support to employees and their families on their work–life challenges.

Employees' health and safety is also an important part of the employee well-being approach. It covers ergonomics, stress management, nutrition, and other well-being matters. Health campaigns are promoted by the company and by the internal women councils for expecting mothers. There are also campaigns around cancer detection, and all these campaigns are extended to the employees' families. To ensure a safe commute, the company provides special services for employees that work in shifts or late hours. Women traveling are also provided with escorts and guards for their safety. In general, employees are educated on the safety guidelines across Indian operations.

10.4.3 Employee Empowerment

The dimension of empowering employees is based on a culture of trust and transparency. A key way to promote employees' empowerment, the company reports, is to focus on the internal transformation. The 2012 Sustainability Report introduced the EFCS 2.0 Phase that represented a shift in which employees took the lead for transformation. It is about the individual taking charge – proactively creating space for growth, expansion, and enrichment. To this end, several programs are launched every year toward building a culture of trust seeking to enable the transformation process. To start, employees are provided with information on the culture, code of conduct, channels for feedback, health and safety norms, and other employee benefit programs.

A singular structure provides opportunities for employees to come together and work toward a common project they are passionate about. It is the Employee Passion Indicative Count (EPIC) on which Nayar spoke on the interview featured above.

These are also Employee First Councils. The councils are a structure for the employees and run by employees. Every year, elections are conducted, and the members of various councils are elected to represent employees that will strategize and implement transformational activities. By 2011, there were more than 2,500 active employees participating in 5,670 projects. Some examples of these projects are Community Service, Talent Council, Sports Council, Wellness Council, Green Warriors, and Women Council.

An Employee First Governance Council portal offers feedback to department heads on policies, programs, and any organization support activities. Additionally, there is a Listen Hour platform, where employees have an opportunity to have face-to-face interaction with their business partners.

The EFCS management philosophy is also based on the premise that there is a need to invert the organizational pyramid. As stated above, Nayar opened the 360-degree performance review process to all employees who a manager might influence. This initiative made it so that anyone who gave a manager feedback could have access to the results of that manager's 360 review. According to the 2011 report, this practice has increased participation, empowered employees, and made the 360 review a development tool, not an evaluative one.

The company continuously monitors annual employee experience through a survey seeking their overall experience on various aspects like organization culture, employee first orientation, work environment, and performance management. A Smart Service Desk system was designed to help employees obtain answers and resolve problems between frontline employees and functional managers. Any employee facing a problem at work can open a trouble ticket, as Nayar stated in an interview, which will be assigned to a manager responsible for its resolution. The company also supports a whistleblower policy to maintain compliance with ethical and legal standards across the company, and all employees are informed about this policy.

There are the U&I Conversations through which any employee can write to the CEO to ask questions ranging from strategy to individual issues. Further, the CEO also offers his blog (www .vineetnayar.com) to interact with employees. The blog is updated regularly and features posts on leadership theories, management practices, and developments in innovation and technology.

There is an annual event, originally called "Directions" in 2012 but renamed "Runway" in 2015, in which the CEO and the leadership team share the vision and strategy of HCL Technologies with all employees. The format of this event is described in the 2012 report as an interactive session where employees can engage directly with management.

The pillar of employee empowerment leads to innovation and customer service improvements. Thus, the company launched a platform for employees to showcase their innovations, and once the innovation is selected through a series of criteria, the employees are encouraged to discuss them with the CEO and management team. There is also a Values Portal that receives ideas from employees on how to improve customer service and a biannual Best Practice Conference, which seeks to adopt best practices across the organization to better serve the customer.

The company classifies employee development programs in technical and soft skills. Training and development make extensive use of online platforms, and some of this training includes knowledge and skills certifications. The leadership development programs aim to equip the next generation of leaders with the required experience to excel in a new managerial position or in a global assignment.

Regarding rewards and recognitions, the company states that it is important to acknowledge empowered employees when they deliver their best. Several initiatives ensure these employees' efforts do not go unrecognized. For example, XtraMiles is a reward and recognition platform that encourages employees to "go the extra mile." What is unique about this platform is that the encouragement comes from colleagues, friends, or peers of the employee. The "02 League of the Extraordinary" recognizes the achievements of the "Difference Makers," who are employees that have received an outstanding rating in their performance reviews for two consecutive years. The "O Infinity League" is made up of superachievers who have received top ratings for two or more consecutive years. The O Infinity recognition includes a ceremony where employees are recognized for their commitment to excellence in the presence of their colleagues and family members. Additionally, there is a practice in which managers reward employees "on the spot" for contributions that are noteworthy. The program is named the HCL SPOT Award.

10.4.4   Innovation through Value Co-creation

This section starts with a thorough statement on how the EFCS management philosophy impacted the structure of the organization and promoted innovation:

> Our Employee First philosophy dismantles the traditional
> hierarchy in the system, empowers employees and builds a

collaborative environment which facilitates new ideas, and possibilities of new ways to solve customer problems. Instead of a few leaders with all the answers, it is a much larger participation through innovation and problem solving leading to significantly larger unlocking of individual potential. Premkumar, S. Senior–Corporate Vice President & President–Financial Services & Healthcare

(HCL, 2011, p. 8)

The concept of empowerment at HCL Technologies goes beyond creating participatory platforms for employees. Shami Khorana, Senior Corporate Vice President, states in the 2011 report that it is about inverting the organizational pyramid and creating a culture of trust and transparency.

Once HCL Technologies understood that value is created within the interface between employees and customers, the philosophy of placing employees first and customers second sought to activate the "value zone." In other words, frontline employees interact with customers and create real value for them, and management supports these efforts. Under this structure, employees are leading decision making.

In 2013, HCL Technologies through new leadership introduced the concept of "Ideapreneur," which refers to employees that collaborate with customers to lead innovation. This approach is based on the EFCS management philosophy taken a step further. The ideapreneurship approach seeks to create an entrepreneurial atmosphere in which employees take the lead in finding solutions and ideas and then lead them to completion.

In 2014, HCL Technologies introduced the initiative of Relationship Beyond the Contract (RBTC) with a trademarked seal that will represent the commitment of the employees with all the stakeholders, including customers. The seal of RBTC ensures that the value the company adds is distinctive. The commitment to take the relationship beyond the contract seeks to ensure that HCL

Technologies understands needs deeply and fosters a transparent dialogue to accomplishing desired outcomes with the partner stakeholders.

The company states that the management philosophy of "Employees First" seeks to create value for the customer through the interface between the employees and customers. Thus, the company declares that it would do everything to enable employees to create the highest possible value. The EFCS is not about making employees happy or comfortable. It is not about employee satisfaction. Those stages in the employees' work experience are passive and do not produce change or innovation. For the company, EFCS is about employee engagement. An employee that is alert to produce value will be better engaged.

10.5 DISCUSSION AND CONCLUSIONS

HCL Technologies is a well-known company because of its management philosophy that supports value co-creation. The company introduced the EFCS approach, and it has inverted the organization pyramid by putting management at the bottom and ensuring that all actions of the company would enable employees to deliver value to the customers. The EFCS and the inverted organization pyramid are supported by three pillars: employee well-being, employee empowerment, and innovation based on value co-creation. Each pillar is made up of specific management and human resource practices (see Figure 10.1 for the identification of such practices in each pillar and the emerging model). The employee well-being pillar is supported by several initiatives, platforms, and programs that help employees share, interact, and exchange ideas and experiences. Employees are empowered because they are the ones that need to make decisions to increase customer value. Innovation is based on the premise that value is co-created through the interaction of the employee and customer.

Along with the EFCS management approach, HCL Technologies has attracted important academic research. In a recent

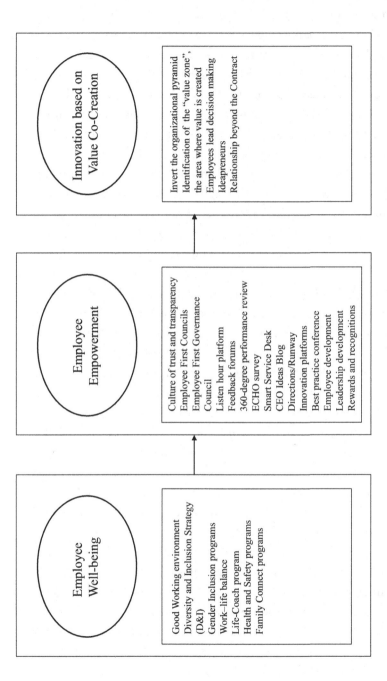

FIGURE 10.1 Inductive model of innovation based on value co-creation through employees

Source: Elaborated by the author.

Symposium of the Journal of Business Ethics on the perspective of aesthetic on human dignity, the editors argued that although dignity is central in humanizing management in organizations, we still are far from understanding its nature (Pless, Maak, & Harris, 2017). The editors concluded that it is the younger organizations that tend to embrace the full concept of treating their workforce like human beings. HCL Technologies was used as an example of hope for human-ism and organizational life because of Nayar's management philoso-phy of EFCS. For the editors, organizational values, vision, and practices in HCL Technologies and in other humanistic companies (e.g., Zappos, USA; Good-Ark, China; Atlassian, Australia) are framed with the management philosophy that employees are human beings with needs and desires (Pless et al., 2017). Thus, the analysis of these companies allows us to advance our understanding of human dignity at work.

Several studies focus on the management and human resource system that shed light on the uniqueness of the EFCS approach. When recruiting externally, a study of major IT companies in India, includ-ing HCL Technologies, showed that the preferred and most cost-effective channels for recruitment included job site/portals, social media like LinkedIn, Facebook, and campus recruitment. The study concluded that a multichannel approach is essential to cover the market for candidates in this industrial sector (Sinha & Thaly, 2013).

A recent study on organizing principles and management systems included interviews with top managers at HCL Technologies that explained how the company experienced a major transformation due to the EFCS management philosophy introduced by Nayar (Birkinshaw, Foss, & Lindenberg, 2014). Before Nayar became the CEO, the company was a second-tier player in the com-petitive market of IT services. Thus, his first challenge was to con-vince all employees that the company was underperforming and in a need for a major change (Birkinshaw et al., 2014). In order to imple-ment the EFCS management philosophy, Nayar implemented a series of specific initiatives to help employees offer a better service to the customers. The study reports how Nayar challenged managers to make their 360-degree surveys public to make them more responsible in front of their employees. One initiative was the "service ticket" program that was designed for employees that needed a managerial response to an uncomfortable issue. The employee could issue a ticket for the matter, and the corresponding manager must offer a solution. The initiative included indicators of tickets opened and the speed of managerial response. For Nayar, these initiatives contributed to the well-being of employees (Birkinshaw et al., 2014). In this vein, the company surveyed employees to identify their passion at work and assign them to a position where they can make use of that passion. The survey was called Employee Passion Indicator Count (EPIC), and the main issues resolved through this survey were collaboration and client service (Birkinshaw et al., 2014). The study further reports that by 2012, HCL Technologies reached an annual growth rate of 24 percent with turnover rates lower than in competitor companies.

A study of the performance appraisal process across nineteen companies in the IT industry in West Bengal, India, including HCL Technologies, shows the effect on employee motivation of the appraisal practice. In general, employees objected to the practice of a forced-choice method that requires the rater to choose from a set of alternative descriptors some subset that is most characteristic of the ratee. For some employees, there were positive outcomes of the appraisal process because it provides growth, recognition, innovation reinforcement, and empowerment. The study also revealed that sometimes there was a gap between performance management policy and its implementation. However, companies showed an active involvement of the line-managers in the appraisal process and a reduction of the intervention of the HR department in this practice (Sanyal & Biswas, 2014).

This case offers an analysis of the management and human resource practices informed by HCL Technologies that show a distinctive characteristic of the EFCS management philosophy. The case

contributes to the value co-creation model by highlighting the importance of the role of the employee in this model. Employees must
actively participate in the value co-creation model. To implement
the value co-creation model, customers and employees need to have
an equal dynamic and central role. It is important that the organization understands the importance of the employees' well-being, the
empowerment employees need for leading innovation, and that
innovation is based on value co-creation in the interface of employees
and customer interactions.

REFERENCES

Birkinshaw, J., Foss, N. J., & Lindenberg, S. (2014). Combining purpose with profits. *MIT Sloan Management Review, 55*(3), 49–56.

GRI. (2019a). About us. Retrieved October 8, 2019, from www.globalreporting.org/information/about-gri/Pages/default.aspx.

(2019b). GRI and sustainability reporting. Retrieved October 8, 2019, from www.globalreporting.org/information/sustainability-reporting/Pages/gri-standards.aspx.

Gummesson, E., Mele, C., Polese, F., Galvagno, M., & Dalli, D. (2014). Theory of value co-creation: A systematic literature review. *Managing Service Quality, 24*(6), 643–683.

HCL Technologies. (2011). Sustainability report 2011. Retrieved October 2019, from https://s3-us-west-2.amazonaws.com/ungc-production/attachments/14411/original/sustainability-report.pdf?1331284444.

HCL Technologies. (2019). HCL Technologies Worldwide, Overview. Retrieved November 10, 2019, from www.HCLTechnologiesech.com/geo-presence#hcl_worldwide.

Kaur, S., Raman, A. V., & Singhania, M. (2014). Human resource accounting disclosure practices in Indian companies. *Vision, 18*(3), 217–235.

Marquis, C., & Qian, C. (2013). Corporate social responsibility reporting in China: Symbol or substance? *Organization Science, 25*(1), 127–148.

National Stock Exchange of India Ltd (NSE). (2019). Business Responsibility Reporting in India: Disclosures and Practices. Retrieved October 9, 2019, from www.nseindia.com/education/content/reports/brr_report.htm.

Nayar, V. (2010, June 18). Employees first, customers second. *The Financial Times Limited.* Retrieved August 25, 2019, from www.ft.com/content/d2d23ab6-7ac2-11df-8549-00144feabdc0.

Pless, N. M., Maak, T., & Harris, H. (2017). Art, ethics and the promotion of human dignity. *Journal of Business Ethics, 144*(2), 223–232.

Prahalad, C. K., & Ramaswamy, V. (2004). Co-creating unique value with customers. *Strategy & Leadership, 32*(3), 4–9.

Ramaswamy, V. (2008). Co-creating value through customers' experiences: The Nike case. *Strategy & Leadership, 36*(5), 9–14.

Saarijärvi, H., Kannan, P. K., & Kuusela, H. (2013). Value co-creation: Theoretical approaches and practical implications. *European Business Review, 25*(1), 6–19.

Sanyal, M. K., & Biswas, S. B. (2014). Employee motivation from performance appraisal implications: Test of a theory in the software industry in West Bengal (India). *Procedia Economics and Finance, 11*, 182–196.

Sinha, V., & Thaly, P. (2013). A review on changing trend of recruitment practice to enhance the quality of hiring in global organizations. *Management: Journal of Contemporary Management Issues, 18*(2), 141–156.

Vuontisjärvi, T. (2006). Corporate social reporting in the European context and human resource disclosures: An analysis of Finnish companies. *Journal of Business Ethics, 69*(4), 331–354.

11 Frugal Innovation in Brazilian Multinationals

Itiel Moraes, Felipe Borini, and Moacir de Miranda Oliveira Jr.

11.1 INTRODUCTION

Multinationals from emerging markets (EMs), especially in Latin America, made a splash on the international scene in the 1970s, stimulated by a context of import substitution. In early 2000, a second wave of internationalization set in around the capture of resources and knowledge. Today, emerging market multinational companies (EMNCs) compete for global leadership through catch-up strategies based on imitation, acquisition, and reverse transference. And yet, while this strategy seizes knowledge and capabilities, innovation is still the engine of competitive advantage and differentiation.

As noted in Chapter 1, the challenges and opportunities generated in EMs drove multinationals to develop innovation mechanisms. A variety of terms have been coined accordingly (low cost, jugaad, shanzhai, reverse innovation, bottom of the pyramid innovation, etc.). Among these, frugal innovation is of note beyond its potential for simply cutting costs. Frugal innovation is an innovation strategy to develop products as good as those already on the market and with a value proposition that is often more sustainable but at a lower cost thanks to internal and open processes with partner organizations.

In this chapter, we suggest that the competitive advantage of EMNCs is achieved through an innovation-aligned catch-up strategy. We report on cases of Brazilian MNCs that placed frugal innovation at the center of this alignment. We conclude by building on the findings and their implications.

11.2 THEORETICAL BACKGROUND

11.2.1 *Frugal Innovation*

Out of the growth in emerging economies, millions have been lifted out of poverty and made gains in purchasing power, giving way to new market segments (Zeschky, Winterhalter, & Gassmann, 2014a). These include the middle class, the "good enough" market, and the low-income market (Gadiesh, Leung, & Vestring, 2007; Govindarajan & Trimble, 2012; Prahalad & Mashelkar, 2010). Consumers in these new segments require innovations and business models that are best suited to their institutional context and economic surplus (Prahalad & Hart, 2002; Prahalad & Mashelkar, 2010).

Some terminologies and concepts thus emerged in an attempt to demonstrate and highlight how innovation takes place in the context of emerging economies (Bernardes, Borini, Rossetto, & Pereira, 2018; von Zedtwitz, Corsi, Søberg, & Frega, 2015; Zeschky et al., 2014a). The types addressed are structurally different with respect to their original motivation, mechanisms, proposition, and value offering. While some solutions may emerge from remodeling an existing product or process, others may be brand new (Zeschky et al., 2014a). This conceptual variety can be summarized as frugal innovation (von Zedtwitz et al., 2015).

At first, the concern was to save resources and minimize environmental impacts so that companies could create robust products with cost advantages and other benefits (*The Economist*, 2010). Here, frugal innovation targeted middle- and low-income segments, especially in EMs. However, studies suggest that bottom-of-the-pyramid consumers, despite income constraints, sought products that did not carry the stigma of poorer markets (Tiwari, Luise, & Katharina, 2016).

Frugal innovators have thus taken advantage of the opportunities offered by digital transformation to significantly reduce costs and improve quality (Kalogerakis, Fischer, & Tiwari, 2017). Frugal innovators deliver high technology at low cost by reducing and leveraging

R&D resources. They bet on alternative technologies and take advantage of open systems architectures (Ray & Ray, 2010).

Put differently, today's assumed frugal innovation value proposition considers not only the low-cost requirements of products, but also innovation capability that manifests the novel, with a sustainable component (Tiwari & Herstatt, 2014; Zeschky, Winterhalter, & Gassmann, 2014b). Based on capabilities, companies yield differential environmental impact, reducing the cost of acquisition, production, and distribution (Hossain, 2017; Rosca, Arnold, & Bendul, 2016).

To encourage this understanding of frugal innovation, companies: (a) focus on core product functionality, meeting or exceeding quality standards; (b) embed a sustainable component in its value chain that results in responsible innovations; (c) intensify the pursuit of cost reduction, including through (d) open innovation networks that reduce the cost of product development and innovation risk (Kalogerakis et al., 2017; Tiwari & Bergmann, 2018; Tiwari et al., 2016).

In this way, frugal innovation is an innovation strategy to develop products as good as those already on the market and with a value proposition that is often more sustainable, but at a lower cost thanks to internal and open processes with partner organizations. The main features of this definition can be summarized as follows:

a) Cost: Frugal innovation aims not only at a price reduction for the consumer but also at economic efficiency in the supply chain (Tiwari & Herstatt, 2012d). Companies must express innovation capacity in cost, so that they can offer cheaper products with other features, maximizing the value paid by the customer (Agnihotri, 2015);

b) Open Innovation: Collaboration with external partners at all stages of the often geographically different industry innovation process for improved quality (Tiwari & Herstatt, 2012a, 2012c);

c) Sustainability Oriented Innovation: Contributions to company performance with increasing pressure for sustainable resource use (Brem & Ivens, 2013).

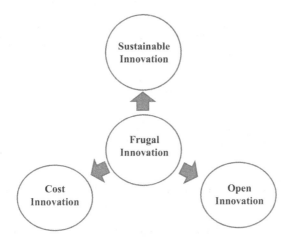

FIGURE 11.1 Strategic dimensions of frugal innovation adopted in the chapter
Source: The authors, based on development.

Frugal products and services can be produced for any consumer group, facilitating accessibility and opening new market segments, regardless of the specific point in the price criterion (Tiwari et al., 2016). Figure 11.1 demonstrates key dimensions. Their application indicates how EMNCs (in this case, Brazilian multinationals) deploy frugal innovation to consolidate competitiveness.

11.2.2 Aligning the Catch-up Strategy with Frugal Innovation

As is well known, the environment surrounding EMNCs is marked by challenges in infrastructure, social development, legal protection, corruption, health, and education (Cuervo-Cazurra, 2007; Meyer, Mudambi, & Narula, 2011), with implications at headquarters and subsidiaries (Cuervo-Cazurra, 2012). While such adversities are evident, they can serve as a competitive advantage by becoming a source of innovation (Prahalad & Mashelkar, 2010; Simula, Hossain, & Halme, 2015). This is the case with frugal innovation. Due to the conditions of their home country, EMNCs are already inclined to

FIGURE 11.2 Strategies of leading global EMNCs
Source: The authors, based on development.

make products as good as those already available in the market and sustainably – i.e., frugal innovations managed at low costs.

The local context of the country shapes and directs the capabilities and competencies to innovate (Murtha & Lenway, 1994; Porter, 1990). In the past, EMNCs suffered a competitive disadvantage with regard to more robust innovation activities (Kothari, Kotabe, & Murphy, 2013; Luo & Tung, 2007). However, EMNCs are currently turning the international market into a springboard for overcoming such disadvantages (Luo & Tung, 2007). They have been aggressively investing in learning and assimilating technologies from multinationals in developed countries (Kothari et al., 2013) to build a high level of absorptive capacity of competences (Lane & Lubatkin, 1998; Mudambi & Navarra, 2004).

This confluence of factors and strategy has ushered in new forms of innovation related to business models, and new capabilities for new frugally oriented products and services (Bhatti, 2012; Bound & Thornton, 2012; Prahalad & Mashelkar, 2010; Simula et al., 2015). With the knowledge and technological capabilities acquired abroad, EMNCs give new life to products and services through frugal innovation. This is exported in the alignment in Figure 11.2, as EMNCs move from a competitive parity stage to a position of competitive advantage.

11.3 METHOD

This study used two research approaches: The first was to conduct case studies using secondary information to verify how the catch-up strategy and frugal combination has been used by the leading Brazilian EMNCs in their markets. The second approach was quantitative in nature, through a survey with the multinational headquarters, in order to verify if the Brazilian MNCs bear this frugal orientation.

The research drew on a survey with intersectional design, conducted in 2015. The questionnaire consisted of twelve questions with five-point Likert scales. The research participants were CEOs, directors, and foreign trade managers. The universe of survey participants was identified through the following data sources: analysis of the project base GINEBRA-Business Management for the Internationalization of Brazilian Companies, secondary database (BCG Global Challengers and Fortune), and business magazines (*PIB* and *Epoca*). In this phase, 210 researchable multinational matrices were identified, to be contacted via email and telephone to participate in the survey. Responses were obtained from 62 headquarters of Brazilian multinationals, about 24 percent of the universe. Factor analysis was used in the review of the results.

The measurement proposal offered with this research is based on the notion that frugal innovation is a multidimensional construct (Rayees, 2017). The dimensions offered by Silva (2018) and used in this research not only encompass the main characteristics of products considered to be frugal but also cause or lead to manifestations of this innovation type (Silva, 2018). Given this, three dimensions were used: cost, open, and sustainability-oriented innovation.

As reported, each dimension is made up of four items measured on a five-point Likert scale. Before measuring the dimensions, the reliability of the questionnaire scales was estimated using Cronbach's Alpha test. All constructs had higher than acceptable indices (0.6). Table 11A.1 in the Appendix shows the operationalization of the measured constructs used in the survey.

11.4   CASES OF FRUGAL INNOVATION IN
BRAZILIAN COMPANIES

As reported, the potential of frugal innovation is not restricted to middle- and lower-class products, as its innovations are not simply cheaper versions of existing technologies or products; they use the appropriate technology available to develop products that meet customer expectations of performance. Thus, the result is not a product aimed at low-income clients per se, as the innovations aim to create a sense of the new, albeit with fewer resources.

This section presents some cases of multinationals that are using frugal innovation to develop new products/services that meet customer expectations of performance at a lower cost. In each of the dimensions of frugal innovation presented, examples of how some Brazilian companies are establishing their competitiveness will be demonstrated.

11.4.1   Natura: Frugal Innovation Pulled by Sustainable Innovation Strategy

Natura & Co is a cosmetic multinational, currently formed by four iconic brands: Natura, AESOP, The Body Shop, and the newly acquired AVON. The company seeks to differentiate itself by generating positive economic, social, and environmental impact with products of natural origin. The Natura brand celebrated its fiftieth anniversary in 2019. Founded in Brazil, it also operates in Argentina, Chile, Colombia, the United States, France, Mexico, and Peru. It has a network of 1.7 million consultants, 45 stores, products in 3,800 pharmacies and is the leading online platform of the Brazilian cosmetics market (Natura, 2016a, 2018).

In 2019, with the acquisition of AVON, the holding company became the fourth-largest beauty group in the world, with annual revenues exceeding US$10 billion. The multinational's brands are aligned with the purpose of promoting, through beauty and social relations, a better way of living and doing business. In the Brazilian market, the company leads in direct sales of cosmetics (Natura, 2018).

The multinational is present in 73 countries and on all continents, with over 18,000 employees. The company has come to benefit from access to knowledge originating from already acquired brands. The company has created networks of excellence, collaboration centers on three strategic themes – digital, sustainability, and retail – to share best practices and build joint actions among group executives around the world (Natura, 2018).

Natura, while strongly focused on sustainability, shows how the combination of catch-up strategy and frugal innovation built a leading global eMNCs. Its strategy begins with the technological catch-up of the world's major cosmetic industries but adapted to the use of local biodiversity. This orientation involves three parts: (a) sustainability for the best product, (b) an inclusive approach to cost-cutting innovation and (c) collaborative development.

a) Sustainability for the best product

The company combined cosmetics, technology, and biodiversity in its innovation. Natura was not held hostage to the catch-up of the major technologies in the cosmetic industry. Thus, Natura was recognized for its ability to use sustainability as a basis for innovation in the cosmetics market, opting for a differential based on Brazilian ecological and cultural biodiversity. The result was a revolution within the company's technology platform and the value of Natura's products. As a result, the brand acquired expression within and beyond Brazil. The company was the first publicly traded company in the world to become a B Corp Company in 2014. Natura is now in the top twenty of the world's most sustainable companies, according to Corporate Knights Global 100 ranking (Natura, 2016a, 2018).

b) An inclusive approach to innovation

To maximize value for customers, shareholders, and society – and significantly reduce the use of financial and natural resources in emerging countries – Natura turned to frugal innovation (Rosca, Bendul, & Arnold, 2015). The company uses the mantle of sustainability to achieve cost efficiency throughout the value chain. Given this, some goals are set: to reduce carbon emissions by 33 percent by 2013, increase production by decreasing water and energy consumption, and use biodiversity as a technological platform (Sebrae, 2016), among others.

c) Collaborative development

Natura has linked sustainable design with traditional and scientific knowledge for product development in an open innovation model – involving a network of national and global partners (Santos, Bianchi, & Borini, 2018). It currently develops projects in a global open innovation network of more than 200 partners, working with suppliers to reduce the impact of products by developing the use chain for recycled materials such as PET and glass (Natura, 2016a, 2018).

Building on the partnerships, in 2012, Natura launched the first cosmetic product with "green polyethylene" packaging in the Brazilian market. The objective was to reduce the environmental impact caused by this type of product. The material, also called "green plastic," was produced from sugarcane, a renewable source of plant energy, unlike ordinary plastic derived from petroleum. This innovation was a partnership between Natura and Braskem petrochemical (Bonatelli, 2010).

The company also built an eco-park for innovation in 2014. It is a technological center in the middle of the Amazon rainforest that researches assets and conducts business in the region, establishing social and environmental sustainability as its mission. This center provides space for partners committed to sustainable development principles, working in an integrated manner and reusing inputs from neighboring companies.

Finally, the company also launched the Applied Research Center on Human Behavior and Welfare in 2016. The center is made up of a network of thirty psychology and neuroscience researchers from the University of São Paulo (USP), the Federal University of São Paulo (Unifesp), and the Mackenzie Presbyterian University (UPM)

(Natura, 2016b). The aim is to structure a solid foundation of knowledge around human well-being from the integration of different areas such as neuroscience, positive psychology, social psychology, and applied health and human sciences. This center is the largest scientific base in the country focused on welfare research and aims to boost knowledge in the area through multidisciplinary research (Natura, 2016b).

11.4.2   Nubank: Frugal Innovation Pulled by High Technology Catch-up Strategy

Nubank is a Brazilian start-up that operates in the financial services segment. It was founded in 2013 with the objective of offering low-cost financial services in an economy where more than 55 million consumers still do not have a bank account. The complexity of the process to open an account was the trigger for the creation of Nubank. The principles of the combination of catch-up and frugal innovation materialized in (a) low-cost orientation to the essentials, (b) the social inclusion of the excluded, and (c) a culture of collaborative innovation.

a) Low-cost orientation to the essentials

Nubank uses technology and design to offer free financial services, including transfers, bill payments, and savings. Many of Nubank's customers are using credit cards or banks for the first time. The company is focused on easy-to-understand products and services, such as credit cards that can be 100 percent managed by a mobile app. The company does not charge annual fees or service fees, which are common in traditional banks in Brazil. This is possible due to the fact that the company does not depend on a physical structure like a traditional bank. In this way, Nubank reduces costs so as to not charge annuity and fees to its customers.

b) In favor of social inclusion of those without a bank account

In Brazil, consumers found it hard to find traditional companies and options without high interest rates. Nubank became that option by way of its customer-friendly technology, bringing safe and simple solutions for users to solve and control their accounts from their smartphones. The company accepts its customers based on the algorithms and the profile of the interested party. As a result, consumers with a good payment history receive lower interest rates. In 2018, Nubank reached a milestone of 5 million credit card customers and 2.7 million account holders. By the following year, the company announced 12 million users across the country, across its products, including credit cards, bank accounts, personal loans, and investments. The company is the most valuable start-up in Latin America and the first Brazilian start-up to approach the US$10 billion mark without going public. That same year, the company began its internationalization process in Mexico and Argentina, with the launch of an international credit card for the Mexican consumer free of annual fees.

c) A culture of collaborative innovation

In 2019, Nubank was the most innovative company in Latin America (Gagne, 2019). Much of this result lies in the maintenance of a start-up culture despite Nubank's breakneck growth. The culture of innovation promotes interactions of professionals from different areas and nationalities, such as the three founders.

Altogether Nubank's workforce includes more than twenty-five nationalities and 30 percent LGBT employees (Desiderio, 2019). The company culture emphasizes agility and rapid feedback. However, beyond internal innovation, companies cannot be closed to new ideas from outside of the company. For instance, The Xpeer Xperience day invites company executives to work in the customer service operation once a year. This experiment serves as a learning experience for executives as they, too, listen to customers and collaboratively think through new product and service strategies.

11.5 SURVEY OF BRAZILIAN MULTINATIONALS

As mentioned earlier, sixty-two multinationals agreed to participate in the survey. Table 11.3 shows the statistical profile of the economic sectors of the participating multinationals. It is found that 51.6 percent of the sample belongs to the manufacturing sector. In Brazil, this sector includes activities related to industrial production, which involves companies that transform raw materials into products for end consumers or other businesses. Companies that transform steel into machines, sugar cane into biofuels, and manufacture consumer goods such as automobiles and clothing are some examples of participants in this sector.

The second-most-significant sector in the sample was that of information and communication, with a 14.5 percent share, which includes the combination of industrial, commercial, and services activities that capture electronically, transmit and disseminate data and information, and sell equipment and products intrinsically linked to these processes. The other sectors with significant representation in the sample were professional and scientific activities at 9.7 percent and extractive industry at 6.5 percent. Table 11.1 presents the general

Table 11.1 *General profile of companies*

Sectors	n	%
Water, sewage, waste management, and decontamination activities	1	1.6
Administrative activities and complementary services	1	1.6
Financial, insurance, and related services activities	2	3.2
Professional, scientific, and technical activities	6	9.7
Trade; repair of motor vehicles and motorcycles	1	1.6
Construction	3	4.8
Education	1	1.6
Electricity and gas	1	1.6
Manufacturing industry	32	51.6
Extractive industries	4	6.5
Information and communication	9	14.5
Transportation, storage, and postal services	1	1.6
Total	**62**	**100**

Source: The authors, based on development.

profile of the sample, in relation to the activities that the companies perform.

To verify the adopted dimensional structure, we resorted to the use of factor analysis. The factorial analysis performed highlighted the three dimensions of the research from the twelve variables used (see Appendix). This technique organized and adjusted the twelve variables according to each previously defined construct. The quality of this adjustment was guaranteed by the KMO–Kaiser Meyer Olkim test index, above the recommended (greater than 0.5). Two other statistical tests were used to ensure that the variables in the survey belonged to the constructs. The first was the Bartlett statistical test, which was significant, and the second was the percentage of total variance explained above 60 percent.

Considering the cost innovation dimension, the factorial analysis confirmed that this construct is formed by the four variables. The analysis of Table 11.2 reveals that the cost innovation strategy most used by the Brazilian multinationals participating in the sample is related to the variable Cost 2. This reinforces that in the development of frugal products, some factors stand out as low-cost production, simpler, cheaper, low-design materials that focus on less sophisticated features, which in turn represent cost innovation (Zeschky et al., 2014a). Thus, when developing frugal innovation, Brazilian multinationals express their ability to innovate in cost by offering cheaper products with other features, maximizing the amount paid by the customer.

Considering the dimension innovation in cost, the sectors that stand out most in this kind of frugal strategy are the manufacturing and information and communication sectors. Among the ten multinationals that had the best score in this dimension, six belong to the manufacturing sector, and two belong to the information and communication sector. Regarding the presence and prominence of the information and communication sector in this dimension, such a result reinforces that low cost does not mean the use of low technologies in the development of new frugal products (Ojha, 2014) as frugal

Table 11.2 *Description of the cost innovation dimension*

Variables	N		Mean	Mode
	Valid	Absent		
Cost 1: The company has invested heavily in innovation to reduce the costs of processes and products/services.	62	0	4.13	4
Cost 2: The company has invested heavily in innovation to reduce costs while increasing and creating functionality in products/services that are valued by target customers.	61	1	4.20	5
Cost 3: The company has invested heavily in innovation to develop cheaper and less-complex products.	61	1	3.84	4
Cost 4: The company has invested heavily in innovation to optimize/increase the scale of production, through the recombination of existing products and processes.	61	1	4.11	4

Source: The authors, based on development.

innovation recombines the technologies of existing components in new ways, creating a change in the price of the package/performance without further investment in the development of new core technologies (Ray & Ray, 2011).

Regarding the sustainable innovation dimension, when analyzing Table 11.3, it appears that the variable Sustain 4 obtained the highest average of this dimension. This reveals that in the development phase of new products and processes, Brazilian multinationals seek to meet the requirements of stakeholders prior to market launch. It also stands out in this dimension that multinationals stimulate the search for sustainable innovation among their employees.

Table 11.3 *Description of the variables of the sustainable innovation dimension*

| | *N* | | | |
Variables	Valid	Absent	Average	Mode
Sustain 1: The company seeks innovations that are sustainable, even if they bring lower returns than traditional products available in the market.	62	0	3.55	4
Sustain 2: In the development of new products and processes, the company seeks better management of natural resources and use of raw materials from sustainable sources (triple bottom line and/or carbon footprint).	62	0	3.77	4
Sustain 3: The company encourages innovation focused on sustainability and challenges its employees to find innovative solutions for new processes and products based on this philosophy.	62	0	3.95	4
Sustain 4: The company seeks to know the perceptions and concerns of different stakeholders (customers, employees, suppliers, trade unions, NGOs) in the product development process.	62	0	4.11	4

Source: The authors, based on development.

The companies' interest in increasing the measurement level of their performance is evident, particularly in relation to social impacts associated with the life cycle of their products and services, as well as the companies' relationship with its stakeholders when they innovate in a sustainable way (Jay & Gerard, 2015). The multinationals with

Table 11.4 *Description of variables of the dimension open innovation*

	N			
Variables	Valid	Absent	Average	Mode
Open 1: The company has mechanisms of integration with suppliers that allow the participation of those in the improvement of new processes and products	61	1	3.62	4
Open 2: The innovation in processes or products has already benefited in some way with collaborative agreements with universities or research centers	61	1	3.54	5
Open 3: Technologies, products, or services that belong to the company domain are accessible and able to be enhanced with customer collaboration.	61	1	3.90	4
Open 4: The company has been engaged in innovation activities such as participation in research consortium and technology transfer agreements with other companies in the sector (strategic alliances and/or joint ventures).	61	1	3.39	4

Source: The authors, based on development.

the highest averages were Moura, Fibria, Nexxera, BR Foods, and Boticário Accumulators.

The third dimension confirmed by exploratory factor analysis concerns open innovation. When analyzing the variables in Table 11.4, it can be seen that individual form was the one that presented the lowest means in its variables. Table 11.4 also reveals that the Open 3 variable was the item with the highest average response, highlighting the interactive character of the open innovation process of Brazilian multinationals.

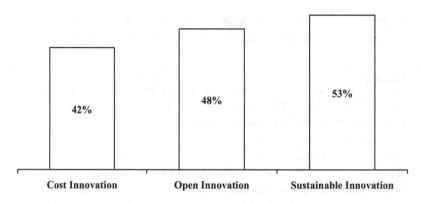

FIGURE 11.3 Dimensions of frugal in Brazilian multinationals
Source: The authors, based on development.

Data from this dimension reinforces the fact that frugal innovations can come from partnerships among companies considered global leaders, entrepreneurs, and local businesses. Often these partners are part of the global chain of world-class companies or part of a global open innovation system crowdsource type (Adriaens, Lange, & Zielinski, 2013). Considering the activities of the most representative economic sectors, the sectors worth noting include manufacturing and information and communication. Companies that stand out include Stefanini IT Solutions, Tupy, Movile, Positive, Fibria, and Embraer.

In this chapter, the factor analysis was initially used to confirm the dimensions of the theoretical framework from the twelve established variables. Moreover, the use of this technique enabled the identification of the most representative multinationals in each factor. By analyzing Figure 11.3, a reasonable balance of multinational participation in each dimension can be seen. Considering the sustainable innovation dimension, 53 percent of Brazilian multinationals are engaged in this type of innovation. Considering open innovation, 48 percent of research multinationals would adopt this model.

Finally, the innovation in cost dimension came to be practiced by 42 percent of the sample.

However, in conceptualizing frugal innovation as the culmination of the three dimensions, the result stands as a warning for EMNCs in Brazil in terms of the catch-up and frugal dual strategies because only 40 percent of the sample brought the three dimensions together at the same time. In other words, more than half of Brazilian EMNCs must move toward a frugal orientation if they wish to position themselves according to the approach we propose here.

11.6 CONCLUSION

The growing participation of emerging economies on the international scene and the prominence of their respective multinationals have drawn the world's attention to the types of innovation that occur in these markets and what models these companies should employ to innovate and compete. This is now more urgent as these multinationals rapidly internationalize and adopt innovative strategies that challenge traditional players in their markets.

From this context, new internationalization theories have attempted to explain this success from the perspective that these multinationals succeed by internationalizing themselves due to access and exploitation of resources available in other markets, especially developed countries. While seeking and possessing these resources is relevant to EMNC strategy, it does not guarantee a competitive advantage for these companies.

Emerging multinationals must still convert this knowledge into new capabilities that the international market does not yet know. Thus, this chapter shows that a strategic orientation based on a catch-up strategy aligned with frugal innovation comprises one of the solutions for the development of competitive advantages and the constitution of global leadership for EMNCs.

APPENDIX

Table 11A.1 *Constructs and variables used in the research*

Research constructs	Code
Cost innovation	
The company has invested heavily in innovation to reduce the costs of processes and products/services and increase productivity.	COST1
The company has invested heavily in innovation to reduce costs while increasing and creating new functionalities of products/services that are valued by target customers.	COST2
The company has invested heavily in innovation to develop cheaper and less complex products.	COST3
The company has invested heavily in innovation to optimize and increase the scale of production, through the recombination of existing products and processes.	COST4
Open innovation	
The company has mechanisms of integration with suppliers that allow the participation of those in the improvement of new processes and products.	OPEN1
The innovation in processes or products has already benefited in some way with collaborative agreements with universities or research centers.	OPEN2
Technologies, products, or services that are the company's domain are accessible and able to be enhanced with customer collaboration.	OPEN3
The company has engaged in innovation activities such as participation in research consortium and technology transfer agreements with other companies in the sector (strategic alliances and/or joint ventures).	OPEN4
Sustainable innovation	
The company seeks for sustainable innovations, even if they bring lower returns than traditional products available in the market.	SUSTIN1
In developing new products and processes, the company seeks better management of natural resources and the use of raw materials from sustainable sources (*triple bottom line* and/or carbon footprint).	SUSTIN2

Table 11A.1 (*cont.*)

Research constructs	Code
The company encourages sustainability-focused innovation and challenges its employees to find innovative solutions to new processes and products based on this philosophy.	SUSTIN3
The company seeks to understand the perceptions and concerns of different *stakeholders* (customers, employees, suppliers, trade unions, NGOs) in the product development process.	SUSTIN4

Source: Silva, 2018.

REFERENCES

Adriaens, P., Lange, D. de, & Zielinski, S. (2013). Reverse innovation for the new mobility (No. 1193). Michigan USA. Retrieved September 2019, from http://deepblue.lib.umich.edu/bitstream/handle/2027.42/100250/102968.pdf?sequence=1.

Agnihotri, A. (2015). Low-cost innovation in emerging markets. *Journal of Strategic Marketing, 23*(5), 399–411. Retrieved September 2019, from https://doi.org/10.1080/0965254X.2014.970215.

Alerigi, A. (2019). Weg desenvolve aeronave elétrica com a Embraer. O ESTADO DE S. PAULO, p. 37. Retrieved September 2019, from https://acervo.estadao.com.br.

ANPEI. (2009). Inovação precisa mirar sustentabilidade. Retrieved September 2019, from http://anpei.org.br/inovacao-precisa-mirar-sustentabilidade/.

Awate, S., Larsen, M. M., & Mudambi, R. (2012). EMNE catch-up strategies in the wind turbine industry: Is there a trade-off between output and innovation capabilities? *Global Strategy Journal, 2*(3), 205–223. Retrieved September 2019, from https://doi.org/10.1111/j.2042-5805.2012.01034.x.

Bedaque, A., Jr. (2006). Alianças Estratégicas e Inovação de Valor: Estudo de Caso dos Jatos Regionais 170/190 da Embraer. 2006. 151 f. Dissertação (Mestrado em Administração) – Pontifícia Universidade Católica de São Paulo, São Paulo, 2006.

Banerjee, P. M. (2013). The "Frugal" in frugal innovation. In A. Brehm & E. Viardot (Eds.), *Evolution of innovation management: Trends in an international context* (pp. 290–310). London: Palgrave Macmillan. https://doi.org/10.1057/9781137299994.

Bernardes, R. C., Borini, F. M., Rossetto, D. E., & Pereira, R. M. (Eds.). (2018). *Inovação em mercados emergentes.* São Paulo: Senac.

Bhatti, Y. A. (2012). What is Frugal, What is Innovation? Towards a Theory of Frugal Innovation. *SSRN Electronic Journal,* 1–45. https://doi.org/10.2139/ssrn .2005910.

Bonatelli, C. (2010). Natura começará a usar 'plástico verde' nas embalagens em outubro. Retrieved September 2019, from https://economia.estadao.com.br/ noticias/negocios,natura-comecara-a-usar-plastico-verde-nas-embalagens-emoutubro,30406e.

Bordo, T. A. (2018). Briga de Gigantes. Retrieved September 2019, from https:// todosabordo.blogosfera.uol.com.br/2018/07/14/embraer-e195-e2-airbus-a220-100-comparativo/.

Borini, F. M., Oliveira Jr., M. de M., Silveira, F. F., & Concer, R. de O. (2012). The reverse transfer of innovation of foreign subsidiaries of Brazilian multi nationals. *European Management Journal, 30*(3), 219–231. https://doi.org/10 .1016/j.emj.2012.03.012.

Bound, K., & Thornton, I. (2012). *Our frugal future: Lessons from India's innovation system.* London: Nesta. Retrieved September 2019, from www.nesta.org .uk/sites/default/files/our_frugal_future.pdf.

Brem, A., & Ivens, B. (2013). Do frugal and reverse innovation foster sustainability? Introduction of a conceptual framework. *Journal of Technology Management for Growing Economies, 4*(2), 31–50. Retrieved September 2019, from http:// papers.ssrn.com/sol3/papers.cfm?abstract_id=2436833.

Cuervo-Cazurra, A. (2007). Sequence of value-added activities in the multinationalization of developing country firms. *Journal of International Management, 13*(3), 258–277. https://doi.org/10.1016/j.intman.2007.05.009.

(2012). Extending theory by analyzing developing country multinational companies: Solving the Goldilocks debate. *Global Strategy Journal, 2*(3), 153–167. https://doi.org/10.1111/j.2042-5805.2012.01039.x.

Cuervo-Cazurra, A., & Genc, M. (2008). Transforming disadvantages into advantages: Developing-country MNEs in the least developed countries. *Journal of International Business Studies, 39*(6), 957–979. https://doi.org/10.1057/ palgrave.jibs.8400390.

Desidério, M. (2019). A chave de inovação do Nubank: bermudas, 25 nacionalidades e 30% LGBT. Retrieved September 2019, from https://exame.abril.com.br/nego cios/a-chave-de-inovacao-do-nubank-bermudas-25-nacionalidades-e-30-lgbt/.

Economist, The. (2010, April 17). The world turned upside down. A special report on innovation in emerging markets. *The Economist.* https://doi.org/10.1093/ nq/s3-VIII.203.419.

Embraer. (2019). Demonstrações financeiras 2018.

Exame. (2019). Mergulhamos na nova Embraer, que se reinventa após venda à Boeing. Retrieved September 2019, from https://exame.abril.com.br/negocios/mergulhamos-na-nova-embraer-que-se-reinventa-apos-venda-a-boeing/.

Gadiesh, O., Leung, P., & Vestring, T. (2007, September). The Battle for China's good-enough market. *Harvard Business Review*, 80–89.

Gagne, Y. (2019). Banking in Brazil is hard. Here's how Nubank is changing that. *Fast Company*. Retrieved September 2019, from www.fastcompany.com/90299054/nubank-most-innovative-companies-2019.

Govindarajan, V., & Trimble, C. (2012). *Reverse innovation: Create far from home, win everywhere*. Boston: Harvard Business Review Press.

Guillén, M. F., & García-Canal, E. (2009). The American Model of the Multinational Firm and the "New" Multinationals From Emerging Economies. Academy of Management Perspectives, *23*(2), 23–35. https://doi.org/10.5465/AMP.2009.39985538.

Hossain, M. (2017, September). Mapping the frugal innovation phenomenon. *Technology in Society*, *51*, 199–208. https://doi.org/10.1016/j.techsoc.2017.09.006.

Jay, J., & Gerard, M. (2015). Accelerating the theory and practice of sustainability-oriented innovation. MIT Sloan School Working Paper 5148-15.

Kalogerakis, K., Fischer, L., & Tiwari, R. (2017). A comparison of German and Indian innovation pathways in the auto component industry (No. 100). Working Paper TUHH. Hamburg. Retrieved September 2019, from https://explore.openaire.eu/search/publication?articleId=od_____718::f1d10f8c335877a190a452d7888011ef.

Kothari, T., Kotabe, M., & Murphy, P. (2013). Rules of the game for emerging market multinational companies from China and India. *Journal of International Management*, *19*(3), 276–299. https://doi.org/10.1016/j.intman.2013.03.007.

Lane, P. J., & Lubatkin, M. (1998). Relative absorptive capacity and interorganizational learning. *Strategic Management Journal*, *19*(5), 461–477.

Le Bas, C. (2016). Frugal innovation, sustainable innovation, reverse innovation: why do they look alike? Why are they different? *Journal of Innovation Economics*, *21*(3), 9. https://doi.org/10.3917/jie.021.0009.

Luo, Y., & Tung, R. L. (2007). International expansion of emerging market enterprises: A springboard perspective. *Journal of International Business Studies*, *38*(4), 481–498. https://doi.org/10.1057/palgrave.jibs.8400275.

Mathews, J. A. (2006). Dragon multinationals: New players in 21st century globalization. *Asia Pacific Journal of Management*, *23*(1), 5–27. https://doi.org/10.1007/s10490-006-6113-0.

Meyer, K. E., Mudambi, R., & Narula, R. (2011). Multinational enterprises and local contexts: The opportunities and challenges of multiple embeddedness. *Journal of Management Studies, 48*(2), 235–252. https://doi.org/10.1111/j.1467-6486.2010.00968.x.

Mudambi, R., & Navarra, P. (2004). Is knowledge power? Knowledge flows, subsidiary power and rent-seeking within MNCs. *Journal of International Business Studies, 35*(5), 385–406. https://doi.org/10.1057/palgrave.jibs.8400093.

Murtha, T. P., & Lenway, S. A. (1994). Country capabilities and the strategic state: How national political institutions affect multinational corporations' strategies. *Strategic Management Journal, 15*(1994), 113–129.

Narula, B. R., & Nguyen, Q. T. K. (2011). Emerging country MNEs and the role of home countries: Separating fact from irrational expectations. MERIT Working Papers 2011-021, United Nations University – Maastricht Economic and Social Research Institute on Innovation and Technology (MERIT).

Natura. (2016a). Relatório de Administração 2016. São Paulo. Retrieved September 2019, from www.natura.com.br.

(2016b). Tudo sobre o nosso Centro de Pesquisa Aplicada em Bem-Estar. Retrieved October 20, 2019, from www.naturacampus.com.br/cs/naturacampus/post/2016-07/centro-bem-estar-perguntas-respostas.

(2018). Relatório de Administração 2018. São Paulo. Retrieved September 2019, from www.natura.com.br.

(2019). Ecoparque: onde nosso núcleo de inovação atua em prol da sociobiodiversidade. Retrieved September 2019, from www.natura.com.br/blog/sustentabilidade/ecoparque-onde-nosso-nucleo-de-inovacao-atua-em-prol-da-sociobiodiversidade.

Ojha, A. K. (2014). MNCs in India: Focus on frugal innovation. *Journal of Indian Business Research, 6*(1), 4–28. https://doi.org/10.1108/JIBR-12-2012-0123.

Oksanen, K., & Hautamäki, A. (2015, October). Sustainable innovation: A competitive advantage for innovation ecosystems sustainable innovation. *Technology Innovation Management Review, 5*(10), 24–30. Retrieved September 2019, from http://timreview.ca/article/934.

Piza, D. (2001, April 8). Embraer consolida globalização. O ESTADO DE S. PAULO, p. 25. Retrieved September 2019, from https://acervo.estadao.com.br/.

Porter, M. (1990). *The competitive advantage of nations.* London: Macmillan.

Prahalad, C. K., & Hart, S. L. (2002). The fortune at the bottom of the pyramid. *Strategy+Business Magazine,* first quarter, *26,* 1–16. https://doi.org/10.2139/ssrn.914518.

Prahalad, C. K., & Mashelkar, R. A. (2010). Innovation's holy grail. *Harvard Business Review, 88*(7–8).

Ramamurti, R. (2012). Commentaries: What is really different about emerging market multinationals? *Global Strategy Journal, 2*(1), 41–47. https://doi.org/ 10.1111/j.2042-5805.2011.01025.x.

Ray, P. K., & Ray, S. (2010). Resource-constrained innovation for emerging economies: The case of the Indian telecommunications industry. *IEEE Transactions on Engineering Management, 57*(1), 144–156. https://doi.org/10 .1109/TEM.2009.2033044.

Ray, S., & Ray, P. K. (2011). Product innovation for the peoples car in an emerging economy. *Technovation, 31*(5–6), 216–227. https://doi.org/10.1016/j .technovation.2011.01.004.

Rayees, F. (2017). A conceptual model of frugal innovation: Is environmental munificence a missing link? *International Journal of Innovation Science, 9*(4), 320–334. https://doi.org/10.1108/IJIS-08-2017-0076.

Rosca, E., Arnold, M., & Bendul, J. C. (2016). Business models for sustainable innovation – an empirical analysis of frugal products and services. *Journal of Cleaner Production, 162*(Suppl), S133–S148. https://doi.org/10.1016/j.jclepro .2016.02.050.

Rosca, E., Bendul, J. C., & Arnold, M. (2015). Frugal and reverse innovation as novel business models having diverse sustainability impact. In *Global Cleaner Production & Sustainable Consumption Conference*. Barcelona, Spain. Retrieved September 2019, from https://elsevier.conference-services.net/viewsecurePDF .asp?conferenceID=3781&loc=files&type=fpaper&abstractID=869862.

Santos, A. B. A. dos, Bianchi, C. G., & Borini, F. M. (2018). Open innovation and cocreation in the development of new products: The role of design thinking. *International Journal of Innovation, 6*(2), 112–123. https://doi.org/http://dx.doi .org/10.5585/iji.v6i2.203.

Sebrae. (2016). Inovação e Sustentabilidade: bases para o futuro dos pequenos negócios. São Paulo. Retrieved September 2019, from https://m.sebrae.com .br/Sebrae/Portal Sebrae/Anexos/inovacao_sustentabilidade.pdf.

Sharma, A., & Iyer, G. R. (2012). Resource-constrained product development: Implications for green marketing and green supply chains. *Industrial Marketing Management, 41*(4), 599–608. https://doi.org/10.1016/j.indmarman .2012.04.007.

Silva, I. M. da. (2018). Capacidades Organizacionais para Inovação Frugal. Universidade de São Paulo. https://doi.org/10.11606/T.12.2018.tde-12062018- 125318.

Simula, H., Hossain, M., & Halme, M. (2015). Frugal and reverse innovations – quo vadis? *Current Science, 109*(9), 1567–1572. https://doi.org/10.18520/v109/i9/ 1567-1572.

Tiwari, R., & Bergmann, S. (2018). What pathways lead to frugal innovation ? Some insights on modes & routines of frugal, technical inventions based on an analysis of patent data in German auto components industry. Working Paper TUHH (Vol. 49).

Tiwari, R., & Herstatt, C. (2012a). Assessing India's lead market potential for cost-effective innovations. *Journal of Indian Business Research, 4*(2), 97–115. https://doi.org/10.1108/17554191211228029.

(2012b). Frugal innovation: A global networks' perspective. *Die Unternehmung (Swiss Journal of Business Research and Practice), 66*(3), 245–274.

(2012c). Frugal innovation: A global networks' perspective. *Die Unternehmung, 66*(3), 245–274. https://doi.org/10.5771/0042-059x-2012-3-245.

(2012d). Open global innovation networks as enablers of frugal innovation: Propositions based on evidence from India. *Die Unternehmung, 66*(3), 245–274.

(2014). Developing countries and innovation. In R. Tiwari & C. Herstatt (Eds.), Aiming big with small cars: Emergence of a lead market in India (pp. 19–39). Heidelberg: Springer. https://doi.org/10.1007/978-3-319-02066-2.

Tiwari, R., Luise, F., & Katharina, K. (2016). *Frugal innovation: An assessment of scholarly discourse, trends and potential societal implications.* [Potenziale, Herausforderungen und gesellschaftliche Relevanz frugaler Innovationen in Deutschland im Kontext des globalen Innovationswettbewerbs.] Hamburg, Germany. https://doi.org/10.1007/978-3-319-46392-6_]2.

von Zedtwitz, M., Corsi, S., Søberg, P. V., & Frega, R. (2015). A typology of reverse innovation. *Journal of Product Innovation Management, 32*(1), 12–28. https://doi.org/10.1111/jpim.12181.

Zeschky, M., Winterhalter, S., & Gassmann, O. (2014a). From cost to frugal and reverse innovation: Mapping the field and implications for global competitiveness. *Research-Technology Management (RTM), 57*(4), 20–27. https://doi.org/10.5437/08956308X5704235.

(2014b). What is frugal innovation? In *The European Academy of Management Proceedings.* Valencia-ESP.

12 Innovation in War and Peace

How Colombian Conflict and Postconflict Triggered Military and Business Model Innovation

Juana García Duque, Veneta Andonova, and María Emilia Correa

12.1 INTRODUCTION

The drivers of innovation in emerging markets (EMs) are diverse. Sociopolitical, economic, and environmental dynamics provide opportunities and challenges that lead EM organizations and companies to innovate under very unique constraints. As a response to these conditions, innovation comes from different classes of organizations and institutions not only to improve economic prosperity but also to alleviate grand societal challenges. For example, income inequality has tremendously grown in China, India, and South Africa, while Colombia is the second-most-unequal country in Latin America, which in turn is the region with the highest inequality in the world. Inequality is often accompanied by different kinds of conflicts, such as diplomatic, economic, military, and migratory tensions or even violent and armed conflicts. These situations set the context for innovation that sometimes directly contradicts Western-centered paradigm, and occasionally produces significantly more progressive solutions for present-day problems than the traditionally prescribed solutions from more prosperous and institutionally organized societies. Against this backdrop, we present the case of military and business model innovation under the conditions of violent conflict and postconflict in Colombia.

Conflict and wars put an enormous demand on a country's resources and also tend to accelerate technological development to adapt tools to solve specific military needs. Later, these military tools may evolve into nonmilitary devices; countries such as the United States and Israel have developed and accelerated their high-tech industries by just such an approach.

In what follows, we examine the cases of three Colombian companies and demonstrate how local challenges can serve as business opportunities for certain types of innovation, as well as how business model innovation can positively impact society. In further detail, we present the innovation drivers in peacebuilding, the types of innovation that emerge from businesses' capabilities and operational transformations, and finally, the main benefits these innovations bring.

We argue that the specific circumstances that fueled and sustained violent conflict for more than fifty years in Colombia gave rise to a change management process that involved a doctrine shift as well as process and military technology innovation. That is, full-fledged managerial innovation in the Colombian armed forces prepared the way for the 2016 peace agreement with the most powerful insurgent group, Fuerzas Armadas Revolucionarias de Colombia – Ejército del Pueblo (FARC-EP). While the postconflict era is also plagued with acute economic and social tensions, Colombian companies have helped alleviate the most painful strains by engaging in business model innovation. Their business strategies involve significant elements of shared value (Porter & Kramer, 2011) and can only be fully understood within the specific context of persistent violent conflict.

12.2 THE COLOMBIAN CONFLICT IN BRIEF

Beginning in the mid-1960s, Colombian armed conflict started with the consolidation of the communist insurgent group, FARC. FARC promoted a Marxist–Leninist agenda of agrarianism and anti-imperialism, becoming the most immediate political problem in the country, despite the fact that there were other leftist insurgent movements. At the time, none of these groups were particularly powerful on their own, but together they posed a thorny challenge for the government.

One of the root causes of the armed conflict was the marginalization of significant portions of the population that were not given meaningful paths toward political and economic development by elites who had neither the mindset nor the capacity to include these marginalized groups in the mainstream (Wickham-Crowley, 1987). Multiple conflicts erupted, including an outburst called the Thousand Day War between 1899 and 1902, in which more than 100,000 people were killed. The climax of these early clashes peaked during a period called La Violencia, a bloodbath between 1948 and 1958 that engulfed almost every corner of Colombia and led to an estimated 200,000 casualties. Looking for protection, some of the population banded together in self-defense, and FARC was born. As time passed, more insurgent groups emerged in different areas of the country, each one with particular tactics and ideological justifications for armed fighting.

In the early years, FARC concentrated its strategy on attacking fixed police positions and local authorities hostile to their cause. According to an army report from 1997, 13 percent of the mayors in Colombia had direct connections to the rebels (Marks, 2002).

Beginning in the 1970s and 1980s, these groups engaged in illegal drug trafficking to fund their activities, leading to further disturbances (Marks, 2002). FARC used the resources gained from the illegal drug trade to heavily invest in military operations. Eventually, drug trafficking became both the main source of income and primary function of these armed groups. Under the command of Manuel Marulanda Velez, alias Tiro Fijo, FARC entered a mobile warfare stage, exhibiting a high degree of tactical and operational coordination both internally and together with another insurgent group, Ejército de Liberación Nacional (ELN) (Marks, 2002).

The size of the threat quickly grew. In 1982, FARC was still a relatively weak organization with 2,000 fighters and 15 fronts. By 1990, it had grown to 5,000 fighters and 43 fronts. By the twenty-first century, the group counted 20,000 combatants among its numbers in 66 fronts and mobile companies that allowed them to embrace mobile warfare and directly confront military units of equal size (Marks, 2002).

The Colombian army was tasked with fighting this growing threat. The government priority has been to guarantee defense rather than active military intervention, which resulted in a field force inadequately equipped for victory. Two additional elements further complicated the military's task: Government policy isolated the rest of society from the internal war, leaving the military to deal with the conflict by their own means, and the political and judicial system was bogged down by rules designed for times of peace. This institutional arrangement was largely insufficient in times of conflict and made warfare a hard and exhausting endeavor for the Colombian people (Marks, 2002).

An estimated 220,000 people were killed between 1958 and 2012, according to the flagship report of Grupo de Memoria Histórica (2013, p. 32). The vast majority of them – 81.5 percent – were civilians. The government's Victims Unit has registered around 8,000,000 victims of the armed conflict.

While violent crime was predominantly restricted to urban areas (Aguirre & Restrepo, 2010), the armed conflict largely concentrated around three rural corridors: the Northern axis, Pacific axis, and Eastern axis (Marcos & Ariza, 2014, p. 2). Indigenous people and Afro-Colombians were more affected by geographic shifts in the conflict (Marcos & Ariza, 2014).

12.3 MANAGERIAL INNOVATION IN WARFARE

Given the situation, a sharp change in the course of military strategy was needed. FARC had switched their approach from terror to guerrilla warfare to mobile war, more and more resembling tactics used in the Vietnam War (Marks, 2002). As a result, the Colombian military expected that FARC would follow the same strategy as the Viet Cong, waging war on all fronts. In fact, FARC and ELN were trained by Farabundo Martí National Liberation Front (FMLN) of El Salvador, who in turn were trained by the Viet Cong and the North Vietnamese Army (Bracamonte & Spencer, 1995; Spencer, 1996).

The Colombian army thus faced an uphill battle against a sophisticated military approach empowered by modern communication gear. At the time, the Colombian army was guided by the American doctrine, according to which warfare was either conventional or unconventional. According to this doctrine, the Colombian war was an unconventional war, that is, a guerrilla war, and as a result, they expected decentralization would prove to be an effective military and organizational approach. The Colombians saw it differently. They believed that the guerilla forces had shifted to a well-coordinated mobile mode of war, and therefore increased command and control were important. The guerillas followed this same approach, coordinating terror attacks and guerilla actions into a unified mobile action. Changing the doctrine in such a significant manner required managerial innovation from the Colombian army as it shifted away from small-scale counterguerrilla actions to mobile war.

In the mid-1990s, the Colombian Air Force and Navy were very small. The police, responsible for law enforcement and not trained for warfare, had 100,000 men located in small posts around Colombia's vast geography. While the army nominally numbered 145,000, only 30,000 of the soldiers were professionals, and only 20,000 of them had actual combat experience. The rest of the army were draftees, of whom only a quarter had high school degrees (Marks, 2002). In sum, the deployment and characteristics of the armed forces could not guarantee military success and forced the organization to innovate.

Former commanders of brigades with combat experience headed managerial innovation in the Colombian armed forces. They understood that the challenges required swift action and preparation for combat at every level. Those who did not meet the requirements were released. This led to a substantial shake-up of the organization, from top commanders down. Military positions were reorganized, and weapons were reassigned. Funding backed up the conversion of

soldiers from conscript to professional status. Administrative formations were turned into combat units. A Rapid Reaction Force was
formed, including the most elite combat divisions. The IV division
was particularly prominent because their area of operations included
the center of FARC combat power. Changes to their internal structure
and the use of tactics learned from the Vietnam War helped to
improve their combat capacity. For example, IV Division prepared
for mobile war by turning three of its formations to airborne status
through in-house training. Another unit responsible for patrolling the
savannah designed an armored truck company equipped with 50-cal
machine guns and an accompanying 106-mm "gun wagon." When
this solution proved effective, they increased the number of these
vehicles to form a brigade (Marks, 2002). The shift in doctrine, change
in command, and to some degree even military technology allowed for
a full-fledged managerial innovation in effectively fighting insurgency. These innovations allowed Colombian armed forces to substantially improve their likelihood of victory in a few years, leading
the FARC to sign a peace agreement in 2016.

12.4   PEACEBUILDING AND BUSINESS MODEL
INNOVATION

We define "peacebuilding" as the development of constructive relationships and initiatives across society by transforming the structural
conditions that generate conflict, in order to establish and sustain
peace in the long term (Hazen, 2007). Peacebuilding initiatives also
aim to tackle systemic multidimensional issues and actors, focusing
on transforming root causes of conflict such as political exclusion,
poverty, lack of resources, and ideological differences. Among the
economic factors that contribute to socioeconomic development in
peacebuilding and conflict resolution are economic inclusion,
employment generation, business creation opportunities, and access
to resources, financing, and land. Private corporations can play a
fundamental role in peacebuilding, as they generate both economic
and social value in their communities. Thus, peacebuilding initiatives

and actions affect businesses at multiple levels, ranging from the company's practices, products, services, and decision-making processes to its relationship with stakeholders.

Extensive literature has established a theoretical and conceptual nexus between the private sector and its engagement with conflict and peacebuilding. Among others, Katsos and Forrer (2014) analyzed a case study in postconflict Cyprus; Jamali and Mirshak (2010) have examined links between MNEs, conflict, and corporate social responsibility (CSR); and Andonova and García (2018) illustrated how emerging MNEs enhanced their competitive advantage by engaging in domestic peacebuilding in Colombia. Despite this important work, researchers have not yet established a coherent linkage between different innovation approaches and their contributions to peacebuilding, or how the postconflict environment encourages companies and organizations to innovate.

The Chamber of Commerce of Bogotá, Colombia, documented companies' willingness to engage in peacebuilding initiatives. A national survey involved more than 1,500 companies from all sectors, with the aim of identifying perceptions about the peace agreement process and their current or possible engagement in peacebuilding initiatives. Small and medium enterprises (SMEs) and large firms both expressed that the private sector should be proactively involved in the construction of peace under the postconflict era. Nevertheless, many of the companies expressed ignorance of governmental peacebuilding programs or how to develop them. Additionally, the majority of large enterprises claimed that they already were involved in peacebuilding through CSR programs, while most SMEs argued that they had contributed through tax payment. Strategically, it appears that large companies engage more in peacebuilding through CSR, and SMEs do so by integrating actions in their business core.

Companies' innovation in peacebuilding can be classified under two recognized innovation types described in the existing literature. The first one is business model innovation, as some peacebuilding initiatives create new business concepts or improve, recombine, and/or change an existing business model (Chesbrough, 2007). Under this definition, the business model is the firm's methods of operation and delivery of value to its stakeholders, as described by Casadesus-Masanell and Ricart (2010). The second type is innovation process and organizational innovation, which includes the creation or modification of business practices, processes, and external relations. In this type of innovation, firms either incorporate new managerial and organizational activities or modify their existing processes. Parallel to both approaches on types of innovation, we include findings on corporate strategies in peacebuilding, described in the study of the Colombian experience by Miklian and Rettberg (2017).

The value of studying peacebuilding in emerging economies and its relationship with innovation lies in the replicability of these initiatives' business models to address other social challenges beyond conflict situations. This study highlights the need to rethink organizational goals beyond the business and have a clear vision of the positive impact that the organization must generate in economic, social, and environmental terms. Such business models fit well with the conscious capitalism movement (Mackey & Sisodia, 2013) and compassionate management (Fryer, 2013) trends, which have been gaining adherents among global corporations such as Starbucks and Patagonia. The concept of conscious capitalism proposes a way of thinking about business, foregrounding its potential to make a positive impact on the world. It invites business leaders and stakeholders to adopt a mindset that helps them identify opportunities for synergies where traditionally they could only perceive trade-offs. Businesses led by conscious leaders aspire to create "financial, intellectual, social, cultural, emotional, spiritual, physical and ecological wealth for all their stakeholders" (Mackey & Sisodia, 2013). These ideas resonate with the framework of shared value (Porter & Kramer, 2011) according to which capitalism is under siege, and companies must take the lead in bringing societies and businesses back together. These ideas meet much skepticism in the Western business world, but they seem obvious and even somewhat belated when viewed in the context of the Colombian postconflict era. In what follows, we briefly describe the most significant features of three highly recognizable Colombian companies' innovative business models that actively participated in not only generating returns for their shareholders, but also transforming the country's societal context.

12.4.1 Bancolombia: Exploring Business Model Innovation

Bancolombia is the largest Colombian financial institution and a part of the financial group called Grupo Bancolombia, which provides diverse banking services and products. The bank is an outstanding multilatina with subsidiaries in six other countries in the Latin American region and is listed on the New York and Colombian Stock Exchanges. It is internationally recognized for achievements related to social development, environmental protection, and responsible governance. Thus, it supports and promotes the Sistema B Movement[1] in Latin America because of its social and environmental sustainability pillars within its business model. Not surprisingly, in 2018 Bancolombia was ranked in the Dow Jones Sustainability Index as the most sustainable bank in the world (La República, 2018).

The Bancolombia Foundation is in charge of creating sustainable and inclusive strategies, both in territories that are marginalized and affected by armed conflict, as well as with vulnerable populations. The foundation seeks to create programs for unbanked communities in remote regions of the country, close gaps between rural and urban areas, improve the agricultural sector, and develop talents in young people through educational programs, among other prosocial aims. Bancolombia adopted a business model around the agricultural sector in which its positive impact on society is as relevant as its impact on the economy.

[1] Sistema B supports the B Corporation or B Corp movement in Latin America, a business innovation tool for companies that generate public good as well as profits for its shareholders. It was created in 2012 simultaneously in Argentina, Chile, and Colombia by Pedro Tarak, Maria Emilia Correa, Juan Pablo Larenas, and Gonzalo Muñoz.

Despite these agricultural roots, Bancolombia has not limited its portfolio to that sector; rather, it has created an innovative business model with social development at its core. In order to improve the economic conditions of small farmers in rural areas, it developed a new risk diversification strategy that allows it to reach this underserved and excluded niche. This business transformation exceeds the typically limited social impact initiatives measured under traditional sustainability indicators. Bancolombia has rethought its success as a large company with more than 100 years of experience into one that also understands its edifying role in society.

Colombia's small farmers lacked resources, including (i) access to credit to purchase and modernize their machinery, (ii) a sustainable source to cover their living expenses during harvest, and (iii) guarantees to cover their risk and attract investors or financial institutions. Bancolombia understood these problems and proposed a credit risk diversification model to their clients that would also benefit the small farmers.

Under Bancolombia's proposal, its clients would lend to small farmers, and the bank would support the payment of these credits by buying all the crop production by these farmers above the market price. The purchase guarantee would be valid for up to ten years. Loans would allow farmers not only to alleviate the costs associated with planting, but also to cover their living expenses while harvesting. In this case, loans were granted for a two-year period, linked with the crop's economic return. After this period, the bank would begin to receive principal and interest payments, creating a win–win relationship in which Bancolombia does not modify the nature of its business. From this experience, the bank and its associated foundation decided to join forces to create this new business model, establishing a two-way continuous learning process that promotes agricultural development and entrepreneurship while bringing new ideas for both organizations.

Currently the Bancolombia Foundation has strengthened this business model through a better understanding of the needs of the rural sector, with a clear contribution to both the economic and social dimensions of peacebuilding. It operates and replicates this business model through the following key strategic actions:

1. Locate a vulnerable population and territory in which there is a high potential for a new agricultural development-specific product.
2. Conduct an investment feasibility study given the available resources according to each case. Special emphasis is placed on understanding the cycles of agricultural production that vary according to products.
3. Establish partnerships with key firms willing to engage these small farmers as their suppliers. This optimizes the value chain by diversifying the associated financial risks.
4. Involve other stakeholders with technical knowledge associated with agriculture to support the projects.

In that way, this business model mitigates causes of conflict, such as exclusion from financial and commercial systems, unemployment, and poverty. Consequently, it positively impacts the socioeconomic conditions of small farmers, their families, and ex-combatants by establishing social cohesion through commercial activity. These peacebuilding initiatives are aligned with one of the most critical negotiating points of the peace agreement, called the Integral Rural Reform (Reforma Rural Integral), that seeks to restitute land to displaced people and encourage agricultural productivity.

Bancolombia is replicating this model with other agricultural products by reaching more regions of the country, especially those where illicit crops are prominent. Bancolombia plans to invest in cocoa and avocado, as these two products are part of the government's agricultural development plans in the postconflict period called Voluntary Substitution Program for Illicit Crops. Creating markets across conflict zones and deep rural areas presents three major challenges described by Anderson, Markides, & Kupp (2010) as (i) lack of legal frameworks, (ii) absence of key infrastructure, and (iii) shortage of skilled people. The bank is aware of these gaps and the need for government support, especially to meet infrastructure needs and enhance connectivity to facilitate commercial dynamics in rural areas.

The new socioeconomic context that creates a favorable environment for firms to innovate is the main driver of such developments. These conditions arise due to the absence of armed conflict, the increase of state presence in rural areas, and the establishment of development plans under inclusive legal frameworks for peacebuilding. Additionally, social and economic demands support the market. Financially, local and global demand for some agricultural commodities such as cocoa and fique fiber is increasing, while engaging the substantial poor and excluded population in rural areas both improves their livelihoods and boosts economic growth.

A theoretical approach to transformation in the Bancolombia business model can be understood in light of the framework described by Cavalcante, Kesting, & Ulhøi (2011) called Business Model Extension. The authors refer to firms in which standardized processes of the core activities are already defined, but the organization adds activities or expands on an existing core activity. In Bancolombia's case, the firm changed both its strategy and the way in which it operates to deliver value to its new and traditional stakeholders. Because creating value for a few is not sustainable or inclusive, managerial practices now focus on generating wealth among vulnerable populations in all territories.

12.4.2 Crepes & Waffles: Interdependency

Crepes & Waffles is a family-owned forty-year-old restaurant chain recognized for its good quality, fair prices, and significant support for women: 93 percent of employees are single mothers, who receive fair salaries, support for family education and housing, and training, both for the job and to increase self-esteem and personal capacity. With over US$100 million in annual sales and 10 percent annual growth, it is the largest food chain in the country.

The family-owned company has traditionally been very responsive to the challenges of related communities. The family's second generation took control of the company during the Colombian peace process. As a result, the company decided to deepen interdependency with the country by redesigning the supply chain toward a regenerative model.

Together with management, shareholders travel the country to identify communities that have been affected by crime or armed conflict or where traditional lifestyles are challenged by aggressive development projects. Rather than forcing communities to adjust their production capacity to the company's needs, the buyers for Crepes & Waffles work to redesign the menu in order to include the products produced by the communities. They offer stable prices over time to allow communities to rebuild their economic capacity and their social capital, and they bring technical support to improve quality and encourage organic and regenerative agriculture as well as ecosystem conservation.

In four years, Crepes & Waffles has developed a mutually beneficial relationship with local suppliers based on trust and the common desire to live in peace, offering safe commercial alternatives to drug trafficking and criminal activities. The company serves over 24 million plates per year, and Crepes & Waffles supports lifestyles for communities and ecosystems as well as commercial viability for communities around the country. The company uses pepper from Putumayo, a territory where drug production has been a main source of income; palmitos from Bojayá and beans from Montes de Maria, regions that suffered horrible massacres; organic lettuce from Boyacá and Cundimarca, where small farmers are being challenged by large agricultural production; cocoa from Tumaco, where arms, drugs, and crime are rampant; and arracacha from Cajamarca, a region threatened by gold mining.

Contrary to traditional expectations, the company has reduced the overall cost of sourcing local products. Initially, supply chain managers received the redesign proposal with distrust. However, the opportunity to personally witness the challenges and to create relationships with people living in the affected communities has been a profound motivation for Crepes & Waffles employees, who continuously find synergies, opportunities for the communities and for the company, and innovations for customers. Crepes & Waffles does not invest in commercial advertising. Only recently have the restaurants provided some basic information about the products and territories, not to promote the brand, but to invite customers to appreciate the beauty and natural wealth of the country. Notwithstanding this understated approach, the dishes developed with the regenerative supply chain model are among the ten highest-margin and most popular products.

The case of Crepes & Waffles exemplifies the proposition presented by DesJardine, Bansal and Yang (2017).[2] This article proposes that the most resilient companies create interdependence, understood as relationships of trust and belonging between companies and the social and environmental systems they inhabit. Interdependence builds stability, allows faster recovery, and leads to greater sharing of visions, values, information, and resources between the various systems. It happens among very diverse actors that further promote flexibility and creativity.

Interdependence is supported by strategic practices, which are social and environmental practices that form part of the core business. They have a long-term horizon, have a commitment of resources, and are part of the company's systems, routines, and structures. They contribute to resilience, and they can help companies recover in the face of crisis by decreasing the severity of an adverse situation and accelerating recovery times. They are correlated with fewer losses, more stable results, and faster recovery, as well as more flexibility against strong changes in the environment. A few examples of such strategic practices include supporting the claims of indigenous peoples, improving working conditions and human rights in the supply chain, increasing diversity among

---

[2] Mark DesJardine, HEC Paris, Pratima Bansal, Western University, Yang Yang, Rowan University; (2019, April). *Journal of Management*, 45(4), 1434–1460.

company employees, as well as committing to product safety, and healthy corporate governance.

Tactical practices, by contrast, seek to improve short-term relationships with stakeholders and adjust to the company's short-term priorities. Organizational systems, routines, or company structures do not change significantly. They support the speed of recovery, but have less impact: They do not build the interdependence between systems that is the basis of resilience, so their impacts are short term. Examples of tactical practices include philanthropic donations and other actions that require few resources, can be executed quickly, and can be stopped without problem because they do not create interdependencies with society or nature.

Large companies in Colombia like Crepes & Waffles are supporting peace and shared prosperity in the country through their business models. Companies like Juan Valdez, the multinational coffee house chain, a cooperative owned by over 500,000 small coffee producers and one of the most recognized brands in the world, and Wok, the restaurant chain that develops supply relationships in 250 communities, analyzed by Lobo, Reffico and Rueda (2012)[3] are developing business models and strategic practices to create interdependency and be active in the peace process in Colombia.

12.4.3 Postobón and CSR

2014 was a year of strategic rethinking for Postobón...we will maintain operational efficiency, contribute to the company's innovation, reinforce value creation...and of course, we will continue with our sustainability model, which every day demonstrates its capacity to transform society. Miguel Fernando Escobar, CEO of Postobón

Founded in 1904, Postobón is part of the conglomerate Organización Ardila Lülle (OAL). This Colombian conglomerate

---

[3] Lobo, Reffico, Rueda. Uniandes 2012.

participates in a diversity of industries such as media (RCN radio and RCN TV), sugar mills (Ingenio Risaralda S.A., Ingenio Providencia S.A. and Incauca S.A.), automotive (Distribuidora Los Coches S.A.), and sports (it is a major shareholder in the football team Atlético Nacional) and operates 123 subsidiaries.

Postobón is a top player in the Colombian soft drinks industry with a 35.9 percent value share and ranked among the top three players in each of the market categories. In 2017, Postobón owned 21 bottling plants, 48 distribution centers and more than 3,000 delivery vehicles. The company operates through franchisees across the Americas and Europe.

Since 2014, the company has changed its role in the soft drinks market, moving beyond traditional products, reinvigorating its CSR initiatives, and undertaking a strategic reorientation at a time when the effects of climate change are increasingly evident, and changes in consumption habits and pressures over categories of sugary drinks become important challenges. Postobón has whole-heartedly embraced the ideas behind shared value (Porter & Kramer, 2011) and has started to experiment with its business model, especially regarding the management of its value chain.

Traditionally Postobón was focused on soft drinks. In 2016, it ranked in the top three places within each category relying on a diversified portfolio of products in bottled water, carbonates, juice, sports and energy drinks, and ready-to-drink tea.

OAL's businesses have a long history of embracing stand-alone CSR initiatives across industry sectors. One such example is the case of Ingenio INCAUCA. As part of its social initiatives, Ingenio INCAUCA built and has supported the operation of a school that provides free education to 150 children, including complementary activities such as arts and sports. Most of these activities, despite addressing the causes of the long-standing violent conflict in Colombia, were not intended to transform the traditional business model of Postobón. This started to change in 2010 when Postobón produced its first sustainability report. Based on the guidelines of the

Global Reporting Institute (GRI), the company made an honest evaluation of their most significant impacts (positive or negative) on the natural environment, Colombian society, and the economy. The underlying understanding was that Postobón as a company could generate reliable, relevant, and standardized information; assess opportunities and risks; and enable more informed decision making to the benefit of both its shareholders and stakeholders (BDS, 2010).

The report contained analyses of global trends and best practices of similar companies, aimed at identifying learning opportunities for Postobón. Later, internal diagnostics were performed to document the company's social responsibility initiatives and to identify future challenges. Thus, a sustainability model that was intended to blend with the traditional business model was developed with eight strategic axes: (1) generation of economic value; (2) corporate governance, ethics, and transparency; (3) human management; (4) environment; (5) sustainable packaging; (6) sustainable production chain; (7) nutrition, health, and well-being; and (8) sustainable relationships with the community.

In 2010, Postobon's most significant societal initiatives were

- "Hit Social": The program consisted of providing support to farmers who owned less than one hectare of cultivated area. Postobón purchased the farmers' fruit harvest at higher prices than the national average. The annual impact was estimated at 3,844 tons of fruit produced by 860 farming families. Farmers also participated in health, recreation, education, and integration programs. This was a major innovation in Postobón's business model. It was also designed to alleviate the most critical tensions in the Colombian agricultural sector, which had traditionally been the drivers behind the long-standing armed conflict.
- Education support: A percentage of the sales of OASIS, a bottled water brand, were used to reduce the school dropout rate. The initiative benefited 14,110 accredited educational institutions, 1,604 public libraries, and 123 universities with 16,500 collections. In addition, the program had financed computers and school kits benefiting more than 6,000 students in 10 departments and 32 municipalities in Colombia.

- Sustainable packaging: The main objective was to reduce the amount of materials used in beverage packaging (both glass and PET) and reduce the environmental footprint of the company. The initiative included the design of a short cap, flexible secondary packaging and biodegradable adhesives. The estimated impact amounted to a reduction of 1,144 tons of sand silica, lime, and aluminum clay.

In 2013, Miguel Fernando Escobar Penagos became the president of Postobón, and in 2014, two years before the peace agreement with FARC, he initiated a new nine-month cycle of strategic planning. Expectations about a possible peace agreement were high, and it was in this context that Postobón adopted a new corporate and competitive strategy for the next ten years, described in a document titled "Great and Ambitious Strategic Goals" (MEGA, by its Spanish acronym). A new company configuration emerged during the first year of MEGA execution. Postobón modified its organizational structure, creating Strategic Business Units and Strategic Services Units. The first level of the company's organization chart was formed by vice-presidencies. As part of the Human Management Vice-Presidency, the Sustainability Division was created with the purpose of planning, directing, and controlling the strategy of sustainability, innovation, and corporate reputation. Its responsibilities included the design of an internal corporate communications plan, the elaboration of an innovation management system, and the execution of initiatives of shared value. The Sustainability Division involved three heads:

- Head of Shared Value: This unit leads initiatives that generate economic and social value across areas and product categories. With the support of different areas of the company, it implements programs reducing the consumption of water and energy and improving the efficiency of waste management, as it expands on existing programs such as Hit Social.
- Head of Corporate Communications: This unit is in charge of reputation management. With the help of the Reputation Institute, every three months it surveys important stakeholders to track their perception of the company. Internally, the company's reputation is measured in the largest cities (Bogota, Medellin, Cali, Barranquilla, and Cartagena), and the process

captures perceptions about the products, innovation, leadership, and community relations of the stakeholders in general.

- Postobón Foundation: This is considered the "operating arm" of the Sustainability Division. The Foundation designs and executes its programs, focusing on improving relations with the communities surrounding Postobón's twenty-one production facilities. It also leads educational initiatives such as the "Agua Oasis" program.

Aligned with the new corporate strategy and organizational structure, Postobón defined its new business model, called "Uno más Todos" (One plus All), based on two guiding principles: mitigation of risks and negative impacts, and creation of shared value. The ultimate objective was the generation of value for Postobón and its stakeholders by seeking a balance between social, economic, and environmental initiatives.

The stakeholders were identified and defined based on the criteria of urgency, legitimacy, and power proposed in the methodology developed by Ronald K. Mitchell, Bradley R. Agle, and Donna J. Wood. The final definition included eight key groups: (1) community, (2) clients, (3) consumers, (4) employees, (5) suppliers, (6) environmental entities, (7) shareholders, and (8) government (Postobón, 2016).

The elaboration of the "Uno más Todos" model was the result of a process of benchmarking and evaluation of different standards, norms, and guidelines in sustainability such as Dow Jones Sustainability Index, Global Reporting Initiative, Global Pact, and CEO Water Mandate. The company fine-tuned the model after evaluating stakeholders' importance, the positive and negative impacts of the industry dynamics, and the sensitivity of the company's objectives to these influences.

Guided by the philosophy behind "Uno más Todos," Postobón identified four key elements to be organically integrated within its business model, as they appeared to give the most significant advantages in a context of peacebuilding.

- "Litros que ayudan" is an alliance with the Colombian Red Cross and e-commerce site Place to Pay. It is a virtual platform (www.litrosqueayudan .com) through which citizens can make donations of water that Postobón doubles through a matching donation to alleviate emergencies such as natural disasters. In 2015, 43,612 liters of water were collected, alleviating eight emergencies and benefiting 15,000 people.

- "Mi pupitre Postobón" is an agreement among Postobón, the National Agency for Overcoming Extreme Poverty (ANSPE), and the Centre for the Promotion of the Book in Latin America and the Caribbean (CERLALC). The program was funded by a percentage of the sales of OASIS bottled water and gave 29 educational institutions 6,410 pieces of furniture for classrooms and libraries that were produced with recycled material Tetra Pak packaging, ultimately benefitting more than 20,000 students.

- "Hit Social," was described above. In 2015, the yearly impact was estimated at 2,40 jobs and 4,310 tons of fruit per year: 1,054 hectares of mango, 365 hectares of blackberry, and 20 hectares of lulo were purchased through this initiative.

- "Mi Bici Postobón" delivers bicycles to children and young students in rural areas where the trip to school takes between forty-five minutes and two hours a day. Beneficiaries are monitored for two years. Bikes only become their property if they use them properly and get positive academic results. The first bicycles were given in 2014 to twenty-two children in Villanueva, Bolívar.

In 2015, Merco (Monitor of Corporate Reputation) included Postobón in its reputation ranking of Colombian companies for the first time. Postobón occupied the 37th position among 100 companies. In 2016, Postobón ascended to 14th position (Postobón, 2017).

After the peace agreement in 2016, Postobón's position looked strong. Significant societal problems had already started to affect the company's understanding of a solid long-term strategy. Climate change triggered extreme weather that increased the volatility in the consumption of Postobón's products and on the supply of water and fruit. After more than fifty years of civil war between the Colombian government and the largest guerilla group, FARC, the peace agreement had just started to be implemented and promised to change the agricultural sector. No one was certain about the mid- and long-term effects of the peace agreement on the business and crime environment in the postwar period, even though many were optimistic. At the same time, the government was looking for new sources of income to finance its commitments in the peace agreement and also improve transportation infrastructure, education, and the bankrupt public healthcare systems. In this context, Postobón's new business model that embraced shared value seemed to address the most urgent societal needs and mitigate the risk of heated domestic debates to raise fiscal income by imposing a tax on sugary soft drinks. Business model innovation is a process burdened with uncertainty and has required courage and determination as well as a firm belief that corporations can be a positive force in a society that looks for a lasting peace and shared prosperity. The synchronicity between the rate of business model innovation and societal transformation has probably been the biggest achievement for the company that has maintained its leading position and strengthened its reputation in turbulent times. Postobón has successfully navigated the pre- and postpeace agreement period while boldly experimenting and leading business model innovation inspired by the philosophy of shared value.

12.5 CONCLUSION AND IMPLICATIONS

The armed forces in Colombia have always been responsible for ensuring the defense of the Colombian state while also playing an important role in internal security and stability, and occasionally participating in missions to guarantee international security. For decades, the armed forces have built the capabilities, resources, and skills to manage their missions and fulfill their duties in these fields, and it is possible that they can be redirected to contribute directly to the competitiveness of the country's economy. Israel may provide such an example, where the mandatory period of national military service serves as a fruitful field of personnel monitoring, development of management skills, and advanced technology management, as well as for teamwork.

Research on innovative business models and strategies toward peacebuilding provides a valuable source of learning for entrepreneurs, large companies, researchers, and policymakers. Successful examples range from operational transformative initiatives, to the ways in which organizations create and distribute value among their stakeholders. The cases discussed above exemplify innovation and peacebuilding that bridge practical and theoretical approaches of both fields. By opening a broader research agenda around this topic, we contribute to a better understanding of unexplored business model innovation questions, including identifying the main drivers of innovation in postconflict and peacebuilding situations.

The cases described above illustrate the type of business innovation that is needed to achieve the 2030 sustainable development agenda, specifically in generating wealth by closing inequality gaps and respecting planetary boundaries. So far, transformations like these have proven beneficial and successful, showing progress and replicability, but they will need to be further monitored for long-term sustainability and success going forward.

The analysis of organizational transformation provides valuable lessons for the private sector. In times of political and social instability, innovation is left behind and not part of the development agenda, leading to progress only toward limited purposes. It is therefore unsurprising that changes in contexts with deep multidimensional challenges, such as armed conflict, lead to substantial innovation. This innovation can arise from different dimensions, but the most important thing is that peacebuilding is one of the fundamental axes in the design, action, execution, and evaluation of its effectiveness. Notwithstanding this evidence, some firms from emerging markets are still reluctant to adopt such new paradigms intuitively and immediately in conflict or postconflict contexts.

REFERENCES

Aguirre, K., & Restrepo, J. (2010). Arms control as a strategy for violence-reduction in Colombia: Pertinence, status and challenges. *Revista Criminalidad, 52*(1), 265–290.

Anderson, J. L., Markides, C., & Kupp, M. (2010). The last frontier: Market creation in conflict zones, deep rural areas, and urban slums. *California Management Review, 52*(4), 6–28.

Andonova, V., & García, J. (2018). How can EMNCs enhance their global competitive advantage by engaging in domestic peacebuilding? The case of Colombia. *Transnational Corporations Review, 10*(4), 370–385.

BDS Consulting. (2010). Identificación de Brechas Postobón S.A.

Bracamonte, J., & Spencer, D. (1995). *Strategy and tactics of the Salvadoran FMLN guerrillas.* Westport, CT: Praeger.

Cavalcante, S., Kesting, P., & Ulhøi, J. (2011). Business model dynamics and innovation: (Re) establishing the missing linkages. *Management Decision, 49*(8), 1327–1342.

Casadesus-Masanell, R., & Ricart, J. E. (2010). From strategy to business models and onto tactics. *Long Range Planning, 43*(2–3), 195–215.

Chesbrough, H. (2007). Business model innovation: It's not just about technology anymore. *Strategy & Leadership, 35*(6), 12–17.

Fryer, B. (2013, September 18). The rise of compassionate management (finally). *Harvard Business Review.*

Grupo de Memoria Histórica. (2013). *¡Basta ya! Colombia: Memorias de guerra y dignidad.* Bogotá: Imprenta Nacional.

Hazen, J. M. (2007). Can peacekeepers be peacebuilders? *International Peacekeeping, 14*(3), 323–338, DOI: 10.1080/13533310701422901.

Jamali, D., & Mirshak, R. (2010). Business-conflict linkages: Revisiting MNCs, CSR, and conflict. *Journal of Business Ethics, 93*, 443–464.

Katsos, J., & Forrer, J. (2014). Business practices and peace in post-conflict zones: lessons from Cyprus. *Business Ethics: A European Review, 23*(2), 154–165.

La República. (2018). Bancolombia, el banco más sostenible del mundo según el Índice Dow Jones. Retrieved September 2019, from www.larepublica.co/empresas/el-banco-mas-sostenible-del-mundo-es-colombiano-2770902.

Mackey, J., & Sisodia, R. (2013, January 14). "Conscious Capitalism" Is Not an Oxymoron. *Harvard Business Review.*

Marcos, R., & Ariza, P. (2014). Colombia: Humanitarian Snapshot as of 15 January 2014. Retrieved September 2019, from www.humanitarianresponse.info/files/snapshot_colombia_EN_jan_2014.pdf.

Marks, T. (2002). *Colombian Army Adaptation to FARC insurgency.* Carlisle, PA: Strategic Studies Institute/Army War College.

Miklian, J., & Rettberg, A. (2017, February 28). From war-torn to peace-torn? Mapping business strategies in transition from conflict to peace in Colombia.

In J. Miklian, R. M. Alluri, & J. E. Katsos (Eds.), *Business, peacebuilding and sustainable development* (pp. 110–128). Abingdon: Routledge.

Porter, M., & Kramer, M. (2011, January–February). Creating shared value. *Harvard Business Review.*

Postobón. (2016). Informe de Sostenibilidad 2015, p. 29.

(2017). Company website. Postobón entre las 15 empresas con mejor reputación. Retrieved May 2017, from www.postobon.com/sala-prensa/noticias/postobon-entre-las-15-empresas-mejor-reputacion.

Spencer, D. (1996). *From Vietnam to El Salvador: The saga of the FMLN sappers and other guerrilla special forces in Latin America.* Westport, CT: Praeger.

Wickham-Crowley, T. (1987). Winners, losers, and also-rans: Toward a comparative sociology of Latin American guerrilla movements. In S. Eckstein (Ed.), *Power and popular protest* (pp. 132–181). Berkeley: University of California Press.

PART III Innovation Outcomes in Emerging Markets

13 Evaluating Outcomes of Innovation in Emerging Markets

Anne Miroux, Lourdes Casanova, and Fernanda Cahen

13.1 MEASURING COUNTRIES' INNOVATION PERFORMANCE

Innovation stands as a key pillar of productivity, competitiveness, and prosperity. Since the 1980s, the role of innovation in economic growth and development has garnered increasing attention from policy-makers and academics worldwide (see Chapter 1) as a growing list of countries continues to embrace science, technology, and innovation policies. As of 2019, thirty-five countries touted Ministries of Science and Technology, including thirteen in Asia and five in Latin America. Meanwhile, countries feel increased urgency to understand the process of innovation. In fact, given the importance of innovation in many countries' overall economic strategies, policies and initiatives that support it are subject to heightened scrutiny (e.g., evaluation tools, rankings, indicators).

In this chapter, we examine both macro performance the progress made by emerging economies in global innovation (Appendix, Tables 13A.1 and 13A.2), and firm-level performance, the evolution of the most innovative companies. We focus mostly on the markets covered in this book and on the E20, a group of top twenty emerging economies selected on the basis of nominal GDP and population (Table 13.1).[1]

---

[1] The E20 (Casanova & Miroux, 2019) is a list of the top twenty emerging economies established by Cornell University's Emerging Markets Institute (EMI). The selection is based on highest nominal GDP, population size, and classification as "emerging" by at least one major international organization. As of 2019, the list includes China, India, Brazil, Russia, South Korea, Mexico, Indonesia, Saudi Arabia, Turkey, Poland, Argentina, Thailand, Iran, Nigeria, South Africa, Malaysia, Philippines, Colombia, Pakistan, and Chile.

Since the early 1970s, tools have been designed to measure a country's innovative performance (see Chapter 1). For example, the National Science Foundation of the United States published the first report on national science and technology (S&T) indicators in the United States in 1973. Early reports emphasized inputs to the scientific process, such as research and development (R&D) funding and the number of students in science and engineering, but did not elaborate much on the results and impacts. This was later corrected by tracking publications and patents. In the 1970s and 1980s, several other developed countries also began to publish reports on S&T indicators. The OECD has played an important role in standardizing these documents by collaborating with Eurostat to develop the *Oslo Manual*, a tool for statisticians and policy makers with guidelines for collecting, reporting, and sourcing data on innovation.

As mentioned in Chapter 1, the *Oslo Manual* (OECD/Eurostat, 2018) provides a wide range of national metrics such as R&D spending, S&T personnel, patents, S&T publications and citations, and exports of high-technology products that relate to innovation. Considered separately, these variables fail to offer a full picture of performance. For instance, R&D spending, number of research institutions, and research staff are inputs to the innovation process and therefore are important, but the relationship between innovation inputs and innovation performance is not straightforward and differs across countries.

Similarly, the number of scientific publications or patents could be seen as indicators of knowledge creation, but their ability to reflect innovation capabilities varies across countries and industries. The use of patents as an innovation indicator, in particular, has been the subject of a long-standing debate due to industries' differences in willingness to patent. Other output indicators may also only partially reflect innovation performance. For example, exports of high-tech goods are a function not only of innovation activity in the economy but also of trade barriers among trading partners. Composite indices combine multiple measures of innovation developed alongside a growing body of literature analyzing these complicating factors (Hagedoorn & Cloodt 2003; Gault, 2013).

Two of the best-known innovation indices are the Global Innovation Index (GII) published in collaboration between Cornell University, the INSEAD business school, the World Internet Patent Organization (WIPO, 2019), and the European Innovation Scoreboard.[2] Other indicators exist, such as the Bloomberg Innovation Index that in its 2019 edition ranked 60 countries (Bloomberg, 2019).[3] This chapter draws largely on the GII due to its global coverage of 129 countries as of 2019 and its broader conception of innovation, as defined by the *Oslo Manual*. The GII moves beyond conceptions of innovation as closed, internal, and localized to encompass types such as "incremental innovation" and "innovation without breakthrough," among others (Dutta, Lanvin, & Wunsch-Vincent, 2019). Further, the GII dovetails with the National System of Innovation approach, which takes into account a wider range of input factors that impact a country's innovation capabilities.

13.2 EMERGING COUNTRIES IN THE GLOBAL INNOVATION INDEX (GII)

The GII incorporates over eighty indicators to track the progress of global innovation across the world and across industries. It averages economies' scores on two sub-indices, the Innovation Input Sub-Index and the Innovation Output Sub-Index to calculate the overall GII score.

The Innovation Input Sub-Index includes five input pillars – institutions, human capital and research, infrastructure, market

---

[2] The European Innovation Scoreboard is produced by the European Commission. It compares the research and innovation performance of thirty-six countries: twenty-seven European Union member countries and selected third countries through a composite index, the Innovation Summary Index (https://ec.europa.eu/docsroom/documents/38781).

[3] Source: www.bloomberg.com/news/articles/2019-01-28/u-s-canada-make-strides-in-bloomberg-2019-innovation-index.

sophistication, and business sophistication, all of which cover defining aspects of the environment needed for innovation in an economy.

The Innovation Output Sub-Index measures the outcome of innovative activities in countries. It includes two pillars – creative outputs and knowledge, and technology outputs.

Based on the GII, developed economies continue to lead in innovation. The top spots are occupied by advanced economies, while emerging markets do not rank high overall. Of the E20 emerging markets, only seven are among the top fifty countries in the 2019 GII. These seven are China, Korea, Malaysia, Thailand, Poland, Russia, and Turkey. None of the emerging economies from Latin America made the top fifty list, though Chile ranks first thereafter (fifty-first). The innovation divide that we still observe reflects the discrepancy in both innovation investments and outputs: Both are still concentrated in a limited number of countries, mostly from developed regions. In addition, only nine E20 economies can be found among the top fifty performers in the Input Sub-Index and eight in the Output Sub-Index. One should note, however, that at the turn of the millennium emerging economies were hardly on the innovation radar screen. Given this historical context, emerging markets have not only experienced economic growth (Table 13A.1), but they have also improved their innovation performance despite their ongoing lag. As noted previously, a few Asian economies have made particular strides in these areas (Korea, China, and India, for instance).

The case of China is unique (see Chapters 2, 4, and 7 and Casanova and Miroux, 2019, 2020). While keeping in mind that year-on-year comparisons of innovation performance based on the GII are impacted by factors such as data availability or changes and adjustments in the variables, we still note China's rapid improvement: From thirtieth in 2011, it rose to twenty-fifth in 2016 and gained more than ten spots in three years to reach the fourteenth position in 2019 – above Japan, France, and Canada and just below Israel and Germany. This performance reflects not only progress in terms of human capital, R&D efforts, general infrastructure, and business sophistication (Table 13A.2), but also the inroads made in terms of knowledge and creative outputs, along which latter dimension China ranked fifth in 2019 (Table 13.3). In 2018 and 2019 (according to our own calculations), China was the global leader in innovation efficiency, as measured by the efficiency ratio: the ratio of the Innovation Output Sub-Index to Innovation Input Sub-Index.

China's upward trajectory in the GII reflects the country's resolute policy of innovation and technological upgrading, particularly since the turn of the century. Delving into specific innovation indicators gives a clearer picture of how far China has advanced in science and technology research. In three key innovation metrics – number of full-time employee (FTE) researchers, patents, and scientific publications – China has overtaken the United States (see Figure 13.1). Tsinghua University, for instance, had the largest number of papers published from 2013–2016 in the top 1 percent most cited papers in math and computing of any university (Stanford University comes in second). Six of the fifteen highest-ranked universities on that metric are Chinese.

Korea is another success story, ranking eleventh in the 2019 GII list, due to steady and significant improvements in the Innovation Input Sub-Index. It is now the highest-ranked economy in the human capital and research pillar, while also maintaining high rankings in knowledge, technology, and creative outputs.

Although India is the seventh-largest economy in the world, it ranks only fifty-second in the GII. Even this ranking represents progress; though year-on-year comparisons of innovation performance based on GII have limitations as noted above, one can observe that India only ranked sixty-second in 2011; it jumped five positions in 2019. India's performance is still hampered by its poor scores on the input side, especially regarding institutions (see Table 13A.2). However, it is doing relatively well on the knowledge and technology outputs (ranked thirty-second) and scores very highly on graduates in science and engineering (seventh), for instance (see Chapter 3 for more on India's NSI).

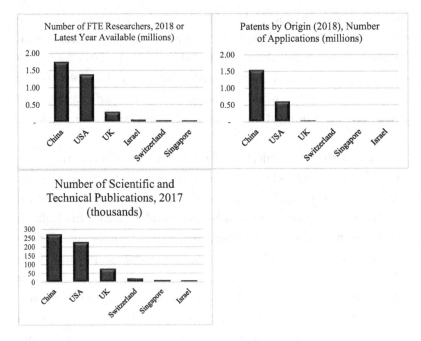

FIGURE 13.1 United States, China, and selected countries in three key innovation metrics
Sources: The authors and EMI team, based on data from UNESCO Institute for Statistics (UIS) database http://uis.unesco.org/ and www.globalinnovationindex.org, accessed November 2019.

Latin America does not perform well overall as a region, with Chile, its highest-ranking country on the GII, only placing 51st in 2019. Perhaps the most surprising aspect of the region's performance is the fact that in several large Latin American economies, output performance is inferior to input: Argentina, Brazil, and Peru, for instance, show a comparatively weak return from innovation investments (Table 13.1). Overall, the region does not fare well in the innovation efficiency ratio; Costa Rica is the strongest Latin American country on that ranking in 33rd place overall, while Mexico, the second, is only 54th. Brazil lags even further behind in 85th place out of 129 countries, an underwhelming performance despite substantial investments in education (OECD, 2018).

Table 13.1 *2019 Global Innovation Index indicators: United States and selected emerging countries*

Country	Overall (score) rank		Innovation efficiency ratio rank (score)		Innovation input rank (score)		Innovation output rank (score)	
USA	3	(61.7)	19	(0.74)	3	(70.8)	6	(52.6)
E20								
• *Asia*								
China	14	(54.8)	1	(0.93)	26	(56.9)	5	(52.8)
India	52	(36.6)	45	(0.64)	61	(44.7)	51	(28.5)
Indonesia	85	(29.7)	77	(0.54)	87	(38.6)	78	(20.8)
Iran	61	(34.4)	16	(0.77)	86	(39.0)	47	(29.9)
Malaysia	35	(42.7)	54	(0.61)	34	(52.9)	39	(32.4)
Pakistan	105	(25.4)	57	(0.60)	113	(31.6)	89	(19.1)
Philippines	54	(36.2)	22	(0.74)	76	(41.7)	42	(30.7)
Saudi Arabia	68	(32.9)	110	(0.42)	49	(46.4)	85	(19.5)
South Korea	11	(56.6)	26	(0.71)	10	(65.9)	13	(47.2)
Thailand	43	(38.6)	40	(0.66)	47	(46.6)	43	(30.7)
Turkey	49	(36.9)	48	(0.63)	56	(45.3)	49	(28.6)
• *Latin America*								
Argentina	73	(31.9)	86	(0.51)	72	(42.3)	75	(21.6)
Brazil	66	(33.8)	85	(0.51)	60	(44.7)	67	(22.9)
Chile	51	(36.6)	84	(0.52)	43	(48.3)	62	(25.0)
Colombia	67	(33.0)	100	(0.46)	58	(45.1)	76	(20.9)
Mexico	56	(36.1)	55	(0.61)	59	(44.7)	55	(27.4)
• *Europe*								
Poland	39	(41.3)	51	(0.62)	37	(51.0)	41	(31.7)
Russia	46	(37.6)	80	(0.53)	41	(49.1)	59	(26.1)
• *Africa*								
Nigeria	114	(23.9)	83	(0.52)	116	(31.5)	105	(16.4)
South Africa	63	(34.0)	94	(0.49)	51	(45.7)	68	(22.3)

Source: The authors and EMI team, based on Global Innovation Index 2019 (www.globalinnovationindex.org/), accessed November 2019.

An examination of some individual indicators highlights aspects of the innovation process and indicates significant transformations in the global innovation landscape. The R&D indicator, for instance, shows how the geography of global innovation expenditures has changed. It also reflects the increased attention paid to innovation by economic actors (both states and firms) in emerging economies, as discussed in prior chapters. In 2017, close to 30 percent of global R&D expenditure came from the top four emerging economies – Korea, India, China, and Russia – up from 8.5 percent twenty years earlier (UNESCO, 2018). China alone accounted for about 23 percent of global R&D expenditures in 2017, having risen to second place as a R&D spender, just behind the United States (see Table 13.2). The

Table 13.2 *Largest R&D spenders (US$ millions), 2017 or latest year available*

#	Country	R&D expenditure	#	Country	R&D expenditure
1	USA	543,249 (2017)	16	Netherlands	18,006 (2017)
2	China	495,981 (2017)	17	Switzerland	17,788 (2015)
3	Japan	175,836 (2017)	18	Sweden	16,742 (2017)
4	Germany	127,105 (2017)	19	Israel	15,254 (2017)
5	South Korea	89,834 (2017)	20	Austria	14,583 (2017)
6	France	62,948 (2017)	21	Belgium	14,179 (2017)
7	India	49,746 (2015)	22	Malaysia	12,412 (2016)
8	UK	47,810 (2017)	23	Poland	11,443 (2017)
9	Russia	42,269 (2017)	24	Singapore	11,114 (2016)
10	Brazil	39,904 (2016)	25	Mexico	11,026 (2016)
11	Italy	32,475 (2017)	26	Denmark	9,195 (2017)
12	Canada	27,179 (2017)	27	Thailand	9,114 (2016)
13	Spain	21,370 (2017)	28	Indonesia	7,720 (2017)
14	Australia	21,199 (2015)	29	Czech Republic	6,896 (2017)
15	Turkey	20,579 (2017)	30	Norway	6,855 (2017)

Source: The authors and EMI team, based on UNESCO Innovations Statistics (UIS) database. http://uis.unesco.org/, accessed November 2019.

Table 13.3 *Number of researchers, top fifteen countries, 2017 or latest year available, and multiplier ratio over a twenty-year period*

	Country	Researchers	2017 or latest year available	Increase over the past 20 years (multiplier)
1	China	1,740,442	2017	3.18
2	USA	1,371,290	2016	1.63
3	Japan	676,292	2017	1.10
4	Germany	413,542	2017	1.80
5	Russia	410,617	2017	0.73
6	South Korea	383,100	2017	3.85
7	UK	289,674	2017	2.00
8	France	288,579	2017	1.86
9	India	282,994	2015	1.90
10	Brazil	179,989	2014	No Data
11	Canada	155,128	2016	1.71
12	Italy	136,204	2017	1.78
13	Spain	133,195	2017	2.58
14	Turkey	111,893	2017	6.19
15	Australia	100,414	2010	1.65

Source: The authors and EMI team, based on data from UNESCO Institute for Statistics (UIS) database http://uis.unesco.org/, accessed November 2019.

number of researchers in emerging economies also grew, as China tripled its number over two decades to a world-leading 1.75 million in 2017, followed by the United States; among E20 countries, India, Korea, and Turkey likewise enjoyed impressive surges (see Table 13.3).

South Korea surpassed all other nations in patent productivity, with 78.2 patents filed per US$ billion of GDP by purchasing power parity (PPP), more than five times the US rate[4] (Dutta et al., 2019). China follows closely behind Korea at 53.7 patents per US$ billion of

---

[4] Based on data on the number of patent applications filed by residents of a country at any given national or domestic patent office.

PPP GDP. Brazil and India performed far less impressively, with only 1.7 and 1.6 patents per US$ billion of PPP GDP, respectively. Based on Patent Cooperation Treaty (PCT) patent applications,[5] the situation is a little bit different: Korea is still in a top position, ranked third after Japan and Switzerland, while China's performance is not very far from advanced economies such as the United States or France and above the United Kingdom and Canada, for instance.

Because innovation tends to be geographically concentrated, the presence of science and technology (S&T) clusters is another indicator of innovation activity in an economy. Emerging economies, here, fare relatively well. Most of the top 100 S&T clusters (based on the number of PCT patents and scientific articles)[6] are in the United States (26 clusters), China (19), and Germany (8) (Dutta et al., 2019). India and Korea with 3 each have the same number of S&T clusters in the top 100 list as Japan. Brazil, Iran, Poland, Russia, and Turkey each have at least 1 cluster in the list. Chinese clusters are particularly well ranked: 2 of them are in the top 5 (Shenzhen/HK and Beijing), and 5 are in the top 25.

The change in the global innovation landscape observed is attributable in large part to the inroads made by emerging market firms into the ranks of the most innovative firms, which we will review in the next sections.

13.3 INNOVATION CAPABILITIES IN EMERGING MULTINATIONALS

A key stakeholder in national systems of innovation is the firm. Emerging market multinationals (EMNCs), global firms with their headquarters in an emerging country, have grown dramatically. The

---

[5] A PCT patent application – or international patent application – is a patent filed under the Patent Cooperation Treaty. The PCT system makes it possible to seek patent protection simultaneously in several countries by filing a single international patent application.

[6] The top 100 clusters are selected on the basis of patent applications under WIPO's Patent Cooperation Treaty and scientific publications included in the Web of Science's SCI Expanded, published by Clarivate (see Dutta et al., 2019).

number of Chinese firms in the Fortune Global 500 ranking expanded from 16 in 2005 to 219 in 2019. At the same time, the number of US companies decreased from 175 to 121. These companies fuel the creation of more stable and better-paid jobs, provide resources to conduct research and foster innovation, and contribute to the development of an ecosystem conducive to the growth of small and medium-size enterprises (SMEs). In this section, we relied on data from the European Commission, PwC, and KPMG to measure EMNCs' performance.

The European Commission publishes data on the 2,500 companies that invest most in R&D. Its 2018 European Union (EU) Industrial R&D Investment Scoreboard shows that these companies, from forty-six countries, have invested a total of about US$814.8 billion (about €736.4 billion), or US$17.6 billion (€16 billion) per country and about US$325.5 million per company (€295 million). This represented 90 percent of the world's total business-funded R&D. Global R&D spending and innovation are overwhelmingly concentrated in a relatively small number of firms: The top 100 companies account for 53 percent of the total spending of the 2,500 firms tracked and the top 500 companies for 81 percent. In 2018, among these 2,500 firms, 778 were from the United States, 577 from the EU, 438 were from China, 339 from Japan, and 368 from other countries (see Figure 13.2). Although all databases have their caveats,[7] this is one of the most comprehensive ones.

The volume of R&D investments is also highly concentrated by country, with companies headquartered in the top three, five, and ten countries accounting for 62 percent, 75 percent, and 91 percent of the total, respectively. Companies from the United States represent 37 percent of the total business-funded R&D investments, those from EU and Switzerland 31 percent, and those from Japan

---

[7] While electricity company State Grid Corporation of China (SGGC) spends about $1.1 billion on R&D (Casanova & Miroux, 2019b) and, as such, it should be ranked number 127, it does not appear in the European Commission database.

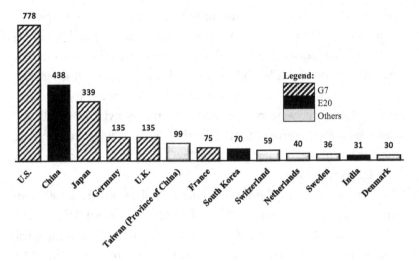

FIGURE 13.2 Countries' number of firms in the 2,500 world's top R&D
investors as per the European Commission data on R&D investments
Source: The authors and EMI team, based on data from the EU 2018 Industrial R&D
Investment Scoreboard (https://iri.jrc.ec.europa.eu).

14 percent. Put differently, those three geographies alone accounted
for 82 percent of the total value of business-funded R&D investments, while those from China accounted for 10 percent of the
total R&D, and Korean companies accounted for only 4 percent.
Considering that China is the second-largest economy in the world,
this is not a particularly high percentage. Chinese companies spend
an average of US$180 million (€163 million) on R&D, but their
American counterparts spend more than twice as much, an average
of US$389 million (€352 million), while companies in the EU
averaged US$383 million (€347 million), and Japanese firms US$326
million (€295 million). In addition, of the top fifty firms, only one is
based in China (Huawei, see Box 13.1), while twenty-two are based in
the United States, eighteen in the EU, and six in Japan. Yet, a change
is taking place.

Chinese firms, for instance, have improved their position substantially compared to prior eras. Chinese company Huawei is today

BOX 13.1 **Huawei**

Huawei Technologies Co. Ltd. is a global telecommunications company that specializes in telecommunications networks, information technology, smart devices, and cloud services. Huawei offers a range of products and services including wireless and fixed networks, cloud computing and services, IT infrastructure, smartphones and other home devices, semiconductors, and services in financing, risk management, and installation of network infrastructure.

Huawei distributes and sells products and provides services in over 170 countries. It has networks that reach one-third of the world's population. As of 2019, it was the third-largest mobile phone producer after Samsung and Apple, and the largest telecommunications equipment producer in the world. Huawei received promotion by the Chinese government in the 1990s, when the company secured a contract to build a national telecommunications network for the People's Liberation Army, aiding in its large domestic presence. Huawei has also expanded its presence internationally through acquisitions and partnerships in Israel, Japan, and other countries. According to the 2018 European Union Scoreboard the firm is the highest ranking in R&D investments from all Chinese firms and number five in the world. It also shows one of the highest growth rates in R&D, spending at 13 percent.

Source: The authors, based on data from Capital IQ and 2019 Fortune Global 500, accessed November 2019.

the 5th-largest R&D spender among the 2,500 firms, behind only Korea's Samsung (see Box 13.2), the United States' Alphabet and Microsoft, and Germany's Volkswagen (see Table 13.4). In 2011, Huawei, already the highest-ranked Chinese company in the European Scoreboard at the time, ranked 41st place overall. That year, of the 250 top firms in the EU R&D Investment Scoreboard, 3 percent of them were Chinese, compared to 9 percent in 2018. The 5 largest Chinese R&D spenders comprise, in addition to Huawei, Alibaba

BOX 13.2 **Samsung Electronics**

Samsung Electronics, part of the Samsung Group, is an electronics manufacturer that specializes in the production of consumer electronics such as phones, tablets, and others; semiconductors; and home appliances. Samsung is the world's largest manufacturer of mobile phones and also has the largest market share in the smartphone market, accounting for 21 percent of the total market as of 2019.

Samsung is heavily focused on remaining a market leader through R&D. In 2018, Samsung spent US$15.2 billion on R&D, more than any other company in the world. The company has over 130,000 patents registered worldwide. Samsung also strategically invests in companies via its Samsung Catalytic Fund. Samsung's R&D activities and investment arm has been focusing on six primary areas: artificial intelligence, cloud infrastructure, device technology, digital health, Internet of Things, and automated mobility.

According to the European Scoreboard (European Commission, 2018) Samsung is the company that invests the most in R&D in the world.

Source: The authors, based on data from Capital IQ and 2019 Fortune Global 500, accessed November 2019.

(ranked 51st), Tencent (see Box 13.3, ranked 61st), ZTE (76th), and Baidu (81st) and account for 28 percent of the total among all Chinese companies. Korean companies are also better represented. The highest-ranking company in 2018 was Samsung, the top seller of smartphones in the world, and Korea also boasted seven other firms among the top 250 most innovative firms. If one extends the list to the top 500, a few other EMNCs make the cut: four from India (Tata Motors [see Box 13.4], Sun Pharmaceutical Industry, Dr. Reddy's Laboratories, and Lupin), three from Brazil (Embraer [see Box 13.5], Vale, and Petrobras), and Saudi Arabia's Saudi Basic Industries, for instance (see Chapters 3, 8, 9, and 11, which illustrate some of these cases). Overall, E20 firms doubled their presence in the top 500 R&D spenders since 2011 from 8 to 15 percent.

Table 13.4 *Top 20 companies in the 2,500 world's top R&D investors, Eurostat, 2018*

#	Company	Headquarters	R&D (€million)	R&D / net sales (%)
1	Samsung	South Korea	13,437	7
2	Alphabet	USA	13,388	14
3	Volkswagen	Germany	13,135	6
4	Microsoft	USA	12,279	13
5	Huawei	China	11,334	15
6	Intel	USA	10,921	21
7	Apple	USA	9,656	5
8	Roche	Switzerland	8,885	19
9	Johnson & Johnson	USA	8,800	14
10	Daimler	Germany	8,663	5
11	Merck US	USA	8,474	25
12	Toyota Motor	Japan	7,860	4
13	Novartis	Switzerland	7,331	18
14	Ford Motor	USA	6,671	5
15	Facebook	USA	6,465	19
16	Pfizer	USA	6,168	14
17	BMW	Germany	6,108	6
18	General Motors	USA	6,087	5
19	Robert Bosch	Germany	5,934	8
20	Siemens	Germany	5,538	7

Source: The authors and EMI team, based on data from the EU 2018 Industrial R&D Investment Scoreboard (https://iri.jrc.ec.europa.eu).

Investment in R&D is also highly concentrated by sector globally, with only four sectors accounting for 76 percent of investments: information and communication technology (ICT) products (24 percent), health industries (21 percent), automobiles and transport (18 percent), and ICT services (14 percent). China has specialized in ICT, which has accounted for 45 percent of spending, followed by 11 percent in automotive and only 3 percent in health. The United

BOX 13.3   **Tencent**

Tencent Holdings Limited is a multinational Chinese conglomerate that specializes in technology, Internet-related services, and artificial intelligence. Tencent offers a variety of products and services including WeChat, TenPay, QQ, and Tencent Games, among numerous others. Tencent boasts over 1 billion customers across its products and services, with a majority based in China. Tencent was the first Chinese technology firm to be valued over US$500 billion in 2017, had the fifth-highest brand value in 2018, and is the world's largest gaming company as of 2019.

Tencent rapidly internationalized its products and services by investing over US$2 billion in expanding WeChat in Asia, Europe, and the United States, creating a global gaming empire, and through diversified investments. Tencent made extensive R&D and venture capital investments, with upwards of US$30 billion since 2015 in over 600 companies worldwide. Tencent continues to remain competitive and applies for over 2,000 patents yearly in China, Japan, the United States, and Europe. With WeChat pay, Tencent is with AliPay (Chapter 5) behind China's leadership in mobile payments.

Source: The authors and EMI team, based on data from Capital IQ and 2019 Fortune Global 500, accessed November 2019.

BOX 13.4   **Tata Motors**

Tata Motors, part of the Tata Group, is an automobile manufacturer specializing in the production of cars, sport utility vehicles, trucks, buses, and defense vehicles, among others. Tata Motors also provides factory automation, financing, and information technology services. Tata Motors is India's largest automobile manufacturer and one of the world's largest automobile manufacturers, selling over 1.2 million commercial units worldwide in 2019. Tata Motors currently offers

BOX 13.4 (cont.)

commercial vehicle products under the brands Tata, Daewoo, Fiat, and Land Rover. The company has an extensive distribution network, with over 6,600 contact points in India.

The company's strategy has included expanding internationally through joint ventures and acquisitions, as seen by Tata Motors' joint venture with Fiat Chrysler and its acquisition of Ford's Land Rover and South Korean car company Daewoo. Tata Motors currently has vehicle assembly plants in six countries and sells products in thirty-seven countries.

Source: The authors and EMI team, based on data from Capital IQ and 2019 Fortune Global 500, accessed November 2019.

BOX 13.5 Embraer

Embraer designs, develops, and manufactures commercial, agriculture, and military aircraft and provides aeronautical services in Brazil, North America, Latin America, and internationally. In its commercial sector, Embraer manufactures jets and planes, provides aircraft services, and leases planes. Embraer is the third-largest producer of civilian aircraft after Boeing and Airbus. In its military sector, Embraer engages in R&D of military defense and security aircraft and its related products and services, including radars, satellites, surveillance and reconnaissance systems, information technology and communications, and more. Embraer's Defense and Security segment alone is present in over sixty countries.

Embraer has been able to keep up with the latest technological and industry developments by forming strategic partnerships with over fifty companies worldwide. As of 2019, Boeing purchased 80 percent of Embraer's commercial aircraft division, later rebranded as Boeing Brasil. Embraer further places emphasis on R&D and invests 10 percent of its annual revenues into R&D. It has over 800 patents in numerous

BOX 13.5   (cont.)

countries worldwide. It is one of only four Brazilian companies in the
2018 European Union Scoreboard.

Source: The authors and EMI team, based on data from Capital IQ and
2019 Fortune Global 500, accessed November 2019.

States has a similar specialization (51 percent of its R&D spending is
in ICT, 27 percent in health, and 8 percent in automotive), while the
EU and Japan are more specialized in automobiles.

To date, US companies are highly dominant within ICT services (software, computer services, Internet, etc.), accounting for
68 percent of total R&D expenditure of the 2,500 companies. The
EU is dominant in automobiles and other transportation with 47 percent of total spending. China does not dominate any one sector, but
claims its largest share in ICT (14 percent). Based on the number of
enterprises, however, enterprises are well represented among the
most innovative firms in electronic and electrical equipment
(accounting for 27 percent of the firms) and auto and parts (22
percent) as well as in tech hardware and industrial engineering (18
percent) (Table 13.5).

PwC publishes the Global Innovation 1000 list of the world's
1,000 largest publicly listed corporate R&D spenders (PwC, 2018).
Though the information does not include state-owned firms (thereby
omitting Huawei and similar Chinese companies), the PwC list parallels the picture that emerges based on EU data: Both indicate the
relatively important presence of EMNCs, especially from China.
Altogether, E20 companies make up close to 23 percent of the firms
in the PwC list, while Chinese companies alone account for 17.5
percent, having doubled their number from eighty-seven companies
in 2012 (Table 13.6). Their R&D expenditure contributed to 8 percent
of the total investment of the PwC listed top 1,000 most
innovative companies.

Table 13.5 *Highly represented industries and countries in the world's top R&D investors*

Industry	Country	Companies
Pharmaceuticals and biotechnology	US	200
	China	33
	Japan	28
	Total	**395**
Technology hardware and equipment	US	99
	Taiwan	51
	China	49
	Total	**269**
Software and computer services	US	148
	China	42
	UK	19
	Total	**268**
Electronic and electrical equipment	China	65
	US	46
	Japan	46
	Total	**240**
Industrial engineering	Japan	38
	US	36
	China	32
	Total	**190**
Automobiles and parts	Japan	36
	China	34
	US	22
	Total	**152**
Chemicals	Japan	36
	US	32
	China	21
	Total	**129**
Healthcare equipment and services	US	53
	Japan	8
	Germany	8
	Total	**90**

Table 13.5 (*cont.*)

Industry	Country	Companies
Others	China	158
	US	142
	Japan	118
	Total	**767**

Sources: The authors and EMI team, based on data from the EU 2018 Industrial R&D Investment Scoreboard (https://iri.jrc.ec.europa.eu).

Table 13.6 *Top ten firms from China,* * *and top firms from other E20 countries, in the PwC Global Innovation 1000 list*

Rank	Company	Country
45	Alibaba	China
59	Tencent	China
77	ZTE Corp.	China
78	Baidu	China
83	China State Construction Engineering	China
84	PetroChina Company	China
89	China Railway Group	China
98	SAIC Motor Corp.	China
100	China Railway Construction	China
101	CRRC Corporation	China
256	Petrobras	Brazil
262	Tata Motors	India
381	Mahindra & Mahindra	India
390	Vale	Brazil
402	Sun Pharma	India
438	Dr. Reddy's Laboratories	India
442	Lupin Ltd.	India
451	Reliance Industries	India
616	Glenmark Pharmaceuticals	India
604	B3 SA	Brazil
(717)	Embraer	Brazil
(892)	Mercado Libre	Argentina

Table 13.6 (*cont.*)

Rank	Company	Country
920	Bharat Heavy Electricals	India
936	Bharat Electronics	India
957	Cipla Limited	India
961	Infosys Ltd.	India
(993)	TOTVS	Brazil

*There are 175 Chinese companies in the list; only the top 10 are included in this table.
Source: PwC, the 2018 Global Innovation 1000 study, retrieved September 2019, from www.strategyand.pwc.com/gx/en/insights/innovation1000.html.

The fintech industry has seen particular innovation from emerging market firms, especially Chinese firms (see Chapter 5). The KPMG 2018 Fintech100 identifies the world's top 100 leading fintech innovators for 2018. The United States is the most-represented country, with 18 companies, followed by the United Kingdom with 12 and China with 11. At the top of the rankings, however, China has more companies in the top 10 than the United States, including 3 of the top 5 firms on the list. Altogether, there are 28 E20 EMNCs in the Fintech100 list, twice the number of firms listed in 2015 (KPMG, 2018). The list includes firms from many other emerging economies such as India, Brazil, Korea, Indonesia, Mexico, Colombia, Argentina, Nigeria, Thailand, and South Africa (Table 13.7).

13.4 GOING BEYOND TRADITIONAL INDICATORS IN EMERGING MARKETS

Three levels of outcomes were identified in the innovation framework for emerging markets in Chapter 1: country performance, company competitive advantage, and social development. The preceding sections of this chapter have focused on the first two innovation

Table 13.7 *Emerging market firms in the KPMG 2018 Fintech100 leading innovators*

Rank[a]	Company[b]	Country
1	Ant Financing	China
2	JD Finance	China
4	Du Xiaoman Financial	China – split off from its parent Baidu
7	Nubank	Brazil
10	Lufax Holding	China
11	OneConnect (PingAn Yizhangtong)	China
12	51 Credit Card	China
18	Policybazaar	India
23	WeLab	China
27	Dianrong	China
36	ZhongAn	China
41	Lendingkart	India
46	GuiaBolso	Brazil
	Other emerging market firms in the list (alphabetical order)	
	Geru	Brazil
	Konfio	Mexico
	PaySense	India
	Ripio Credit Network	Argentina
	ThisIsMe	South Africa
	Tiger Brokers	China
	Tpaga	Colombia
	Wallet.ng	Nigeria
	WeBank	China

[a] KPMG lists 100 of the most innovative companies, but only ranks the first 50.
[b] 50 leading.
Source: The authors, based on KPMG, the 2018 Fintech100, https://h2.vc/wp-content/uploads/2018/11/Fintech100–2018-Report_Final_22–11-18sm.pdf.

outcomes. In both dimensions, we have seen how emerging markets have now moved from imitators to leadership positions. China has been able to grow significantly in recent years and rival the United States on many national innovation dimensions. Companies such as the Korean Samsung have become globally competitive and have assumed leadership positions in key technology domains.

It is interesting to note that the country and firm-level successes in many emerging markets have been driven by innovation (on growth and innovation see Rosenberg, 2006; Fagerberg, Srholec, & Verspagen, 2010; Mühleisen 2018, among others). The economic growth (Table 13A.1) experienced by emerging markets such as Korea and China can be linked as a source or a result to their policy emphasis on technological innovation. Since the 1970s Korea, and China in the last decade mainly, have pursued potent, deliberate, and consistent policy for technological upgrading and innovation (see Chapters 4 and 7). Some experts claim that the sustained high growth of the so-called Asian miracles is the result of a technology and innovation policy with ambitious goals set by the state and applied consistently (Cherif & Hasanov, 2019). On the other end of the spectrum, in Latin America, for example, the government efforts have been much less marked. And as compared with Asia, few Latin American firms, for instance, are among the top R&D investors in the world.

Social development is also an important outcome of innovation that has special significance in the context of emerging markets, especially given their relatively high levels of poverty and inequality. Preceding chapters in this book have provided examples of specific types of innovation that tend to be more oriented toward social development in emerging markets: frugal innovation, reverse innovation, business model innovation in conflict-torn areas, as well as social innovations. These types of innovations have played an important role in improving the quality of lives of citizens in emerging markets. Social development has also been enabled by the spread of new innovation enablers in emerging markets. For example, while venture capital has been vital in the creation of innovation ecosystems globally, microfinance and mobile payments have played an important role in sustaining grassroots innovation, creating wealth for many micro and small entrepreneurs, including a large number of women. This has helped improve the living standards of families and aid social development in emerging markets.

Innovations in emerging countries have often arisen in resource-constrained environments, within limited R&D budgets, and frequently focused on local markets. As a result, their innovations typically followed modest, less spectacular paths, as in the case of frugal innovation (Chapter 11) and did not engage in the traditional race for intellectual property rights. Such innovations tend to be underreported or underrecognized by traditional innovation metrics, such as R&D expenditures, patents, or trademarks. Most indicators available, including those cited in this chapter, would not reflect those types of innovation, and though efforts are being made, empirical research has yet to come up with the means to measure them adequately (see Santamaría, Nieto, & Barge-Gil, 2009; Cuervo-Cazurra & Un, 2010; Barge-Gil, Jesús Nieto, & Santamaria, 2011; Spieth & Schneider, 2016; Clauss, 2017). In the preceding chapters of the book these types of innovation and their impacts have been highlighted.

The focus of this book has been on how many emerging markets have moved from imitation to leaders in innovation. While some emerging markets such as China and Korea have reduced their innovation gaps with developed markets, their success has also shown the divide in innovation success across emerging markets. Better measures are needed to evaluate the multifaceted dimensions of innovation in emerging markets so that appropriate policy measures can be put in place by decision leaders from the public and private sectors. Today emerging markets need to learn not just from developed countries but also from their peers across other emerging markets as a path for sustainable growth.

Table 13A.1 General information on selected emerging countries using the United States as reference (2018) (countries covered in the book are bolded)

Country	Population (million)	GDP rank	GDP (bn US$)	GDP/ capita rank	GDP/ capita (US$)	GDP Growth (%)	Researchers	Total Patent Application	R&D expenditure (% of GDP)
US	327.2	1	20,494.1	9	62,641	2.86	1,371,290 (2016)	597,141	2.8 (2017)
E20									
• Asia									
China	**1,392.7**	**2**	**13,608.2**	**68**	**9,771**	**6.60**	**1,740,442 (2017)**	**1,542,002**	**2.1 (2017)**
India	**1,352.6**	**7**	**2,726.3**	**143**	**2,016**	**6.98**	**282,994 (2015)**	**50,055**	**0.6 (2015)**
Indonesia	267.7	16	1,042.2	115	3,894	5.17	56,950 (2017)	9,754	0.2 (2017)
Iran	81.8	188	–	188	–	0.00	51,961 (2013)	12,823	0.3 (2013)
Malaysia	31.5	35	354.3	62	11,239	4.72	73,537 (2016)	7,295	1.4 (2016)

Table 13A.1 (cont.)

Country	Population (million)	GDP rank	GDP (bn US$)	GDP/capita rank	GDP/capita (US$)	GDP Growth (%)	Researchers	Total Patent Application	R&D expenditure (% of GDP)
Pakistan	212.2	39	312.6	154	1,473	5.43	69,769 (2017)	892	0.2 (2017)
Philippines	106.7	37	330.9	126	3,103	6.24	18,481 (2013)	4,300	0.1 (2013)
Saudi Arabia	33.7	18	782.5	38	23,219	2.21	No data available	4,004	0.8 (2013)
South Korea	51.6	12	1,619.4	31	31,363	2.67	383,100 (2017)	209,992	4.6 (2017)
Thailand	69.4	25	505.0	81	7,274	4.13	83,349 (2016)	8,149	0.8 (2016)
Turkey	82.3	19	766.5	71	9,311	2.57	111,893 (2017)	8,038	1.0 (2017)
• Latin America									
Argentina	**44.5**	**24**	**518.5**	**60**	**11,653**	**-2.51**	**54,046 (2016)**	**3,667**	**0.5 (2016)**
Brazil	**209.5**	**9**	**1,868.6**	**74**	**8,921**	**1.12**	**179,989 (2014)**	**24,857**	**1.3 (2016)**
Chile	18.7	40	298.2	54	15,923	4.02	8,993 (2016)	3,100	0.4 (2016)

Colombia	**49.6**	**38**	**330.2**	**87**	**6,651**	**2.66**	**4,305 (2016)**	**2,223**	**0.2 (2017)**
Mexico	**126.2**	**15**	**1,223.8**	**69**	**9,698**	**1.99**	**29,921 (2013)**	**16,424**	**0.5 (2016)**
• Europe									
Poland	38.0	21	585.8	56	15,424	5.15	96,497 (2017)	4,849	1.0 (2017)
Russia	144.5	11	1,657.6	61	11,289	2.25	410,617 (2017)	38,364	1.1 (2017)
• Africa									
Nigeria	**195.9**	**29**	**397.3**	**142**	**2,028**	**1.94**	**5,677 (2007)**	**338**	**0.2 (2007)**
South Africa	**57.8**	**32**	**368.3**	**88**	**6,374**	**0.79**	**27,656 (2016)**	**6,915**	**0.8 (2016)**

Sources: The authors and EMI team, based on World Bank (2019) (https://data.worldbank.org) and World Intellectual Property Organization (www.wipo.int/portal/en/index.html), and the UNESCO Institute for Statistics (http://data.uis.unesco.org/), accessed November 2019.

Table 13A.2 *Global Innovation Index Input and Output Indicators, selected emerging countries using the United States as reference (2018) (countries covered in the book are bolded)*

Country	INPUTS					OUTPUTS	
	Institutions rank (score)	Human cap. & research rank (score)	Infrastructure rank (score)	Market sophistication rank (score)	Business sophistication rank (score)	Knowledge & technology rank (score)	Creative rank (score)
US	11 (89.7)	12 (55.7)	23 (59.2)	1 (87.0)	7 (62.7)	4 (59.7)	15 (45.5)
E20							
• Asia							
China	**60** (64.1)	**25** (47.6)	**26** (58.7)	**21** (58.6)	**14** (55.4)	**5** (57.2)	**12** (48.3)
India	**77** (59.5)	**53** (33.5)	**79** (43.0)	**33** (56.3)	**65** (31.0)	**32** (33.5)	**78** (23.5)
Indonesia	99 (53.2)	90 (21.3)	75 (44.2)	64 (48.8)	95 (25.7)	82 (17.6)	76 (24.0)
Iran	116 (48.8)	43 (37.6)	68 (46.0)	100 (40.0)	113 (22.6)	46 (27.2)	45 (32.5)
Malaysia	40 (71.6)	33 (44.2)	42 (51.8)	25 (57.8)	36 (39.3)	34 (32.1)	44 (32.8)
Pakistan	100 (53.1)	116 (12.5)	120 (27.3)	102 (39.6)	96 (25.5)	70 (20.6)	104 (17.6)
Philippines	89 (56.0)	83 (24.6)	58 (48.5)	110 (38.3)	32 (40.9)	31 (33.7)	63 (27.7)
Saudi Arabia	104 (51.3)	29 (45.5)	55 (48.9)	47 (51.9)	48 (34.3)	87 (17.0)	86 (21.9)
South Korea	**26** (79.7)	**1** (66.5)	**15** (61.6)	**11** (64.3)	**10** (57.6)	**13** (50.2)	**17** (44.1)
Thailand	57 (65.8)	52 (34.7)	77 (43.6)	32 (56.5)	60 (32.3)	38 (31.3)	54 (30.0)

• *Latin America*							
Argentina	**86** (56.7)	**42** (38.7)	**69** (45.8)	**111** (37.9)	**57** (32.6)	**78** (19.2)	**77** (24.0)
Brazil	**80** (58.9)	**48** (36.0)	**64** (46.8)	**84** (44.2)	**40** (37.6)	**58** (23.0)	**82** (22.8)
Chile	39 (73.0)	57 (32.5)	50 (51.0)	49 (51.7)	53 (33.1)	61 (22.9)	66 (27.2)
Colombia	**61** (64.0)	**78** (27.0)	**47** (51.3)	**53** (50.4)	**58** (32.6)	**76** (19.5)	**85** (22.3)
Mexico	**66** (62.8)	**54** (33.4)	**59** (48.3)	**57** (49.9)	**73** (29.4)	**50** (25.5)	**55** (29.2)
• *Europe and Central Asia*							
Poland	37 (73.6)	40 (41.2)	38 (53.8)	65 (47.9)	38 (38.4)	39 (30.9)	46 (32.4)
Russia	74 (60.9)	23 (48.3)	62 (47.1)	61 (49.4)	35 (40.0)	47 (27.1)	72 (25.1)
Turkey	85 (57.4)	46 (36.3)	41 (52.2)	52 (50.8)	71 (29.5)	59 (23.0)	40 (34.2)
• *Africa*							
Nigeria	**114** (49.3)	**119** (11.3)	**122** (26.6)	**88** (43.4)	**85** (26.7)	**106** (14.0)	**101** (18.8)
South Africa	**55** (65.9)	**65** (30.4)	**83** (41.1)	**19** (58.6)	**55** (32.7)	**57** (23.9)	**91** (20.8)

Source: The authors and EMI team, based on Global Innovation Index 2019 (www.globalinnovationindex.org/), accessed November 2019.

REFERENCES

Barge-Gil, A., Jesús Nieto, M., & Santamaria, L. (2011). Hidden innovators: The role of non-R&D activities. *Technology Analysis & Strategic Management*, 23(4), 415–432.

Bloomberg. (2019) U.S. and Canada make strides in Bloomberg 2019 Innovation Index. Retrieved November 2019, from: www.bloomberg.com/news/articles/2019-01-28/u-s-canada-make-strides-in-bloomberg-2019-innovation-index.

Casanova, L., & Miroux, A. (2020). *The era of Chinese multinationals: How Chinese companies are conquering the world*. San Diego, CA. Academic Press. Elsevier.

(2019). *Emerging Markets Multinational Report 2019. Building constructive engagement*. Ithaca, NY: Cornell University. Retrieved November 2019, from www.johnson.cornell.edu/Emerging-Markets-Institute https://hdl.handle.net/1813/66978.

Cherif, R., & Hasanov, F. (2019). *The return of the policy that shall not be named: Principles of industrial policy*. Washington, DC: International Monetary Fund. Retrieved November 2019, from: www.imf.org/en/Publications/WP/Issues/2019/03/26/The-Return-of-the-Policy-That-Shall-Not-Be-Named-Principles-of-Industrial-Policy-46710.

Clauss, T. (2017). Measuring business model innovation: conceptualization, scale development, and proof of performance. *R&D Management*, 47(3), 385–403.

Cuervo-Cazurra, A., & Un, C. A. (2010). Why some firms never invest in formal R&D. *Strategic Management Journal*, 31(7), 759–779.

Dutta, S., Lanvin, B., & Wunsch-Vincent, S. (Eds.). (2019). *Global innovation index 2019: Creating healthy lives – the future of medical innovation*. Ithaca, Fontainebleau, and Geneva: Cornell, INSEAD, and WIPO.

European Commission. (2018). *EU R&D scoreboard: The 2018 EU industrial R&D investment scoreboard*. Seville: European Commission. Retrieved November 2019, from https://iri.jrc.ec.europa.eu/sites/default/files/2019-11/346814f1-e2e0-4b48-9562-0cbb2ee7c601_0.pdf.

Fagerberg, J., Srholec, M., & Verspagen, B. (2010). Innovation and economic development. In B. Hall & N. Rosenberg (Eds.), *Handbook of the economics of innovation* (Vol. 2, pp. 833–872). Amsterdam: Elsevier.

Gault, F. (2013). *Handbook of innovation indicators and measurement*. Cheltenham: Edward Elgar Publishing.

Hagedoorn, J., & Cloodt, M. (2003). Measuring innovative performance: Is there an advantage in using multiple indicators? *Research Policy*, 32(8), 1365–1379.

KPMG. (2018). The Fintech100 – Leading global fintech innovators. Retrieved November 2019, from: https://h2.vc/wp-content/uploads/2018/11/Fintech100-2018-Report_Final_22-11-18sm.pdf.

Mühleisen, M. (2018, June). The long and short of the digital revolution. *Finance & Development, 55*(2), 4. Retrieved November 2019, from www.imf.org/external/pubs/ft/fandd/2018/06/impact-of-digital-technology-on-economic-growth/muhleisen.pdf.

OECD. (2018). OECD science, technology and innovation outlook 2018. Adapting to technological and societal disruption. Retrieved November 2019, from www.oecd.org/sti/oecd-science-technology-and-innovation-outlook-25186167.htm.

OECD/Eurostat. (2018). *Oslo Manual 2018: Guidelines for collecting, reporting and using data on innovation* (4th ed.). Paris: OECD Publishing. https://doi.org/10.1787/9789264304604-en.

Pohjola, M. (2000). *Information technology and economic growth. A cross-country analysis*. Research Paper 173. World Institute for Development Economics Research. Helsinki: The United Nations University. Retrieved November 2019, from www.wider.unu.edu/sites/default/files/wp173.pdf.

PwC. (2018). The 2018 global innovation 1000 study. Retrieved November 2019, from: www.strategyand.pwc.com/gx/en/insights/innovation1000.html.

Rosenberg, N. (2006). Innovation and economic growth. OECD. Retrieved November 2019, from: www.oecd.org/cfe/tourism/34267902.pdf.

Santamaría, L., Nieto, M. J., & Barge-Gil, A. (2009). Beyond formal R&D: Taking advantage of other sources of innovation in low-and medium-technology industries. *Research Policy, 38*(3), 507–517.

Spieth, P., & Schneider, S. (2016). Business model innovativeness: Designing a formative measure for business model innovation. *Journal of Business Economics, 86*(6), 671–696.

UNESCO. (2018). Innovations statistics (UIS) database. Retrieved November 2019, from http://uis.unesco.org/.

World Intellectual Property Organization (WIPO). (2019). WIPO statistics database. Retrieved November 2019, from www.wipo.int/portal/en/index.html.

World Bank Data. (2019). Retrieved October 2019, from https://data.worldbank.org.

Conclusions

*Emerging Markets Becoming
Innovation Leaders*

Lourdes Casanova, Anne Miroux,
and Fernanda Cahen

Innovation began to emerge as its own field of study in the 1960s, but it did not garner attention from scholars across a wide range of disciplines until the later years of the twentieth century. Recently, experts in fields ranging from economics to social sciences to business studies have explored innovation's role as a driver of growth and social change, and innovation is now widely considered central to economic growth and development. Outside of academia, policymakers, business leaders, and even the public at large have increasingly embraced innovation. Innovation policies figure high in the policy agendas of many countries, and "innovative nations" and "knowledge-based economies" are becoming keywords in today's economic policy manifestos.

This expansion of interest in the subject partly reflects changes in the geography of innovation since the early 2000s, marked by the increasing role of emerging economies. Some of the most creative ideas have come from emerging markets, and a number of firms from these regions have become global leaders, with brands known to consumers all over the world. Emerging markets no longer merely copy innovations made in advanced economies; they now lead in a number of areas of innovation. Not only have they generated new business and organizational models, or products and services that better meet the needs of their local markets, but they have also developed new technologies and research and development (R&D)-based high-tech products and services. Some of these innovations are truly disruptive, impacting emerging economies and firms and markets in developed countries alike and creating new arenas of global competition.

We have described this phenomenon as a shift from copycats to leaders and organized its analysis under the framework for innovation in emerging markets in Chapter 1 and discussed in the subsequent chapters. Our collective goal was not to offer an exhaustive examination of each of these components, but rather to illustrate them through concrete case studies, sometimes uncovering firm or industry experiences that remain unknown or underreported, or exploring exceptional (or uncommon) situations such as innovation in conflict zones. Taken together, these examples show the need for analysis that reaches beyond emerging markets known for innovation such as China or Korea, and explores less-well-charted territories. The diversity of the cases selected points to our first conclusion: Emerging economies have a solid, authentic, and often original culture of innovation.

As elaborated across the various chapters of this book, multiple factors have enabled emerging markets' culture of innovation to thrive, including the strong supporting hand of the government, most notably observed in the case of China. State involvement can take on many different forms; however, many of them may be less direct and of a lesser magnitude than in the case of major Chinese SOEs. The lesser-known case of INVAP, the Argentinian firm in the nuclear industry – a high-tech domain – demonstrates this point (Chapter 7). Another important driver of innovation in emerging countries is their specific industry context and the capabilities and characteristics of their firms. In India, for example, catch-up processes, industry history, and path dependency have played critical roles in industries as varied as pharmaceuticals, wind turbines, and auto parts (Chapter 3).

Enterprises are at the core of the innovation process and become even more crucial when the institutional context is lacking and government support for innovations is weak. A number of emerging economies in the Balkans (Chapter 6) display these characteristics; in these countries, government R&D investment is modest, and the research sectors and technology transfer systems are limited. Despite these challenges, strong entrepreneurial ecosystems have developed that have played a crucial role in generating an impressive innovation momentum, leading to improved economic performance and visible gains in international innovation rankings. Even in countries where the state plays a substantial role, the value that enterprises place on innovation, the ways they develop their innovation capabilities, and their level of collaboration with universities and other enterprises matter, as illustrated in the analysis of Chinese firms undertaken in Chapter 2. Similarly, the evolution of firm-level capabilities in a technology and R&D-based sector such as pharmaceuticals (Chapter 8) sheds some light on the challenges faced by emerging market firms in their efforts to move from copycats to leaders.

While emerging markets have become innovators in strategic industries, their innovation capabilities have been most prominent in IT-related activities, especially e-commerce and mobile payments. Alibaba's Alipay may be the best-known example, but cohorts of start-ups from emerging countries are just a step away from becoming unicorns, with the power to disrupt entire segments of IT-related services. Mercado Libre, Flipkart, and Jumia (all examined in Chapter 5) are examples of e-commerce unicorns innovating in emerging markets in the face of sizeable challenges, while firms such as Tencent and Huawei have already reached the status of global behemoths and innovators in strategic areas, such as 5G.

In addition to new enterprises emerging as champions of innovation, countries are also improving their innovation capabilities. A detailed examination of several emerging economies ranked in the Global Innovation Index (GII) shows how deeply and broadly the geography of innovation competitiveness has changed over the last decade, largely in favor of emerging economies (Chapter 13).

Until now, many emerging countries' innovations have arisen in resource-constrained environments, within limited R&D budgets, and frequently focused on local markets. As a result, their innovations typically followed modest, less-spectacular paths, as in the case of frugal innovation (see Chapter 11) and did not engage in the traditional race for intellectual property rights. Such innovations tended to be underreported or underrecognized by traditional innovation metrics, such as R&D expenditures, patents, or trademarks. Business model innovations that arise when, for instance, firms have to adapt to local environments (as in the case of e-commerce and mobile payments) are relatively common in emerging economies, as are organizational innovation (Chapter 10) and social innovation. Accurately measuring such innovations remains a significant challenge in the absence of updated methodological and statistical frameworks to assess innovation in all of its dimensions. Despite such undermeasurement, the economic and social impact of these "invisible innovations" on the populations and communities in many emerging countries has been profound, as illustrated in Chapter 5 (e-commerce) and Chapter 12 (innovation in Colombia's conflict and postconflict zones).

As yesterday's copycats become today's leaders in innovation, the multiplicity of approaches that they have followed provides additional insight into what makes a successful innovator. Globally, innovation has now become a two-way street, along which mature economies and emerging ones can learn from each other. We hope that this book contributes to this evolving global dialogue.

Index

Printed in the United States
by Baker & Taylor Publisher Services